ENDS OF WAR

ENDS OF WAR

The Unfinished Fight of Lee's Army after Appomattox

Caroline E. Janney

THE UNIVERSITY OF NORTH CAROLINA PRESS

Chapel Hill

*Published with the assistance of the Fred W. Morrison Fund
of the University of North Carolina Press.*

© 2021 Caroline E. Janney

Designed by Jamison Cockerham
Set in Arno, Scala, Cutright, and Ophir
by Tseng Information Systems, Inc.

Jacket illustrations: Front: *Rebel Prisoners on Their Way to the Rear,
Captured by Gen. Sheriden at Five Forks April 3d, 1865*, photograph by Brady's
National Photographic Portrait Galleries; front flap: *Marching Prisoners
over the Mountains to Frederick, M.D.*, by Alfred R. Waud; back: *The Battle
of Gettysburg—Prisoners Belonging to Gen. Longstreet's Corps Captured by
Union Troops* by Edwin Forbes. All courtesy Library of Congress.

Manufactured in the United States of America

The University of North Carolina Press has been a member
of the Green Press Initiative since 2003.

LIBRARY OF CONGRESS CATALOGING-IN-PUBLICATION DATA
Names: Janney, Caroline E., author.
Title: Ends of war : the unfinished fight of Lee's army
after Appomattox / Caroline E. Janney.
Description: Chapel Hill : The University of North Carolina Press, [2021]
| Includes bibliographical references and index.
Identifiers: LCCN 2021003641 | ISBN 9781469663371 (cloth ; alk. paper)
| ISBN 9781469663388 (ebook)
Subjects: LCSH: Confederate States of America. Army—Demobilization.
| Reconstruction (U.S. history, 1865–1877) | Social conflict—Southern States—
History—19th century. | United States—History—Civil War, 1861–1865—
Peace. | United States—Politics and government—1865–1877.
Classification: LCC E668 .J363 2021 | DDC 973.7/3013—dc23
LC record available at https://lccn.loc.gov/2021003641

Portions of this book have appeared in various forms in the following publications:
Caroline E. Janney, "Free to Go Where We Liked: The Army of Northern
Virginia after Appomattox," *Journal of the Civil War Era* 9, no. 1 (March 2019):
4–28; and "'We Were Not Paroled': The Surrenders of Lee's Men beyond
Appomattox Court House," in *Petersburg to Appomattox: The End of the War
in Virginia*, ed. Caroline E. Janney, vol. 11 of the Military Campaigns of the
Civil War series (Chapel Hill: University of North Carolina Press, 2018).

For

CAMPBELL

the last of Ewell's Corps

THE END CAME, TECHNICALLY, AT APPOMATTOX.

But of the real difficulties of the war the end was not yet.

The trials and the perils of utter disorganization were still to be endured.

George Cary Eggleston, CSA

Contents

Figures & Maps

ENDS OF WAR

Introduction

At dawn on April 9, 1865, Lt. Col. David G. McIntosh pulled his battery of the South Carolina Pee Dee Light Artillery up the hill overlooking the village of Appomattox Court House and awaited orders. To the front, the firing was growing hotter as the Confederates pushed back Maj. Gen. Philip H. Sheridan's troopers. The road to Lynchburg might soon be opened. But the sudden appearance of a Union column emerging from the woods on an elevated chain of hills surrounding the Army of Northern Virginia foretold a different outcome.[1] Closing in on both the right and left flanks, the Union army was pushing the rebels back, trapping them in the small valley. Confederate hopes of breaking through the lines vanished.[2]

Observing a flag of truce passing along the lines, McIntosh considered his options. Should he stay with his command and accept whatever a surrender might bring? Or could he refuse to lay down his arms, to remain true to his country? It took only a moment to decide. He could not bear the thought of witnessing the spectacle of surrender. With no time to tell his men goodbye, McIntosh and seven of his comrades headed for a wooded ravine behind them, slipped away, and made their escape from the field.[3]

Upon reaching the open country, they spurred their mounts on, galloping as fast as the weak animals could carry them. Yanking off their badges of rank and disguising their uniforms as much as possible, they passed through a swamp and up the steep slopes along the Appomattox River before leading their horses on foot for several miles to the southeast. Throughout the afternoon they trudged on, forcing a Black man they picked up to accompany them for safety. Finding a secluded spot, they decided to halt and wait for nightfall to cover their further progress. Then in the distance, they heard a salute of guns. Gen. Robert E. Lee had capitulated. The Army of Northern Virginia would be surrendered, but McIntosh and his comrades were not ready to quit.

At dusk they mounted their horses and rode in an easterly direction trying to avoid the Union campfires dotting the landscape. Exhausted and soaked, they approached a home in the early morning hours and began beating on the door. When an older African American woman answered, they demanded directions to Pamplin's Station. She pointed back toward the road from which they had just ridden. Frustrated, they asked who lived on the premises. "Colonel Cheatham," she replied. Assuming that they were in Confederate territory, they ordered her to wake him. But when the colonel came to the door wearing a blue uniform blouse, the fugitive Confederates realized the woman had betrayed them. Thinking fast, McIntosh and his comrades introduced themselves as Union general Philip Sheridan's scouts in search of their camp. The weary colonel gestured toward the campfires in the distance, then bid them goodnight and headed back to bed.[4]

With daylight approaching, and still passing themselves off as Sheridan's scouts, McIntosh and his comrades pushed on through the rain, bribing another Black man to pilot them past the lines of the Union Fifth Corps before arriving safely along the banks of the Staunton River on the afternoon of April 10. If this pace continued, they would reach Gen. Joseph E. Johnston's army in North Carolina in short time and pick up their arms once more.[5] As it was for so many others in Lee's Army of Northern Virginia, their war had not ended at Appomattox.

Conventional wisdom has long held that the surrender at Appomattox served as the final act of the Civil War, as the moment that helped forge a smooth transition from war to peace.[6] If Appomattox was not *the* closing scene of the war, then it has fit into a series of final acts, including the assassination of Lincoln on April 14 and the Grand Review of the Union armies in late May. Each event seemed to flow inevitably into the next, each reflecting a certainty that the massive bloodletting of war would soon be coming to an end.

More recently, historians have begun to challenge the notion that Appomattox and the other Confederate surrenders marked a distinct historical break between the war and Reconstruction. Instead, they argue that the formal military war shifted the violence into new forms of resistance, such as the Ku Klux Klan.[7] Yet jumping too quickly from the surrender at Appomattox to the political decisions in Washington or the violence of the post-war South has obscured the ways in which the disbanding of Confederate armies shaped all that followed.

If we slow down the pace, taking the story frame by frame, looking at events as they unfolded day by day *after* Appomattox, we see a far more contentious, uncertain, ambiguous, and lengthy ending to the American Civil War. Slowing down the narrative highlights the anxieties of Union and Confederate soldiers, civilians on the home front, and government officials. It underscores the complexity of decisions made by the U.S. army, civilian authorities, and soldiers from the Army of Northern Virginia as well as the unintended consequences of those decisions. A more detailed accounting of the spring and summer of 1865 reveals the unanticipated problems and chaos that flowed from well-meaning actions and inconsistent choices that set the tone and expectations for years and even decades. Rather than serving as a clear ending to the conflict, the surrender of Lee's army brought into stark relief many of the legal, social, and political questions that had plagued the war from the beginning.[8] Even more importantly, what followed the surrender would offer the first real test of how a democracy might end a civil war and highlight the fractures in that democracy that would haunt generations to come.

To be certain, Appomattox represented the capitulation of the Confederacy's most important army, Lee's Army of Northern Virginia.[9] But even that statement can prove misleading. As Bvt. Maj. Gen. George H. Sharpe, provost marshal for the Army of the Potomac, observed only a month after the surrender, "A large number of Lee's army were not paroled at Appomattox."[10] Of the approximately 60,000 men available to Lee after the evacuation of Petersburg and Richmond on April 2 (which included those in trenches surrounding Petersburg along with the various units from the Richmond defenses), only 26,000 to 28,000 were paroled between April 9 and 12 at Appomattox. Accounting for the approximately 11,530 casualties sustained between April 2 and 8, a conservative estimate would suggest that at least 20,000 of Lee's men dropped out of the ranks after April 1, escaped the Union cordon on April 9, or otherwise refused to surrender themselves.[11]

Their reasons were as varied as the men themselves. Many had been footsore and starving stragglers unable to keep up with the relentless pace of Lee's army as it pushed west. Others believed that there was little use resisting any further and elected to go home. Some simply hoped to forgo the humiliation of surrendering. Much of the cavalry had managed to ride past the Union troopers blocking the road to Lynchburg, while other artillerists and infantrymen slipped from the lines that day, refusing to acquiesce or be conquered. All told, for nearly 17,000 soldiers from the Army of Northern Virginia, the war did not end in the now famous village.[12]

What would happen to those soldiers? When Union general-in-chief Ulysses S. Grant set his pen to paper on April 9, he had a wealth of experience and precedent to guide him, but he had not paused to consider precisely to *whom* his terms might apply. Would it include all those not at Appomattox? Grant and others insisted perhaps the terms *should* apply to others, if only to prevent legitimate Confederate soldiers from casting their lot with guerrillas and continuing the war for years, if not decades, to come. Grant's primary goal was and continued to be the restoration of the Union. He believed that paroling as many Confederates as quickly as possible would serve as the best means for achieving peace and reconciliation.

But rather than assuaging Grant's concerns, the dispersal of Lee's army inflamed fears of roving bands and marauders. In this instance and countless others that would follow Appomattox, Grant, Secretary of War Edwin Stanton, President Andrew Johnson, Attorney General James Speed, and other government and army officials would make decisions shaped by the immediate context of moment. Most of these decisions were well intentioned, but as is so often the case, both their short- and long-term implications had not been considered. Each new choice led to new questions and more improvising.

Underlying all of this was ambiguity about whether the war had in fact ended. There had been no armistice that called for the end of all fighting, no treaty dictating the terms of peace signed by the political leaders of both sides. Appomattox was *not* the legal end of the war, only the capitulation of a single army. Both nineteenth-century and contemporary legal scholars have discussed this at length, pointing out that the *surrender of armies* is distinct from the termination of a *state of war* between the two sides.[13] In the days, weeks, and months that followed April 9, this issue loomed large. Civilians, government officials, Union military authorities, and paroled Confederates wondered just what it meant to parole a rebel soldier. Would the conditions of paroles remain in effect indefinitely? How long would paroled Confederates be required to register with local provost marshals? Would they ever be allowed to travel beyond the confines of their homes or home states again? Perhaps most importantly, was a parole a blanket amnesty, as some northerners feared and many Confederates expected? Were paroles and their protections limited to wartime? If the war was declared over, would the surrender terms continue to protect paroled Confederate soldiers from prosecution by the federal government? While many Union officials and legal theorists argued that rebels could be prosecuted *after* the war, they recognized that declaring the war over too soon would prevent the United States from utilizing war powers that still appeared necessary to enforce emancipation. Long after Appomattox, decisions on wartime as a legal state mattered to both Confederate soldiers and newly emancipated African Americans.[14]

This book considers the extraordinary difficulties of forging peace in the wake of a civil war. It is the story of simultaneous endings and beginnings, quickly radiating beyond the small village of Appomattox Court House, Virginia, and the armies that met there. As Lee's soldiers took to the paths, roads, rivers, and railway lines that led away from Appomattox, they carried the ambiguity of the surrender with them. They took that uncertainty to small farming communities and to cities like Richmond, bursting at the seams with refugees; to the mountains of the newly created state of West Virginia; to Unionists' abodes in Washington and Baltimore; to North Carolina, where a Confederate army remained in the field; and to a million other places across the South and North. Disbanding Lee's army marked the first and most important step in an enormous process of demobilizing all the armies of the Confederacy that was, in many ways, as important as mobilizing the men had been in 1861. Rather than a single event that unfolded solely at Appomattox, the surrender of Lee's army was scattered, staggered, and confusing. It involved tens of thousands of men across a vast landscape and proved far more drawn out than many at that time—or since—have understood.

This is also the story of civilians, free and enslaved, who were entangled with Lee's dispersing army. Hundreds of African American men still accompanied the Army of Northern Virginia at its surrender. They, too, wanted desperately to go home. Some would have a choice in how they did so. Others would not. Conversely, some Confederate sympathizers welcomed hungry soldiers into their homes as heroes. Others allowed them only to sleep in their barns. Some harbored those who had not yet been paroled, helping them evade Union authorities. Others formed vigilante committees and ran unwelcomed returning rebels out of their communities. In surrender as in battle, the war proved to be as much about those at home as about those who fought.

While civilians and government officials had a hand in bringing the war to a close, soldiers—both Union and Confederate—proved the most important actors. Those in the Army of Northern Virginia hailed from every state in the Confederacy as well as from the loyal border states of Maryland, West Virginia, Kentucky, and Missouri. Collectively and separately, they made decisions about whether to stay with the army or escape; how and when to travel home; to seek paroles; to turn themselves in to local provost marshals and risk the possibility of being detained; to return to their homes in Unionist regions; to beg for food or steal it; and, for some, to force their former slaves—now free men—to accompany them home or assist them. Some were well-known officers who hailed from the slaveholding ruling class. Others represented the middling class as farmers or printers. Still others had entered the army poor and went home even more so. Some willingly conceded defeat. Others sought desperately to continue the fight.

Union soldiers—especially Grant and his high command—likewise shaped the contours of this story. They issued orders for patrols to search for guerrillas or unparoled Confederates, arresting and executing some and perhaps letting others slip away. They forbade rebels from traveling through loyal regions. They offered transportation—or denied it. This is, therefore, a story of individuals as much as armies and bureaucracies.

Union and Confederate soldiers alike had participated in an extraordinarily wrenching experience of war, and all grappled with what the next steps might be—for them personally and for their country. This book neither examines nor excuses the motivations or purposes of Confederates as soldiers; rather, it explores the war's ending as a pivotal period that shaped all that followed, from Reconstruction to the present. Questions of Confederates' status and place in the Union lingered for years and even decades after Appomattox, but the first few weeks and months after April 9, 1865, proved critical in establishing the parameters within which these questions would—and could—be answered. Perhaps most importantly, the immediate aftermath of Appomattox confirmed that a deep and abiding commitment to the Confederacy had not ended with the surrender. In some ways, it had only begun.

1

Unraveling

The routes leading west from Petersburg and Richmond were a gruesome sight in early April 1865. The final week of March had brought torrents of rain to Southside Virginia, swelling creeks and streams and leaving roads clogged with ankle-deep mud. Rival armies likewise flooded the countryside. Anyone witnessing the scene might have easily discerned which would be victorious. As Robert E. Lee's Army of Northern Virginia tramped west, desperately hoping to find passage south to its Confederate allies commanded by Joseph E. Johnston, Ulysses S. Grant's Union forces pursued their quarry, growing in belief that four years of war could be brought at last to an end.

Lee's army appeared to be dissolving into the landscape. Soldiers had abandoned their mud-choked muskets. Cap boxes and cartridges lay strewn in a mad confusion. Discarded clothing, cooking utensils, personal baggage, blankets, and papers soaked with rain littered the way, while the dead and wounded filled the woods. Burning and broken-down wagons, ambulances, and caissons mired in the thick sludge became obstacles to avoid, as did the dead and dying horses and mules that had hauled them.[1]

Near the rear of Lee's thinning ranks marched James "Eddie" Whitehorne of the 12th Virginia. Now twenty-five years old, Whitehorne had grown up on his family farm in Greensville County, near the North Carolina border. In June 1861, he enlisted as a private in Company F, the Huger Greys, and by August he had won promotion to corporal and then first sergeant. But there his rise through the ranks ended, as would much of his time in the field. During the war's second year, terrible rheumatism forced him to take extended periods of leave. Rejoining his regiment in the spring of 1863, he fought at Chancellorsville and Gettysburg, only to have a shell fragment

7

smash both his legs on the second day of fighting. Incapacitated until June 1864, he rejoined his comrades, but only weeks after returning to the field, he was hit again in the leg at the battle of the Crater. Following two more months of medical furlough, he finally returned to the 12th Virginia in October. Now he found himself in a column fleeing west after abandoning the Confederate fortifications between Richmond and Petersburg in the early morning hours of April 3. In an all-night march he had covered more than twenty-three miles before crossing the Appomattox River by pontoon boat near Goode's Bridge. Exhausted and in terrible leg pain, Whitehorne confided in his diary, "I have a growing fear I shall not be able to keep up tomorrow."[2] But on he pressed.

Many of his comrades had decided differently. Desertions had been a problem in the army throughout the winter. From the camp of the 8th Virginia, E. Augustus Klipstein informed his wife in early February that four deserters from Stewart's Brigade had been executed. "They had better have remained faithful to the cause of their country, but there are a great many croakers and a good deal of dissatisfaction in the army," he wrote. But he understood why: "The prospect of another bloody campaign and short rations are doing its work."[3] Union forces enticed their foes to leave the siege lines as well, including offers of free transportation to the North and government employment. Other surrendering rebels received twenty-six dollars for turning over their guns and equipment to the U.S. forces. "I think that is pretty good inducements," wrote one Union soldier in early March. "They say they will *desert* by *Brigades* when there is a move."[4]

With the approach of the spring campaign season, the situation had become so untenable that on March 27 Lee issued what would prove his last order before the surrender, threatening to execute any man who so much as joked about deserting. "Those indulging such jests will find it difficult on a trial to rebut the presumption of guilt arising from their words," Lee warned, commanding that his order be read to each company once a day for three days and to every regiment at dress parade once a week for a month.[5]

But the desertions continued as the army abandoned Richmond and Petersburg. On the afternoon of April 3 near Namozine Church, General Sheridan reported that his cavalry had captured nearly 1,200 rebels, informing Grant that the surrounding woods were "filled with deserters and stragglers."[6] An officer with the 7th United States Colored Troops (USCT) observed that the proximity to home seemed to induce Virginia Confederates to give up the fight sooner than their comrades from farther south. "They say

Appomattox campaign, April 2–9, 1865.

that the whole Rebel forces that belong in Virginia will desert Lee as soon as he leaves for North Carolina," the officer wrote to his wife.[7]

Benjamin Sims of the 17th Virginia was one such deserter. Even before the retreat began, the conscript from Louisa County fled along with much of his regiment at Five Forks on April 1. "We take to the woods, every man for himself," he scribbled in his journal, adding that he had joined up with two of his company about a mile from the field. Unable to find a spot to cross the Appomattox River on April 2, he and a comrade decided to go home. But even those from farther afield elected to abandon their units.[8] The number of stragglers captured by pursuing Union forces daily ran in the thousands, and stories came from all directions of Confederates taking to the woods and heading home, some in small groups, others in large squads.

Each day, Union confidence surged. For nearly three years, Union troops had struggled to defeat Lee's seemingly unbeatable army. Now Federal cavalry reported that the rebels had been forced to destroy countless wagons, caissons, and munitions as they fled. Propelled forward, Union troops marched twenty to thirty miles a day in the mire, striving to ignore hunger and exhaustion. "My feet are full of blisters, and I am played out," wrote one weary soldier to his father. But weariness did not mean they would quit. As one Union artillerist declared, they could taste the opportunity to finally "bag Lee."[9]

After another all-night march through more heavy rain, on April 6 Lee's army advanced southwest until a fight erupted along the banks of Sailor's Creek. From Brig. Gen. Reuben Lindsay Walker's artillery train, James Albright witnessed the scene along a rise just across the creek. "I have never seen such confusion," he confessed that evening, "nor anything so nearly approaching a rout." When the quartermaster, commissary, and hospital wagons tried to cross a small gorge along the creek, they piled upon each other, and men struggled to pull weak horses and mules up out of the soggy creek bottom. Soon there was no choice but for the Confederates to abandon yet more precious ordnance, ammunition, and other stores.[10]

Albright could not have fathomed such a scene four years earlier. Born in Greensboro, North Carolina, in 1835, he had apprenticed himself at the age of sixteen to the printer of the *Greensboro Times*, a weekly literary paper. Quickly learning both the mechanics of printing and writing, by 1857 Albright could claim a byline as a coeditor along with his childhood friend C. C. Cole. Throughout the secession winter of 1860–61, Cole and Albright continued to publish their paper, voicing their support of the Union and opposition to secession. But in the aftermath of Fort Sumter and Lincoln's

The Last of Ewell's Corps, April 6, 1865, based on a sketch by Alfred R. Waud.
In *Battles and Leaders of the Civil War*, ed. Robert Underwood Johnson
and Clarence Clough Buel, vol. 4 (New York: Century, 1887), 721.

call for 75,000 troops, they threw the full measure of their support behind the Confederacy. "We were born and reared in this town," they wrote in an editorial that spring, and "therefore, North Carolina shall be first in our heart and the Confederate states, second — and for these we will battle, no matter who assaults them." Demonstrating his loyalty to his state and new country, Cole enlisted in the spring of 1861 along with other members of the Guilford Grays. But unlike most of the young men who marched off to war, Albright had a young wife and three-year-old son. He would stay in Greensboro as the sole editor and owner of the weekly paper.[11]

For the next year, Albright fought the war through words. Each week the *Times* reported from the Virginia battlefields, reprinted messages from President Jefferson Davis, and called on the town's women to help gather provisions for their soldiers. In the spring of 1862, with Confederate conscription looming, the newly widowed Albright recognized he could no longer remain at home. Closing down his printshop and securing someone to take care of his young son, in late April he joined the 13th Battalion North Carolina Artillery (soon transferred to the 12th Battalion Virginia Artillery), where Albright found himself detailed as an ordnance sergeant for the entire battalion.[12]

Three years later, the thirty-year-old looked around him to see the Army of Northern Virginia crumbling. As night began to fall along the banks of

Little Sailor's Creek, Albright and the rest of the army managed to slip away, but the battle had proven especially costly at a moment when Lee could little afford to lose any more men. His army had sustained approximately 7,700 casualties (compared with only 1,148 among Union forces), in addition to nearly 300 wagons and ambulances. Eight generals had been captured, including Lt. Gen. Richard S. Ewell and Maj. Gen. George Washington Custis Lee, the commanding general's oldest son. Witnessing the disorganized mob from high ground overlooking the creek late that day, Lee quietly exclaimed, "My God! has the army been dissolved?"[13]

The losses from those taken prisoner or killed and wounded proved catastrophic enough. But another 1,450 Confederates escaped the field, failing to rejoin their commands. Among them was Maj. Joseph G. Blount of the Macon Light Artillery. Deployed on a ridge above Sailor's Creek, his gunners had attempted to help Maj. Gen. John B. Gordon's Second Corps hold off the Federals. When it became clear that this would be impossible, Blount and his battery left with their two remaining guns and headed west toward Lynchburg.[14] So too did countless others, including Richard Chapman and William H. Reed of the 32nd Virginia. The departures, Albright observed that evening in his diary, would soon ruin Lee's army.[15]

Even with the attrition, the Union high command recognized the tenacity with which Confederates continued to fight. Sheridan insisted that Sailor's Creek proved "one of the severest conflicts of the war, for the enemy fought with desperation to escape capture, and we, bent on his destruction, were no less eager and determined." Faced with annihilation and starvation on one hand or surrender on the other, one Union soldier observed that the Confederates continued to "cling to General Lee with childlike faith" as they pressed on west toward Farmville and looked for their opportunity to turn south toward General Johnston.[16] But still the Confederate ranks thinned. After another night march, the third in five days, thousands of stragglers dropped out of the column, some simply collapsing along roadbeds, others wandering listlessly through Virginia's dripping woods. Trailing behind Lee's men, the lead division of the Union Second Corps picked up individuals and entire squads, many literally sleeping on the side of the road.[17] Hustled to their feet, the men reversed their march back toward Richmond. Now that Union prisoners had been liberated from Libby Prison, the bluecoats happily refilled it with Lee's men, one soldier estimating that upward of 3,000 rebels now occupied the wretched site.[18]

By the time Grant arrived in Farmville on the afternoon of April 7, he recognized that Lee could not hold out much longer. Desertions alone suggested that his army was disintegrating. But the capture of thousands of prisoners at Sailor's Creek and elsewhere accompanied by the destruction of so many wagons convinced Grant that the time was right to end the fighting. At 5:00 P.M., sitting on the brick front porch of the Randolph House (later called the Prince Edward Hotel), he issued a note inviting Lee to surrender. "The results of last week must convince you of the hopelessness of further resistance," Grant began. "I feel that it is so, and regard it as my duty to shift from myself the responsibility of any further effusion of blood by asking of you the surrender of that portion of the Confederate army known as the Army of Northern Virginia."[19]

Just after nightfall, the flag of truce appeared in front of Confederate lines bearing Grant's letter. At the Blanton House in Cumberland County, Lee took the note, read it silently, and then, without uttering a word, passed it to Lt. Gen. James Longstreet. "Not yet," Longstreet replied. Lee trusted the general he called his "Old War Horse" perhaps more than any other senior officer. He assured Lee that it was not yet time to capitulate. With such encouragement, Lee responded to Grant that he was not ready to surrender; even so, he wondered what the terms of surrender might entail. Until he heard from Grant, however, he would continue to press his army west.[20]

Another night march made Eddie Whitehorne's leg throb with pain, yet on he marched even as others seemed to melt into the countryside. William Gordon McCabe, a twenty-three-year-old staff officer with the 1st Company of the Richmond Howitzers, ascribed the attrition to cowardice rather than fatigue. "This is one of the very saddest days of my life," he wrote on April 7. "When I see the crowd of stragglers and then look across at the Blue Ridge and think that I must give up this beloved Virginia because of the faint-heartedness and cowardice of these men, who have deserted their colors, my heart bursts with a sob. I am willing and ready, if God spares my life, to follow the old battle flag to the gulf of Mexico. If our men desert it, and I am not killed, I shall be forever an exile," he vowed. "If we lose our country," he surmised, "it is our own fault." He would do his best, however, to prevent such an outcome, arresting scores of laggards along the route.[21] Other officers resorted to more desperate measures to keep men in the ranks, including threats to shoot those who appeared eager to depart. Some soldiers could not be compelled to continue even under threat. But most marched on, determined to press the fight.[22]

Just south of Appomattox Court House, an exhausted and famished James Albright had settled down into camp near the station along the South Side Railroad.[23] Traveling with Walker's reserve artillery train, Albright and others now led the Confederate column, crossing the headwaters of the Appomattox before passing through Appomattox Court House, a village that consisted of a post office in the general store, a handful of homes, and its central feature—the courthouse. Reaching a rise about a half mile above the railroad station around 3:00 P.M. on April 8, the artillerists unharnessed their few remaining horses and mules, lit campfires to cook their paltry rations, and lay down on the ground to sleep. Suddenly, the cry of Union cavalry startled them. The lead element of Sheridan's troopers, under Bvt. Maj. Gen. Wesley Merritt, was upon them in an instant, sent to capture the waiting supply trains and to cut off Lee's escape route west.[24]

Albright joined the fray, scrambling to help push the Union cavalry back. But pandemonium quickly ensued. Panicked officers and soldiers rushed around in madness, at least one artillery captain hiding behind a stump on his knees before Gordon McCabe chased him to the rear with his saber. With darkness blanketing the battlefield, the Federals proffered one more charge, canisters exploding all along the line. Finally, Walker ordered the guns withdrawn to the north toward Red Oak Church near Oakville, staff officers riding from the rear to the front instructing men to take care of themselves. Hearing these orders, several batteries elected to escape, dragging their guns with them if they could, abandoning those that could no longer be fired or pulled. Hurrying back to his camping spot, Albright shoved his clothing in a bag, destroyed his letters, and tore the name off his pocket diary so that "no Yank could say he had 'a rebels diary' by the name of Albright." Then with his captain and one wagon, he abandoned the field and headed west toward Lynchburg rather than face the prospect of surrendering.[25]

On the night of April 8, Lee assembled what would prove his last council of war. With the moon casting a bright glow, Gordon, Longstreet, and Maj. Gen. Fitzhugh Lee of the cavalry gathered around a crackling fire, where Lee recounted his exchange of letters with Grant. He had received reports that Union forces now blocked the road south of Appomattox Court House. If it was only cavalry, the Confederates might hope to push past them. But if Federal infantry proved to be in their front, they would have no choice but to surrender. Taking all of this in, Fitz Lee offered his uncle one caveat: if surrender seemed imminent, he would try to extricate the cavalry with the hopes of fighting another day.[26]

Near midnight, a courier arrived at Grant's headquarters with Lee's response. Despite Lee's hedging tone that insisted that he was not yet ready to yield but only to discuss "the restoration of peace," Grant knew Federal forces now squeezed the Army of Northern Virginia from the south and west. If the generals met, Grant was confident he could compel a surrender within an hour. But his chief of staff, Brig. Gen. John A. Rawlins, had been incensed at the tone of Lee's letter, and the former lawyer reminded Grant that he had no authority to arrange terms of peace. "Your business is to capture, or destroy Lee's army," Rawlins counseled. Grant agreed, but at the moment his head was throbbing from a migraine, and he needed sleep. He would respond to Lee's letter in the morning.[27]

Around 3:00 A.M. on Palm Sunday, April 9, what remained of Lee's army roused once more and fell into line. Under the cover of darkness and a dense fog, men who had covered more than 100 miles in a week began to move west along the Stage Road, hoping to break through the enemy that encircled them. Catching up with Lee during the ride, Brig. Gen. Edward "Porter" Alexander halted with his commander to take in the landscape two miles east of Appomattox Court House. They could surrender, Alexander observed. But he advised instead that they cut their way out, scatter to the woods and bushes, and then try to join Johnston, or the men might return to their home states with their arms and report to their governors. Delay might yet provide more time for foreign intervention from France or Britain, but once they received news of Lee's surrender, neither nation would intercede. Perhaps most important, if Lee's army surrendered, every other Confederate army was sure to follow. "The one thing left us now to fight for is to try & get some sort of *terms*," Alexander stressed, "not to be absolutely helpless, & at the mercy of the enemy." He knew the United States would never recognize the Confederacy as a sovereign nation, but he thought individual governors might be in a position to negotiate with the Federal government. Rather than succumb to the mortification of what would surely be Grant's demand for unconditional surrender, Alexander thought it best to flee the field.[28]

Lee listened patiently before explaining that if he turned his army loose, the men would have no rations and be subject to no discipline. They would turn to plundering and robbing to survive. "The country would be full of lawless bands," he cautioned. He also knew that the United States would not tolerate the dispersal of rebel forces, especially its leaders. "The enemy's cavalry would pursue in the hopes of catching the principal officers, & wherever they went there would be fresh rapine & destruction." Lee would not unleash this guerrilla-style war on the South. Plus, he assured Alexander, "Grant will not demand unconditional surrender. He will give us as honorable terms as we have right to ask or expect."[29]

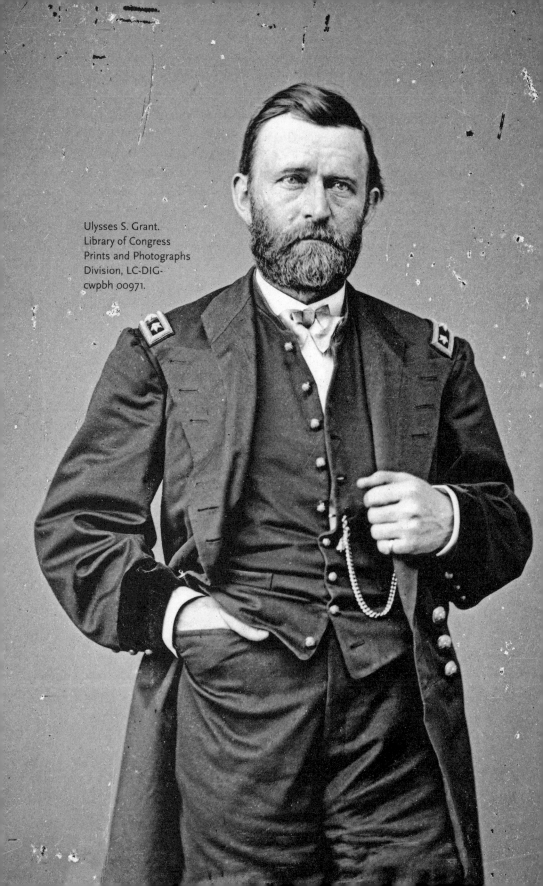

Ulysses S. Grant.
Library of Congress
Prints and Photographs
Division, LC-DIG-
cwpbh 00971.

Around 8:30 A.M. Lee started to the rear to confer with Grant, as his letter of the previous day had promised. Lee and his aides had just passed the rear guard when they met a member of Union major general George Gordon Meade's staff bearing Grant's reply. Grant began by informing Lee that he had "no authority to treat on the subject of peace"; that was a political matter, not a military one. Grant could negotiate only the surrender of Lee's army. But, he added, he was equally anxious for peace, as was the entire North. The moment had come for Confederates to lay down their arms. With his army encircled, Lee knew he now had no other choice. Turning to Col. Charles Marshall, his closest aide, Lee instructed him to write Grant and request a meeting to deal with the surrender of his army.[30]

Like Alexander, those in the ranks were not so convinced that Grant was "a man of mercy." Throughout the retreat, many had feared that if forced to surrender they would face scorn and imprisonment. They knew well the reputation of "Unconditional Surrender" Grant. "That we should be subjected to abhorrent humiliation was conceived as a matter of course," explained one cannoneer. As members of the Confederacy's most celebrated army, he and others worried that they might be subjected to the "exultation of a victorious foe, such as we had seen pictured in our school books, or as practiced by conquering nations in all times." Many believed it probable that "after an ordeal of mortifying exposure for the gratification of the military," they would be "paraded through Northern cities for the benefit of jeering crowds" before being sent to prison camps.[31]

Although few men in the ranks knew it, Unionists had indeed celebrated when Lincoln returned to Washington after his visit to Richmond on April 4 with 600 Confederate prisoners guarded by members of the 28th USCT. "It is retributive justice all the way through," abolitionist Julia Wilbur observed from Alexandria. "Lincoln comes to W[ashington] like the conquerors of old bringing his captives with him." To avoid such a fate, many of Lee's soldiers had contemplated plans to escape, including cutting their way out by using the guns of the men who had fallen in front of them. Many did more than discuss escaping. In February, Augustus Klipstein had chastised deserters, but faced with the prospect of surrender he now abandoned the army. Rather than seeing themselves as deserters to their cause when surrender became imminent, thousands of Lee's men calculated that leaving might be the best means of both preserving their individual honor and displaying their loyalty to the Confederate nation.[32]

Among those who refused to capitulate were remnants of Brig. Gen. Reuben Lindsay Walker's artillery train. Six miles to the north of Appomattox Court House, they were preparing breakfast in their camp near the Red Oak Church on the morning of April 9. More than half of Walker's train had been destroyed or captured in the previous day's clash with Maj. Gen. George A. Custer's cavalry. Nearly two dozen guns had been captured at Appomattox Station, while another two dozen had escaped toward Lynchburg. Fewer than five dozen pieces remained that morning when a courier arrived from Lee. Rumors circulated through camp that Lee had asked Walker to join him at daybreak with the artillery if he could. If Walker found this impossible, those under his command who favored continuing the contest were to report to the mountain town of Lincolnton, North Carolina, where they would receive further instructions. While Walker rode off to Lee's headquarters hoping to learn more, the batteries began to hitch up and move out into the road. But when he returned, all movement halted. There was no way they could escape the Federal cordon.

Determined that the best way to fight was to ditch the main army, strike off in small groups, and reorganize at a later date, Walker's men prepared to leave. They spiked and buried some guns in a gully-washed ravine near the church to prevent the Federals from capturing their artillery pieces. They cut down the carriages, chopped limber chests and wheels into small kindling, and unharnessed the horses before disbanding the companies. Col. C. E. Lightfoot of the Surry Light Artillery informed his men he would not surrender the command but disband it, leaving them all to their own devices. But first, he ordered each of his drivers to take his best horse and give the other to a cannoneer so that the men might have some way to travel home. Mounting the horses, the men rode north toward the James River in small groups. Off marched members of Martin's Battery. Away rode men from the Surry Light Artillery. Some were headed home. But others, including Gordon McCabe, Harry C. Townsend, Charles Friend, and at least twenty other members of the 1st Company of the Richmond Howitzers broke into several squads, bound for Lincolnton. "Every officer and man weeping," McCabe wrote. "All promised to join us in N.C.," where they would continue the fight.[33]

Even as officers from both armies began to mingle near the steps of the courthouse in the village awaiting a meeting between Grant and Lee, two of Fitzhugh Lee's three cavalry divisions were galloping west toward the Blue Ridge, refusing to await the terms. Separated from Gordon's infantry, around 11:00 A.M. Fitz Lee, accompanied by Maj. Gen. Thomas L. Rosser and Col. Thomas T. Munford's troopers, pressed farther north and west, where they encountered another line of Union cavalry. Rushing forward in a saber charge with the rebel yell echoing across the valley, they slammed into the Union line. All of a sudden, the road to Lynchburg was clear. The infantry might be trapped. But the cavalrymen under Rosser and Munford had another prospect. If they desired, they could continue west and hope to fight another day.[34]

When the flags of truce began to appear, Munford elected to confer with the enemy. With a canteen of peach brandy tucked in his saddle, the thirty-four-year-old cavalry officer along with two staff officers rode out to speak with Union major general Ranald S. Mackenzie, who informed him that Lee was at the moment negotiating the terms of surrender with Grant. Munford asked if he might communicate with Lee to determine whether the cavalry, now in the rear of Union lines, would be included. If it was, he would cheerfully submit. But until he had proof, he felt at liberty to withdraw his troopers. The peach brandy made its rounds among the men, but the Union officers could not give Munford any answers. Mounting his horse, he nodded and thanked the men for their civility, then rode back to his command.[35]

While Munford held his conference, many of his men had settled on their own course of action. Seeing the ceasefire as an opportunity to avoid the humiliation of surrender, some of Maj. Daniel A. Grimsley's 6th Virginia Cavalry troopers began leading their horses to the rear under the guise of finding a stream to water their mounts. Federal officers in their front complained that the rebels were violating the truce by permitting men to leave the line. But what recourse did the Confederates have when even the officers began to flee? Obtaining permission to go to the woods and camp, Grimsley and several others of the command decided instead to head toward their homes in northern Virginia.[36]

After meeting with Mackenzie, Munford returned to discuss the situation with Fitz Lee and Rosser. Perhaps they genuinely worried that they would not be included in whatever terms Grant would extend to Lee. Maybe they believed, as Fitz Lee later suggested, that escape was essential because the men owned their own mounts and could not afford to resume their postwar lives without them. Alternatively, they may have held out hope that the cavalry might yet continue the struggle. Whatever their rationale, the three officers agreed that their troopers would not surrender that day. Instead, the cavalrymen swung up into their saddles once more and cantered west on the road to Lynchburg. A few miles from Appomattox they halted at a crossroads. One way led to a ferry over the James River, the other to Campbell Court House and Lynchburg. While most of Brig. Gen. William H. F. Payne's brigade headed toward the river along with much of the horse artillery, intending to disperse, Munford's old brigade accompanied by the Maryland Cavalry agreed to reconvene in Lynchburg.[37]

Throughout the morning of April 9, hundreds, perhaps thousands, of artillerists and infantrymen fled the field.[38] Some artillery batteries did so as units, taking their canon with them. Twenty-eight guns from the artillery of Richard H. Anderson's division headed for Lynchburg.[39] But others, such as those of Capt. John J. Shoemaker, Lt. Charles R. Phelps, and Lt. Marcellus N. Moorman, along with many of the men of Shoemaker's Artillery, abandoned their guns before leaving.[40] Among the infantry, many struck off with only one or two comrades. "A great many save themselves the humiliation by escaping as best they may," a signalman scribbled in his diary that evening, adding, "Some Genls tell their men to save themselves if they can."[41] The unshakable loyalty of Lee's troops had finally unraveled not only because of exhaustion but also because of individual honor and a sense of duty to the cause.

2

The Terms

Resting alongside the remnants of the 12th Virginia during the ceasefire, Eddie Whitehorne pulled out his diary and began to write. "Sad is a poor word to describe how I feel," he confessed. After four years as a soldier, he could not imagine what a potential surrender might mean. All he knew was how to drill, march, and fight. How would he return to farming or working in a store when he had thought of nothing for the past four years except staying alive, whipping the enemy, or preparing for the next battle? But it was more than life after the army that gave him pause. Unlike his comrades who feared punishment upon surrender, he was pondering all that had been lost. "To think we have been toiling, suffering, bleeding for our country and for the freedom to govern our states as we wish and then to be forced to surrender," he lamented. To surrender meant abandoning the Confederate quest for independence. It meant that so many of his comrades and leaders had died in vain. "It is humiliating in the extreme," he admitted. "I'd rather be killed than go back to Pleasant Shade and tell them we were subjugated."[1]

Lee had assured artillery general Porter Alexander and others that Grant would offer honorable terms, but like his men, he had no way of knowing whether Whitehorne's fears were warranted. Waiting inside Wilmer McLean's parlor along with his staff officer Charles Marshall and two of Grant's aides, he proved a striking figure in his full-dress uniform complete with sash and sword. If he was to be taken prisoner, he would at least look the part of a noble general.[2] Around 1:30, Grant, with his personal staff, arrived at the edge of Appomattox Court House, clad in his officer's sack coat with only the shoulder straps of a lieutenant general and in mud-spattered pants, his headquarters wagon having failed to keep up in the mad rush to capture the rebel army. Climbing the home's broad steps, Grant entered the handsomely outfitted parlor and met Lee face to face for the first time in the war.[3] After some idle small talk, Grant informed Lee that the terms he offered were the same as those indicated in his letters: Confederate soldiers would lay down their arms and not take them up again until properly exchanged. Again, the conversation drifted to other topics before Lee interrupted Grant, asking for the terms in writing. While other members of Grant's staff exited the parlor, Grant called for Lt. Col. Ely Parker to bring him writing materials. Seated at a small oval table, Grant bent over his manifold order-book, which allowed him to make three copies, and with a cigar in his mouth began to compose.[4]

Rolls of officers and men were to be made in duplicate, one copy to be given to the Union army and the other to be retained by Confederate officials. The officers would give their individual paroles not to take up arms against the United States government, while each company or regimental commander would sign a parole on behalf of his command. The arms, artillery, and public property of the Confederate army were to be turned over to the Union forces, but officers would be permitted to keep their personal sidearms and baggage.

During the previous days' exchange of letters, Grant had refused to concede anything except the surrender of the men on parole. But now in the room with Lee, he added a provision. It was to be the most important of the surrender: officers and men would be allowed to return to their homes, "not to be disturbed by United States authority so long as they observe their paroles and the laws in force where they may reside."[5] Contrary to his reputation and nickname, or even to the fears of those in Lee's ranks, Grant did not demand an unconditional surrender. Instead, he offered the terms he thought would produce what he sought most: the capitulation of Lee's army, which he hoped would be followed by the rapid surrender of all other Confederate forces.

Although many would applaud his magnanimous and generous approach, almost from the moment he penned the agreement Grant found himself on the defensive. Why had he been so lenient? Why had he not demanded an unconditional surrender? Had he afforded protections to the rebels beyond his capacity as a military commander? For the rest of his life, he would be forced to justify himself for decisions seemingly made in the moment. As he famously wrote in his memoirs, "When I put my pen to the paper I did not know the first word that I should make use of in writing the terms. I only knew what was in my mind, and I wished to express it clearly."[6]

It was true that no government official dictated the terms. Nor were they

inspired by any subordinate. Grant's words might have flowed forth sponta-
neously, but as his military secretary Lt. Col. Adam Badeau later explained,
the terms were not the result of chance, carelessness, or indifference: "They
were the legitimate outgrowth of Grant's judgement and feeling; the consequence of all that had gone before; embodied then for the first time, because
then for the first time the necessity for the embodiment had arrived."[7]

Grant needed to look no further than the American Revolution for an example of how a civil war might end. In October 1781, George Washington's
Continental army had surrounded British forces under Lord Cornwallis on
the Virginia Peninsula by land and (thanks to the timely arrival of the French)
by sea. In keeping with European tradition, Washington paroled most of the
officers, allowing them to retain their sidearms and personal baggage. The
common soldiers, however, would receive no such paroles. After turning
over their arms and accoutrements in a formal ceremony, they marched off
to internment camps in Winchester, Virginia, and Fort Frederick, Maryland.
There they remained for months with inadequate food, clothing, or quarters before being relocated to equally hideous prison camps in Pennsylvania. Struggling to house and feed the Yorktown prisoners, even in an abysmal
way, in June 1782 Congress voted to sell the German prisoners into inden-
tured servitude and further reduce the rations of the British prisoners. Not
until peace negotiations had been secured in May 1783—nineteen months
after the surrender at Yorktown—would the 6,000 British prisoners be released.[8]

   At West Point, the young Sam Grant likely studied the lessons from the
Revolution as well as the laws of war penned by Emmerich de Vattel. The
eighteenth-century Swiss jurist stressed that warfare should be conducted
"with great moderation and generosity" and "extreme politeness." Hoping
to avoid the cycles of retaliation that followed when one side claimed moral
justness, Vattel urged enemies to separate the means from the ends of war, to
embrace a moral neutrality, and to avoid retaliation and retribution.[9]

   Grant may have studied theories of war in the classroom, but sitting
across from Lee in McLean's parlor he might have also recalled his first direct experience with surrender—one shared by Lee. As a second lieutenant with the 4th Infantry during the Mexican War, Grant witnessed Gen.
Zachary Taylor compel the surrender of Mexican forces at the provin-
cial capital of Monterrey in September 1846. Certain that the fighting was
now over and trusting that a generous peace would help end the war, Tay-

lor agreed to an eight-week armistice before allowing the Mexican forces to keep their weapons and evacuate the city. While President James K. Polk derided the terms as too lenient, Taylor's soldiers praised his generosity.[10] But the war was not nearly as final as Taylor believed. When Gen. Winfield Scott's initial demand for a surrender was refused at Veracruz in March 1847, he bombarded the garrison into submission. After forty-eight hours of shelling, the carnage within the city's walls proved ghastly, leaving smoldering buildings, starving women and children, and hundreds of casualties of both civilians and soldiers. If stories of civilians relegated to eating donkeys were not enough, in the days following the surrender U.S. troops rioted, setting fire to a nearby settlement after they had robbed and raped several inhabitants. The surrender at Veracruz had offered a glimpse of a less than ideal capitulation — of one that might spiral out of control, bringing more chaos than closure.[11]

Grant likely also had in his mind the surrenders of two other rebel armies he had orchestrated during the present war. At Fort Donelson on February 16, 1862, Brig. Gen. Simon B. Buckner had requested the appointment of commissioners to agree upon terms of capitulation as well as an armistice until the commissioners could conduct their meeting. But Grant informed his former West Point and Mexican War comrade that "no terms except unconditional and immediate surrender" would be accepted. Grant promised that the approximately 12,000 prisoners sent north to camps would be treated well and provided rations. Invoking tradition, he allowed officers to retain their sidearms and personal baggage but required all horses and public property be turned over to Union authorities. Departing from European and the Revolution's practice of formal surrender ceremonies, however, there would be no formal parade, no stacking of arms. Nor would Grant demand the surrendering officer's sword, as European custom had long held.[12] He would not inflict unnecessary humiliation on men he hoped might one day be his countrymen again. But there were limits to Grant's magnanimity. When Buckner grumbled that his men had been treated unfairly by Union troops who took their blankets and appropriated officers' sidearms, Grant fired back that "every thing belongs to the victors."[13]

By the summer of 1863, at Vicksburg along the banks of the Mississippi, Grant had another Confederate army in his grip. On July 3, Confederate lieutenant general John C. Pemberton requested an armistice in order to arrange the terms of capitulation. Grant echoed his Donelson terms, rejecting negotiation. But when the two commanders met, Pemberton refused Grant's demand of an unconditional surrender.[14] After consulting with his subordinates, Grant proposed slightly revised terms. His officers had convinced him to parole the nearly 30,000 surrendering Confederates rather than incur the cost of shipping them off to prisoner-of-war camps on the condition that they refrain from any further military service against the United States until formally exchanged.[15] Early in the morning on July 4, Pemberton consented.

Grant's choice to parole the Confederates relied upon both custom and the laws of war. European tradition had long held that prisoners of war might be released upon their oath not to bear arms against those who captured them until exchanged for an enemy soldier. Under an elaborate prison cartel system developed in 1862, Union paroled prisoners were held in their own army's parole camps until exchanged, while Confederates went home to await exchange. A parole, therefore, served only as a conditional freedom that relied heavily upon a soldier's honor, especially in the case of Confederates who had been sent home. Those who violated their paroles faced execution if recaptured. A parole, however, said nothing about the enemy's obligation to the parolee; the onus rested entirely on the prisoner. Grant calculated that the paroled Vicksburg Confederates would return to civilian life rather than report for exchange. His leniency, he hoped, would "make them less dangerous foes during the continuance of the hostilities, and better citizens after the war."[16]

All of this history must have weighed on Grant's mind as he sat in Wilmer McLean's parlor.[17] Years later he would observe that he thought the Confederate cause "one of the worst for which people ever fought." Yet his magnanimous terms reflected the rules of warfare he had learned both in the classroom and on the battlefield. He would not hold the rebels' cause against them and seek retaliation or retribution.[18] Just as he had done at Vicksburg, he would parole the surrendering Confederates.

Perhaps most importantly at Appomattox, Grant's terms were not his alone but also those of his president.[19] Lincoln's Proclamation of Amnesty and Reconstruction issued on December 8, 1863, had established the president's lenient position on reunion. The proclamation allowed every Confederate below the rank of colonel to obtain an absolute pardon by laying down his arms and taking an oath of allegiance to the United States. In meeting with Grant, Maj. Gen. William T. Sherman, and Rear Adm. David D. Porter aboard the *River Queen* in late March, Lincoln had made clear that he desired an easy peace and liberal terms. He hoped that the Confederate soldiers might quickly return to their farms or businesses, and as such, he wanted no retaliation or revenge. In a more poetic fashion, the president's second inaugural address had summed up his position: "malice toward none."[20]

Yet Grant remained well aware that he was limited to negotiating military topics, not political ones. When Lincoln had met with Confederate leaders on February 3 at Hampton Roads to discuss peace, General-in-Chief Grant was not permitted to attend. He was reminded of this the following month when on March 2 Lee inquired as to whether Grant might be willing to discuss "an end to the calamities of war." Grant had consulted Secretary of War Edwin Stanton, who conveyed Lincoln's stern instructions: the lieutenant general was to have "no conference with General Lee unless it be for the capitulation of Gen. Lee's army, or on some minor, and purely, military matter." He was not "to decide, discuss, or confer upon any political question."[21] Grant assured the secretary that under no circumstances would he exceed his authority and then declined to meet Lee.[22] His response to Lee on April 8 had reiterated the fact that he could not negotiate peace.

Although Lee had not asked, Grant was likewise aware that he could not address the status of the enslaved people — perhaps hundreds — who remained with Lee's army. At Vicksburg, six months after the Emancipation Proclamation, Pemberton had requested that in addition to their sidearms, his officers be allowed to retain their personal property — including their slaves. Grant officially refused to allow Confederates to take their slaves with them, but when pressed as to whether "servants" who wished to leave with their rebel masters might do so, he replied that "no compulsory measures would be used to hold negroes."[23] During the Vicksburg campaign, freeing the slaves had been part of the military strategy of striking at Confederate resources. Yet Grant said nothing about the enslaved men at Appomattox. Lee's surrender signaled the demise of the rebellion, but a military convention could not resolve the question of emancipation.[24]

Politics, military tradition, and the laws of war all influenced the terms Grant would offer Lee, but so did pragmatism. It simply was not feasible to hold all of the men of the army as prisoners. (Ironically, Union soldiers captured by Confederates during the Appomattox campaign would be sent to Camp Parole in Annapolis. Unlike their defeated foes, these soldiers from the victorious army would not be allowed to return home immediately.) It was equally untenable to disband the men without any restraints upon them. Instead, as he had done at Vicksburg, Grant opted to consider them paroled prisoners of war forbidden from raising arms against the United States. Indeed, General Orders No. 100, known as the Lieber Code, held that the penalty for breaking one's parole was death. The rolls to be created of all those paroled at Appomattox would be imperative for enforcing such provisions should any Confederate again dare to take up arms against the United States.[25]

Grant's most original and noteworthy addition to the terms was the provision that Confederates would be allowed to return to their homes undisturbed, as long as they did not break laws in force locally. No previous surrender had included such language, but it was couched in the laws of war. Grant was no lawyer, yet he understood that having treated Confederates as enemy belligerents throughout the conflict (as opposed to rebellious citizens or criminals), the Union could not punish them. Enemy soldiers could be defeated but not prosecuted. Rules of civilized warfare held that once a war was over, there was no need to punish a vanquished enemy.[26] By including this provision, Grant tacitly acknowledged Lee's soldiers as enemy combatants who could not be tried as traitors for waging war. Significantly, he included this line without Lee's request.

Since 1865, many have credited Grant's terms as a gesture of benevolence meant to bring wayward rebels back into the fold.[27] His immediate concern, however, was the prospect of protracted and irregular-style war — the type General Alexander had suggested to Lee on the night of April 8. History revealed that civil wars could cascade into years of reprisals and retaliation.[28] Judicious and generous terms, Grant hoped, would do much to avoid such an outcome. The terms Grant set forth were tools for achieving his military objective of forcing the surrender of Lee's forces — an objective that he and Lincoln believed would help bring peace. Ending the fighting and bringing the Union back together remained their paramount goal. Grant firmly believed that punitive or humiliating terms would hinder this process. But in adding the provision that the Confederates would be allowed to return to their homes undisturbed, Grant had inadvertently opened the door for a much broader interpretation of paroles, one that would have significant consequences in the weeks and months to come.

While Union officers quietly filled McLean's parlor, Grant walked over to Lee and handed him the manifold order-book. As he read, Lee brought his own experiences and expectations of surrender with him from his time at West Point and in Mexico. But he had no experience in surrendering a force. Even when badly outnumbered, his army had always triumphed, or at least survived to fight another day. Now he wondered what history might say. He also thought of the men who had endured so long under his command. Would his soldiers be subjected to harsh conditions? Would they face persecution? Prosecution? He knew the onus to protect them fell on his shoulders.[29]

In this light, Lee made one edit to Grant's original text, adding the

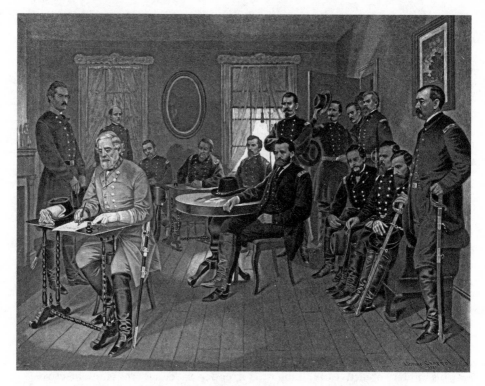

The Surrender of Lee by Alonzo Chappel. This 1885 print highlights Lee as the main figure. Many elements of the room are accurate, including the number of tables and Lee's one aide, Col. Charles Marshall. But it features men at the wrong tables and inaccurately portrays Grant's dress. Library of Congress Prints and Photographs Division, LC-DIG-ppmsca-59361.

phrase "until properly exchanged" to Grant's parole terms. This was no mere correction or oversight. It held important military implications and revealed both Grant's and Lee's understanding of the surrender.[30] Grant *had* included language about an exchange in his letter to Lee the previous day. But sitting across from the rebel general, he neglected to do so because he believed Lee's surrender signaled the beginning of the end of the war. There was no need for a prisoner exchange if the war had concluded. Lee's emendation, however, left open another outcome. Should the armies in North Carolina, along the Gulf, and west of the Mississippi prevail, Lee's men might be needed once more. They might be exchanged to fight another day. Lee's modification signaled a fleeting bit of hope. Grant's concession of the point, however, indicated his confidence that the war was almost over. So did his promise to allow Lee's artillery and cavalry to keep their mounts.[31]

While their staff drew up the final copies, Lee and Grant spoke briefly about the specifics of the surrender. Each appointed three officers to oversee the details. Grant selected Maj. Gen. John Gibbon, Bvt. Maj. Gen. Wesley Merritt, and Maj. Gen. Charles Griffin, while Lee selected Lt. Gen. James Longstreet, Maj. Gen. John B. Gordon, and Brig. Gen. William N. Pendleton. With this settled, Lee requested rations for his starving men, to which Grant readily agreed. Before leaving, Lee asked one more thing. Despite the generous terms, he recognized that passions among his men ran deep. Might the two armies be kept separate in order to prevent "unpleasant individual rencontres that may take place with a too free intercourse?" Again, Grant nodded in agreement. Around 3:00 P.M., the generals rose, shook hands, and Lee departed.[32]

By 4:00 P.M., word of Lee's surrender had reached the Union lines, and the enthusiasm could not be contained. When General Meade and his staff rode among the troops waving their caps, the soldiers went wild. Thousands of Union kepis flew through the air, men cheered at the top of their lungs, and a few hearty souls tossed their comrades in blankets. South of the village, a brigade of USCT soldiers likewise celebrated, firing a volley in joy. All along the lines, the batteries sounded a national salute. Just before dusk, the troops received orders to go into camp and send for rations and supplies suited to a celebration. Around campfires brimming with laughter, the victorious soldiers enjoyed a raucous supper with their superiors before improvising some fireworks from artillery ammunition chests.[33]

Even amid the jubilation, the weight of events was clear to every soldier in blue who had stormed the heights at Fredericksburg, held the high ground at Gettysburg, or survived the horrors of Spotsylvania's Bloody Angle. All knew well that Lee's army had been the main strength of the Confederacy — its primary source of inspiration and hope for independence. And now it was no more. "So ends the great rebel army: *the* army of the rebellion," declared one Union colonel. He wished, however, that Lee's army had been defeated in a decisive battle and utterly annihilated. As it was, the rebellion appeared worn out rather than suppressed. Some of his comrades agreed. "There are many unsubdued spirits among them yet, and large numbers will scarcely regard their parole," predicted another U.S. soldier. Mesmerized by the glowing embers of his campfire, he could not help but wonder if such an ending might not yet encourage rebel sentiment.[34]

Across the Appomattox River that evening, many of Lee's men took to their diaries, recording their range of emotions. "Some were crying, some cursing and some praying," observed one South Carolina soldier; "mourning of every kind took place."[35] Another admitted that he could barely bring himself to write of their disgrace. "I am broken down mentally and physically," he continued, "never dreaming that I could have undergone so much and all for naught."[36] Observing the glow of a thousand Union campfires marking the lines encircling Lee's men, Eddie Whitehorne summed up the feelings of many: "Last night we were free soldiers of the Southern States; tonight, we are defeated men, prisoners of war of the Northern States."[37]

As Whitehorne and others settled into their camps that night, around ten o'clock Secretary Stanton ordered a grand national salute. Although the news failed to reach many posts so late on a Sunday evening, from countless U.S. army headquarters, fortifications, and arsenals, including the Military Academy at West Point, guns rang out to celebrate Lee's surrender. Private citizens, too, celebrated, including the African American residents of Alexandria who placed candles in their windows, lit bonfires, and marched through the streets in a procession. Grant and the men under his command were well on their way to ending the rebellion. Soon the citizen soldiers who had saved the Union hoped they, too, would return to their homes.[38]

While his own men remained in the field to ensure that the war was indeed over, Grant's terms had promised that Lee's men would be allowed to return to their homes immediately. But Lee and Grant had failed to discuss the specifics of this process. After his meeting with Grant on April 9, Lee began to worry about the logistics of getting his men home. Early on the morning of April 10, he drafted a letter to the Union general-in-chief asking for guidance.[39]

Before departing for Washington that morning, Grant decided that he should meet with Lee once more. This time there was little formality. Halting on a slope just northeast of the courthouse, the two generals sat astride their horses for nearly half an hour discussing a few more details while their principal officers held back, out of earshot.[40] The previous day, Grant knew he had been restrained by military imperatives and had not been at liberty to discuss political questions. But with the Army of Northern Virginia's capitulation secured, he now pressed on issues of the entire Confederacy. Given Lee's stature — not to mention his position as general-in-chief — Grant suggested that he might influence all the Confederate forces to surrender. Surely if he advised such a course, others would heed it. But Lee demurred; he, too, would have to consult his president.[41]

Lee turned instead to the concerns that had plagued him the previous evening: unlike the surrender at Vicksburg, where Confederates headed

Lithograph depicting Grant and Lee talking on the morning of April 10, 1865.
Library of Congress Prints and Photographs Division, LC-DIG-pga-01671.

back into their own territory, his men now would be forced to move through Union lines to return home. How could he be sure that their paroles would be honored and that they would not be arrested or treated as deserters? Calling General Gibbon to them, Grant explained that Lee was "desirous that his officers and men should have on their persons some evidence that they are paroled prisoners." Lee concurred, observing that he wanted to do all in his power to protect his men.

Gibbon informed them his corps had a small printing press from which blank forms could be struck off. After the passes had been filled out and signed by their officers, they could be distributed to each officer and man with Lee's army. Lee agreed, then turned back to Grant. The previous day, Grant had exempted private horses from the surrender. But Lee explained that his couriers, along with most of the cavalry and artillery, had likewise supplied their own mounts. Would they, too, be allowed to retain their horses? Yes, Grant replied. Much of the South had been destroyed over the past four years, and these men would need horses to plant their spring crops. They could keep them. Once more, Lee had prevailed in negotiating more protections and provisions for his men.[42]

In addition to affording Lee's men proof that they had been paroled,

Grant would order his armies to allow Lee to move through their lines upon presentation of his parole pass. "General Lee will be permitted to visit Richmond at any time unless otherwise ordered by competent authority," Grant instructed, "and every facility for his doing so will be given by officers of the U.S. army."[43]

Before heading toward Burkeville Junction around noon, Grant offered the surrendering Confederates one more provision. Special Field Orders No. 73 stated that "all officers and men of the Confederate service paroled at Appomattox Court House who to reach their homes, are compelled to pass through the lines of the Union armies, will be allowed to do so, and to pass free on all Government transports and military railroads."[44] The order was as practical as it was generous. By sending the paroled prisoners to their homes as quickly and efficiently as possible, Grant hoped the war's end would come more swiftly.

After Lee and Grant parted, the six commissioners convened at the McLean House to discuss the details of the surrender. Grant did not directly oversee the commissioners' agreement, but he offered guidance that reflected the same principles that shaped the terms he offered Lee, most especially his pragmatism. With Gibbon recording their decisions, the six generals first discussed the disbanding of Lee's men. That they would relinquish their arms and flags was a given. Grant had insisted that unlike at Donelson and Vicksburg, there would be a formal surrender ceremony in which the Confederate troops would march by brigades to a designated point (apparently not yet determined), where they would stack their arms and turn over their flags, sabers, and pistols. The question remained, however, as to the best way of getting the men to their homes as quickly and efficiently as possible. Perhaps Longstreet shared Lee's suggestion that the troops should be sent in "detachments under their officers to points near their homes or to points from which they may reach their homes by rail." Or maybe this proved to be the most practical way of dispersing nearly 28,000 men. Regardless of its origin, the agreement's first term stipulated that after stacking their arms and flags, the Confederates were to "march to their homes under charge of their officers, superintended by their respective division and corps commanders." The subsequent terms necessitated that horses and other property belonging to the Confederate government would be turned over to the U.S. authorities but allowed officers the use of wagons and ambulances to transport their private baggage (which would be returned to the nearest U.S. quartermaster once the officers reached their final destinations). As Grant had promised Lee earlier that morning, couriers and mounted men of the artillery and cavalry would likewise be permitted to return home with their personal horses or mules.[45]

These terms proved rather extraordinary. Rather than sending the rebels home under Union guard or ordering them to disperse immediately, the U.S. army authorized—in fact, required—the Confederates to maintain the appearance and even command structure of an army as they made their way home. Such was both an unusual concession to a defeated foe and incredibly pragmatic. If the enlisted men no longer carried weapons (the chief marker of a military force), then would it not make sense to send them home in organized groups, under the watchful eye of their officers? Would this not prove much more orderly than a mass dispersion of nearly 30,000 men into the surrounding countryside?

The final clause of the agreement, however, would prove crucial. Who was to be included in the surrender? Grant had instructed that prisoners captured prior to Lee's capitulation were not to be paroled. Stragglers picked up by Union troops following in their wake or men captured at the battles of Sailor's Creek, High Bridge, or Cumberland Church were supposed to be sent to Union prisons. Such proved the fate of Adam C. Howren of the 5th Florida, captured on April 6 at High Bridge before being sent to City Point. While his comrades continued their march west, learned of Lee's surrender, and ultimately received their paroles, he awaited a steamer bound for the prison at Point Lookout, Maryland (a prison from which he would never be paroled). Brig. Gen. Eppa Hunton had likewise been captured at Sailor's Creek. While the rest of Lee's army moved west, he and other captured officers, including Lt. Gen. Richard S. Ewell, likewise headed east to City Point and subsequently north toward Fort Warren prison in Massachusetts.[46] Prisoners captured before April 8 were not included in the surrender.

But what of the others—the stragglers or those who had evaded surrender? The commissioners conceded that Lee's army had been plagued by desertions and men falling out of line since they left Petersburg and Richmond. Should they be included? What of the cavalry who had escaped with Fitz Lee, Rosser, and Munford—should these men be permitted the same terms as those who had capitulated when called upon to do so? General Gordon believed so. Rising to his feet and launching into an impassioned speech, he pointed out that the Confederates had been treated liberally so far. Should they not continue to give the most generous interpretation of the terms as possible? Should not all of Lee's men be included under the agreement? Throughout Gordon's animated plea, Longstreet sat silently. But when Gordon finished, Longstreet offered a clarification: the terms should include all of Lee's troops *except* any cavalry that had made its escape and any artillery more than twenty miles from Appomattox at the time of the surrender. The other five concurred, adding in the agreement's final wording that the surrender included all those operating with Lee's army on April 8. Around 8:30 that evening, their work done, the commissioners signed the agreement.[47]

Grant either had come to a similar conclusion as to who was to be included or had read the agreement within a half hour. That afternoon while en route to Burkeville, the general-in-chief received an urgent telegram from Secretary of War Stanton asking whether Rosser (who Stanton apparently did not know had joined Lee's main body) and the troops operating in Loudoun County (namely, Col. John S. Mosby's partisans) were to be included in the surrender, or only those under Lee's "immediate personal command." From Prospect Station at 9:00 that evening, Grant responded. "All prisoners captured in battle previous to the surrender stand same as other prisoners of war, and those who escaped and were detached at the time are not included." Grant had cast his net more narrowly than the commissioners in asserting that any who escaped—not only cavalry, but also artillery and infantry—or were detached should *not* be included. But in this same telegram to Stanton, he showed flexibility, a flexibility that appeared repeatedly in the coming days and weeks. Here again was his desire to end the war once and for all. Although the terms he had penned on April 9 had *not* included those who escaped, deserted, or were detached, he believed they *should* extend to "all the fragments of the Army of Northern Virginia" as well as to General Johnston's army in North Carolina.[48]

Generosity flowed naturally from a winning commander whose principal goal, as it was for most of the loyal citizenry, was ending the fighting and restoring the Union. But it was more than generosity that motivated Grant's decision. Paroled soldiers would be accounted for, included on lists kept by Union authorities. To parole them was to have a record of them. Perhaps more importantly, soldiers who broke their paroles might be executed. Paroling Lee's men might deter them from continuing the rebellion by other means.

Yet even as Grant's response made its way through the telegraph wires to Washington, thousands of Lee's men streamed away from Appomattox vowing never to surrender—no matter how generous the terms.

3

Flight

By mid-morning on April 9, the artillery and cavalry units who had cut their way past the Union lines began galloping into Lynchburg. Members of Brig. Gen. Reuben Lindsay Walker's artillery who had escaped Sheridan's attack at Appomattox Station on April 8 and ridden west arrived just before noon. Soon the commands of Capt. John J. Shoemaker, Lt. Charles R. Phelps, and Lt. Marcellus N. Moorman, along with many of the men of Shoemaker's Artillery, joined them heading to the fairgrounds, where they spiked their remaining guns and dismantled the carriages. Once finished, Shoemaker asked for volunteers. Who would be willing to go with him to North Carolina and continue the fight alongside Gen. Joseph E. Johnston? Lieutenants Phelps and Moorman stepped forward. Fifty others followed. The rest elected to go home and await further word.[1]

Throughout the day and into the evening, thousands more Confederates poured into the bustling city. Among them rode former printer turned artillerist James Albright of North Carolina. Approaching Lynchburg around 5:00 P.M., Albright discovered other troops had ridden in from the west. Maj. Gen. John D. Imboden had arrived with his cavalry brigade on April 6, and Maj. Gen. Lunsford L. Lomax's division of cavalry had reported from the Shenandoah Valley the previous afternoon to reinforce the local provost marshal, Brig. Gen. Raleigh Colston, in case Lee made it all the way to Lynchburg. But the news did not appear promising. Rumor had it that the troops left at Appomattox had surrendered and "all hope was gone."[2]

As more Confederate soldiers reached Lynchburg, with them came confirmation of Lee's surrender. The news struck civilians as hard as it did Lee's soldiers. "There are no words to express the bitterness and poignancy of the grief I now feel," wrote nineteen-year-old Mary Washington Cabell, daughter of a local minister. "If my death could have averted the blow I must now record, it would have been willingly given." About 1,000 cavalry troopers made it out before the surrender, she estimated. As they streamed by her house throughout the day, she observed that "their hearts seem broken, yet their bearing is firm and manly. They say they could not stay and see Lee go up and deliver himself to the Yankees." Indeed, Mary wished that she might have the same liberty as the horsemen — to simply ride off. "As much as I love [Virginia]," she wrote, "I wish to go away, for now everything has changed."[3]

With soldiers streaming in from the east, wounded troops from the city's hospitals roaming the streets, and civilians uncertain of what was happing, tensions mounted. A few crazed soldiers placed straw under their caissons and lit them.[4] Civic leaders dreaded to think their town might dissolve into rioting, so they shuttered businesses and suspended all services in the city for the evening. But fearing the impending arrival of Union troops, some frightened citizens began tossing Confederate money and cotton bonds into the canal. Their own pockets empty, the soldiers began fishing it out. For others, whose stomachs yearned for sustenance, money was not enough. Initiating a pattern that would continue for many of Lee's men as they made their way home, they set their sights on Confederate stores. "Irresistible raids were made on the commissary and other buildings," an army surgeon reported. When those stocks were gone, the men turned to looting "clothing, tobacco, and shoes" from the canal boats and warehouses.[5] The provisions had been stockpiled by the Confederate government for its soldiers, and even if the bulk of Lee's army had surrendered, those still in the field insisted they were entitled to them. They remained Confederate soldiers, and they would take whatever they needed, what they believed rightfully was owed to them.

By evening, several officers recognized that as order in the ranks dissolved, they needed to abandon the fairgrounds and move their troops across the James River to bivouac for the night in order to protect the city. Once there, Rosser, Munford, and the other officers gathered around the small campfires to debate their options. At twenty-nine, Rosser had been born in Virginia but moved with his family to the Texas frontier as a teenager. In 1856, he received an appointment to West Point and was weeks shy of graduating when he returned south to join the Confederate forces in 1861. Commissioned a first lieutenant in New Orleans's Washington Artillery, he headed to Virginia, where he would remain for the war. Fighting in the Shenandoah Valley in the fall of 1864, he was promoted to major general before returning to Petersburg, where he commanded a cavalry division.[6] Five years older than the brash West Pointer, Munford had attended the Virginia Military Institute. When Virginia seceded, he naturally threw his lot in with his state, serving first as a lieutenant colonel in the infantry before joining the cavalry. In March 1865, he had taken command of Fitz Lee's cavalry division, but the Richmond native still held only the rank of colonel, his commission having never been confirmed before the capital fell. Ill feelings had existed between the men since 1863, when Rosser had been promoted over the older Munford.[7] Their escape from Appomattox would do nothing to heal such deep wounds.

The two officers, therefore, made no plans to coordinate their next moves. Having heard rumors that Lee had escaped Appomattox with a portion of the army and gone to Danville, Rosser elected to disband his unit and send the men home to await further instructions. He would ride on to Danville and confer with Lee. Munford would head toward Roanoke to see his three surviving children, his wife and one child having died during the war. From there, he would decide what came next. In the meantime, members of his command, including the 1st Maryland Cavalry, were instructed to go where they pleased until April 25, when they would rendezvous at the cattle scales in Augusta County.[8]

Pvt. William L. Wilson of the 12th Virginia Cavalry was among those in Rosser's Division who awaited word on the north side of the James that evening. "The whole command is in confusion," he wrote. "No attempt scarcely is made by the officers to control the men." He believed most of his comrades would strike out for home in the morning, but some of the division's officers had advised otherwise. Col. Matt D. Ball had instructed the men of the 11th Virginia Cavalry "to retain their formation" and attempt to join General Johnston in North Carolina, because General Rosser had learned on good "authority that Gordon had simply surrendered 8000 men while Gen Lee had escaped." Col. Elijah V. White, however, told his men of the 35th Virginia Cavalry Battalion "to go to their homes in the Valley and recruit their horses, when, should a Southern Army really exist, he would lead them to it." In other words, they had two options: return to their homes and await calls to reassemble, or press south and continue the fight with Johnston's army. Wilson cast his lot with Colonel White. "I shall return to the Valley and await developments there," he concluded before adding, "It is impossible to prolong the struggle on this side of the Mississippi."[9] Appomattox had not been the end. For thousands who had escaped the surrender, a belief in their ultimate vindication and the power of rumor prevailed.

By the morning of April 10, a great many of those who had gathered in and around Lynchburg had dispersed. "Almost all of the Virginia soldiers appear to have gone to their homes, or to other points of safety, there to be ready to fight more if need be," observed a member of the 12th Virginia Cavalry. Military stores that could not be carted off were destroyed so that they would not fall into Union hands, and those in the hospitals who could leave did so. But the Confederates had not given up all hope. "Very few are so much whipped as to favor the abandoning of the cause," the cavalryman noted, adding that it was not just those from Virginia who harbored such thoughts. "The Southern soldiers from Lee's army appear to have the same intentions, and no doubt most of them will go to their homes, if possible, before joining Johnson [sic]."[10]

Like his comrades, the trooper could fathom only two options: going home to await calls for the next fight, or heading south to join Johnston. But others saw a different option: quitting the war and going home. Some had not even attempted to make it to Lynchburg. Bound for their homes in northern Virginia, Daniel Grimsley and his men of the 6th Virginia Cavalry stopped at a farmhouse where they "pressed an old negro into service" to guide them under the cover of darkness to the James River.[11] To the south in Pittsylvania County, Col. William Nelson's artillery battalion elected to disband rather than continue the fight. Parking the artillery pieces and distributing the horses among his men, Nelson bid them farewell.[12]

Even many who had gathered in Lynchburg simply called it quits. On April 9, Caldwell Calhoun Buckner of the 7th Virginia Cavalry had ridden with Rosser's command from Appomattox, impressing any horses he could find along the way. But Buckner did not remain with the diehards long. Only two days later, having made it as far west as the Staunton River, he determined "to return and start back" toward his Orange County home. Perhaps he had never been as devoted to the cause as some of his younger and wealthier comrades. The thirty-six-year-old had been at best a reluctant Confederate. During the spring of 1861, he "did all in his power to prevent the secession of his native state," and while his fellow Virginians marched off to war, he remained at home raising his thoroughbred stock until conscripted in January 1864.[13] He had no desire to continue the fight. Like the vast majority of those who escaped the surrender at Appomattox, he would go home.[14] His war had ended.

Even some of those who decided to head south to General Johnston ac-

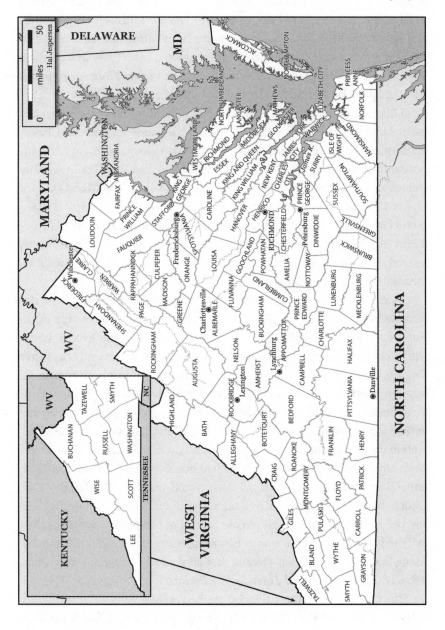

Virginia
counties,
1865.

knowledged that the dispersal of troops meant the end of the Army of Northern Virginia. James Albright lamented the inglorious ending. Instructed by an officer at Lynchburg to take their horses, fill up on rations, and "go if we did not want to be captured before daylight," he had said his hasty goodbyes and headed south. "Twas a sad hour and a humiliating one for those of us who believed we had done our duty," he confessed to his diary that evening. "We felt death were preferable." Along with a few other North Carolinians he would press on, bound for Greensboro and whatever fight might be left.[15]

Others remained uncertain as to whether the Army of Northern Virginia had in fact capitulated. The artillerists who had disbanded at Red Oak Church on the morning of April 9 had heard rumors that Lee wanted them to reconvene at the hamlet of Lincolnton in western North Carolina. If there was any chance this might be the case, they would gather there. On Monday, April 10, Pvt. Charles Friend and a party of six others from the 1st Company, Richmond Howitzers traveled south, taking turns walking and riding the few beleaguered artillery horses that remained. Selecting a slightly different route, sixteen other members of the 1st Company had elected Corp. Edward G. Steane as their leader before striking out on foot toward Lincolnton.[16]

Harry C. Townsend was among those who followed Steane south, determined to continue the fight. Townsend had been devoted to the cause from the beginning. In 1861, the eighteen-year-old clerk still lived at home with his parents when he enlisted in the Richmond Howitzers only days after Virginia seceded. The following spring during the Peninsula campaign, he was wounded and subsequently captured at Williamsburg. For more than three months he remained a prisoner until finally exchanged in August, just in time for Antietam. During the years that followed, he saw action at Fredericksburg, Chancellorsville, Gettysburg, and the bloody battles of the Overland campaign. Through all of this, he had not lost the will to fight. Instead, under Steane's leadership, on April 9 Townsend and the others left Red Oak Church bound for the James River, hoping to put it between themselves and any Union soldiers who might pursue them. For more than four miles they marched west through the woods before halting near an old tobacco barn. Along the banks of the small stream, they cooked what few rations they had left, washed, and hunkered down for the evening.[17]

The next morning, the artillerists pushed on in much the same manner as they had during the previous week. After preparing a small breakfast, they "took up the line of march" toward the James. Reaching the home of one of their colonels in Bedford County, Townsend and his companions exchanged coffee for eggs from the colonel's slaves before compelling one of them to ferry the artillerists across the river. Here, only a day's march from the surrender field at Appomattox, men and women remained enslaved and subject to the whims of the Confederate army. Despite declarations in newspapers to the contrary, Lee's surrender had not resulted in the liberation of most enslaved people. Their war continued, too.[18]

Now safely across the James, Townsend and the others took the road toward Amherst Court House. All along the route they began to encounter stragglers from Lee's army who brought news that the general had indeed surrendered. But belief overshadowed fact. "We paid no attention to these rumors," Townsend observed in his diary, electing instead to march on. They arrived in the small village of New Glasgow on April 11, where a colonel confirmed the accounts of Lee's surrender. More importantly, they learned that the terms had included those within twenty miles of his lines at Appomattox. They debated their options. Some of the men believed that they should remain in Amherst County and obtain more information. Others wanted to continue their journey to Lincolnton. With offers of lodgings and generous gifts of sorghum, meal, bacon, and buttermilk from the locals, the men decided they could wait at least one night to make their decision.[19]

Waking early the next morning they agreed to continue their trek. With bellies full of eggs, pies, and pastries from the locals, they set their course due west toward the hills surrounding Buffalo Springs. Ascending the western slopes of the Blue Ridge, Townsend paused to take in the magnificent scene spread out before them. Below lay a picturesque valley greening with the spring rains. Encircling them stood the blue mountains, their cloud-capped peaks rising high into a perfect April sky. How could such beauty coexist with war?, Townsend wondered. Would this tranquil place soon be blighted by desolation and ruin? He could not waste more time on such thoughts, and turning, he climbed on alongside his comrades toward Robinson's Gap.[20]

Others headed toward North Carolina with the full knowledge of Lee's surrender. The same William Gordon McCabe who had berated stragglers during the army's flight from Petersburg rode west through sheets of rain with plans to cross the Blue Ridge before heading south to Johnston. Accompanied by several other artillerists, the small party had stopped at the house of a "good rebel woman" near Lynchburg on April 9 for supper before continuing their trek. With a cold rain pelting down upon them, they finally halted in the early hours of April 10, tied their horses, and took a brief rest on the muddy road. At daybreak, they rode on, stopping again at a loyal Confederate home for breakfast before crossing the mountain near Campbell Court House.

With pen in hand that evening, McCabe reflected on both the past and the future. "We will join Johnston, if we are not captured before we reach him," he wrote his future wife. "If he capitulates and there is any other organized force in the field, I will join that, if God spares my life." But he had more than just defiance on his mind. He seethed at his new situation, blaming it on those who proved far less devoted than he and his fellow artillerists. "The capitulation of the Army was brought about entirely by the cursed straggling of the men and some cowardly infantry officers," he fumed. He could not yet comprehend that all was lost. "How can we look you Virginia girls in the face again?" he wondered. "This State is not conquered, only over run; and the flame *will* break out within 20 years." If he survived that long, he vowed to "offer my sword once more to the Right." While Lee and most of his men had rejected dispersing the army at Appomattox in order to continue fighting, McCabe presaged a battle that could outlast such military decisions.[21]

Some 150 miles to the northwest in the Shenandoah Valley, the town of Winchester bustled with energy. Around midnight on April 10, a telegram had arrived announcing Lee's surrender. As word spread, Union soldiers along with the town's Unionist civilians thronged the streets, parading up and down, cheering and huzzahing until their voices broke. Cheer after cheer lifted to Grant, to Sherman, and to the savior of the Valley, Phil Sheridan, before a thirty-four-gun salute rang out from the 1st Maine Battery. The headquarters of Maj. Gen. Winfield Scott Hancock had been brilliantly illuminated as artillerists launched rocket after rocket in raucous celebration. Civilians and soldiers soon congregated around headquarters calling for Hancock to offer a few words. But amid the din of the crowd, the amused general could hardly quiet them enough to offer much of a speech. Instead, he proposed three cheers for their country before a band struck up a lively rendition of "Down with the Rebel and Up with the Yanks."[22]

The excitement continued through the morning hours and into the afternoon when Hancock received orders from Secretary of War Stanton to print and circulate the final surrender terms within the lines of the Middle Military Division, an area that covered much of the lower Shenandoah Valley extending into Maryland and West Virginia. But it was not merely an announcement that Stanton wished conveyed. In keeping with Grant's desire to end the rebellion as quickly as possible and his instructions to include all of Lee's men, the secretary instructed Hancock that "all detachments and stragglers" from the Army of Northern Virginia who turned themselves in to Union authorities would be paroled under the same conditions extended to those at Appomattox and be permitted to return home. Those who did not surrender, Stanton explained, should be captured and held as prisoners of war.[23]

By the following afternoon, circulars posted throughout the lower Shenandoah Valley reproduced the entire exchange of letters between Lee and Grant, while newspaper columns announced the parole terms. "Every military restraint shall be removed that is not absolutely essential," Hancock promised, "and your sons, your husbands, and your brothers shall remain with you unmolested." Those who failed to surrender, however, would be captured and treated as prisoners of war. He added one more word of caution especially to those who had harbored marauding bands: "Every outrage committed by them will be followed by the severest infliction," he declared. "It is for you to determine the amount of freedom you are to enjoy."[24]

In Washington, meanwhile, Union chief of staff Maj. Gen. Henry W. Halleck worked feverishly on the afternoon of April 10 to inform the other Union commanders throughout Virginia and Maryland of Secretary Stanton's orders. Halleck instructed Maj. Gen. Christopher C. Augur, commanding the Department of Washington, to send a cavalry force and section of artillery to Virginia's Northern Neck, a peninsula on the western shore of the Chesapeake Bay bounded by the Potomac River to the north and the Rappahannock River to the south. There, Union cavalry would distribute copies of the correspondence between Grant and Lee. All detached parties and stragglers—no difference was to be made—who complied with the conditions of the surrender would be paroled and allowed to return to their homes. Those who did not would be brought in as prisoners of war. Once Augur's men had broken up "all hostile organizations on the Neck," they were to return to Washington.[25]

There was a caveat to Stanton's instructions. He explicitly informed Hancock, Augur, and his other commanders of the one exception: "The guerrilla chief Mosby will under no consideration be paroled," he ordered.[26]

In May 1861, John Singleton Mosby enlisted in the Confederate army as a private in the 1st Virginia Cavalry. A lawyer prior to the war, Mosby had no military training, yet by March 1863 the physically unassuming twenty-nine-year-old had risen to prominence as the commander of the 43rd Virginia Cavalry Battalion, a partisan ranger unit sanctioned by the Confederate government and supported by Lee. Most of Mosby's Rangers hailed from Fauquier, Loudoun, Fairfax, and Prince William Counties in northern Virginia, where they engaged in raids — usually by small bands of men — on Union camps and supply trains in northern Virginia, in the Shenandoah Valley, and into southern Maryland. The battalion's success marked it as the most effective use of such troops in the war. "My purpose was to threaten and harass the enemy on the border and in this way compel him to withdraw troops from his front to guard the line of the Potomac and Washington," Mosby later explained. "We created so much anxiety that the planks on the bridge across the Potomac were taken up every night to prevent us from carrying off the Government."[27]

Guerrillas and bushwhackers had thwarted Union efforts from Missouri to Virginia the entire war. Yet Mosby was quick to point out that his was a regularly sanctioned partisan unit that hewed to the lawful use of mobile forces. Unlike Missouri guerrillas, he did not target Unionist civilians, and his Rangers observed an established command structure complete with commissions. The Union soldiers who encountered Mosby, however, saw little difference between his command and guerrillas elsewhere. The Rangers wore only gray jackets (not uniforms with insignia) and returned to civilian populations after strikes for food, shelter, and intelligence. They drew almost no supplies from Richmond but armed and equipped themselves entirely with their plunder. Most importantly, by the summer of 1864 they had acquired a reputation for especially brutal killings of Union soldiers. A New England soldier, attempting to recount the terror that Mosby's men inflicted, explained that the rebels had slashed one Union soldier's throat from ear to ear, while "another was found lifeless hanging from a tree by his feet head downwards." "I think you can hardly call us very bad names in view of the atrocities by these infernal traitors," he wrote.[28]

Only days after taking command of the new Army of the Shenandoah in August 1864, General Sheridan ordered his army to rid the Valley and northern Virginia of the "cutthroats and robbers" by exterminating "as many of Mosby's gang" as possible. Despite Sheridan's determined efforts, the raids continued. In mid-August, after Mosby's men attacked a Union wagon train outside of Harpers Ferry, burning six wagons, Grant had grown increasingly frustrated. "The families of most of Mosby's men are known, and can be collected," he instructed Sheridan. "I think they should be taken and kept at Fort McHenry, or some secure place, as hostages for the good conduct of Mosby and his men. Where any of Mosby's men are caught *hang them without trial.*" Grant tempered his instructions in a second message to Sheridan, ordering him instead to arrest all men under the age of fifty and hold them as prisoners. But his message was clear: Mosby's men needed to be stopped.[29]

The situation reached a fevered pitch as summer gave way to fall. In late August, a detachment of Mosby's men discovered thirty members of the 5th Michigan Cavalry burning private homes near Berryville, Virginia. Rather than hold them as prisoners, they "herded their captives into a ditch and shot them to death point blank." Mosby claimed he operated as a regular, if detached, unit of Lee's army, but these actions clearly violated the laws of war. The atrocities continued when Mosby's men mortally shot a wounded Union lieutenant outside of Front Royal, Virginia, even as he tried to surrender. Incensed, soldiers under Maj. Gen. George A. Custer retaliated when they captured then hanged or shot six of Mosby's men near Front Royal. Mosby did not respond immediately, but in November he selected seven prisoners from Custer's command to execute in retaliation. Mosby then informed Sheridan that there would be no more executions "unless some new act of barbarity shall compel me reluctantly to adopt a course of policy repulsive to humanity." No more executions followed, but Sheridan would take the war to Mosby's home territory, burning hundreds of barns and grist mills as well as seizing thousands of cattle, sheep, hogs, and horses. "The task was not a pleasant one," a Union cavalry captain admitted, "for many innocents were made to suffer with the guilty, but something was necessary to clear the country of the bands of Guerrillas that were becoming so formidable."[30]

A few days before Christmas, a Union bullet finally found its target in Mosby. Despite reports of his death that circulated in both northern and southern newspapers, the famed Gray Ghost survived. So did Sheridan's campaign to exterminate him. Union officials began to believe, however, that capturing the Rangers and refusing to exchange them was as effective, if not more so, than hanging them. By April 1865, more than 180 of Mosby's Rangers remained in northern prison camps. But with new recruits constantly joining the ranks, including those from the Northern Neck, where he had extended his reach in January, his strength remained between 300 and 400 men.[31]

Confronted with rebels who seemed to flout the laws of war when it suited them, it is little wonder that Stanton and Halleck ordered Hancock and others to exclude Mosby and his men from the Appomattox terms. But when Stanton consulted Grant about this decision on the afternoon of April 10, the general-in-chief had other thoughts. Recognizing the potential threat the Confederate irregulars still posed, Grant informed Stanton that he hoped Hancock might "try it with Mosby."[32]

Grant's position could hardly have been more different from his stance the previous August, when he had ordered Sheridan to execute Mosby's

Col. John Singleton Mosby (*standing, second from left*) and some members of Mosby's Rangers, 43rd Virginia Cavalry Battalion. Library of Congress Prints and Photographs Division, LC-DIG-ppmsca-35436.

men without trial. But now everything had changed. With Lee's capitulation, Grant hoped that all rebels would soon lay down their guns, including the partisan rangers. And yet, perhaps it was his conversation with Lee earlier that misty morning along the Appomattox Stage Road that had swayed his thinking. Grant later recalled that Lee had pointed out "that the South was big country and that we might have to march over it three or four times before the war entirely ended."[33] Had this given Grant pause? If the cycles of retaliation continued with Mosby and other guerrillas, even with the surrender of the main armies the war might never end. Indeed, earlier that day Union officials reported that some of Mosby's men had crossed the Blue Ridge with intentions of capturing and plundering Hancock's trains south of Winchester, another company had been sent to Maryland on a raid, while yet another battalion had attempted to steal U.S. horses and mules in Fairfax County. This continued threat necessitated that Mosby and his men be brought in as quickly as possible.[34]

On April 11, as nearly 300 Rangers gathered in their home territory around Fauquier and Loudoun Counties, Hancock's chief of staff forwarded Mosby copies of the exchange between Grant and Lee, offering them the same terms conferred upon those at Appomattox. Although Hancock awaited a reply, he was hardly surprised that none arrived. With their fine steeds and pistols, Mosby's command proved more likely to disband than formally surrender. After two days of waiting, Hancock issued a circular on April 13 stating in no uncertain terms that if Mosby failed to respond immediately, Union forces would unleash their wrath on his civilian supporters. Anxious that Mosby might well continue to ignore the summons, the following day Hancock mobilized a force of cavalry and infantry to comb Loudoun and Fauquier Counties with instructions to seize any horses found in the possession of "people whose loyalty is not undoubted" and, most importantly, to arrest every able-bodied man who could not produce a parole. Similar instructions hailed from the Department of Washington, where the commander of the 16th New York Cavalry was ordered to clear northern Virginia of detached bodies of rebels and guerrillas. In the event that his troops encountered such men, the colonel was to offer them the same terms granted to Lee's main force. "If they refuse the terms proffered they will of course be attacked and captured or destroyed if possible," ordered General Augur.[35] The partisans had been a thorn in the side of Federal forces for far too long. They would not — could not — be allowed to continue their rampage. If they did, the war might drag on indefinitely.

Even as Union officials offered Mosby's Rangers the opportunity to surrender themselves and receive the same generous terms extended to Lee's main army, many of those who had fled the field at Appomattox remained determined to carry on the fight. On April 12, a Virginia cavalry major wrote to his mother from Pittsylvania County along the Virginia–North Carolina border, informing her that he had not been subjugated. He expected to remain in the area for another month and then to head south, perhaps to Texas. "I will follow the fortunes of the Confederacy as long as there is any hope of retrieving our fallen fortunes," he explained. "If all our efforts to achieve independence fail, I shall leave the country & find a home for you in some other land. We will carry our household goods to some new Virginia," he promised. But he remained optimistic: "I can not believe that our cause will ultimately fail." More than two weeks later he wrote again from the mountains of Rockbridge County. He still planned to start soon for Texas but had hoped to visit her before departing. In order to do so, however, he would have to go to Richmond, surrender himself, and seek a parole. "But even my duty to my mother would not justify me in surrendering my person or my principles to the enemies of my country," he informed her. "I embraced the cause of the South when it was prosperous & triumphant; I will not desert it now that it is downfallen & perhaps hopeless, & if I can do nothing more for it here, rather than make terms with the conquerors of my country, I will exile myself to some foreign land."[36]

J. H. "Ham" Chamberlayne agreed. Among those escaping Appomattox with David McIntosh, on April 12 the twenty-seven-year-old artillery captain had paused to write his brother and sister who remained in Richmond. Although fatigued, he was safe and well with McIntosh in Halifax County, near the North Carolina border. Assuring his family that he was no shirker, he explained that they had not fled until the firing ceased and preparations began for a surrender. "We refused to take part in the funeral at Appomattox C. H. & cut or crept our way out," he defiantly explained. They were bound for Joseph Johnston's army, but if they could do nothing there, he would head to Mississippi and hoped to make it to Texas by summer, as he had "no notion of laying down my arms." He instructed his brother to seek out letters from Walter Taylor or any of Lee's other staff members that might be able certify his promotion to captain, as his commissions had been burned during the retreat. But his thoughts were not only of himself. Be sure to look after the stocks and try to recover the family farm in Maryland, he reminded his brother. Then conceding that he might never see them again, he bid his siblings goodbye. "I am not conquered by any means & shall not be while alive—My life is of no further value—Farewell to my beloved Virginia."[37]

Chamberlayne's letter had not yet reached his sister Lucy by the fifteenth, but having no word from him, she was certain she knew what he had done. Writing to a mutual friend, she asked that he tell her brother she approved and blessed him. "Tis what I would have done under like circumstances," she insisted. Elsewhere in the capital city, other Confederate women shared her sentiments. Seventeen-year-old Lelian Cook had witnessed the arrival of paroled men day after day. But she found her spirits lifted by word that only 8,000 soldiers had surrendered at Appomattox, and more important, Fitz Lee's cavalry troopers were not among the surrendered. They had cut their way out, she informed her diary, "and I suppose they have gone to Johnston." While many of the "artillery boys" had all returned home, she still had not heard from her uncle Will or his battalion, which left her optimistic. "Though we are defeated at the present," she wrote, "I hope our people are not yet subdued and it will be all for the best in the end. I believe God is on our side." Even in the wake of Appomattox, many Confederate women refused to lose faith in their cause.[38]

General Rosser agreed. Lee might have surrendered, but that did not mark the end of the Confederate cause. The government had not capitulated, nor had any of the other major armies surrendered. Having temporarily disbanded his division at Lynchburg, on the rainy morning of April 10 Rosser and his staff rode toward Danville, where rumor had it they might confer with President Jefferson Davis about the prospects of continuing the fight. The president had departed by the time the general arrived, but Rosser found another audience in John C. Breckinridge, former general, now secretary of war. Agreeing that there might yet be hope, Breckinridge instructed Rosser to return to central Virginia and round up all of his troopers who had not yet been paroled.[39]

Breckinridge's admonition that Rosser enlist only those *not yet paroled* underscored the value the Confederate leadership still placed on the parole oath. Paroled soldiers had pledged not to resume fighting until they had been exchanged. To break one's parole was not only a failure of personal honor but a violation that would result in imprisonment or execution.[40] Hewing to the code of military conduct and the laws of war, Breckinridge was adamant that only those soldiers who had avoided surrender could continue the fight, no matter how desperate the rebels might be for more troops.

Spurring his horse northward, Rosser rode to Staunton, where he issued a proclamation on April 12 from what he declared the headquarters of the Army of Northern Virginia. Having promoted himself to the rank of lieutenant general, he called upon his men to shoulder their muskets once more "and return to the field to meet the arrogant invader who had insulted you, robbed you, murdered your dearest friends and relatives, outraged your fair women, despoiled your homes, and dishonored all that is most dear and sacred." He would lead the men against this dastardly foe, he promised, and would never surrender "until the purple current ceases to flow from my heart, or until you are a free, independent and happy people!" He further declared, "If we are true to ourselves and to honor, we can never abandon a cause we have so nobly sustained for the last four years." True men, he reminded them, would never "kiss the rod that smites us or bend our knees to our bitterest foes." "Rise like men and come to me," he commanded, instructing companies and regiments to assemble at Charlottesville, Staunton, or Lynchburg "without delay."[41]

Rosser's calls to fight on proved all the more striking in light of his position on Mosby and other partisan rangers. From his Shenandoah Valley headquarters in January 1864, he had urged the War Department to abolish the partisan ranger system. "Without discipline, order, or organization," he

Maj. Gen. Thomas L. Rosser. Rosser and much of the Army of Northern Virginia's cavalry escaped the Union cordon at Appomattox on April 9. On April 12, Rosser issued a proclamation from Staunton, Virginia, calling on those who had evaded surrender to join him in continuing the fight. F. Trevelyan Miller, ed., *The Photographic History of the Civil War*, vol. 4 (New York: Review of Reviews Co., 1911), 75.

wrote Lee, they roamed throughout the country "a band of thieves, stealing, pillaging, plundering, and doing every manner of mischief and crime." "They are a terror to the citizens and an injury to the cause," he maintained.[42] Yet his dispersal of the cavalry and calls for them to rendezvous and rise up again against the "dastardly foe" smacked of the guerrilla warfare Lee had cautioned Brig. Gen. Edward Porter Alexander against at Appomattox. Sending the men home to their respective states would force them to rob and plunder for sustenance, Lee had warned. The countryside would teem with lawless bands. Fresh rapine and destruction, not peace, was sure to follow.[43] But Rosser called on his men to assemble by company and regiment. In his estimation, there would be order for the fight that still loomed.

Avoiding Union troops was imperative for every rebel who refused to surrender themselves — for Rosser's cavalrymen who planned to reconvene, for those bound for North Carolina, or for any simply hoping to make their way home.[44] With the Blue Ridge Mountains to their west, James Albright and his fellow artillerists rode southwest on constant lookout for soldiers in blue. "Yanks reported in Franklin and Henry counties," he noted in his diary on a rainy April 11 morning. He would have to "run through," he observed, sarcastically adding, "without capturing any of them."[45] Albright tried to make light of the situation, but he and others knew full well that their position was precarious at best. "As we have no parole pass we are uncertain what would be our fate in the event of our capture," a Confederate signalman scribbled in his diary on April 12; "consequently we avoid the Yanks as we would a pestilence."[46] Having not yet heard Grant's offer to extend the terms to all of Lee's men, those who had escaped feared the worst.

For some, these fears were soon realized. While Albright traveled south, Benjamin Jones and seven others from the Surry Light Artillery who had disbanded at Red Oak Church headed toward their home in Virginia's Tidewater. Rather than following the more direct route due east that would lead through Union lines, the men set off on a circuitous route that took them northwest through Amherst and Nelson Counties before turning east through Albemarle and Fluvanna Counties. Reaching the outskirts of Richmond on April 16, they proceeded north, "passing Mechanicsville in time to escape a train-load of Federals, and on down by the battlefields of Cold Harbor," where memories of the previous year's fighting were renewed by the "blackened ruins, earthworks, forest destroyed, bridges, mills, and homes burned." All along the way, they had lodged with sympathetic civilians who shared what food they could spare.[47]

For more than a week, the party had managed to stay together and avoid Union patrols. But that soon changed. Discovering a canoe along the Chickahominy, George C. Holmes and Thomas Williams paddled downriver, hoping to procure a larger boat upon which they might all travel. But choked with fallen timber, the river proved impassable, and the two quickly became separated from their small party. Their separation proved disastrous. Unable to find a way down the clogged river, Holmes and Williams gave up and proceeded to Richmond, where they were arrested for evading surrender on April 18 and sent to Point Lookout, Maryland, to remain for several months.[48]

The same fate awaited several other members of the Surry Light Artillery. When three men departed on horseback from the small group with whom they had been traveling and rode into Richmond, they too were taken as prisoners of war and sent to Newport News. Twenty-year-old Charles C. Richardson and six of his traveling companions had managed to cross the James River at Scottsville in Albemarle County on their way home to Sussex County. But upon reaching Chesterfield County, they had seen bluecoats on the other side of the Appomattox River who offered a canoe to carry them to the southern shore. Whether it was hunger or another reason that compelled them to agree is unknown, but Richardson and his fellow artillerists—none of whom had parole passes—quickly found themselves confined to a tobacco barn in Dinwiddie County. Here they were kept for two nights and a day before being transported under guard by railcar to Petersburg, where they were again imprisoned.[49]

The remaining members of the Surry Light Artillery had no idea what had befallen Richardson and the others, but they remained vigilant as they tramped east. Managing to find a small boat of their own, five of the men had slowly made their way to the confluence of the Chickahominy and James, where they discovered Union gunboats stationed every mile or so guarding the stream. Only three miles from home, they determined to wait for darkness. That night, they wrapped their oars to prevent making any sound and set off silently across the James. "At last," Benjamin Jones recounted, "our little craft grated upon the sands of old Surry shore!" On Tuesday the eighteenth, the men reached their home in Charles City County, where they finally learned the fate of their comrades who had remained at Appomattox. "All of them have surrendered," Jones reported. "It was this that we feared and that made us so resolved to thread our way homeward without falling into the hands of the foe, and thus of being delayed indefinitely, until it might suit the convenience of the Federals to permit us to proceed onward."

Their fears, however, were not confined to white Union soldiers. "Our party was the first to reach home," he declared, "and we have had no experience with Yankee blackguard or negro insolence! This alone is worth all the pains the longer way has cost us." For Jones and his comrades, the possibility that Black soldiers might visit them with revenge or retaliation could not be separated from the disintegration of the Army of Northern Virginia.[50]

Even with the dispersal and unraveling of Lee's army, remnants still existed. More than a week after Appomattox, at least 12,000 soldiers from the army had yet to surrender.[51] Mosby and his men remain unconvinced that the Confederate cause was lost. Like others, they wondered if Johnston's army might break free of Sherman's grip in North Carolina and offer a lifeline to the Confederacy. Some, like Townsend, McCabe, Chamberlayne, and Albright, headed south or west, determined to join Johnston in his fight. Others bided their time at home, awaiting a renewed call for battle. Still others simply went home. All were uncertain what would follow. But most acknowledged that though crumbling into chaos, there had been no end to the Confederate nation.

4

Waiting

The rain that continued to fall throughout the day on April 10 seemed fitting for the defeated Confederates still encamped around Appomattox Court House. Exhausted, famished, and unable to break out of the Union lines, they had surrendered. Yet like so many of those who had escaped the previous day, Kena King Chapman still held out a glimmer of hope that the cause might yet survive. The twenty-five-year-old second lieutenant from Smithfield, Virginia, had been committed to the Confederacy from its earliest days. He had enlisted in April 1861, joining the 19th Battalion Virginia Heavy Artillery in 1862, and with the exception of the previous week's retreat, he had spent the entire war within the fortifications surrounding Richmond. Now the senior officer left in his brigade, Chapman found himself tasked with writing out its parole list. But he remained optimistic. "There is life in the old land yet," he observed, "and I cannot believe that the southern people are yet subjugated. From what I can hear the enemy desires peace as much as we do but will agree to nothing but unconditional submission on our part."[1] In his estimation, that submission had not yet been achieved.

Bivouacked on the hills to the east of the village awaiting their paroles, Lee's men finally had time to reflect. In letter and diaries, they revealed a range of emotions, from despair and exhaustion to relief and defiance. Some fumed about those who had fled or avoided capitulation while they had remained steadfast to the end. Others acknowledged the generosity of Grant's terms only to seethe at the sight and sound of their Union conquerors. Some watched as the enslaved men attached to the army contemplated their own futures. Most embraced the tenor of Lee's farewell address, conceding that the quest for southern independence had been thwarted by insurmountable northern resources. But at least a few, like Chapman, retained faith that the Confederacy might yet survive. Together they waited, unsure what the next few weeks, months, and years might bring but quite certain that they had fought the good fight.

Lee's men could not help but notice how few men remained. Edward Valentine Jones of the Richmond Howitzers wondered what had become of the "25,000 muskets that flashed in the sunlight the day we left Richmond. . . . Many have been captured, some killed in the daily engagements, some wounded, and oh I blush to say it, a number — nor are they few — have thrown away their guns and now seek refuge in the rear." Eddie Whitehorne likewise observed that "Hungry, sick, weak men have dropped out by the thousands," speculating that only 8,000 to 10,000 infantrymen stood in the ranks on the morning of April 9.[2] Although the disorganized state of the commands made any real accounting impossible, Lee likewise estimated that fewer than 8,000 infantrymen and several thousand cavalry and artillerists had been present.[3] Among the 23rd South Carolina, Corp. John Forrest Robertson could count only 17 men with rifles in the entire regiment. All along the arduous retreat, thousands of men — many of them unarmed — had dropped out of the ranks. When the dinner bell rang that evening, however, many of those who had taken to the woods or failed to keep pace rolled into camp to receive the rations of biscuits and beef sent by Grant. With a great bit of compassion, Robertson concluded that "all without doubt did the best they could, so charity covers the doings of the weaker ones."[4]

Not all felt so generous. Speaking to his division that evening, Brig. Gen. James A. Walker rebuked those who had fled earlier in the day only to return once the fighting had ceased. "This morning I led into battle seven hundred good and true men," he began. "This afternoon, my muster rolls showed me fifteen hundred." Where had these men been during the battle?, he demanded. Mincing no words, he condemned those who had taken to the woods as "sulking cowards!" Anticipating Lee's farewell address the next day, Walker implored those who remained in the ranks to go home with a clear conscience, knowing that the cause had failed through no fault of theirs. But he warned them to be wary of their comrades who had not shown such devotion. "You well know those who were not with you," he continued. "If you meet them in the social circle, avoid them, if on the walks of business, distrust them, and if at the altar of your God, turn from them. For the man who would forsake his country and her cause in the hour of greatest need would sell his God."[5] Capt. Frank Potts of Lt. Gen. James Longstreet's staff likewise minced no words on stragglers. "We have proven ourselves unworthy of independence," he wrote his brother only days after the surrender. "The great mass of people sighed for the fleshpots of Yankeedom, and deserted the leader of whom they were not worthy."[6]

Some who returned could more easily avoid being labeled cowards, including cavalry chief Maj. Gen. Fitzhugh Lee. Although he had ordered his command to disperse and return to their homes, Fitz Lee and five of his staff officers had ridden to Farmville, where they surrendered themselves on April 11 to Maj. Gen. George Meade, who ordered them back to Appomattox. Climbing into their saddles once more, Lee and his staff turned their mounts northwest toward the village they had escaped only two days prior. The next afternoon, they rode up to the McLean House and requested a meeting with Maj. Gen. John Gibbon. "Going to the door," Gibbon later recounted, "I found Gen. Fitz Lee seated on his horse, looking as I thought, somewhat uneasy." The two men had not seen each other since Lee's time as a West Point cadet under the Union general. "I could only think of a little rollicking fellow dressed in cadet-grey whose jolly songs and gay spirits had been the life of his class," Gibbon recalled. Calling out a cheery hello, Gibbon ordered Lee to dismount and join him. In the McLean parlor, Lee related the details of his escape on the ninth before inquiring of his staff officer Charles Minnigerode Jr. who had been wounded during the battle. After more pleasantries, Lee accepted his former instructor's offer to spend the night in the comfort of the home. Lying on the floor, he slept more soundly than he had in years.[7]

Fitz Lee's subordinate Brig. Gen. William P. Roberts likewise returned to Appomattox a few days later. Upon receiving orders on April 9 to withdraw from the field, Roberts had directed his brigade of North Carolinians and Georgians to disband and head toward their homes. Within a few minutes, every trooper had heeded his advice. "Shortly thereafter I traveled South, accompanied by one of my men," he later wrote, "but upon reflection I felt it my duty to return to Appomattox, which I did, and surrendered to the officer in command, General Gibbon."[8] Along with Fitz Lee, Roberts found his name included on the Appomattox parole lists with at least twelve other officers who reported themselves for parole after the departure of their commands.[9]

Whether they arrived in Appomattox in order to avoid charges of cowardice and prove their honor or because they were desperate for rations, those who returned offered visible proof the army had unraveled over the previous week. And yet a refrain of utter shock at the surrender reverberated through the diaries and letters of those who remained. Edward Valentine Jones conceded the steady attrition in the ranks during the march west, but he had been blindsided by news of the surrender. "What fatal change had come over the once gallant army of Northern Virginia," he asked himself.[10] This mixture of frustration, failure, and disbelief would not be left on the field. It would not be supplanted by memories of a peaceful reconciliation born in the McLean parlor. Instead, these emotions would seed a strident defense of Lee, his army, and the Confederate cause for decades to come.[11]

Robert E. Lee's final address to his soldiers simultaneously echoed and fostered these sentiments. He had muttered only a few words to his troops when he returned from the McLean House, but later that evening he asked Col. Charles Marshall to draft a farewell order that might be delivered before the army disbanded. The next day, commanders instructed their men to fall into formation without arms to receive General Orders No. 9.[12] The men stood in silence as their officers read Lee's words lauding the loyalty, valor, and "unsurpassed courage and fortitude" of "the brave survivors of so many hard-fought battles." Directed at those who remained in the ranks, not those who had fled or deserted their comrades in the push west, he assured them that the surrender was through no fault of their own. Instead he insisted that the army had been "compelled to yield to overwhelming numbers and resources." "You will take with you the satisfaction that proceeds from the consciousness of duty faithfully performed," he advised, "and I earnestly pray that a Merciful God will extend to you His blessing and protection."[13]

Lee's message was layered with meaning that his soldiers surely grasped. His reference to "overwhelming numbers" conjured images of mercenaries and foreign hirelings who had fought not for some righteous cause but for money, while "resources" called to mind the industrial might of the North. Both served as an indictment of northern society and stood in juxtaposition to the agrarian South, whose soldiers had "remained steadfast to the last." Yet even the "valor and devotion" of Lee's men could not stop the Union war machine.[14]

Here, only a day after the surrender Grant hoped would quell the rebellion, the foremost Confederate leader set forth two of the central tenets of what would come to be known as the Lost Cause: Confederate soldiers had been devoted, honorable, and chivalric; and the Confederacy had not been defeated on the field of battle but had been overwhelmed by the Union's forces and matériel. They might have succumbed to a superior military power, but might did not make right. Defeat had not rendered their cause immoral or its soldiers less than heroic.[15]

The farewell struck a chord deep within the men, and many hoped to preserve the words for posterity. Officers requested their own copies of the orders, approaching the general to ask for his signature. Some of the rank and file likewise hoped to capture the moment and stopped to scribble down his words in their diaries and letters. But not all heralded them as a final farewell. After transcribing the order into his diary, artillerist Eugene Henry Levy of Louisiana observed that "hope yet remains." Like others, he held out faith that France would intervene, just as it had done during the American Revolution. "When the Lilly of France is borne against the grasping Eagle the name of our venerated chief will act as a talisman to call the sons of the South once more to strive for national independence," he wrote; "God grant that the day is not far distant."[16]

Amid a steady rain the men headed back to their camps. At least a few bands tried to soothe spirits, moving among the troops and serenading them. Musicians from the 4th North Carolina gathered near the headquarters of Gen. Robert E. Lee and Maj. Gen. Bryan Grimes and struck up "Parting Is Pain." Others called for more stirring rebel songs, including "Bonnie Blue Flag" and "Dixie." Soon the valley hummed with familiar tunes, both lively and morose.[17]

While the Confederates hunkered down in their soggy camps awaiting paroles and enjoying much-needed rations and rest, the Union forces who had marched just as hard to capture the rebel army found themselves once again on the move. On the morning of April 10, Sheridan's troopers departed for Burkeville, the junction of the South Side and Richmond & Danville Railroads, where they might head south to assist Maj. Gen. William T. Sherman in North Carolina. On Tuesday the eleventh, soldiers of the Second and Sixth Corps followed the cavalry to Burkeville, while those of the Twenty-Fifth Corps returned to Richmond. Only the Fifth Corps from the Army of the Potomac and two divisions from the Army of the James's Twenty-Fourth Corps would remain on-site to oversee the printing of parole passes and receipt of surrendered property.[18]

Watching the Union troops depart, many Confederates hoped that they would be allowed to stack arms in their camps and simply leave the field after being paroled. But before riding toward Prospect Station that morning, Grant had insisted upon a formal surrender parade. This occasion—the surrender of *the* Confederate army, *Lee's* army, was much too important not to mark with some formality.[19] As such, the first item in the commissioners' agreement stated that the "troops shall march by brigades and detachments to a designated point, stack their arms, deposit their flags, sabers, pistols, &c."[20] Just as the British troops had formally done at Yorktown, the conquered Confederates would be forced to perform the ritual of defeat.

Grant's pragmatism shaped both the timing and pace of the surrender ceremonies, including which troops would be paroled first. If the men in Lee's ranks were starving, their horses proved equally ravenous. But there was no grain or hay to spare for the rebels' horses. The cavalry and artillery, therefore, needed to be paroled as quickly as possible for the sake of both man and beast. On the afternoon of April 10, even as the commissioners still met to determine the final terms, Gibbon ordered Bvt. Maj. Gen. Ranald S. Mackenzie to send a brigade of U.S. cavalry to the road north of the village where they would receive the sabers, accoutrements, and other arms of the Confederate cavalry units that had not escaped.[21] More than 1,000 cavalrymen rode into the village under the lead of Col. Alexander Cheves Haskell, where all but the officers paused to deposit their arms and colors.[22] Having surrendered their arms and received their blank parole passes, the men were free to leave. The next morning, April 11, the men of the artillery hitched up their guns and marched into the village, where they handed over their guns to John Turner's division of the Twenty-Fourth Corps. The infantry was set to follow.[23]

In his drenched and muddy tent, Eddie Whitehorne still waited. "We have no idea when we will be paroled." He had heard rumors that his division would be among the last, even as most of the cavalry and artillery had received passes and departed. Other infantrymen likewise wondered when their turn might come. "We are still in suspense not knowing when we will get off," noted William Alexander of North Carolina.[24] The parole lists had not yet been finalized. Neither had the passes been printed. Gibbon's press had been taken to General Sharpe's headquarters at Clover Hill on the morning of April 10, but it would take time to produce the estimated 30,000 blank parole passes needed. The press would have to run all night and perhaps throughout the next day. Knowing that this would be too much for the few soldiers tasked with running the press, Gibbon issued a call for more printers who might keep the press going so that they all might get to their homes as quickly as possible.[25]

While Gibbon's press hastily churned, Confederate regimental and company commanders labored in their respective tents to prepare the parole lists. Rather than have individual soldiers sign a parole of honor, commanding officers would compile a roll of all the men still with them and sign on their behalf. Duplicates of the completed lists were to be prepared, with one copy to remain with the Confederates and the other to be turned over to General Sharpe, provost marshal of the Army of the Potomac.[26]

In the coming weeks and months, Sharpe and other provost marshals would play a pivotal role in the disbanding of Confederate forces far from the field at Appomattox. The law enforcement arm of the military, provost marshals policed soldiers and civilians. On the Union home front, they arrested civilians suspected of disloyalty, hunted down deserters, enlisted volunteers, and enforced the draft. Those attached to the army were appointed by line officers, ranged in rank from lieutenants to generals, and functioned more like military police. They oversaw a passport system for those traveling through the lines, detained prisoners of war and deserters, and, most importantly for the post-Appomattox period, retained records of paroles and oaths of allegiance.[27]

The lists demanded by General Sharpe seemed a simple request, but it proved incredibly daunting. Commands had become so entangled during the retreat that it was nearly impossible to ensure that each soldier appeared on the roll of his assigned regiment, let alone company.[28] Making matters even more complicated, after Lt. Gen. A. P. Hill's death at Petersburg on April 2, his corps had been added to that of Longstreet's, while the men of Lt. Gen. Richard Ewell's corps found themselves assigned to Maj. Gen. John B. Gordon after their commander's capture. Many of the officers and men simply had no idea as to which command they officially belonged. Moreover, some troops had been abandoned by their general officers, who left the men to fend for themselves after filling out their own papers. They would have to make do the best they could, even if that meant attaching themselves to another unit.[29] Many found themselves included on the lists with men from entirely different brigades, divisions, or even corps.[30] When some without officers attempted to turn themselves in to Union officials, they were sent back to Confederate lines to be paroled by any commanding officer. Confederate provost marshal Maj. David B. Bridgford thus recorded the names of 190 unattached noncommissioned officers and privates who had been cut off from their commands, and upon his return to Appomattox on April 11, Fitzhugh Lee directed his adjutant general to parole another 136 men deprived of commands.[31]

If some men appeared on lists with units other than their own, others who had already left would later find themselves listed as present.[32] In at least one instance, two men who escaped Appomattox were included on the roster of those paroled. Sgt. Berry Benson of the 1st South Carolina

(McCreary's) had been captured nearly a year earlier at Spotsylvania and spent several months in Elmira Prison before escaping by tunneling to freedom. Back with the Army of Northern Virginia, he could not fathom returning to prison — a fate he thought likely, given the impending surrender — and convinced his brother, Blackwood, to leave with him. Rifles in hand, the men crept through the brush, crawled through ditches, and hid in a fence corner to elude the Federal pickets. In doing so, they stumbled across a young North Carolina soldier named Higgins who had the same idea. Together, the three men crossed to the north side of the James River before turning south in the hopes of joining Johnston's army. But even as they made their way around Federal lines, the Benson brothers were being added to the roster of those surrendered on April 11 by McGowan's Brigade.[33]

Whether they were included by mistake or purposefully listed because they had been engaged in the fight on the morning of April 9 remains unclear. Regardless, their account suggests that the final list of 28,231 paroled Confederates completed on April 15 almost certainly overestimated the number present.[34]

"As yet," John Anderson of South Carolina wrote his father from his campsite at Appomattox, "we have had none of the Yankee's bravado of triumph."[35] This aligned with orders from Grant and his fellow officers. "We were ordered to treat them as 'erring brothers,'" observed a Maine volunteer, sparing the rebels the "humiliating scenes which a foreign foe would have been compelled to undergo." Not that he had any great sympathy for the rebels. "The fact that they are not foreigners is not due to any lack of effort on their part," he remarked. The Union forces had already been forced to share their rations, even though they were existing on half rations themselves. What more was to be asked? "If we are to be so tender," the Mainer sarcastically quipped, "perhaps we should have surrendered to them, for it must be excessively humiliating for these high-toned Southerners to surrender to us mean, craven-spirited Yankees."[36]

Some of Lee's men conceded that Grant's terms had been very liberal. As Kena King Chapman confessed, contrary to their fears that they would be heading off to prisoner-of-war camps, "we are all to be paroled and sent to our homes there to remain until exchanged." Few had taken this for granted. Grant's terms, combined with the rations, came as both a surprise and a relief.[37]

But acknowledging Grant's magnanimous terms did not soften their distaste for the enemy. In fact, many of the enlisted men became increasingly embittered by the Yankees' behavior as they waited for their paroles. On Monday morning, several Union soldiers approached the rebel camps for a closer look, and later in the afternoon, officers began to ride among the tents. Some senior officers like George Gordon Meade had requested to visit with old friends like Robert E. Lee, but others appeared to relish the opportunity to parade triumphantly through their defeated foes' camp. Dr. Henry J. Millard of Massachusetts considered the surrender the "happiest day" of his life and enjoyed the "privilege" of riding through Lee's army while the troops were still in possession of their arms.[38] Such was the fruit of victory, but it particularly galled one North Carolinian. "Our hearts have been today frequently stirred up upon seeing the conquering Yankee Officers riding about," he wrote.[39] Capt. Henry Chambers could not contain the bitterness he felt toward the victors. He only hoped for some "terrible retribution" to "come upon this motly crew who have waged upon us so unjust, so barbarous a warfare!"[40]

On April 11, General Gordon gathered his Second Corps for a final farewell. While he was sending them home, this might not be the end, he observed. There might yet be another outburst between the sections. Perhaps it would happen in five years. Maybe ten. But if and when it happened, Gordon asked his men, could he count on the old Second Corps to rally once more? Would they again respond to their country's call? The response, wrote one soldier, "was a universal shout of yes."[41]

Worried that such sentiments could devolve into violent altercations, Union leadership tried to prevent escalating animosities. In order to avoid disputes between the surrendered Confederates and Maj. Gen. E. O. C. Ord's African American troops, Ord had kept the Black soldiers in the camps behind their white comrades and sent them from the area before the formal surrender on April 12.[42] Even without the conflict that surely would have followed an encounter between the rebels and their former slaves, there was no mingling with the enemy among the enlisted men.

While the Black Union soldiers marched away from Appomattox, the African Americans who remained in Confederate camps could not help but wonder about the status of their own freedom. In 1861, nearly one out of every twenty to thirty Confederate soldiers brought a slave with him to manage gear, cook meals, mend and wash clothing, and tend to horses. "Think of it," observed a private from the Richmond Howitzers, "a Confederate soldier

Unidentified group of Confederates posing in Virginia with an African American man, most likely an enslaved body servant. PA0382, John L. Nau III Collection, Small Special Collections, University of Virginia.

with a body servant all his own, to bring him a drink of water, black his boots, dust his clothes, cook his corn bread and bacon, and put wood on the fire." Others employed free Black men to perform the same labor as slaves. Brig. Gen. Edward Porter Alexander had done just this in late 1861 when he hired fifteen-year-old Charley Crowley in Loudoun County. Young Charley would spend the remainder of the war with Alexander as a servant and groom to his horses.[43] A personal slave made some of the hardships of camp life at least a bit more tolerable for a significant number of rebels.

The number and percentage of body servants declined over the course of the war, but facing a shortage of manpower, the Confederate government in April 1862 began debating the use of Black men as teamsters, musicians, and cooks. The Confederate Congress subsequently authorized officers to enlist four cooks per company. Such men, the bill explained, "may be white or black, free or slave persons," with the provision that "no slave shall be so enlisted without the written consent of his owner." Once "enlisted" the cooks were to be "put on the muster roll" and paid at the same time and place as the rest of the company.[44] At least some companies obeyed these orders, such as the Goochland Light Artillery. In the fall of 1864, the unit included at least five Black men on its muster roll. Among them was Frederick, who had joined as a cook at Richmond in February 1863. Perhaps he had been owned by a member of the unit, or maybe he had been a freeman known by someone in the battalion. The lack of a surname makes it impossible to learn more. Regardless, Frederick and several other Black cooks were noted "present" on the company muster rolls through February 1865, just before the unit disbanded.[45]

Those listed by name on company rolls were almost certainly men who were either free or permitted by their masters to offer their services (perhaps in the hopes that owners would reap a financial gain). Still more bodies were needed. States took the lead in allowing the impressment of enslaved men, but beginning in the spring of 1863, the Confederate Congress authorized the army to impress slaves. In addition to constructing fortifications, digging ditches, serving as teamsters, working burial details, and repairing roads, the army directed conscripted slaves to serve as nurses and cooks — all labor that freed Confederate soldiers for combat roles.[46]

By April 1865, many impressed slaves had managed to escape to Union lines. But hundreds of African Americans — free and enslaved — remained with the Army of Northern Virginia. Given the practice of including Black men on the muster rolls, it is hardly surprising that some commanders included the names of African American men remaining with the army at Appomattox on the parole lists. Among those still present with the Donaldsonville (Louisiana) Artillery's Company B were three "servants" — L. Leport, Jonathan Mamply, and Jonathan Semple — and a cook, H. Blum. In Gary's Cavalry Brigade, W. H. Mauldin included the names of five "free boys" and two slaves, all described as teamsters. Although he failed to list them by name, Capt. H. C. Thornburn of the Third Corps Quartermaster's Department likewise certified that he had under his charge sixteen "negroes — slaves in public service." The 18th Georgia Battalion listed four musicians and four cooks, including Scipio Africanus, a cook who had enlisted at Savannah in November 1862 with the consent of his owner, and Joe Parkman, a musician from Green Island who had been with the army since March 1862.[47]

In addition to those who labored for the army were hundreds of privately owned enslaved men. Among them was Charley, General Alexander's hostler and servant. General Longstreet's slave Jim camped among the men bivouacked along the hills surrounding the courthouse, as did Maj. Giles B. Cooke's slave William.[48] Maj. Henry Kyd Douglas fumed that his "boy, Buck," had absconded with his horse and hand trunk during the fighting on April 9, but he quickly found another unnamed enslaved man in camp to fill Buck's place.[49] Company grade officers and enlisted men, too, could still claim the presence of their slaves. Accounting for the men in his mess after the surrender, William Abernathy, a courier with the 17th Mississippi, noted that among the twelve men in the mess who had begun the war, only he and his "body guard, an old negro named Simon," remained.[50] George, an enslaved man who served as a cook for courier Thomas Devereux of North Carolina, likewise continued with the army on April 9.[51] Foreshadowing the Lost Cause tributes to so-called faithful slaves, John Crawford Anderson of the 13th South Carolina informed his father that his valet and cook, Peter, "still proves true and says he will never desert the cause, but is very much elated at the idea of getting home."[52]

There is no record of Peter's emotions as he waited in the camps with Lee's men, but it is likely his private sentiments accorded with other African Americans who christened April 9 as "freedom day." Thomas Morris Chester, a Black war correspondent from the *Philadelphia Press* embedded with the Army of the James, celebrated the 2,000 soldiers of the USCT who had participated in the final battles, which gave "Lee's forces as trophies to the Union army." One of those soldiers, William H. Harrison, recognized that if circumstances had been different, he might have been camping alongside Lee's army rather than with the Union army. Born in Richmond, he had accompanied his owner to war with Lee's army as a body servant until he was captured in 1863, brought to Knoxville, and forced to fight in the Union army. But from the Union ranks, he could proudly claim his part in destroying slavery. "I was with General Grant when Lee surrendered at Appomattox," he later recalled. "That was freedom."[53]

On nearby farms and plantations, enslaved men and women likewise celebrated the surrender as culmination of the long, arduous process of emancipation. Not far from Appomattox, Samuel Spottford Clement and the other field hands could hear the "boom of the cannon and the crack of musketry" and prayed that the Yankees might prevail. Four days later, his owner gathered the slaves and informed them they were free. In Pamplin, Fanny Berry recalled that she and other slaves burst into song when they learned that Lee had surrendered with the assistance of the USCT. At that moment, she declared they "knew dat dey were free."[54]

On the afternoon of April 11, Turner's Division of Gibbon's Twenty-Fourth Corps, which had been supervising the ceremonies, left Appomattox for Lynchburg to secure its surrender. But the men of Lee's infantry had not yet turned over their weapons, munitions, and battle flags. Around midnight,

Brig. Gen. Joshua Chamberlain, now in charge of the 3rd Brigade, 1st Division, of the Army of the Potomac's 5th Corps, received word that he would oversee the surrender parade and receive the guns and flags.[55]

Like Grant, the rebel chieftain would not participate in the formal surrender. Instead, on the gray morning of Wednesday, April 12, Union headquarters ordered a detail of cavalry from the 4th Massachusetts to escort Lee and his staff toward Richmond.[56] As Lee, his aides, and a single wagon bearing their personal belongings started east, a chorus began to echo across the valley. Throughout the camps of the Army of Northern Virginia, the rebel yell commenced, spreading from one regiment to another and then back again. Men seemed to appear from everywhere, raising their hats and cheering their general in a refrain that moved even the cavalrymen of the 4th Massachusetts. The ovation, observed escort Sgt. William Arnold, "seemed to me a wonderful manifestation of confidence and affection for this great military chieftain."[57]

Back in Appomattox, Chamberlain's lone division formed along both sides of the Lynchburg Stage Road. Across the small valley the men could see Lee's infantry breaking camp one last time. Down came the small shelter tents, and then, slowly, the gray mass formed into columns, flags aloft, and began to move.[58] John Gordon's Second Corps took the lead, marching down the muddy hill and across the shallow waters of the Appomattox. As the Confederates advanced up the Stage Road toward the courthouse, Chamberlain called the Federal columns to attention. Orders were given to shoulder arms, and the Union soldiers raised their rifles to their shoulders in a sign of respect. A soldier in the 155th Pennsylvania observed that it took nearly six hours for all the Confederates to complete the stacking. "Not an unkind word was spoken to them," he noted, adding that "some of their color bearers shed tears when they delivered up their colors."[59] A special correspondent stationed with the Army of the Potomac's Fifth Corps was equally moved by the morose scene. "A more wretched and painful sight I have never witnessed," he wrote.[60]

Among those laying down arms was Eddie Whitehorne. Earlier that morning he had fallen into line along with the remaining members of the 12th Virginia before marching nearly two miles toward the village. Ascending a gentle hill, he saw two Federal lines, one on each side of the road. "Our men marched up boldly and stacked arms and did not seem to mind any more than if they had been going on dress parade," he noted. "They did not look at us, did not look defiant, did not make disrespectful remarks." Instead, at least in Whitehorne's mind, it was the rebels who remained defiant. "The Yanks are afraid of us now," he assured himself, "and that will make them hate us all the more in future years. If we meet one in the road he will always get out of our way."[61] The humiliation of surrender had not deterred Whitehorne's bravado. If anything, it strengthened his contempt for the Union victors.

Unlike Whitehorne, some of Lee's men who had remained at Appomattox simply refused to take part in the surrender ceremony. After the Confederates left, the 118th Pennsylvania had scoured the woods where the rebels had camped, collecting muskets and other discarded munitions of war. In many locations they found more than just a few broken rifles or haversacks. Indeed, it appeared as if entire battalions had stacked their arms and left the field, refusing to participate in the formal surrender or wait for their paroles. The volume was such that one Union soldier estimated that, if all of these Confederates had remained, it would have swelled Lee's ranks to more than 50,000 men.[62]

After stacking his musket alongside the remnants of Mahone's Division, Eddie Whitehorne settled down for the evening. Until the parole lists were completed, no one was supposed to leave. Famished, exhausted, and simply wanting to sleep, he initially groused when a lieutenant disturbed him at ten o'clock. But the news was good. The blank paroles had just arrived from the Union printing press, and the lieutenant required Whitehorne's assistance in filling out those for the 12th Virginia, Company F. If they completed them immediately, the men could depart for home as soon as they liked. "I needed no persuasion," the young sergeant wrote, "so I jumped up and borrowed a pen and bottle of ink from one of the men." Scrounging up a scrap of tallow candle, he quickly went to work, inscribing the names of the eighteen men still with the company before rushing to have the commanding officer sign the papers and obtain the parole passes. "I now have my parole in my pocket," he scribbled in his diary. Pausing, he added, "Two signatures on a piece of paper—one in the spring of 1861 which made me a soldier—the other in the spring of 1865 which makes me ———."[63] Whitehorne could not find a word to finish his sentence. Just what would be his status—his place— in this post-Appomattox world?

Whitehorne had every reason to worry. Even as the Confederates prepared to head home, word reached Washington of the terms and raised the first doubts about whether the paroles would operate as a blanket pardon. "I do not blame Lee's being received on parole," Francis Lieber wrote Senator Charles Sumner on April 11. But Lieber worried about the legal implications. "You put a rebel beyond trial for treason when you receive him according to the laws of war, as a prisoner of war, and parole him," he warned.[64] For Lieber and others, Grant seemed to have overstepped his bounds.

5

Procession of Defeat

Capt. William Henry Harder of the 23rd Tennessee left Appomattox on the morning of April 13. The thirty-five-year-old had served through the entire four years of war. In 1861, he had raised a company of nearly 100 men from the Cedar Creek area of Perry County, Tennessee. Outfitted in uniforms sewn by Harder's mother and other local women, the company marched off to war, seeing action at Fort Donelson and then Shiloh, where Harder was wounded and taken prisoner. He spent the next few months recovering at Camp Douglas before returning to his command in the fall of 1862. During the next two years, Harder and his men fought at Stones River and Chickamauga before being sent east in 1864, where they were ordered to the trenches around Petersburg. And so it was that this western regiment surrendered with Lee.[1]

Just as Harder had led his men off to war, he now led them home. Leaving by way of the Lynchburg Road, he and the sixty-three remaining members of the 23rd marched alongside a group of nearly 1,000 other Confederate soldiers bound for southwest Virginia and Tennessee. Falling into column, the regiment headed west, traipsing in silence through the Federal lines for nearly a mile. As they passed the rear guard, Harder observed that the Confederates were now "free to go where we liked." But the men did not break from the ranks. Instead, on they marched, four abreast, brigade following brigade, regiment after regiment. They had gone to war as communities, and many would return the same way. In their final act as soldiers, they marched home from battle.[2] The surrender of the Army of Northern Virginia would not serve to demarcate between past and future as much as Unionists hoped or Confederates feared.

Having deposited their rifles, flags, ammunition, and artillery with the Federals, most of the Confederate rank and file left Appomattox with few accoutrements of an army. Enlisted men kept their blankets, haversacks, and canteens — if they had not abandoned them along the flight from Petersburg or Richmond. Some lucky men carried little hand axes they wore tucked in their belts — axes that had been so crucial in throwing up breastworks at the Wilderness, Spotsylvania, and Cold Harbor and in the trenches at Petersburg.[3] And a few managed to collect rifles along the roadside that had been abandoned the previous week.[4]

Eddie Whitehorne and his two companions had a relatively short distance to travel to their Greensville County home. Taking the road bearing southeast from Appomattox Court House, they started for home at daybreak on Thursday, April 13. For miles they tramped along muddy, puddle-filled roads, finally crossing the South Side Railroad at Pamplin's Station. Stomachs aching, they rejoiced upon discovering a mill. But the flood of soldiers ahead of them had already collected all of the meal as quickly as it poured into the tub. If luck failed their appetites, the arrival of a neighbor, William Hays of Harris's Brigade, offered at least a bit of relief. Riding a lame horse, Hays offered to let the men take turns walking and riding, alleviating the pain and discomfort caused by their blistered feet for several miles, even as the poor old beast lumbered along slowly. Just before nightfall, providence again shone on them when a gentleman agreed to let them camp along his property, while his wife offered the starving soldiers freshly baked bread.[5]

Even though thousands of men like Whitehorne who hailed from Virginia would leave in pairs or small parties, a substantial number initially marched away from Appomattox, as did Harder, with their divisions, brigades, regiments, or companies.[6] The ninety-eight enlisted men who remained with Griffin's Company, Salem Flying Artillery, gathered after the surrender ceremony to begin their eighty-plus-mile trip to Roanoke.[7] At six o'clock in the morning on April 13, nearly 350 Alabamians of Battle's Brigade were up and ready to march, heading through the Union lines toward Appomattox Station. From there, they planned to follow the South Side Railroad until they reached a train. At the invitation of their colonel, Edwin L. Hobson, Pvt. Edward Valentine Jones of the 3rd Company, Richmond Howitzers, who had been separated from his battalion during the retreat, elected to join the ranks of the Alabamians and head toward Richmond. It was too dangerous, Hobson had observed, to travel alone through a country occupied by the enemy. Rumors swirled that several men had been killed and many others robbed. Suffering from an ulcerated sore throat, the twenty-year-old artillerist accepted the colonel's offer, finding a mule to carry him alongside the Alabama foot soldiers.[8]

More regiments and brigades left on Thursday, April 13. Away marched the remnants of Wilcox's Division—Lane's, Thomas's, Scales's, and Mc-Gowan's Brigades of South Carolinians. Bound for North Carolina tramped two brigades of Tar Heels under the command Maj. Gen. Bryan Grimes.[9] Perhaps as many as 400 members of Hood's Texas Brigade struck out for Danville, where they hoped to catch cars that would take them southwest to New Orleans or Galveston. Not needing to go quite so far west as their Texas brethren, however, more than 100 members of the 3rd Arkansas ventured southwest toward Chattanooga, while many of those in Company K followed Capt. A. C. Jones toward Fort Monroe to find a steamer bound for New Orleans.[10] This was no longer the Army of Northern Virginia. It had largely come unraveled over the course of the retreat. But remnants of the once formidable force, still bound together by an esprit de corps, military conventions, and orders from the surrender commission, remained to march away from Appomattox.[11]

Likewise heading south in columns marched Bratton's Brigade of South Carolinians, the largest brigade surrendered at Appomattox with more than 1,500 men.[12] In a statement published in the Richmond and South Carolina papers in early February 1865, the men of the brigade acknowledged that Lee's army had experienced reverses, but they remained committed to Confederate independence. After four years of witnessing what they described as atrocities committed by northern troops, there was no way they could return to the Union. "The outrages upon us by a base and unprincipled foe," the South Carolinians had declared, "have created an impassable gulf between the two sections, which must forever prevent all union or affiliation between them." They expected that "no concession on our part would be accepted by them short of a state of complete subjection, which would be worse than death."[13] Grant's generous terms had done nothing to change their sentiments.[14]

As spring winds began drying the mud-clogged roads, the entire countryside appeared to be on the move. Formerly enslaved men and women, white refugees, and sutlers traversed the region and flowed into small towns as well as big cities, as did the remnants of Lee's army.[15] Confederates in pairs, companies, and brigades marched away from Appomattox in every direction. Like Bratton's Brigade, most of those from the Carolinas, Georgia,

Tennessee, Mississippi, Alabama, Louisiana, Arkansas, and Texas started south. Some kept to the roads, but others followed the muddy ravines, hog trails, or streambeds that kept them off the beaten path. Some headed west toward the Blue Ridge to begin their trek southward, but a great many traveled due south to Danville, the closest railhead where they might catch a train to Greensboro.[16] Those pointed east and north encountered a landscape wracked by four years of fighting. Though greening with the spring rains that continued throughout the second week of April, the countryside lay barren. Scarcely a fence post could be found in central Virginia, and the fields had grown up with broom sage and brush. Pastures remained empty, most of the sheep, cattle, and hogs long since provender for the massive armies that had devoured the region for nearly four years.[17] For those bound for Richmond and Petersburg, the roads proved a gruesome reminder of the past week's flight. Broken wagons and discarded rifles littered the muddy and rutted roadbeds, while wet and rotting horse carcasses filled the air with a putrid odor.[18]

Some Confederates took pause at such sights, observing that the passing of these armies might be the last they would ever witness. On Thursday, April 13, George Bernard of the 12th Virginia and his two traveling companions stopped to watch several wagons wending their way along the rough roads up the Shenandoah Valley. Here was "an organized party of Confederates . . . quartermaster, or wagon-master, and teamsters, still in the faithful discharge of their duty, solemnly and slowly moving to their point of destination in obedience to the orders of some superior officer." They proceeded along, Bernard thought, "as if nothing had happened." Such sights in the days and even weeks after Lee's surrender served as a reminder that the war was ending if not yet ended.[19]

The Union troops, too, were once more on the move. Most of the army had left Appomattox on April 10, bound for Petersburg or City Point. But members of the Fifth and Twenty-Fourth Corps who had stayed behind to oversee the surrender and paroles left in the days that followed. Toward Farmville rolled wagons and ambulances with their white covers carrying both Confederate arms and wounded soldiers. Off marched the infantry and artillery, driving cattle over the gentle hills. In the evenings, they paused while campfires lit up the night sky, only to resume their journey the next morning. Again, they tramped eastward along the South Side Railroad, trekking across a country stripped of everything and cut up by wagon ruts, reaching Burkeville, where the remnants of the Second and Sixth Corps already bivouacked.[20]

"The roads are full of paroled rebels going home," Union corporal Henry C. Metzger informed his father on April 14, yet he remained on the march. "I would not have missed this trip for a good deal, but would like to be out of service as soon as peace is declared. I don't want to be in the army when the fighting is over." Metzger and other Union enlistees like him had fought as citizen soldiers who swore to defend the nation. Once the Union had been saved, they expected to go home, having no desire to serve as an occupying force.[21] Even in mid-April, his was a common refrain from the camps of Union soldiers. Their defeated foes were headed home, but the victorious Union soldiers would have to wait. "I dont know what they intend to do with us," observed Albert G. Harrison of the 14th New Jersey Infantry from camp near Burkeville. "We dont get any papers, so we hear nothing but rumors."[22] Uncertainty abounded—for Union and Confederate alike.

Despite orders from General Gibbon instructing soldiers of the Twenty-Fourth Corps to abide by the surrender agreement, Confederates remained cautious and wary of the terms, uncertain that they would protect them.[23] Only a short distance from Appomattox, a Union sergeant ordered Carlton McCarthy and another artillerist to halt and show their paroles. "It was the first exercise of authority by the Federal army," McCarthy observed—and a stark reminder that Lee's men remained in a precarious position.[24] Many had heard stories of comrades who had been refused passage, had been held by Union authorities, had seen their personal horses and mules taken, or had been hanged for violating their paroles.[25]

Even with their passes in hand, Joseph A. Graves of the Bedford Light Artillery and his twenty comrades elected to take a more circuitous route south through Campbell Court House rather than head directly home, "fearing lest we should be detained in Lynchburg by an examination of our papers."[26] Other departing rebels observed the Union troops from a distance. "Saw a squad of Yankee cavalry at this place," Eddie Whitehorne reported from Prince Edward County on April 14. "They did not have anything to say to us."[27] Efforts to keep their distance were not lost on Union troops. A New York cavalryman patrolling the area south of Petersburg saw hundreds of Lee's men passing by on the roads each day. "Most of them avoided our column, emerging from the woods and spreading over the fields in all directions, battle-worn veterans in dingy gray and butternut, silent and cast down," he noted.[28] Deep-seated bitterness and distrust motivated them to keep their distance.

But necessity often required parolees to seek out Union troops. Heading toward Burkeville to catch a train, twelve members of the Norfolk Blues stopped at Farmville, the nearest post where Confederates could secure rations from Union supply trains, on April 13. There they found "a mob of half satisfied and insolent looking Yankees" along with "dirty, and ragged, yet proud and defiant looking Confederate soldiers." Dismayed by the filth of the once-thriving town, the men presented their parole passes to the local provost marshal for one day's rations before heading on along the South Side Railroad. At Burkeville, a group of Floridians likewise requested rations from the provost marshal. "They saw we were starving, so they did not weigh or measure it, but gave it to us in piles, for they were sorry for us, in our starved condition," recalled one soldier. But passes did not guarantee there would be any rations to receive. By the time the men from the Norfolk Blues arrived in Burkeville, Federal soldiers had doled out all of the available provisions.[29]

Some of Lee's men sought out Federal posts to accept Grant's offer of free carriage on government transports and military railroads when necessary to reach their homes. Many of those going to Richmond or the Virginia Tidewater followed the tracks nearly fifty miles southeast from Appomattox to Burkeville. A junction of the Richmond & Danville Railroad and South Side Railroad, the town consisted of a three-story clapboard hotel that had been used as a Confederate hospital for the past year, a depot, and two small houses. In the days after April 3, the U.S. Army had rebuilt the railroad between Burkeville and Petersburg, which further opened passage to U.S. headquarters at City Point. Showing their passes to the Union troops now occupying the station, hundreds of weary and footsore Confederates climbed aboard and on top of the crowded boxcars.[30]

Among those who found passage was artillery general Porter Alexander. On the morning of April 12, he had left Appomattox on horseback with a mixed party of Federals and Confederates, including Confederate major generals John B. Gordon and Cadmus Wilcox, bound for the railroad depot.[31] There, he turned over an artillery horse to the Federal quartermaster, and the party boarded a "jammed & packed" train to City Point, where the brigadier general planned to catch a steamer to Richmond.[32]

Situated on the confluence of the James and Appomattox Rivers, City Point had served as the Union headquarters throughout the siege of Petersburg. But even as Grant was ordering the massive war machine to slow down, the river port still bustled. Transports moved up and down the waterways, conveying supplies to the army, while all along the shore, Union surgeons tended to the sick and wounded in tents that stretched for miles. Into this

Docks at City Point, Virginia, where paroled Confederates caught steamers heading to Richmond, Baltimore, and points south. Library of Congress Prints and Photographs Division, LC-DIG-ppmsca-33286.

well-oiled, fully manned Union base trickled Thomas Halstead of the 61st Virginia and thousands of other filthy, tattered, and weather-beaten parolees. Finding his way to the provost marshal's office, Halstead stood in line. Reaching the window, he fished the pass from his pocket, placed it on the sill, and awaited his stamp. With such government sanction, he climbed aboard the steamer for Norfolk, hoping he would be home by dinner.[33]

Requiring civilians and soldiers alike to carry passes had become a necessity of war. Confederate soldiers, like their Union counterparts, had been required to show passes when they returned home on furlough or otherwise left their commands. And much to the dismay of many, civilians were required to present a government-issued passport for all railroad travel within the Confederacy during much of the war. When the Confederate Congress adjourned in Richmond, Senator John W. Lewis of Georgia complained that he had to first find someone who could identify him to accompany him to the provost marshal's office, where he would be met with a soldier bearing a bayonet. Once he obtained the pass, he would travel to the train station, again to be met by soldiers, and be obliged to show his pass yet again. It did not seem proper, he observed, that he could not travel to his home "without obtaining a pass like a negro." Senator Williamson S. Oldham of Texas likewise likened the passport system to the passes required of slaves and free African Americans. Although a "free citizen," he grumbled he "was not allowed to go from [Richmond] . . . to North Carolina without going to the Provost Marshal office and getting a pass like a free negro."[34] In comparing their plight to that of African Americans, Confederates neglected to acknowledge that theirs was but a wartime measure that would surely terminate with the end of the war.

Yet much as slave passes had both allowed and restricted the mobility of enslaved men and women, parole passes represented a new and uncertain position for Lee's men.[35] Now prisoners of war, their passes allowed them to travel home—but only to their homes. Presenting one's parole pass for rations or transportation and having it stamped by a U.S. (as opposed to a Confederate) provost marshal provided a stark reminder that Lee's men were not yet free civilians. They were not truly "free to go where they liked." Instead, they remained paroled prisoners—prisoners who would likely never be exchanged.

Even with a parole pass, the promise of easy passage did not always prove to be the reality. Throughout the region, both the Union and Confederate armies had destroyed locomotives, torn up rail lines, and burned bridges. Even where U.S. engineers had managed to rebuild portions of the track, the hastiness of the repairs combined with the high volume of demand hampered travel. Alongside 300 other members of Battle's Brigade, Edward Valentine Jones reached Burkeville Junction around noon on April 14. When their colonel asked the provost marshal when a train might arrive, he learned the times were sporadic. The men would have to wait.

Their wait proved a godsend when the colonel procured rations, including cans of condensed milk—a novelty in the South. "It is put up in tin boxes holding one pint each, is about the consistency of thick paste, and diluted with water, forms milk. We found the paste very rich and sweet, quite as good as preserves to our Confederate palates," Jones explained in his diary. "How these Yankees do live."

Before sunlight the next morning, a train came puffing into the station bearing a freight of crackers for the army. Once unloaded, the Confederates clamored to fill the cars, pushing and shoving their way as torrents of rain began gushing from the skies, soaking those forced to ride on the top. But soon the wet rebels found themselves ordered to disembark. Union soldiers needed to be transported to City Point. Climbing down from the cars, they waited once more in the mud-clogged railroad town. It would be at least twenty-four hours before another train arrived.[36]

Although they looked like companies, regiments, or even brigades marching away from yet another battle, the men in the ranks and their commanders recognized the limits of unit cohesion in the wake of surrender. Both practical matters and individual motivations ensured that the command structure often lasted little more than a few days. After only one day's march along the sodden roads, Brig. Gen. Samuel McGowan halted his brigade of South Carolinians at a farmhouse. Unable to procure more than a single ear of corn, he had no other choice but to disband his command.[37] Bratton's Brigade likewise began to disperse after only a few days.[38] Leading the brigade's 1st South Carolina, Col. James R. Hagood understood that without money and no longer possessing the authority of the Confederate government to confiscate goods, he had no way of providing for the men. Having marched some twenty-four miles away from Appomattox, he could conceive of no other plan than to give each man his parole pass and allow him to get home the best he could. That evening as the men clustered around their campfires, Hagood and the officers decided to fill out the blank paroles for every man present. Early on the morning of April 14, the brigade gathered to distribute passes before splintering. Some traveled on in squads of six to twelve men, while others like Col. Asbury Coward's 5th South Carolina or those of the Palmetto Sharpshooters marched on in a fairly large and organized group.[39]

The decision of Bratton's Brigade to distribute the passes after leaving Appomattox proved quite common. Although many men had received their parole passes in the camps before departing the surrender site, commanders who planned to leave as units had held on to the passes as a way of maintaining control or leverage over soldiers no longer bound by Confederate martial law. On the morning of Friday, April 14, Lt. G. H. Mills of the 16th North Carolina called his remaining men together to dole out the passes, informing them that they would be better served in their efforts to find food and shelter if they could escape the crowded roads.[40] Having the parole passes in hand would prove crucial for individual soldiers. Without them, they had no evidence that they had surrendered. These slips of papers allowed them to pass through Union lines when necessary to reach their homes, to secure passage on a U.S. railway, and to prove that they were prisoners of war protected by the terms Grant had offered at Appomattox.

Yet paroles held meaning beyond the practical status they might convey. For the men who had remained with Lee through Appomattox, they offered proof of honor. They served as a reminder than a soldier had retained faith in his commander and the Confederate nation. The passes embodied a spirit of loyalty and devotion unmatched by thousands of their comrades.[41] Indeed, they knew all too well that deserters from their army roamed the countryside. Near Campbell Court House on April 14, Lt. Abner Cox of the Palmetto Sharpshooters and the remaining members of Bratton's Brigade listened as the locals shared harrowing stories of fellow Army of Northern Virginia men scouring the countryside and pillaging homes by holding civilians at gunpoint. To Cox, such men were a disgrace. He could only scoff when one of Maj. Gen. George Pickett's men approached the officers and asked for a parole. Deserters and cowards, in his estimation, deserved no such accommodation.[42]

The Black men who had been deployed in support of the Confederate military effort faced many of the same daunting tasks as their former masters in making their way back to their loved ones. One of the first dilemmas would be how and where they would travel. Many left Appomattox on their own. But at least some former slaves accompanied the paroled Confederates as they trekked away from the surrender site. Jim continued on with Lt. Gen. James Longstreet and his aide Thomas Goree. An unnamed enslaved man departed Appomattox with members of 16th North Carolina.[43] In late April, William Fulton of the 5th Alabama Battalion noted that "some of the company negroes" were still traveling with him and several of his comrades near the Catawba River in North Carolina (yet Fulton's reference suggests that others elected not to travel with the white Alabamians).[44] Ostensibly free in the wake of the surrender, the servants turned freedmen who traveled with their former masters might have found it pragmatic to continue on with the Confederate soldiers. African Americans were headed back to *their* homes—back to *their* families—and traveling with white men might have offered at least some measure of protection or security. But equally as important, the fear and terror that undergirded slavery did not dissipate with Confederate surrender. African Americans remained cautious and apprehensive about exercising their freedom.[45] Regardless of why they chose to stay in the company of white men, their presence allowed Confederates to assert that slaves remained loyal to their former masters and the rebel cause, a myth that would only grow in the years and decades that followed.

But African Americans also struck out on their own. Most left with little record of their destination, such as cavalry captain Henry Carter Lee's "boy Wilson," who departed at some point between April 9 and 11.[46] Charley Crowley, a slave from Loudoun County hired by Porter Alexander in late 1861, however, informed the general of his whereabouts. After leaving Alexander at Appomattox on the morning of April 12, Crowley had found a mule that he rode to the nearby railroad junction. With ten dollars in gold provided by Alexander, Crowley boarded a train bound for Petersburg with about 5,000 Union soldiers, both white and Black. But his experience aboard the train revealed just how tense and unpredictable the situation remained after the surrender, even for a former slave. "When I told them I was a servant in the Rebel Army," he wrote, "I came very near being shot by some of the colored soldiers." Only the intervention of "some white friends" saved his life.[47]

Having watched the Confederates march away from Appomattox, General Gibbon assured Grant the source of the fighting had been terminated. "I believe all reasoning Men on both sides recognize the fact that slavery is dead," he observed on April 13.[48] But emancipation had not been one of the terms of surrender and had not yet been secured by the Thirteenth Amendment's ratification. While most slave owners bitterly conceded they were no longer entitled to control the flesh of other humans, at least some soldiers remained intent on protecting their property. Only days after the surrender, cavalry adjutant Robert Hubard of Buckingham County, Virginia, attempted to hide both horses and "3 or 4 Negroes" from occupying Union troops.[49] Maj. Henry Kyd Douglas, still fuming that his "boy, Buck," had absconded from Appomattox with his horse and personal baggage, later wrote that his first purpose upon leaving the surrender field was "to go in search of my man and my properties." Taking another unnamed "servant" with him, he left in the company of several other officers bound for Charlottesville, determined to find Buck.[50] Even in defeat, these men failed to acknowledge the Emancipation Proclamation. For them it had been a moot point.

While Confederate soldiers sought to protect their human property, the presence of United States Colored Troops served as a stark reminder of both slavery's demise and the rise of a new social order for white southerners.[51] The greatest nightmare of white southerners, slaveholders and non-slaveholders alike, had long been that of a slave uprising. For many Confederates, the USCT represented just this: armed Black men sent into the South with northern sanction to kill white men, a fear that had escalated after Confederates surrendered their weapons. Paroled Confederates clearly felt the reversal of antebellum power. Near Burkeville, Edward Jones and members of Battle's Brigade had caught up with the Union Twenty-Fifth Corps, whose ranks were "composed entirely of Negro troops — darkies of shade from the light mulatto to the coal black African, all well armed and equipped and the soldiers of the enlightened U.S. government. . . . We must have passed fifteen and twenty thousand of them," he observed before adding, "They are commanded by white officers and in their marching and martial appearance certainly reflected great credit upon their drill masters." It seems hardly coincidental that Jones elected to describe the officers in these terms; such well-trained African American soldiers could only be the product of "masters." [52] Other paroled Confederates were less impressed by the USCT soldiers they encountered. Upon reaching Petersburg on April 17, chaplain William Wiatt asserted he had been "grossly insulted by a Negro soldier." The next day at City Point, he was "insulted again by a Negro soldier." Such was not the deference white men expected from African Americans.[53]

While some of Lee's men complained about Black soldiers, others later claimed to have responded with deadly force. When Pvt. Hartwell Koon of Finegan's Florida Brigade accused a USCT sentinel of kicking him while the parolees awaited an ocean transport at City Point, tensions quickly escalated. Another Floridian struck the Black soldier in retaliation before an officer, who had been allowed to retain his sidearms per the surrender terms, ran his sword clear through the Black guard. Such actions might have been overlooked by Confederate authorities, but the paroled soldiers realized that in a post-Appomattox world, they could be charged with war crimes by the U.S. government. They hurried back to a nearby ship to avoid getting caught, but escaping without penalty must have emboldened the band of Floridians. Still waiting for their ship to depart City Point on April 17, they ventured ashore, where they learned of Lincoln's assassination. Seeing the rebels amid the mourning services, several African Americans minced no words, cursing the parolees "in a very vile language." Again, the Floridians claimed to respond with deadly violence, David L. Geer of the 5th Florida recalling years later that "some of the boys strung up those coons on the pickets that made the fence around the park." Evading punishment once more, they climbed aboard the U.S. transport *Wilmington* on April 22, bound for Savannah.[54]

On its face, Geer's account seems improbable. Even if the Confederate officer was armed, the enlisted men would not have been, whereas the Black soldier would have had a gun. Moreover, it is unlikely that such brutalities would not have been noticed by white Union soldiers. If Geer fabricated the account decades later, that is significant in itself. But evidence does exist of Confederate soldiers murdering Union soldiers. From Richmond in late

April, Thomas Morris Chester reported that "rebel officers continue to strut about in the uniform in which they delighted to murder Union soldiers, in a spirit which is almost beyond the degree of loyal forbearance." There were likewise several cases of white southerners tried by military commissions in the spring of 1865 for assaulting and murdering Black soldiers. In April, a military commission sentenced guerrilla Samuel Nance (and possibly a veteran of the 47th North Carolina) to death for killing a soldier of the USCT in Winchester, Tennessee. The following month, Union authorities arrested Charles Zeringue, a veteran of the 30th Louisiana who had fought with the Army of Tennessee. Zeringue was found guilty of killing a Black private at Vick's Plantation in Louisiana.[55]

Given the centrality of violence to slavery, it is little wonder that defeated white southern men resorted to deadly force in response to what they perceived as the slightest provocation from Black men who now held positions of authority—and guns. Yet these violent encounters also underscored the degree to which wartime atrocities by Confederates against the USCT continued after April 9, 1865. The Confederate army had often disregarded and, in numerous instances, sanctioned murders of African Americans. When the United States began enlisting Black men as soldiers, the Confederate government vowed it would not treat captured Black troops as prisoners of war. Instead, they were to be turned over to state authorities for reenslavement or to be tried for insurrection (the punishment for which was the death penalty).[56] Practice in the field proved more varied and often more barbaric than that proposed by Richmond, offering more latitude for officers and enlisted men alike. At New Market Heights in the fall of 1864, for example, members of Hood's Texas Brigade captured several men of the USCT and took them as personal slaves rather than sending them to prisoner-of-war camps.[57] At the battle of the Crater in July 1864, some of Lee's soldiers sold surrendering Black soldiers into slavery, including John H. Butler of the 23rd USCT, who was purchased by a Mr. Durfy of Charles County.[58]

But some Confederate officers refused to give quarter, executing surrendering Black troops at the battles of Milliken's Bend and Saltville; in Kansas, North Carolina, and Arkansas; and perhaps most infamously at Fort Pillow. The Army of Northern Virginia was not exempt from committing such atrocities. Encountering Black soldiers for the first time in May 1864, a trooper in the 9th Virginia Cavalry wrote home that a few Black prisoners were taken, before adding, "It is needless for me to say what became of them."[59] At the battle of the Crater, Lee's men shot men of the USCT in the head and slit their throats long after they had surrendered.[60] None of these actions had been punished by the Confederate army. In fact, Porter Alexander defended the army's actions at the Crater. "The general feeling of the men toward [black soldiers'] employment was very bitter," he explained. "The sympathy of the North for John Brown's memory was taken for proof of a desire that our slaves should rise in servile insurrection & massacre through the South, & the enlistment of Negro troops was regarded as advertisement of that desire."[61] Artillery colonel Willy Pegram justified such killings. "It seems cruel to murder them in cold blood, but I think the men who did it had very good cause for doing so," he declared. More importantly, he believed fighting—and killing—Black troops motivated Confederates. "I have always said that I wished the enemy would bring some negroes against this army. I am convinced, since Saturday's fight, that it has a splendid effect on our men."[62]

As Lee's men made their way farther and farther from Appomattox, in every direction, they could increasingly envision their civilian lives. Around campfires, they fantasized about their first home-cooked meal. They debated whether it would be too late to plant corn and oats upon their arrival. And privately, some wondered how their families would receive them. For all the thought they gave to their lives as civilians, both practical concerns and custom ensured that many of the habits, practices, and even language of martial life remained on the trip home. Just as they had in their wartime diaries, paroled soldiers, even those traveling in groups of only two or three, described their mode of travel as "marching" and referred to meals as "rations"—words most would not have chosen in the antebellum years.[63]

Above all, food filled soldiers' minds, if not their stomachs. Even though the Confederate government had been hard-pressed to secure enough provisions for its armies, especially during the retreat from Petersburg and Richmond, in mid-April a handful of government stores remained scattered across the region. But some were more willing than others to part with their scarce stashes. After marching for two days, several members of the 4th North Carolina proved especially fortunate in drawing some meat from a commissary southwest of Appomattox in Henry County, Virginia.[64] Outside Liberty, Virginia, William Henry Harder and the other officers commanding those bound for Tennessee directed a mill operator to turn over any remaining Confederate flour. The owner promptly complied.[65]

Other commissary agents refused to cede their supplies before relenting under threat. On Thursday, April 13, to the northeast of Appomattox a crowd of paroled soldiers pressed the ex-Confederate commissary of subsistence at

Buckingham Court House to provide any remaining rations. Initially hoping to keep the wares for himself, the agent finally relented and allowed the men to help themselves.[66] A similar event played out farther to the north in Orange County. After learning of the surrender, former quartermaster Maj. William Burton Richards had absconded from Charlottesville with five of the best mule teams and a load of other Confederate goods. But just outside the small town of Orange Court House, his merry ride came to an abrupt halt when he was met by a squad of unparoled troopers in the Black Horse Cavalry. Taking four of the wagons piled high with much-needed provisions, one of the cavalrymen informed Richards that "he ought to be d———d glad to get off with one wagon and a whole skin."[67]

A day's march south from Appomattox, Maj. Gen. Bryan Grimes and what remained of his division came upon a small country store, where nearly a hundred paroled men and several local women had gathered. The shop had served as a distribution center for needy soldiers' wives to obtain rations, and the women had arrived that morning to collect a small lot of meat. The paroled men insisted that they would leave the meat to the women, but they demanded that the owner turn over his stores of cowpeas to them. When he refused, claiming that the peas were to be sent to the Confederate quarter-master in Danville, Grimes threatened force to obtain the much-needed nourishment. Still possessing his sidearm, clad in the uniform of a general, and commanding — however tenuously — soldiers, Grimes insisted that he maintained the power to impress goods from civilians — especially those bound for the Confederate government. Grimes promised the man a receipt, and the store owner finally relented, prompting a scramble among the sol-diers. They shoved peas in their haversacks and pockets and filled empty con-tainers they found in the store. And one ingenious young soldier pulled off his pants and made them into a sack by tying the legs together at the ankles. "Off he marched," recalled an amused comrade, "with the peas in the forked sack around his neck."[68]

Yet with tens of thousands of Confederate soldiers traversing the countryside, civilians, not government stores, bore the brunt of providing sustenance. For those on the home front only a few days' walk or ride from Appomattox, the flow of soldiers in and out of their homes seemed endless. Even a piece of bread might have been more than many families could spare. By the fall of 1864, invading and friendly armies had stripped much of the land bare and disrupted supply networks, leaving communities seeking basic foodstuffs. Early in 1865, commissary agents continued to impress bacon, beef, corn, flour, potatoes, and other goods across the South, even as many farmers withheld their provisions to avoid impressment at low prices. Compounding circumstances, army officials regularly denied requests to ship materials across state lines in an effort to ensure that commissaries had enough provisions for the troops. Between the devastation wrought by the armies and the impressment agents, communities from Virginia to Georgia suffered miserably.[69]

The significant number of soldiers who headed south from Appomattox through the Virginia counties of Campbell, Bedford, Pittsylvania, Henry, and Patrick had a good degree of luck in acquiring provisions, however, because this region had avoided the presence of armies throughout the four years of fighting. Near South Boston on the Virginia–North Carolina border, General Grimes, his courier Thomas Devereux, and several other staff officers came upon a comfortable-looking white house set in a grove of budding trees. There was little to eat, the home's owner informed them, as he had been feeding Lee's soldiers all morning. But calling Eliza, an older enslaved woman who had not yet learned of her freedom, he ordered her to feed the soldiers. "I never enjoyed a meal more," recalled Devereux, although he failed to comment on Eliza's continued status as a slave.[70]

Lee's men were conscious of the toll the war had taken on civilians like their own families, and most were grateful to those who willingly shared their meager cupboards. Before leaving Appomattox, Brig. Gen. William Ruffin Cox informed the men of his brigade that they should seek out "people of means" along their route home for food. If such individuals refused to help the homeward-bound men, Cox advised them to "take enough to get along with, but to treat the people with great respect."[71] For those who kept diaries on their trek home, documenting the names of those who willingly opened their homes and pantries became commonplace.[72] Four days' travel from Appomattox, a "big hearted Virginian" took in William Fulton and other members of the 5th Alabama, providing them food and lodging for the evening. "His name was J. A. Burwell," Fulton wrote, "and I am sure he can never know how we appreciated his generosity, for words were too weak to express it."[73] At each stop along the route to North Carolina, John Willis Council carefully, and thankfully, recorded the names of those who offered shelter and food—as well as those who did not, such as Grif Adams, "a rich man near Paxton" who refused the soldiers accommodations on the night of April 11.[74]

While homeward-bound Confederates frequently recorded the names of white southerners who assisted them, they rarely did the same when they relied upon African Americans, at least not in contemporary accounts. In

Pittsylvania County, Virginia, several South Carolina soldiers recorded that they had the "good fortune" to encounter a Black man who sold them twelve quarts of rice. Accounts written years later occasionally added such memories. Twenty years after the fact, several officers from New Orleans's Washington Artillery recalled that forty miles from the surrender field, they halted near Cumberland Court House to purchase cornbread and milk from an individual they described as "a kind-hearted old negro woman." If the soldiers coerced such assistance, they did not feel compelled to mention it in their diaries and reminiscences.[75]

While homeward-bound Confederates relied upon those on the home front, so too did civilians rely upon the soldiers. As the paroled men fanned out from south-central Virginia in every direction, they carried with them news of the army's surrender. In hamlets and towns, in farming communities and cities, soldiers confirmed rumors of the capitulation and, more importantly for Confederate families, information about fellow soldiers. With few southern newspapers printing, word of mouth proved the best — and often only — source of information about the state of the war and loved ones. Confederate families in particular proved keen to open their doors and, to the extent possible, their pantries to the soldiers.[76] Parents, siblings, and wives hoped that some other family would do the same for their homeward-bound kin. But just as important, doing so might help them glean news about husbands, brothers, and sons — and afford the possibility of sending letters with soldiers to family and friends farther afield.[77] The disbanding Confederates would serve a vital link in the southern communications network.

The arrival of some soldiers and not others proved vexing for families at home. By the evening of April 14, Willie Penn of the 42nd Virginia had made it as far as his brother-in-law's Patrick County home. Willie had not been paroled at Appomattox, but he did bring word that two of his younger brothers had been captured by the Union and taken prisoner. The next evening, he arrived at his mother's home to find it brimming with at least thirteen homeward-bound soldiers, some of whom suffered from debilitating wounds and were unable to travel any farther. For three days, Mary Penn had been feeding and tending to convalescing strangers, all the while worrying about her own sons. If her ministrations brought relief to the soldiers, they in turn brought her some measure of relief when they shared rumors that Thomas had been aboard the ambulance train recovering from jaundice when last seen. He might still be alive. Still, there was nothing about young Joe. As the soldiers were "passing and calling" and attempting to "eat us out of house & home," Mary vacillated between despair and hope. "We are now in Yankee lines & power," she wrote her daughter, Eliza, but all may not be as bad as feared; "if I can only get my dear children together again I feel we can live anywhere." The unknown was simply unbearable. "Dear boys I do trust they are safe & will get home in a short time but this suspense is so bad," she confessed. For all of Mary Penn's anxiety, she remained defiantly optimistic. Many of the soldiers passing through told her they were on their way to Gen. Joseph E. Johnston's lines—at Lee's request. "They say they can't see how any one would do otherwise than take the advice," she explained to Eliza. And from this she took solace: "There is still hope left for our independence," she declared.[78]

Yet Lee's soldiers carried more than news to the home front. They also brought chaos and disorder. Only a few days after the surrender, Confederates began arriving in Danville, Virginia, first in pairs, then in small bands, and eventually in regiment-strength groups. In the span of a few hours on April 13, more than 3,000 tramped across the wooden railroad bridge into the tobacco town situated on the North Carolina border that had served as the seat of the Confederate government until April 9. More importantly, Danville offered the prospects of a working rail line south into the Carolinas and of supplies shipped south from Richmond by the fleeing Confederate government. Desperately hungry, nearly 2,000 of Lee's men gathered near the railroad depot, where they began demanding provisions. Fearing that mob violence might overtake his city, Mayor James M. Walker pulled a pistol from his coat and fired at the ringleader. Whether purposefully or not, Walker missed, promptly dispersing the crowd.[79]

During the week that followed, thousands more soldiers arrived in the city perched on the bluffs above the Dan River. For several days, the men flowed out just as they flowed in. But the system broke down when the railroad superintendent failed to find someone to pump water for the engines. Without water, the trains could not leave, so the soldiers remained. On Monday, April 17, a train filled to the brim with passengers, both inside and on top, waited below the water tank at the depot when a tremendous explosion shook the entire town. An enormous cloud of smoke rose from the Confederate arsenal, the air carrying with it shards of glass, fiery chunks of wood, and human flesh. As the smoke abated, both soldiers and civilians rushed toward the harrowing scene, hoping to save those caught in the blast, even as powder kegs and artillery shells continued to detonate. The following day, nothing remained of the building but a huge crater. Fourteen lay dead, at least one of whom, Pvt. G. C. Gregg of the 13th Georgia, had been paroled at Appomattox.[80]

Even as Danville smoldered, Lee's men continued to file toward the border city. Arriving on April 18, Abner Cox of the Palmetto Sharpshooters and his comrades learned that Col. Asbury Coward of the 5th South Carolina had managed to secure 1,300 rations for members of Bratton's Brigade as well as railroad transportation to Greensboro. But the colonel had bad news as well. A government warehouse and private property had been destroyed "by a worthless mob of citizens and paroled soldiers." As much a warning as praise, he told his men he knew them well enough to be sure that none had ventured into the city and participated in any looting or destruction. With that, the men fell into line again and prepared to pass through the wrecked town in search of another station farther down the line. "The Brigade marched through in perfect order, and bivouaced 3 miles below the town," observed Cox that evening in his diary. With rations aplenty, they halted for a hearty meal, drawing full allotments of bacon, meal, salt, and even molasses. Returning to their columns, they marched on, crossing the state line before boarding the train at Pelham, North Carolina, headed for Greensboro. Rumor had it, there were more supplies to be found in that city, and perhaps even Johnston's army.[81]

For most of the week following Lee's surrender, rain had pelted Eddie Whitehorne as he and his companions crossed central and southeastern Virginia. But on Sunday, April 16, the sun once again shone. The day marked one week since the surrender, a memory that Whitehorne confessed continued to "hurt like an open wound." But the warm rays combined with the familiar sights of his home county lifted his spirits. Three miles from home, he parted ways with his last traveling companion. "Here I left Bass," he wrote that evening in his diary, "and was alone for the first time in years." For nearly four years, the twenty-five-year-old had marched, eaten, slept, and fought alongside other soldiers — other men. Now all of that had come to an end. At home he would not be alone. His parents, along with ten siblings (seven of whom were sisters), awaited. This would be a domestic world far removed from the masculine confines of the camp and battle line.[82]

In the days that followed, Eddie busied himself clearing fields and planting crops. Harrowing rows on Saturday morning, he glanced up to see the welcome sight of his friend Bass riding back from town with a wealth of news. A Bostonian by the name of Simeon Parssons had arrived to open a store, Bass reported. The Masonic Lodge would reorganize and meet again soon. All of the church bells had been melted down for cannon, but the preachers had returned from the army, and services would resume as usual the following day. Of all the news the former sergeant brought, Whitehorne dwelled on one bit: "Bass also said the boys were going to get together and form a Confederate Veterans Organization." Though he had not quite yet accustomed himself to the stillness, the quiet, of peace, he was gradually coming to terms that his life as a solider was past. "It seems I am a veteran," he wrote in the last entry of his wartime diary. And after a series of dashes, just as he had done when contemplating what his parole pass meant, he added, "Suppose I'll attend the meeting."[83]

Whitehorne and the thousands of others returning home from Lee's army remained uncertain as to what their status might be beyond that of veteran. Would their paroles hold? Would they be prosecuted for treason? If not, would their status as citizens — with the rights and protections afforded by the U.S. Constitution, a constitution they had forsaken — be recognized? As the coming weeks and months would reveal, being a civilian did not make one a citizen, and being paroled might not offer the protection many had assumed.

6

Urgent Pursuit

Around 7:30 on the night of April 13, General Gibbon telegraphed Grant announcing that the surrender of Lee's army had been completed. He estimated that 25,000 to 30,000 men had been paroled, while 147 artillery pieces, 10,000 small arms, and 71 flags had been received.[1]

Despite Gibbon's report, both Confederate and Union officers recognized that a significant portion of Lee's men had not yet surrendered. Estimating troop strength had always been a guessing game, but Grant and his officers knew that Lee had commanded nearly 60,000 on April 1. During the fighting that ensued on the march west between April 2 and 8, Lee's army had sustained approximately 11,530 casualties, but only 28,231 men had been officially paroled at Appomattox. Some 20,000 men who should have been paroled were missing.[2] Perhaps much of Lee's army *did* still exist.

Hoping to end any further Confederate resistance, Grant and his officer corps extended the generous Appomattox terms to any of Lee's soldiers willing to surrender themselves. In the days and weeks that followed April 9, thousands of Lee's men would complete the process of surrender and paroling that had begun at Appomattox. Some arrived at Union posts like Farmville or Winchester, Virginia, of their own accord, deciding that it was in their best interest to turn themselves in to Union provost marshals throughout the region. Some did so at railroad junctions such as Burkeville in order to receive rations or transportation from the Union armies. Others found themselves hunted down by the U.S. cavalry with little choice but to acquiesce. Regardless of Confederates' reasons in seeking or accepting paroles, their ability to do so reflected the inclusiveness, flexibility, and generosity of the Appomattox terms. Ensuring that all of Lee's men surrendered themselves remained one of Grant's topic objectives.

Nothing impeded this goal more than the continued threat of guerrilla warfare. The dispersal of Lee's army had inflamed fears of roving bands and marauders. Along the Northern Neck, up and down the Shenandoah Valley, in the counties just north of Richmond, and across the Potomac into Maryland, the U.S. cavalry hunted down partisans, especially those of Col. John S. Mosby's command. Securing the surrender of those who had remained in Lee's ranks until Appomattox would not be enough. If Grant and the War Department could compel all rebel soldiers to turn themselves in, especially those with intentions of waging a guerrilla-style war, perhaps the rebellion would truly come to an end. That was certainly the hope of Union troops who fanned out from Appomattox, close on the muddy trails of so many of Lee's men.

Thirty miles to the southeast of Appomattox Court House, Farmville became a beehive of activity in the days after the surrender. The small town boasted a mere 1,500 residents, several churches, and, according to one Union soldier, "a number of fine residences." For most of the war, Farmville saw little action. In 1862, the Confederate government had established the General Hospital in the town's tobacco factories and warehouses. With capacity for 1,500 soldiers, the complex attended to those who suffered from chronic diseases and to convalescents from overcrowded Richmond hospitals. But early April 1865 found it inundated with thousands of newcomers. Confederate soldiers wounded in the previous days' battles filled the hospital complex, while civilians thronged the streets. Hearing that the Union troops had been ordered to issue rations to the destitute, impoverished citizens from the surrounding countryside poured into town to beg some small pittance.[3]

The Union soldiers sent to Farmville not only would help feed the hungry but also would continue the work of paroling Lee's army begun at Appomattox. On April 10, Lt. Col. Thaddeus L. Barker and a brigade from the Ninth Corps began issuing paroles from his headquarters in a Main Street storefront. A temporary provost marshal, Barker paroled at least 1,827 Confederates over the next eleven days. Some were prisoners captured during the fighting on April 8 and 9. Among them was Pvt. Henry T. Bahnson of the 1st North Carolina Battalion Sharpshooters, who had been among those captured by Union cavalrymen on the morning of April 9 "near a little white house." Indeed, Bahnson proved lucky to be a prisoner at all. After his capture, he encountered a USCT soldier whom, he later admitted, he taunted. The Black soldier would have none of the rebel's disrespect, leveling his gun at the captured Confederate. Only the quick reflexes of a white Union soldier spared Bahnson's life. Having escaped certain death, he was equally surprised to learn that after a week of captivity, he would be paroled in Farmville.[4]

In addition to those captured at the battles around Appomattox on April 8 and 9, nearly 600 of those paroled at Farmville had been patients in the town's hospital — some admitted only days earlier. Some proved to be hospital workers — doctors, nurses, and clerks — as was the case with S. S. Keeling, who had spent much of the war as a clerk and later a steward in Richmond-area hospitals.[5]

But the vast majority of the more than 1,800 parolees between April 10 and 21 were not patients or prisoners captured in the previous days' fighting. Instead, men from the ranks who hailed from Virginia, Alabama, North Carolina, South Carolina, Georgia, Maryland, and Tennessee arrived in the Prince Edward County town, where they signed paroles that provided the same conditions as those given to their comrades who had remained in the ranks. Such was the case for Pvt. Bradford Ivey of the 16th Georgia, who had enlisted in July 1861 and served as a teamster for much of the war. Pvts. J. B. O'Neal of the 27th North Carolina and T. J. Howell of the 44th Virginia also turned themselves in at Farmville, while the remainder of their units had surrendered at Appomattox. Almost entire regiments, too, surrendered in the tobacco town, including eighty members of the 3rd Virginia Cavalry, forty-eight members of the 18th Virginia Infantry, and twenty-seven from the 41st Alabama. Whether they had been stragglers hoping to find some extra provisions after the escape from Petersburg, had intended to abandon the army for good given its dismal prospects, or had fled along with much of the cavalry and artillery, many of Lee's men decided it was in their best interest to surrender.[6]

About sixty miles to the west, more than 3,500 rebels waited in Lynchburg to decide their course of action. Among them remained Frank Lobrano, a twenty-seven-year-old native of Italy who had fought with New Orleans's famed Washington Artillery. As the rain beat down in torrents, Lobrano and his companions hunkered down at the Norvell House, one of the city's most prestigious hotels, still debating their options. When eight Union scouts of the 5th Pennsylvania Cavalry led by Lt. Terrence Fitzpatrick rode into town on the April 11, Lobrano did not flee. Having heard that Lee's men would be entitled to the same paroles as those who had surrendered at Appomattox, he and the others waited. The municipal leaders proved far less resigned to fate. Recognizing that U.S. forces might help restore order, they sent three representatives back with the troopers to offer the town's surrender. The next day, approximately 250 cavalry troopers under General Mackenzie wound their way up the river road to Main Street, where the mayor and city council surrendered the city. With an immense crowd pushing in to get a glimpse of the exchange, Union authorities assured the locals that they would make every effort to protect private property.[7]

But Grant had ordered all warlike material carried off or destroyed. Immediately, U.S. forces began to take stock of the Confederate military resources. Among the stores were fifty-six field pieces, six heavy guns, forty mortars, seventy-five caissons, 15,000 muskets, twenty-five locomotives, a vast quantity of railroad property, several hundred sabers, a large quantity of ammunition, and niter beds. Despite the looting of April 9, a great deal of commissary and quartermaster stores also remained. Arriving on April 13, Bvt. Maj. Gen. John W. Turner ordered Union soldiers to raze several buildings along the canal used as a laboratory and ordnance storage before setting fire to four or five canal boats filled with government supplies. The rations were to be spared. Finding flour, salt, cornmeal, and bacon, as well as hay and grain for their horses, Turner's men distributed the provisions among their own troops, paroled prisoners, and the city's destitute citizens.[8]

If Turner's objective was ensuring that the rebels had no resources to continue their fight, central to this was compelling the surrender of the thousands of Confederate soldiers still lingering in the town. In a practical step, the U.S. troops chose the former office of the Confederate provost marshal to establish their parole office. And just in case the beleaguered rebels might need help in finding the building, an enormous U.S. flag that measured no less than twelve feet by twenty stretched across Main Street to mark the site.[9]

During the next five days, Turner reported that he issued approximately 5,000 paroles in the city.[10] As with Farmville, the lists included men from the numerous hospitals and various invalid corps, but the vast majority were soldiers whose units had either surrendered at Appomattox or disbanded. Like at Farmville, most of those who surrendered in Lynchburg did so as units, a fact not lost on General Mackenzie. "Quite a number," he reported, surrendered in their "company organizations."[11] While thirty members of the Louisiana-based Washington Artillery surrendered at Appomattox, at least forty-two men from the battalion, including Frank Lobrano, sought paroles in Lynchburg on April 13. Sixty members of Lynchburg's own Otey's Battery, twenty-one from the 2nd Maryland Battery (Baltimore Light Artillery), and thirty-nine men from the 11th Virginia—all units that had been present at Appomattox on the morning of April 9—likewise presented themselves for parole. In the days that followed, Virginia's parolees proved to be the most numerous, supporting the claims of those who had believed men closest to home had been more likely to abandon the ranks during the retreat or refuse to surrender. But soldiers from every state represented in the army arrived. Men from the 61st Alabama, 5th Florida, 49th Georgia, 48th Mississippi, and the 7th Tennessee, among others, drifted into the city, where the provost marshal compiled their names in lists, just as Confederate regimental and company officers had done at Appomattox.[12]

Arriving in Lynchburg on Friday, April 14, General Gibbon could not have been more pleased. "This place is filled with Rebel soldiers," he observed, yet the change in their sentiment proved remarkable. Several local officials had requested, indeed implored, the U.S. troops to remain in town and preserve the order after the pillaging of April 9. Taking quarters in the college buildings, Gibbon had the opportunity to chat at length with Prof. James P. Holcombe, a law professor at the University of Virginia, Confederate congressman, and Confederate commissioner to Canada. Holcombe assured Gibbon that his opinions had changed completely, and he was now "in favor of a reconstruction of the Union." Relieved to hear such encouraging news, Gibbon took out pen and paper and immediately jotted out a pass for Holcombe to go find Confederate congressman William C. Rives so that they might jointly address the local community on the subject. "I think we are on the right road to peace," Gibbon mused, "if the President will only come out in a liberal, magnanimous proclamation." Other than the women, who remained "the most rabid" and refused to appear on the streets, Gibbon felt confident that the end of the war was at hand. The soldiers "have all pretty well given up the cause as lost and have expressed themselves as very much astonished at the way they have been treated, as it is so much better than expected."[13]

Even with the arrival of more Union troops throughout April 14 and 15, Confederates continued to pour into the town. Most were those who had avoided surrendering at Appomattox. But some were men who had been paroled at Appomattox, including Lt. Gen. James Longstreet, accompanied by his aide Thomas Goree. Having overseen the last of the surrender process, the general hurried to Lynchburg where his wife, Louise, and two young sons, Garland and Robert Lee, had been residing.[14]

Still other arrivals had not even been in the Army of Northern Virginia. At least eighty-nine of the men who sought paroles in Lynchburg hailed from the western armies and had only recently been released from the prisoner-of-war camps at Point Lookout, Maryland, and Johnson's Island in Ohio.[15] Why had so many gathered in the Lynchburg area? Was it merely speculation on their part that Lee would make it to Lynchburg, where they hoped to offer their services — or at the very least find rations? Did they expect to find working rail lines heading west toward their homes in Kentucky or Missouri? Or was there an agreement among these men to meet in the Piedmont region? Whatever the reason, the presence of so many suggests more than mere coincidence.[16]

With passes in hand, those who had escaped on April 9 were now free to go home. For New Orleans bound Frank Lobrano, this meant retracing his steps back toward Appomattox. Around eleven o'clock on the morning of April 13, he struck out for the small village, arriving around seven o'clock to find it still teeming with Union soldiers tasked with collecting the detritus of war left behind by the departing Confederates. Lobrano and the other members of the Washington Artillery camped for a single night at the surrender grounds. The next morning, with the sun finally peeking out from behind the clouds, they joined hundreds of other Confederates in their trek eastward.[17] Following the South Side Railroad, they passed through the now bustling town of Farmville. Men in blue stood guard around the town's businesses, but others wearing shades of butternut and gray passed through the muddy streets. Some, like William Wiatt, had been paroled at Appomattox and now stopped in the hopes of drawing rations of bread, coffee, and perhaps, if they were lucky, a little sugar.[18]

The provost marshals in Farmville and Lynchburg continued to parole a steady stream of rebels, even though they had not yet received an official copy of the Appomattox terms. Instead, like other comrades in the field would do in the days and weeks that followed, they relied on their own judgment. Some were paroling all rebels, including those captured before the surrender, which Grant had explicitly forbidden. Others offered transportation and rations, while some refused aid to any Confederate. Slow communication, overlapping military jurisdictions, and individual personalities all contributed to improvisation and inconsistent policies. When and where a rebel sought a parole mattered a great deal.

On the afternoon of April 14, from the headquarters of the Army of the Potomac, General Meade's chief of staff finally beseeched Maj. Gen. Charles Griffin to explain the exact terms of the paroles. "Do you give them transportation anywhere?" he asked. "How about rations?" That evening, Griffin responded, clarifying that at Appomattox, they had taken the paroles of officers on behalf of their units, not the paroles of individual enlisted men. He explained that Grant's order permitted paroled soldiers to travel free on all government transports and military railroads when it was necessary to pass through Union lines to reach their homes. But he noted that "this order has been construed by us very liberally where officers and men have manifested an intention to go home and remain there, which large numbers have done."[19] Provost marshals might apply an exceptionally lenient reading of the surrender terms if it meant ending the rebellion and getting the rebels home as quickly and efficiently as possible.

As the Union army moved east across Virginia, it established more paroling sites, including one at Burkeville, sixteen miles southeast of Farmville. Many Confederates who had escaped—or otherwise failed to arrive at—Appomattox traveled to this key railroad junction in order to get papers that allowed them to board the trains and receive rations. In a four-day stretch from April 14 to April 17, the provost marshal recorded 1,614 names. While they came to Burkeville primarily seeking transportation and food, as with Lynchburg, the vast majority of Confederates paroled in the village arrived with other members of their units. At least sixty-one men from the 1st Virginia Reserves, fifty-seven from the 9th Virginia Cavalry, forty-nine from the 10th Alabama, twenty-four from the 10th Florida, and twenty-three from the 30th North Carolina made their way to the railroad village in search of papers.[20] With passes in hand, they joined others like Frank Lobrano catching the cars bound for City Point. From there, those from Southside Virginia and North Carolina could more readily walk home, while those heading to the Deep South hoped to board steamers bound for Savannah and New Orleans.[21] If lucky, they might be home soon enough to get a late spring planting into the ground.

———

Having returned to Appomattox from Lynchburg on April 14, satisfied that peace was nearly secure, General Gibbon settled down for the evening in the McLean House. He was completing the final reports when his chief of staff let out a gasp of horror. A dispatch had just arrived from Washington with the most horrific and unbelievable news: Lincoln had been shot at Ford's Theatre. The wound was fatal, and he could not possibly survive the night. No one yet knew who the culprit was nor how many had been killed. Some said that Secretary of State William H. Seward and his son Frederick had likewise fallen victim to the assassin's hand. What of Vice President Andrew Johnson? Had he been killed as well? Doubts surfaced as to whether there

While there are no extant photographs of provost marshal offices in 1865, they might have resembled this one at Aquia Creek along the Potomac River in northern Virginia, 1863. Library of Congress Prints and Photographs Division, LC-DIG-ppmsca-12567.

was any viable government in Washington, and many began to ask if this was yet a new stage of a war they had believed to be nearly finished.[22]

On Easter Sunday, word arrived in central Virginia confirming that Lincoln had died at 7:22 the previous morning. Writing from Appomattox, Union surgeon Daniel Nelson erupted with indignation. "Retribution will follow them," he declared in a letter to his wife back in Massachusetts; "rebel and rascal are synonymous too often."[23] At Burkeville, Pvt. Albert G. Harrison informed his parents that the news had rekindled vengeful feelings toward Lee's men. "It fills every Soldier's heart with the most bitter hatred against a Rebel," he wrote. But more to the point, gone were the magnanimous gestures of a few days prior: "If it is our lot to get in another engagement before the expiration of our term of Service, the old double Six will not show any mercy or take many prisoners, and that is the best way to serve them, kill all we catch, for the advantage now is ours."[24] Not far from Harrison's camp, a Union artillerist agreed. "This is the result of the leniency of our government to armed rebels," he lamented. "The country is overrun with them."[25] Worried that the Union troops might seek revenge, Federal commanders throughout the region rushed to prevent any acts of retaliation. In

Farmville, Brig. Gen. Joshua Chamberlain ordered a double guard placed around the entire camp and instructed regimental commanders to recall all of their men, allowing none to leave. "It might take little to arouse them to frenzy of blind revenge," he cautioned.[26]

Rage engulfed Unionists from the northern home front to Union army camps. In Washington, as word that paroled rebel soldiers had committed the crimes raced through the capital's streets, angry crowds vowed revenge on any and every white southerner, some threatening to visit the Old Capitol Prison to lynch all the rebel officers confined there.[27] A Boston woman informed her cousin in China that the assassination had ensured that "the people will now be satisfied with nothing less than death or perpetual exile for the leaders."[28] In his camp with the Ninth Corps, David Lane of the 17th Michigan observed that "imagination cannot paint the whirlwind of revengeful wrath that swept over the army" or "the strong desire, openly expressed, to avenge [Lincoln's] death by annihilating the people whose treason brings forth and nourishes such monsters. Woe to the armed Rebel, now and henceforth, who makes the least resistance," he warned.[29] Union soldiers far from Appomattox concurred. Charles Lynch reported that members of the 19th Connecticut believed that rebel leaders had incited the murder and so cried for their heads.[30] From Alabama, another Federal soldier told his wife that the rebel officers were in a state of perpetual fear. "They are afraid that Andy Johnson will hang the last one of them," he observed, adding that "if he would I truly believe he would be doing the world a kindness."[31]

In Baltimore, Bvt. Brig. Gen. William W. Morris worried about the effect Confederates' returning to Maryland was having upon the city. Commanding the Middle Department during Maj. Gen. Lew Wallace's temporary absence, Morris knew all too well that Baltimore had long been filled with disloyal residents. Some 20,000 Marylanders had served in the Confederate armies, and now many of the survivors sailed into the harbor each day, exacerbating tensions. As early as April 12, Morris had asked Grant whether all soldiers paroled by Lee's surrender might be required to report to the provost marshal upon entering the city, register their names, and discard their Confederate uniforms. "Unless some such order is issued the streets will be filled with rebel uniforms and women parading with them and the result will be trouble," he warned Grant. Having read the terms of surrender, however, he wondered whether such an order would conflict with the terms of their parole.[32]

When word reached Baltimore in the early morning hours of April 15 that Lincoln had been assassinated by city native and actor John Wilkes

Booth, Morris immediately placed the department under martial law. He forbade the departure of all trains and boats. He ordered patrols of the harbor and all borders and the arrest of any person arriving from Washington. And even though he had yet to hear from Grant, Morris demanded that all rebels in the department report to the provost marshal, where their papers would be examined. Only those whose former residences lay within the city limits would be allowed to remain. "Paroled prisoners of war (rebels)," he added, must abandon their treasonous Confederate uniforms within twelve hours of arriving in the city. "Any violation of this order will be promptly noticed by arrest and imprisonment, whatever the conditions of the parole may be," Morris promised. This included paroled soldiers from Lee's army. Given the state of hysteria enveloping the region, he vowed to override the Appomattox paroles if necessary.[33]

Morris was not alone in ordering rebels to register with the local provost marshal and discard their rebel uniforms. Nor were these policies confined to loyal states. In occupied Petersburg, Col. George C. Kibbe likewise demanded that all paroled prisoners arriving in the city register their names and have their paroles countersigned in order to receive passes that would allow them to remain within Union lines. Paroled prisoners in Washington were instructed to register with the local provost marshal and report back every ten days. Failing to do so meant breaking their parole (which could be punished by execution). At Norfolk, the provost marshal declared that persons found wearing any clothing, emblem, or badges of the "insurgent forces" would be arrested. None of these new orders had been requirements of parole under the Appomattox terms but were improvised by officers in the field. In the wake of the assassination, U.S. commanders throughout Virginia, Maryland, West Virginia, and Washington, D.C., replicated such orders, hoping that they might help quell the rebellion.[34]

In the hours after Lincoln's death, the War Department issued orders directing Union officers throughout Virginia to arrest "all persons coming into the lines."[35] Commanding the Middle Military Division, Maj. Gen. Winfield Scott Hancock warned his subordinates that the president and (mistakenly) secretary of state had been mortally wounded by assassins. "The object of the order," he explained, "is if possible to secure the arrest of the assassins who are attempting to make their escape."[36]

Hancock recognized that hundreds if not thousands of Lee's men had taken to the hills and hamlets of the Shenandoah Valley without paroles. His announcement of April 10 offering the same terms as those given at Appomattox had already induced at least thirty-five Confederates to turn themselves in at Winchester. But the possibility of assassins escaping south through the Valley heightened his sense of urgency. Just that morning he had received word that a regiment from Maj. Gen. John D. Imboden's irregular cavalry force was on its way in, and he had authorized Bvt. Maj. Gen. Alfred T. A. Torbert to send a detachment of cavalry up the Valley to seek out rebels who had not yet signed paroles. But Hancock worried that Washington's orders to arrest all those coming into the lines might dissuade more unparoled soldiers from surrendering. Telegraphing Maj. Gen. Henry W. Halleck at the War Department, he asked whether the offer extending the same surrender conditions to those not at Appomattox remained in effect. Were Confederates who sought to avail themselves of the surrender opportunity to be detained? Paroles denied? If Washington cracked down too hard, would that suspend the paroling process? Would news of Lincoln's assassination revitalize the rebel effort? If so, all the work done thus far in the name of ending the war might be undone.[37]

While Hancock awaited word from Washington, he directed that the paroling continue. But he instructed his provost marshals to include information that had not been collected on the parole lists at Appomattox, Lynchburg, Farmville, or elsewhere before the assassination: a physical description — age, height, complexion, and hair and eye color — not unlike descriptions found on passports issued by the U.S. State Department since the 1820s.[38] Perhaps this information would be helpful in confirming paroles — or in identifying those who had been involved in the assassination.

Lincoln's assassination had ratcheted up calls for revenge and led to more stringent measures in loyal border regions such as Maryland and Washington. Yet rather than suspending the paroling process, the president's murder made it all the more pressing that the remnants of Lee's army who had not surrendered do so, willingly or not. The need to end the war immediately — to quash any further acts of rebellion — necessitated ensuring that every Confederate had surrendered. Grant would stand by his parole terms, even as other loyal Unionists came to question them.

After Lincoln's assassination, it was not enough to wait for Confederates to surrender themselves. Whether motivated by rage or fear, in Washington commanders sent orders to patrol the countryside in search of unparoled rebels. In the early morning hours of April 15, Brig. Gen. William H. F. Payne found himself among those hauled in by Federal cavalry. Wounded near Petersburg on March 30, Payne had returned to his Fauquier County home when he learned of Hancock's offer to parole all those of Lee's army and sent for his aide on April 14 with instructions that he go to Fairfax Court House and offer the general up on parole. Before Hancock could grant a parole, at 3:00 A.M. on April 15, Federal troops had surrounded Payne's Warrenton home amid cries from Unionists to hang him. The general believed he had voluntarily surrendered and was due the same parole offered to Lee's other soldiers, but as the manhunt for Lincoln's assassins intensified, the local Union provost marshal thought differently. Rather than allow him to remain free, Union troops arrested Payne, confiscated his sword and horse, and sent him to Washington's Old Capitol Prison — "locked up for his own safety." Aboard a train from Alexandria to the capital, abolitionist Julia Wilbur saw the general looking "shabby and dirty" with his arm in a sling. The "bare-headed Gen. Payne," she informed her diary, "looked as little like a Genl. as you [could] well imagine." Despite his repeated appeals and warnings that his treatment might well discourage others such as Colonel Mosby from surrendering, Payne would not be released. Instead, on April 21, he found himself on his way to yet another prison, this one at Johnson's Island, Ohio.[39]

To the west in the Shenandoah Valley, General Hancock ordered the cavalry to seek out rebels wherever they might be congregating. Leaving their camp near Opequon Creek on Sunday, April 16, a detachment of Union cavalry headed south toward the village of Strasburg, where they believed members of the 23rd Virginia Cavalry would surrender. The Virginia horsemen had been part of a detached group from Lee's army that comprised the meager and largely scattered forces of the Valley District by the spring of 1865. Two days earlier, Lt. Col. Charles T. O'Ferrall had disbanded the 23rd, leaving the men to their own devices. Although a representative of the Virginia horsemen had promised Hancock that the entirety of the regiment would surrender, when the Union troopers arrived in Strasburg on April 17, the 23rd Cavalry was nowhere in sight. Whether news of Lincoln's assassination had emboldened some to continue the fight, or whether they just lost nerve, the vast majority of the regiment failed to appear. Instead, individual men such as George H. Murphy arrived over a two-day period to surrender.[40] If most of the 23rd Virginia Cavalry did not show, the provost marshal found plenty to keep him busy. "A great many stragglers from the Army of N. Va. had congregated there," reported the Union commander, each of whom would be paroled until word from Washington directed otherwise.[41]

From Strasburg, the Union cavalrymen continued up the Valley toward Mount Jackson, leaving an escort in the small village of Woodstock to parole more stragglers. In the wake of the assassination, word continued to spread among Confederates that Hancock's men would parole any and all who availed themselves of the opportunity. From his home in Staunton, the as yet unparoled mapmaker Jedidiah Hotchkiss observed that "many are disposed to go and seek this parole." Hotchkiss, however, remained unconvinced that he should do so just yet.[42]

Union commanders were particularly keen on securing the paroles of officers, including Col. Thomas T. Munford. After departing Lynchburg on April 10, Munford had ridden west. His wife and seven-year-old son had died only two years earlier, and he longed to see his three surviving children, now staying with relatives near Roanoke. He had stopped briefly at his Bedford County home on April 13, where he found a message awaiting him from General Mackenzie requesting that he report to the Union headquarters in Lynchburg. Promoting himself to the rank of brigadier general now commanding Lee's Cavalry Division, he declined until he could ascertain his status. "I was at no time within your lines, nor did I expect to surrender my command or myself," he wrote. Until he had proof that Lee had included his command in the surrender, he would not capitulate. "I shall follow our old flag and defend it until we are free," he declared. "My men do not believe they could have been surrendered." If, however, Mackenzie could furnish him with sufficient evidence to the contrary, he would submit. But not until then. "If this paper could be sent to General Lee it would obviate many difficulties," he closed. "My desire is to act in good faith, but I will take the risk until it is made clear."[43]

Although Munford was not disposed to seek a parole, many of the cavalry who had fled Lynchburg decided otherwise. Whether they had not yet heard General Rosser's April 12 proclamation calling for them to reassemble or whether they had simply decided to call it quits remains unclear. But on April 18, twenty-seven members of Company D, 12th Virginia Cavalry, presented themselves to the provost marshal in the Valley hamlet of Mount Jackson. For more than a week the men had stayed together as a unit, led by Capt. Henry Walper Kearney. Now, however, they were ready to surrender. The following day, April 19, thirty-five men from the 1st Maryland Cavalry, men who had escaped Appomattox with Munford, gathered seven miles to the south, where they signed paroles in New Market. On April 20, nine more Maryland troopers surrendered themselves in the small town.[44] Unlike so many of Lee's men who were daily arriving at Federal posts throughout Virginia, these were not local men who had already returned to their homes. Instead, many in Company D hailed from Shepherdstown, a village in Jefferson County claimed by both Virginia and West Virginia in 1865, while other companies of the 1st Maryland Cavalry had been organized at Baltimore and Williamsport, Maryland; Pittsburgh, Pennsylvania; and Washington, D.C. In other words, either these Confederates were reluctant to return to their homes in the loyal states, or they were awaiting calls to reconvene.[45]

The number of Confederates arriving at Union posts each day surprised even those of the Union cavalry contingent, forcing them to establish two offices, one in New Market and the other in Mount Jackson. Quickly exhausting his supply of blank parole passes, Col. Marcus A. Reno reported that in a matter of several days, the cavalry detachment had paroled 1,465 men, collecting sixty-six carbines, fifty-seven sabers, twenty pistols, and "but few horses." "The number paroled by me was not large in as much as I had to take every man's individual parole," the Union commander observed, adding, "It would be a labor of months to effect it thoroughly." Still, he estimated that there were some 2,000 to 3,000 rebel cavalrymen scattered throughout the Valley from New Market to Staunton and in the smaller valleys to the west and east. "Of these the better portion will come in to take their paroles," Reno predicted. But he did not believe Federal force was warranted. Such matters would soon settle themselves because the ravages of war had left little on which locals might subsist. "The necessity for labor is imperative and the season for farming just opening will go far toward producing peace and greetings throughout the Valley," he concluded.[46]

Reno was not surprised, however, at the low numbers of guns surrendered—paroled Confederates wanted to assure themselves of some form of protection. Throughout the war, deserters and lawless men had proven a problem. The disbanding of Lee's army only heightened such anxieties. As one homeward-bound parolee observed, the landscape seemed "infested with deserters who commit depredations upon the citizens . . . and travelers."[47] They worried not only about skulkers and deserters but also about raiders whose loyalties were unknown. Along the North Carolina border in Patrick County, P. W. Watkins warned his brother about raiding parties that had swept through the countryside during the first week of April taking "some negroes and horses." But the dissolution of the Confederate army disturbed him more: "I fear deserters will be very troublesome now no one [is] here to stop them." Mary Penn likewise described more attacks by raiders in the county. Not only had they absconded with all the government meat, but they also had proceeded to burn private dwellings, leaving women and children with nothing but the clothes on their backs.[48]

With such reports reaching Union posts throughout Virginia, Grant and others continued to worry about guerrillas and roving bands—both rebel deserters and those who had never spent a day in the ranks. At least some Union soldiers acknowledged that Lee had sought to prevent such marauding. "He might have dispersed his army in small bands, and scattering them round have suffered them to devastate and pillage the country," conceded a Union soldier's newspaper only a day after Appomattox. Yet even though Lee had surrendered, they cautioned that straggling bands of guerrillas might continue to plague the South for months to come, "murdering small parties without quarter."[49]

The marauders' range proved wide-sweeping. Throughout early April, attacks continued along the lines of the South Side Railroad; in the counties just north of Richmond; in the Shenandoah Valley; and, along Virginia's Northern Neck, on the peninsula between the Rappahannock and Potomac Rivers. Only days after Lee's surrender, Maj. Gen. Christopher Augur sent Federal cavalry to the Northern Neck, where he offered to all detached bodies of rebels the same terms as granted at Appomattox. "If they refuse the terms proffered," Augur instructed, "they will of course be attacked and captured or destroyed if possible."[50] Across the Potomac River near Leonardtown, Maryland, Union scouts reported "a party of well-armed rebel soldiers" with designs on seizing a Chesapeake Bay steamer.[51] In western Maryland, Bvt. Maj. Gen. William H. Emory likewise reported that "a large number of stragglers and deserters from the enemy" had gathered near Huttonsville. "I have sent out cavalry to prevent them from organizing into bands of robbers & to bring in such as are troublesome," he reported on April 13.[52] Union soldiers supported any measures necessary to remove the guerrillas from the field. "No effort will be spared to capture them and once captured, that punishment will be meted out to them that their offense deserves," observed a Union newspaper, before adding, "A short shrift and a long rope is the best medicine for these gentry and should be the motto of those employed in hunting them down."[53]

Union officials, however, drew a distinction between the vast majority of Lee's soldiers and such ruffians. From the headquarters of the Peninsula District, comprising the counties between the York and James Rivers, Bvt. Brig. Gen. Benjamin C. Ludlow enlisted civilians and paroled Confederates to help him root out the illegitimate bands of armed men. In an effort to distinguish between those who were and were not paroled, and therefore "legitimate," Ludlow beseeched men belonging to any organized company who had returned to their homes to register their names at the posts established throughout the district. But it was not enough that paroled soldiers register. The Union army needed their assistance. "Those men whose experience in war renders peace more dear," Ludlow noted, could help prevent "the attacks of men who take advantage of the present state of affairs for the purpose of private gain or private revenge."[54] While the U.S. government repeatedly refused to recognize the Confederacy as an independent nation, Union soldiers were willing to differentiate between legitimate Confederate soldiers and the illegitimate bands that terrorized the countryside.

Mosby's Rangers made such a proposition more difficult and remained the chief concern for the Union command in and around Washington. Since Appomattox, informants had reported Mosby's whereabouts as far south as the outskirts of Richmond and as far west as Front Royal, Virginia. No one seemed quite sure where the Gray Ghost would appear next. By the Saturday of Lincoln's death, rumor had it that Mosby was riding through Leesburg and its vicinity, attempting to induce all stragglers to join his command.[55]

The next day, Easter Sunday, the tide seemed to be changing. General Hancock had waited impatiently for a response from Mosby since his first offer to accept his surrender on April 11, and the colonel had finally sent word that he was ready to discuss surrendering his command. From his headquarters in Winchester, Hancock telegraphed Washington to inquire as to his limits in negotiating terms.[56] Secretary of War Stanton agreed that a meeting with Mosby was necessary, but he urged wariness. "It may be needless to caution an old soldier like yourself to guard against surprise or danger to yourself," he wrote, "but the recent murders show such astounding wickedness that too much precaution cannot be taken." Yet Stanton also believed the partisan ranger might be of use. "If Mosby is sincere," he observed, "he might do much toward detecting and apprehending the murderers of the President."[57]

Halleck responded to Hancock that Grant had authorized the paroling of Mosby and his men under the same terms as those agreed upon with Lee. But with the assassination overshadowing every decision, Halleck added a condition that had not appeared in the Appomattox terms. Those whose former homes lay in the loyal states or the District of Columbia would not be permitted to return on parole alone: "Persons from these places must take the oath of allegiance and get special permits from the War Department before they can return."[58]

Halleck did not conjure this policy out of thin air. Rather, it was based on precedent established during the war, especially in Maryland. Like other border states, Maryland had a divided populace. Over the course of the fighting, military authorities had ratcheted up control over Confederate sympathizers in the state. In 1863, the provost marshal of Baltimore, Col. William S. Fish, forbade the publishing or selling of Confederate music or images of Confederate leaders, banished some editors to southern states, and arrested several dozen private citizens under suspicion of southern loyalties. Maryland civilians themselves took up the question of rebels in their midst in the 1864 constitution. Drafted by the Unionists who controlled the state, the new constitution outlawed slavery, reapportioned the general assembly based on white inhabitants only (rather than include a fraction of enslaved people), and disenfranchised anyone who had displayed a hint of southern sympathy.[59] Rebels were not welcome in Maryland.

But did these instructions apply only to Mosby's men?, Hancock wondered. Or to all paroled soldiers of the Army of Northern Virginia desiring to return to loyal states? Many of those arriving within Hancock's division were from West Virginia, and he thought it best to allow them to proceed home without taking an oath of allegiance. What of those from the loyal states such as Missouri, men who had already been paroled? Would they be allowed to go home without taking the oath? The legal uncertainty was unsettling to Hancock. "It is necessary to have this matter clearly understood," he wrote Halleck on April 18, "as they come in understanding that they are to have the terms given to Lee's army." He believed it would be best to let those from West Virginia, and even Missouri, to travel home, but he did draw the line at Maryland and the District of Columbia. To travel there, he insisted, rebels should be required to take an oath of allegiance.[60] Still having received no word directly from Grant, Hancock elected to detain all officers and soldiers bound for northern locales, even those who had willingly surrendered and received their paroles, until he heard otherwise.[61]

Grant was not convinced of Halleck's determination to prevent rebels from returning to the loyal states. Writing to Secretary Stanton on April 17, Grant explained that he believed it better to parole Mosby's men (as well as other known partisans such as John W. Mobberly's detachment of Elijah V. White's 35th Virginia Cavalry Battalion) as prisoners of war in loyal states such as Maryland than allow them to remain "at large as guerillas" in the disloyal states. He did, however, agree that any paroled prisoner returning to a loyal area be required to register his name and residence with the provost marshal nearest his home—yet another condition that had been added since the surrender at Appomattox.[62]

Halleck and Hancock had struck on both legal and political questions raised by Grant's terms: what to do with the approximately 75,000 men from the loyal states of Kentucky, Missouri, and Maryland who had fought for the Confederacy.[63] It was one thing to send paroled soldiers home to states that had seceded. There, the majority of the population had been in rebellion, and the terms for recognizing civil governments were still up for debate. But what of those states that had not been in rebellion against the government? Would paroled Confederates be allowed to return to those states? Would taking the oath in which one declared himself loyal to the Union — far different from a parole in which a soldier promised to lay down his arms and abide by the laws — satisfy Unionists in those states? Tensions surrounding returning rebels were especially high in the Washington, D.C., Maryland, and West Virginia corridor in the wake of Lincoln's assassination. Booth, many of his coconspirators, and those who allegedly helped them escape were from the border state of Maryland. And at least one report noted that on his escape, Booth had secured shelter from rebel sympathizers by claiming to be a Confederate wounded at Petersburg trying to get home to his family in Maryland.[64] Such incidents provided proof that threats to the Union remained, even if Lee's army no longer existed.

As Grant and Halleck debated this question, Hancock proceeded in his quest to disband Mosby's Rangers. The general refused to see the rebel colonel, but he authorized cavalry officer Brig. Gen. George H. Chapman to meet with Mosby and offer the same terms as given to Lee's men, including the provision that men could keep their privately owned horses but not their arms. Chapman was to impress upon the colonel that with his surrender, *all* guerrilla operations were to cease. Reports of independent raiding parties operating in the Blue Ridge Mountains had reached Hancock, and Chapman was to warn Mosby that it would be in his interest to encourage those to stop as well. Finally, Mosby and his men should know that any retaliatory actions taken against the Union-sympathizing people of the region would be met with a swift response by Union forces.[65]

On the morning of Tuesday, April 18, General Chapman along with an escort of two cavalry regiments cantered toward Millwood, a village not far from the West Virginia line. For more than two years, no Union soldier had been safe in the region. But Mosby had sent word of a truce. There was not a picket to be seen, not a scout or vidette in the vicinity. Riding into the village, the Union escort gathered at a large farmhouse, where the soldiers waited along the porches and on the lawn under the branches of budding trees. At noon a bugle sounded, bringing every man in blue to his feet. To the east, a column of mounted men emerged from the woods. Wearing his best uniform astride a sorrel mare, Mosby rode at the head of a column of nearly sixty men—all on the finest horses left in northern Virginia.[66]

General Chapman met Mosby as he dismounted, the two men clasping hands. After introductions, they sat down to a meal provided by the home owner and turned to business. Mosby expressed sincere regret concerning Lincoln's assassination and declared he had no desire to spill more blood. But he informed Chapman that he was not yet convinced the Confederate cause was lost. If he learned that Johnston's army had been defeated, he would disband. Indeed, he had already advised his Rangers that each was free to seek an individual parole, and more than a dozen had already done so in Winchester. But he would not surrender them as a unit. Nor would he surrender. If defeat proved imminent, Mosby planned to leave the country. Give me ten days, Mosby requested, to see what might become of Johnston. Chapman agreed to suspend hostilities for another forty-eight hours, a period ending at noon on April 20.[67]

When Grant learned of Mosby's refusal to surrender, he erupted. "If Mosby does not avail himself of [t]he present truce," the general-in-chief instructed Hancock, "hunt him and his men down. Guerillas, after beating the Armies of enemy, will not be entitled to quarter."[68] Grant had long insisted that guerrillas remained the chief threat to peace, but rumors that Mosby was complicit in Lincoln's assassination only fueled his desire to smash all elements of irregular resistance. Talk in Washington claimed that Mosby had met with Booth in the capital, and some suggested that the assassins had crossed the Potomac and were endeavoring to make their way to Mosby's band. Indeed, Lewis Powell, alias Lewis Paine, who had attempted to assassinate Secretary Seward, had been one of Mosby's Rangers before deserting in January 1865.[69]

On April 20, just before the truce expired, Mosby and twenty of his men again met with Union officials in Millwood. But this time, rather than a general, Hancock sent a staff officer. When he refused to allow new terms or an extension of the truce, Mosby became agitated. "Tell General Hancock it is in his power to do it, and it is not in my power to resist it; but I will not accept a parole before Joe Johnston has surrendered," he thundered. Standing abruptly, he signaled to his men. They all rose, mounted their horses, and galloped off.[70]

But Mosby knew the time had come to disband his Rangers. The next day, he summoned his men to an open field just north of Salem. At noon, officers ordered the men to mount and form a line. Riding up and down the line, Mosby listened while his lieutenants read his farewell address to the men: "The vision that we have cherished of a free and independent country has vanished, and that country is now the spoil of the conqueror," it began. Just as he had promised General Chapman, the slight and wiry colonel was electing to disband the Rangers rather than surrender them to the enemy. Although he claimed he was no longer their commander, he sounded a refrain similar to Lee's at Appomattox. "I part from you with a just pride in the fame of your achievements and grateful recollections of your generous kindness to myself. And now at this moment, in bidding you a final adieu, accept the assurances of my unchanging confidence and regards."[71]

Not surprisingly, Mosby's flowery prose omitted any mention of his Rangers' more egregious acts. Like so many of the farewells offered in the war's closing days, he emphasized only the heroism and devotion of his men. In doing so, like Lee, he helped lay the groundwork for a postwar canonization of Confederates in the very moment of their nation's death.

Mosby's final act as colonel complete, he and six of his men turned south toward Richmond to continue the fight. The great majority of his men, however, rode northwest to the Union garrison at Winchester. By the evening of April 22, at least 380 Rangers and most of the officers had been paroled, including Mosby's second in command, Lt. Col. William H. Chapman. "He is as important as Mosby," Hancock wired Stanton that night before departing for Washington, "and from conversation had with him, I think he will be valuable to the Government hereafter." Moreover, some of Mosby's own men were now in pursuit of the guerrilla chief—motivated by a $2,000 reward offered by the commanding general.[72] With the stroke of a pen and the recording of their names on the parole list, Mosby's Rangers could claim absolution for all they had done. Equally as important, the Union leadership's pursuit of guerrilla forces that had consumed them since Lincoln's assassination was finding success.

Yet even with the increasing number of parolees and the disbanding of Mosby's command, Munford remained determined to continue the struggle. His refusal to surrender himself to General Mackenzie on April 17 raised a key question: had the terms included Confederate cavalry outside the Union lines? Mackenzie deferred the query to General Gibbon, the senior officer on the commission appointed by Grant to arrange the terms at Appomattox. From his headquarters in Burkeville, Gibbon responded directly to Munford. "The surrender of the Army of Northern Virginia shall be construed to include all the forces operating with that army on the 8th instant, except such bodies of cavalry as actually made their escape previous to the surrender," Gibbon explained. "The question, therefore, as to the actual escape of your command is left to your decision."[73]

Munford had no intention of capitulating. Instead, on April 21—the same day Mosby disbanded his command—Munford issued a stirring special order intended to rally his men. He explained that he had just received a communication from President Jefferson Davis ordering them into the field again in defense of their liberties. "Our cause is not dead," he intoned. In language that sounded much like Rosser's April 12 proclamation, he reminded his men of the atrocities committed by the Union, of the "devastated fields, our burned homesteads, our violated daughters, and our murdered thousands." "Their present pretend policy of conciliation is but the cunning desire of the Yankee to lull us to sleep, while they rivet the chains . . . which they will surely make *us* wear *forever*," he warned. Rejecting any pretense to reconciliation, he entreated his soldiers to "teach our children eternal hostility to our foes."

Underscoring the limited nature of Lee's surrender, Munford informed his old brigade that there were more men from the Army of Northern Virginia who had escaped the Federal lines and returned home than were surrendered at Appomattox. (Munford was wrong. Union provost marshals would parole nearly 17,000 men from Lee's ranks at other locales by mid-July, but more than 28,000 were paroled at Appomattox). "You have never been surrendered!" he declared. Having cut their way out before the surrender was completed, "you, together with the majority of the cavalry[,] are free to follow your country's flag." He beseeched them to rally once more. And only a week after Lincoln's assassination, he employed the Virginia motto— the same words reportedly shouted by John Wilkes Booth: "Virginia, our beloved old Commonwealth, shall yet stand triumphant and defiant, with her foot upon her tyrants prostrate, and her proud old banner, never yet sullied, with its 'Sic Semper Tyrannis' streaming over her." Be ready to assemble at a time and place to be disclosed, he commanded.[74]

Fewer and fewer of Lee's men were inclined to follow Munford's lead, choosing instead to lay down their arms and seek out a paroling station. At cities such as Winchester, Norfolk, and Lynchburg; in the small towns of Farmville, Black's and White's Station, Millwood, Columbia, and King George Court House; and throughout the Shenandoah Valley, Lee's soldiers continued to trickle in to paroling stations, sometimes in groups and often as individuals. By April 22, no fewer than 7,000 had chosen to do so, filling the roads of Virginia with their comings and goings.[75] From her home in Middleburg, Catherine Hopkins Broun watched the steady stream of Confederates make their way to and from Winchester to be paroled. "It was really heartbreaking to see the young men," she scribbled in her diary. "I saw them in tears and heard some said [sic] they would rather be shot than take it but they are compelled, for [if they did not surrender] everyone would be taken as prisoner of war and the houses burned they were found in."[76]

For Confederate soldiers and their civilian supporters, however, surrendering to U.S. forces did not mean admitting that their cause was wrong. "Gen. Lee 'surrendered' no rights of conscience, no sentiment or feeling of affection for his country," a Valley newspaper reassured its readers on April 21. "We are still proud of our country (aye, if possible, prouder than ever), and still love it with a devotion intensified by her misfortune." Seeking paroles did not make Confederates "Union men." Instead, it offered a path toward peace, the chance for desolated fields to produce once more and for soldiers to return home to their families. At least that was the hope of most.[77]

But no Virginia locale would feel the weight of the paroling and disbanding more so than the former Confederate capital, Richmond.

7

A Rebel Capital No More

On Monday, April 17, artillery ordnance officer Kena King Chapman and ten of his men could finally see the spires of Richmond's churches. They had followed the James River east for five days, bound for the capital, where they hoped to find friends and family who might assist them before they continued their journey toward their homes in Smithfield, Virginia. But upon reaching a bridge three miles outside of Richmond, a Union guard halted them. Even with parole passes in hand, the guard, under orders from the provost marshal general, refused to allow the Confederates to pass, ushering them down Westham Plank Road to the nearest Union headquarters for the night. The next morning, a Union captain informed the men that if they were not Richmond residents, they could not enter the city. Yet Chapman persisted. After much cajoling, the officer finally conceded on the condition that Chapman and his men report immediately to the adjutant quartermaster. Following orders, they went directly to the quartermaster's office. Go on, he informed them. You are already paroled. He had no further use for them.[1]

That same day, Pvt. Edward Valentine Jones of the Richmond Howitzers and Col. Edwin L. Hobson of Battle's Brigade arrived on the outskirts of Petersburg. They had endured a wretched ride in a boxcar used for transporting army horses from Burkeville, but even with their Appomattox paroles, they needed to register with the Petersburg provost marshal. When they sought passes to travel on to Richmond, a Union guard refused Hobson because he was an Alabamian. Only residents could return, the guard insisted. The next day, Jones, who hoped to pick up clothing and other items he had left with a cousin in Richmond prior to the retreat on April 2, pre-

Union soldiers standing on two pontoon bridges on the James River, Richmond, April 1865. Note the guardhouse where Confederates like Kena King Chapman likely showed their parole passes. Library of Congress Prints and Photographs Division, LC-DIG-ppmsca-33356.

vailed in getting passage for both of them to the outskirts of the capital city. After crossing the pontoon bridge from Manchester, a guard ordered all the paroled prisoners to fall in line. They were to be marched to the provost marshal's office, and nonresidents were to be sent home. Again, Hobson was refused entry into the capital. Having none of it, the colonel slipped past the guard and rushed into the hustle and bustle of the crowds. Jones attempted to pass as well but was halted; he was forced to march with the column before he, too, successfully slipped out of line.[2] If caught, they could have been charged with breaking their parole, but like thousands of others, they disregarded the Union policy in the hope of finding friends and family who might offer food and shelter.

The city that greeted the Confederates proved a far cry from its antebellum or even war days. "Such a scene of desolation I never witnessed, whole squares both upon [Cary Street] and Canal and Main lay in ruins, in some places they were still smoking," observed Jones. Chapman concurred. "Old Richmond is sadly changed," he noted, "all business portions of the city being a heap of ruins." In the entire valley stretching south from Franklin Street to the James River, scarcely one building stood. The great shops and warehouses now lay as masses of crumbling walls and rubbish. Every railroad

A Rebel Capital No More

entering the city had been destroyed, the three bridges spanning the James burned by the evacuating Confederates. Trains now stopped across the river in Manchester, passengers forced to go by conveyance or foot across the pontoon bridges. Even a Union officer reported that the "once beautiful city" now "presented a hopeless picture of desolation." Retreating Confederates had torched the city, but foreshadowing Lost Cause revisionism, Chapman blamed the Union immigrant hirelings and Black soldiers for the destruction.[3]

The presence of so many free African Americans proved more devastating for resident Lucy Muse Fletcher. "From the Cemetery to James River and from Brook Avenue to Rockettes the city is peopled with negroes and Yankees," she bemoaned. Even as Fletcher decried this "galling sight," her condescending and biting words could not help but convey the festive spirit enveloping Richmond's African American community. "The streets are thronged with negroes of all shades from the pretty mulatto in her jaunty hat and fur bellows to the dusty and ragged cornfield drudge who with soiled garments and streaming headgear is making her way into the square to enjoy the music of 'Yankee Doodle' and 'Old John Brown,'" she wrote. Young boys frolicked in the capitol square, tumbling down the grassy hills, as young girls jumped rope and rolled hoops throughout the grounds "This is Yankee *civilization*!" Fletcher sarcastically quipped, before adding, "I hope they enjoy each others society for our citizens are rarely seen on the streets."[4]

Unlike many of their rural counterparts who had either not learned of their freedom or remained tentative as to how they might claim it, African Americans in Richmond demonstrated no uncertainty. They had witnessed the USCT, many of the soldiers former slaves, march into the Confederate capital on April 3 before gathering on Broad Street near Lumpkin Alley, site of the slave jails and auction houses. Among the soldiers stood Garland H. White, a formerly enslaved man from Virginia who had escaped to Ohio before joining the 28th USCT as a chaplain. Called on to give a speech by his comrades, he complied. "I was aroused amid the shouts of ten thousand voices," he recalled, "and proclaimed for the first time in that city freedom to all mankind." Within the cells of Lumpkin's jail, enslaved men began to chant, "Slavery chain done broke at last!" The crowd soon joined in, and the USCT rushed to release the prisoners. Moved to tears, White could not continue his speech. Instead, he waded through the vast crowds where he found an aged woman inquiring for a man by his name who had been taken from her and sold when he was boy. Amid the occupation of Richmond, he was reunited with his mother. Four days later, a grand jubilee meeting was held in the First African Church on Broad Street, where not a seat could be found. News of Lee's surrender only heightened the elation. African American war correspondent Thomas Morris Chester observed that "nothing can exceed the rejoicings of the negroes since the occupation of this city. They declare that they cannot realize the change; though they have long prayed for it, yet it seems impossible that it has come. . . . The highest degree of happiness attainable upon earth is now being enjoyed by the colored people of this city," he wrote. Whether a longtime resident or a newcomer from the surrounding counties, those in Richmond enjoyed a brief moment of true liberation.[5]

It was not simply that Black men and women were now free, but the sight of their former masters as prisoners offered powerful evidence that the racial order had been uprooted by war. When a large group of captured rebels escorted through the streets by USCT halted in front of Libby Prison, one of them spotted his former slave now in a blue uniform. Stepping out of the ranks, the Confederate called to him, "Hallo, Jack, is that you!" The USCT guard glared back at the prisoner. "Why Jack, don't you know me?," pressed the rebel. "Yes, I know you very well," the guard replied, "and if you don't fall back into that line I will give you this bayonet." With a musket now pointed at him, the Confederate said no more.[6]

Maj. Gen. E. O. C. Ord was well aware that white Richmonders despised the presence of both African Americans and Union troops in *their* city. Upon establishing his headquarters in Jefferson Davis's recently vacated mansion on April 13, the Department of Virginia commander informed Secretary of War Stanton of his intentions to be "kind to the submissive" and to "make the military rule acceptable." As such, his first official act was to order all soldiers of the USCT to leave the city and move to a position south of Petersburg, an act in keeping with his previous record toward Black soldiers but also meant to placate white Richmonders. He next instructed the coal, canal, and Fredericksburg Railroad companies to resume operations so that food and fuel might flow into the capital. He granted passes home to civilians on the same terms given by Grant to Lee's army. Finally, with Grant's permission and the arrival of the department's provost marshal Bvt. Maj. Gen. Marsena R. Patrick, Ord began paroling thousands of sick and wounded Confederate soldiers who had been convalescing in the city's thirteen hospitals and their medical personnel. "Confederate surgeons should be notified to turn over their sick to our medical officers and return to their homes as speedily as possible," Ord instructed. Like other Union commanders throughout the state, he offered to parole any rebels who surrendered themselves.[7]

Many in the city noted Ord's kindness and generosity. Perhaps it was

Gen. E. O. C. Ord with his wife and child at the residence of Jefferson Davis in Richmond. In the doorway is the table on which the surrender of Gen. Robert E. Lee was signed at Appomattox. Library of Congress Prints and Photographs Division, LC-DIG-cwpb-02930.

Ord's personal background that shaped his approach. In early January 1865, Grant had tapped him to take command of the Army of the James, despite his reputation for personal and political infighting, partly a result of his well-known Democratic loyalties. Or, he may have simply been trying to implement Grant's magnanimous policies in an effort to facilitate reunion and reconciliation.[8] But some locals speculated that his wife (who may have had Virginia connections) influenced his friendly feelings toward Confederates in Richmond. "She is a lovely person," John Francis Heath wrote from the city, "& we deem ourselves fortunate in being in the hands of so humane an officer as her husband. She has a great deal of influence on her husband & uses it in our favour."[9]

Ord's reluctance to obey Grant's orders to arrest the mayor and members of the city council in the wake of Lincoln's assassination only heightened Confederates' fondness for the general. Equally telling was his response to Grant's order on April 15 that all paroled officers and surgeons be arrested until they could be sent beyond Union lines unless they took the oath of allegiance. Less than a week after his assurance that Lee's paroled men would not be disturbed by U.S. authorities, Lincoln's murder had made Grant willing to retract this portion of the surrender terms. Ord responded immediately to his general-in-chief that arresting Lee and his staff, who had returned to the city earlier that day, might reopen the rebellion. He would risk his life to ensure that the paroles were kept. Four hours later, a calmer Grant withdrew his order in the name of peace.[10]

That same day, Republican congressman Elihu B. Washburne of Grant's Illinois district telegraphed Lincoln — not yet knowing of his death — from Richmond urging calm. He had just arrived from the field at Appomattox, where he had witnessed the surrender. He had been impressed with the rebels' compliance and wrote Lincoln that it was not necessary to call an extra session of Congress. "I believe it would only lead to evil," he warned, worried that Democrats in Congress might undermine emancipation. The Radical Republican had spoken to the Democratic Ord upon arriving in Richmond, who concurred, endorsing the telegram. "The change in sentiment here, after contrasting the past tyranny with the present unexpected good order and freedom, makes me think your proclamation of emancipation will be supported by a majority in Virginia," noted Ord.[11] The president, in conjunction with his generals, could oversee the war's conclusion, including emancipation without congressional interference.

In the days that followed, Confederate soldiers streamed into Richmond almost as quickly as they had rushed out ten days prior. Some were paroled soldiers returning to their homes; others were passing through en route to residences farther east; some were stopping for a short time before catching steamers to places as far away as New Orleans, Mobile, and Texas; and still others were hoping to get passes to travel north to Washington, Baltimore, or New York.

The great majority of arrivals, however, proved to be unparoled soldiers from the Army of Northern Virginia. Even before Provost Marshal Patrick established his office at the custom house on April 13, Union officials had

Custom house standing among ruins in Richmond where Marsena
Patrick, provost marshal general, established his headquarters.
Note that the columns at the right of the photo are draped with
mourning crepe following Lincoln's assassination. Library of Congress
Prints and Photographs Division, LC-DIG-cwpb-02771.

administered several hundred paroles. Between the hours of one and three
o'clock each day, Lee's men could be found waiting to surrender themselves
at the Female Institute on the corner of 10th and Clay Streets.[12] The labor
only intensified after Patrick's arrival. "There is a world of work to do, and I
hardly know where to begin," Patrick observed. One thing was certain: with
the impeding influx of more rebels, he needed to clear out those who could
not claim residence in the city. On April 16, he ordered patrols to gather all
Confederate officers and men who did not have authority to remain in the
city as well as those who were residents who continued to lounge in public
places. "They must be instructed to go at once to their homes and remain
there." This provision of the terms had to be enforced, or the city would be
overwhelmed with graycoats.[13]

In the days that followed, Confederates continued to enter the city,
some as individuals but most in small groups with other men from their regiment. Most were Virginians. Among them, at least seventy-four men from
the 3rd Virginia Infantry, fifty-two from the 3rd Virginia Cavalry, and thirty-
one from the 53rd Virginia Infantry arrived. But fragments of regiments from

North Carolina, Georgia, Louisiana, Florida, South Carolina, Mississippi, and Alabama also sought paroles. By month's end, at least 1,610 soldiers from Lee's army would surrender at the former Confederate capital.[14]

Such was not the homecoming most had imagined. Rather than a victory parade, Lee's men entered their former capital to find Union soldiers crowding the city. "Officers in blue were lounging about in *our* usual haunts," observed a member of the New Orleans–based Washington Artillery. The presence of Union troops at the Spotswood Hotel particularly galled Lee's men. The newest and finest hotel in the city, the Spotswood had become synonymous with the rebel cause. Located two blocks south of the capitol building, throughout the war it welcomed Confederate military and political leaders, spies, profiteers, and the South's elite who gathered amid the sweet smells of bourbon and cigars. The five-story brick building had been spared from flames on April 3 by a lull in the wind, but it now housed men in blue — an unwelcome change for the paroled Confederate officers and the Army of Northern Virginia medical director, R. J. Breckinridge, who took their meals at the hotel. Around the supper and breakfast tables, gray and blue mingled, the gray appearing to outnumber the blue as tensions mounted. "Some rows having occurred," one Confederate related understatedly, "we were politely requested to leave."[15] After one such a fight, Provost Marshal Patrick issued orders on April 18 declaring that all paroled Confederate soldiers (including officers) as well as Union soldiers not on duty were forbidden from wearing their sidearms and revolvers.[16]

The conflicts between Union and Confederate soldiers were caused in part by the bravado of the defeated rebels. "They sport their best suits of gray with a degree of arrogance which should not be tolerated — more with the bearing of conquerors than routed vandals, as they are," Thomas Morris Chester reported from Richmond. At the very least, he thought, they should be "divested of the treasonable uniform so offensive to loyal tastes." Each day, more Confederates arrived, including Gens. Fitzhugh Lee, Henry Heth, Porter Alexander, and George Pickett. "The effect upon the population is not very pleasant," Chester testified on April 16. Even after Lincoln's assassination, the rebels seemed to grow bolder, their utterances of disloyalty louder. "The rebels continue to strut in their uniform, and in many cases make remarks which are offensive to Union soldiers," he noted. But unlike Bvt. Brig. Gen. William Morris in Baltimore, Ord had not issued an order prohibiting the rebel uniform (Chester speculated that the rationale was not because Union generals failed to recognize the propriety of forbidding the rebel uniform, but they "rather tolerated them" in order to "more readily capture cer-

A Rebel Capital No More

Confederates from Lee's army flocked to Richmond, often gathering in public places such as around the Washington Monument on the capitol grounds. Library of Congress Prints and Photographs Division, LC-DIG-cwpb-01277.

tain chieftains who had forfeited their right to be at liberty"). Such decisions continued to reflect the local and regional nature of military commands.[17]

Ord had a more pressing problem. In a city already swollen with wartime refugees plus thousands of newly emancipated men and women from the surrounding countryside, the influx of both paroled and unparoled Confederate soldiers verged on disastrous. "Two hundred or 300 men a day are arriving to give themselves up, lay down their arms, and be paroled under the order I have issued," General Ord reported. But this was stressing a city already brimming with more than 25,000 similarly situated white and Black women and children. Ord was doing the best he could to alleviate the situation: he had distributed rations to more than 15,000 people, including at least 500 paroled Confederates; ordered the canal, road, and mill companies to resume work; hired nearly 1,000 African American men along the docks—some to load and unload government vessels and others to shovel and cart off the rubble of war; and employed nearly 300 African American women as seamstresses with the Quartermaster's Department.[18]

In addition to these measures, Ord struggled to reduce the number of people in the city. He had encouraged the destitute to leave, but his primary concern lay with the Confederate soldiers who filled every corner of the city, from the docks to the capitol square. His chief action had revolved around doling out passes for Confederate officers and men to return to their homes, in some cases via northern cities. With the southern railroad system in shambles, some concluded that their fastest route home would take them to Washington, Baltimore, or New York, where they might catch a steamer bound for a southern port or a railroad headed west toward Kentucky or Tennessee. Ignoring the fact that a state of war continued to exist, Lee's men operated as if things had returned to their prewar norms. For his part, Ord had endorsed requests to travel north, believing that it would help alleviate Richmond's congested streets and having the utmost confidence that the defeated rebels would not dare commit crimes in the North.[19]

Among those seeking passage north was Lee's artillerist Porter Alexander. Since departing Appomattox, Alexander's intentions had been to go to Brazil, where he would offer his services in the war against Paraguay. In order to do so, he needed to first journey to Washington, where he hoped to speak to the Brazilian minister. Although Lee had advised him against such a plan, Alexander persisted and called upon Ord for a permit to travel to Washington. Ord, too, warned Alexander that he should avoid heading to the capital, especially in the wake of Lincoln's assassination. But the artillerist "decided to risk it." With pass in hand, on April 17 Alexander boarded a steamer, which sailed down the James and up the Potomac, landing him in Washington the next day.[20]

The more Grant learned of Ord's liberal policies in the wake of the assassination and with the murderers still on the loose, the more he became irate. On April 18, he admonished Ord to cease providing paroled Confederates passes to travel north. "Paroled prisoners belonging to N.C., S.C., Georgia, Florida, Alabama, and in fact all of the southern states must get to their homes through the Country. Those at [F]t Monroe must be turned back," he ordered. They had been granted passes to travel through Union lines when necessary to reach their homes, but the U.S. government had not undertaken "to pay their passage nor permit them to travel a roundabout way, through the loyal states for their convenience." They seemed to overlook the fact that a state of war still existed. Several large Confederate armies, including Gen. Joseph E. Johnston's, remained in the field. Grant would not — could not —

condone such travel. Union officials would immediately desist in providing transportation *and* rations.[21]

Ord, who believed he was acting in the spirit of Appomattox, pushed back. To deny paroled Confederates passage north would strand a large number of destitute soldiers in Richmond. Detailing the web of challenges they faced, he pointed out to Grant that railroad and canal routes that might lead them home had been destroyed; there were few horses or mules to provide transportation; their money was worthless; and they were starved. Some claimed homes in Maryland, northern Kentucky, or Tennessee. Others had no homes to which they could return, including those from Hampton and along the North Carolina coast, where freedmen's colonies had been formed. "They are coming here by the thousands — Many of them have wives and children here," Ord wrote. "It is important to get them away from here. If I am not authorized either to feed them or send them away by the most expeditious routes I cannot be responsible for consequences."[22]

Returning from Lincoln's funeral, Grant minced no words in his reply to Ord. "We cannot undertake to bear all the hardships brought on [in]dividuals by their treason and rebellion," he asserted on April 19. Again, Grant reiterated his position: he had never agreed to furnish homes, subsistence, or transportation to the men of Lee's army. He had allowed for them to pass through Union lines — *in former Confederate territory* — when necessary to reach their homes. In other words, the paroles granted them freedom of movement within the seceded states. And while Grant had promised that no fares would be collected on government transports moving through the South, this had not been an invitation for Lee's men to "come within our lines and stay there at public charge" or a promise "that men going to N. C. or Ga. should be furnished a pleasant passage through the North and Coastwise to their homes." To ensure that his point had been heard, Grant ordered Maj. Gen. Henry Halleck, Ord's newly appointed superior as commander of the Military Division of the James, to Richmond the following day to oversee enforcement of the instructions.[23]

Grant's orders had an immediate impact on every soldier in Richmond, whether he donned the blue or the gray. Provost Marshal Patrick found himself roused from his bed with instructions to send guards to Fort Monroe, where they were to intercept any boats heading north with rebels. There they found nearly 3,000 paroled Confederates crowded along the wharf awaiting government steamers that would carry them south to New Bern, Savannah, Mobile, and New Orleans.[24] But others hoped to travel north. Among them stood Capt. William Wardlaw of South Carolina. Having made his way from

Appomattox to Richmond, where he had obtained a passport to travel to Baltimore, on April 19 he learned he could not sail north. Like other gray-clad soldiers, he had assumed that upon surrendering he would be free to travel anywhere in the United States he pleased. It was as if the rebellion had never happened. But Union authorities were not so quick to agree. While the fighting might be nearing its conclusion, legal and political questions of ending the rebellion remained.[25]

Tensions in the capital continued to swell. "Our not permitting Rebels to go North," Patrick observed, "has raised the mischief here." Ord persisted in his pleas to Grant. On the afternoon of April 20, he telegraphed the general-in-chief inquiring as to what should be done with the thousands of paroled Confederates awaiting steamers at Fort Monroe bound for New Orleans and Mobile. An increasingly frustrated Grant fired back again, seemingly reversing the policy he had laid out on April 10: the rebels would *not* be furnished transportation by the government. Not to the North. Not even to the South. Again, invoking the language of his previous day's commands to Ord, Grant explained that "it was no part of the arrangement that they should receive transportation or be allowed to pass through our lines except when to reach their homes it was necessary to do so." The men of Lee's army whose homes were south of Richmond would have to travel over land. If they elected to come within Union lines, Grant warned, they would do so "either as prisoners of War who surrendered their paroles or as persons desirous of quitting the rebel cause and taking advantage of the Presidents Amnesty."[26] They had three choices: travel home with the scarce resources they had, take the oath of amnesty to the United States, or submit to prison.

Only eleven days after the surrender at Appomattox, the limited and evolving meaning of the paroles was becoming apparent. They had not guaranteed Lee's men free movement. Nor had they ensured government transportation or rations. Paroles had not restored the rights of U.S. citizenship. Only oaths of allegiance could do this. And it remained to be seen whether paroles truly protected rebels from prosecution for treason. As Frank Potts of the 1st Virginia informed his brother, he was now a "subjugated rebel, who has no nation, no rights and no greenbacks."[27]

Upon arriving in Virginia, Halleck saw immediately that Ord had been correct about Richmond's refugee crisis. Something needed to be done immediately to alleviate the suffering. Per Grant's instructions, he could not send Confederate soldiers north, but he would do his best to take care of the civilians, authorizing women and children transportation aboard railroads to points south of the former Confederate capital. "Those wishing to go in

A Rebel Capital No More

other directions will be conveyed out of the city in ambulances to certain convenient points to be designated by you," Halleck instructed Ord, adding that "no one will be permitted to come to the city in public conveyances."[28] Halleck's orders, however, said nothing about paroled soldiers. Although a burden on the city's resources, Halleck well knew that there were thousands more unparoled rebels who might yet turn themselves in to the occupying Union forces.

8

To Johnston's Army

By Friday morning, April 14, Harry Townsend's party of sixteen men from the Richmond Howitzers had crossed the North River and started toward Natural Bridge. After a short stop to bathe in the cool, crisp waters, the men marched on toward the Buffalo River, where a local shared a copy of Lee's General Orders No. 9. The order gave them pause. They had been six miles north of Appomattox Court House at Red Oak Church during the negotiations. But did Lee's surrender include them? Some believed it did and urged the party to return to Lynchburg and give themselves up to the Yankee authorities. But others insisted that they were not surrendered. Unable to come to an agreement, the group elected to split. Nine headed back toward Lynchburg, but seven, including Townsend, pushed on toward Lincolnton, North Carolina, where they would rendezvous and continue the fight.[1]

At dawn, Townsend woke to a cold rain. If the rain was expected, the arrival of five of the men who had left the group the previous day was not. Shortly after the men had separated, the party returning to Lynchburg had met Brig. Gen. William N. Pendleton, chief of artillery and one of the three Confederate officers on the surrender commission. Although he was a paroled prisoner, he informed the men that they had misinterpreted Lee's order. They were not surrendered. It was their duty to go on to North Carolina and join Johnston's army. Four of the men no longer had the will to fight, but five of the group immediately retraced their steps and set out to find those who had continued their trek to Lincolnton.[2]

Over the next few days, the cold spring rain drenched the earth while the dozen men continued their southwest march along the eastern edge of the Blue Ridge Mountains. At nights, Confederate civilians opened their homes, allowing the men to rest in comfortable beds for the first time in months, or at the very least to warm themselves in front of the hearth while sleeping on the floor. Along the way, nature tried desperately to thwart their efforts with the swollen waters of the James costing them a thirty-dollar ferry ride. Yet their lack of supplies proved the greatest obstacle. At the towns of Buchanan and Fincastle they had hoped to find the Quartermaster's Department willing to provide rations and clothing. But neither location had anything left to spare. Instead, the men relied upon civilians to feed them, and a few bought fabric on credit to replace their torn, filthy uniforms with a fresh set of clothes.[3]

By the morning of April 18, the group had reached Big Lick (present day Roanoke), where a quartermaster agreed to meet them and discuss the possibility of acquiring horses. But upon hearing that cavalry officer Thomas T. Munford was in town, the group set off to ask his assistance. Quickly gaining an audience with him, they learned that he would be of little help unless they joined his command. They demurred. The artillerists remained determined to reach Lincolnton. Disappointed that they would not join him, Munford agreed that should they find any government horses along their way, they were authorized to impress them. Leaving Big Lick, the men crossed the Blue Ridge Mountains toward North Carolina, where they planned to take up the fight once more.[4]

As Townsend and his party traversed western Virginia, Lt. Col. David G. McIntosh, Capt. Ham Chamberlayne, Maj. Gen. James L. Kemper, and several other artillerists who had escaped Appomattox had headed due south, crossing the North Carolina border on Thursday, April 13. "The negroes all seem to be free here or to think themselves so," observed McIntosh upon reaching Milton, North Carolina. Regardless of the enslaved peoples' status, the party remained determined to reach Johnston. On they rode, passing through Red House, Leasburg, and Prospect Hill before striking Johnston's column at Haw River Station.[5] Their war was not over.

While Lee's paroled and unparoled men dispersed from Appomattox, the soldiers of Johnston's army were attempting to defend North Carolina against Maj. Gen. William T. Sherman's troops. But on April 10, as Johnston pulled his army back toward Raleigh, Capt. Samuel T. Foster of Granbury's Texas Brigade began hearing of Lee's capitulation. With men of the Army of Northern Virginia streaming through the Carolina countryside, the rumors abounded, offering Johnston's men inconsistent and often conflicting re-

David G. McIntosh was among the artillery officers who escaped the surrender at Appomattox and rode south, hoping to join Gen. Joseph E. Johnston's forces. Jennings Cropper Wise, *The Long Arm of Lee*, vol. 2 (Lynchburg, Va.: J. P. Bell Company, 1915), 736.

ports. Some suggested that Lee had surrendered only a few men, leaving the great bulk of his army "scattered all over the country," while others reported that he had surrendered "42,000 men, and himself with them."[6] Despite such accounts, Johnston's army continued its retreat through a bitter rain, abandoning Raleigh and slogging west through Hillsborough and Chapel Hill toward Greensboro, a major rail center.[7]

A mere forty-five miles to the south of Danville, Virginia, Greensboro had offered one last bit of hope for soldiers in Lee's army. For those who had absconded from Appomattox, they thought they might find Johnston still ready to fight. They would offer their services and defeat Sherman's bummers. For those who had received their paroles, they expected to secure more rations from Johnston's quartermasters and commissary.

Jefferson Davis likewise held out hope. On the afternoon of April 11, a train bearing Davis and his cabinet pulled into the Greensboro station, where the Confederate president met with Gen. P. G. T. Beauregard and other members the Confederate cabinet aboard his coach. The situation was dire, Beauregard explained, and the president should prepare for the worst.

Davis was undeterred. Although there had been setbacks, he insisted the fighting should continue, even if that meant taking the war to the Trans-Mississippi, where Gen. Edmund "Kirby" Smith still led an army. Frustrated with Beauregard's response, Davis summoned Johnston from his headquarters in Raleigh at midnight. The next day, Johnston joined Beauregard for another meeting. Even together, the two generals (in whom Davis rarely had confidence) could not convince him that the end was upon them. As they stood to leave, Davis informed them that he expected news of Lee's army to arrive with Secretary of War John C. Breckinridge that evening.[8]

With Johnston's army stretched some fifty miles between Durham Station and Greensboro, rumors of Lee's demise poured in from all directions. On April 11, officers of the 1st Georgia Regulars attempted to rally their troops by informing them that Lee and his army were holding their own along the banks of the Appomattox after causing Grant to lose more than 30,000 men. But only four days later, the Georgians learned the painful truth when they encountered some of Lee's men on their way home. "The announcement ruined the morale of Gen. Johnston's Army," observed W. H. Andrews, adding that after such news, "it was nothing more than a howling mob."[9]

On April 12, as Lee's infantry formed in lines for the formal surrender parade, Breckinridge brought Davis official news of the army's capitulation. Conferring with Gens. Johnston and Beauregard, the three agreed the end was at hand. But when they met with Davis, he refused to relent. He refused to believe that the Confederacy had been defeated. While terrible, the latest disasters were not fatal. "I think we can whip the enemy yet if our people will turn out," Davis declared. No one spoke. Both the generals and Davis's cabinet knew otherwise. Finally, after much urging, Johnston replied, "It would be the greatest of human crimes for us to attempt to continue the war." The Confederacy had no money or credit, no arms to put in the hands of its soldiers, and no ammunition to load their rifles. "The effect of our keeping the field would be, not to harm the enemy," he declared, "but to complete the devastation of our country and ruin of its people." The only possible choice was to negotiate for peace. With a majority in agreement, the reluctant president dictated a letter to Sherman requesting a temporary suspension of operations to "permit the civil authorities to enter into the needful arrangements to terminate the existing war."[10]

Sherman, too, received word of Lee's surrender on April 12. As he expected, two days later upon reaching Raleigh, he received Davis's letter alongside a request for a meeting. Sherman agreed before dashing off a tele-

J. H. "Ham" Chamberlayne
as a captain of the
artillery. Chamberlayne
and Chamberlayne, *Ham
Chamberlayne*, 256.

gram to Grant promising to extend the same terms the general-in-chief had offered Lee and to "be careful not to complicate any points of civil policy."[11]

With no knowledge of the impending conference, David McIntosh and Ham Chamberlayne hurried toward Johnston's headquarters. Locating the general near the south bank of the Haw River on April 14, they offered their services. "He made no direct reply to my tender," McIntosh observed, "said he had more artillery than he knew what to do with." Still, the colonel was impressed with Johnston's quiet demeanor. "He evinced no surprise or excitement in speaking of Lee's disaster," McIntosh noted. Johnston invited them to stay with him closer to Greensboro that night, to which they readily agreed.[12]

Riding into Greensboro, McIntosh and Chamberlayne found the railroad town in a state of commotion. In the spring of 1861, Greensboro had been a quiet village with barely 2,000 residents. But four years of war had witnessed a boom. In May 1864, the Piedmont Railroad opened, providing

To Johnston's Army

a vital link between Lee's army in Virginia and supplies in the Deep South. Along with the trains came the military warehouses and more people. Throngs of refugees had poured in from Virginia and coastal North Carolina since 1862, while Sherman's march through South Carolina had driven more to Greensboro in the winter of 1865.[13] By early April, both Johnston's and Lee's soldiers added to the chaotic streets.

Passing through the town on their way to Salisbury, artillerists from Bachman's South Carolina Battery were among the first to enjoy the largesse of the military stores. They discovered quantities of tobacco hogsheads lining the main street and witnessed the destruction of an entire trainload of liquor belonging to the Medicinal Department. As a detail knocked in the heads of the barrels, whiskey flowed down the street from the depot. Determined not to let such a prized commodity go to waste, the boys of Bachman's Battery filled anything they could—canteens, camp kettles, and any other vessel that would hold the precious liquid.[14]

In the days that followed, parolees from Lee's army, those who had escaped Appomattox, and many from Johnston's ranks streamed into the swollen city in search of food and supplies. By April 15, with the help of the free-flowing liquor, all sense of control had evaporated, and in a scene reminiscent of Danville only two days earlier, mobs began looting. A crowd composed of soldiers, desperate civilians, and former slaves first gathered on South Elm Street, where they ransacked a Confederate storeroom. Quartermaster Maj. Samuel R. Chisman raced into the warehouse waving a torch and vowing to light a powder keg if the pillagers did not disperse. Convinced that he would make good on his word, the plunderers scrambled to exit the building as fast as they could.[15]

Abandoning the first warehouse, the mass swarmed the state stores on the corner of Market and Elm Streets, carting off bacon, sugar, corn, clothing, blankets, and shoes. Lacking the bravado of Chisman, the state quartermaster beseeched Beauregard for help. The general responded immediately, ordering Lt. Col. Alexander C. McAlister's North Carolinians to disperse the mob. The Tar Heels had been detached from Lee's army in February and sent south to round up deserters and haul them back to the ranks. Now they found themselves ordered to fire into the pillagers, some of whom had been their comrades only a few months prior. Yet as soon as McAlister's men had scattered the first crowd, another group of soldiers, this time men from Brig. Gen. George G. Dibrell's Division in Johnston's army, descended on the warehouses and opened fire on the North Carolinians. McAlister's command returned fire, killing a trooper from Dibrell's cavalry and wounding three more. After a few more shots, the looters fled, leaving the North Carolinians standing guard over the ransacked warehouses.[16]

The decision to fire on the pillagers, which included Confederate soldiers, spoke to the desire of Beauregard and other officers to maintain order. Just as Grant and Sherman worried about guerrillas and partisans, Confederates recognized that disbanding the rebel armies had the potential to spiral into unbridled destruction. Lee had warned Alexander that such might result if his army scattered rather than surrendered. Before departing Appomattox, multiple officers had cautioned their men against pillaging and stealing. Now only days later in Greensboro, Beauregard had authorized the use of force in order to rein in the chaos and offer some semblance of order.

Failing to secure any horses or quartermaster stores in Greensboro, McIntosh, Chamberlayne, and their small party rode southward through High Point, pressing on to Salisbury, still determined to tender their services to the Confederate cause.[17]

As McIntosh and party departed, another of Lee's escaped artillerists arrived in his hometown. "The town is in a perfect uproar—the Yankees expected every minute," James W. Albright observed. Riding through the frenzied streets, he headed first to his home. There he found his father as well as his brothers, Daniel and Bob, the latter of whom had reached home only a short time earlier, having remained with Lee's army and receiving his parole at Appomattox. "*At home once more*—no one but a soldier of 3 years knows how much these words mean," Albright wrote later that evening. But his comfort in having his family united again was quickly overshadowed by the turmoil of the city.

Amid such fear, soldiers from both Lee's and Johnston's armies continued to seek out provisions. The pillaging had ceased, Albright noted, but "goods of the army are going in every direction." Hoping to secure clothing and provisions for himself, he rode down to the quartermaster's office, where he encountered many friends and former comrades drawing rations along with shoes, socks, and blankets. But upon returning the next day, he found the quartermaster "as stingy as if he expected the war to last another three years." Despite the tightfisted quartermaster, rumors swirled through the city that Johnston was preparing to surrender.[18]

The next morning, Albright reported to General Beauregard, who still commanded Confederate forces in Greensboro. Albright told the general about the last bitter fighting in the trenches at Petersburg, of the blistering push westward, of his escape from Appomattox Station on April 8, and of his journey south to Johnston's lines. When he finished, Beauregard asked precisely where Albright had been on the Sunday of the surrender. West of Appomattox bound for Lynchburg, he responded. Beauregard shook his head. You were included in the surrender of Lee's men, he told the artillerist. Albright could not participate in military efforts in Greensboro or anywhere else. If Johnston's army was forced to evacuate the city, Albright was obligated to remain until paroled by Union forces. Just as Beauregard would use force to prevent rioting, he would uphold the honorable rules of civilized warfare. Finally acknowledging that his fight was finished, Albright went home.[19]

Countless others from Lee's army reached Johnston's lines only to receive similar news. For more than a week, Gordon McCabe, Richard Walke, and Joseph McGraw had ridden south, determined to continue the fight. Stopping occasionally to rest, without blankets or oilcloths, they were nearly delirious for want of sleep as they continued their push toward Johnston's lines. After nearly 230 miles, they reached the advance of his army on April 17 and reported for duty. "We could get literally nothing to do," McCabe wrote from Greensboro, "and furthermore were considerably disgusted to find many officers of rank very badly whipped."[20] Capt. John J. Shoemaker and approximately fifty members of Stuart's Horse Artillery were likewise refused. Turning north, they retraced their path to Lynchburg. "We started back to Old Virginia and became plain citizens once more," Shoemaker recalled.[21]

On the morning of April 17, General Johnston mounted his horse near Hillsborough and rode toward Durham Station to meet General Sherman. Stepping inside the small weatherboard farmhouse of James and Nancy Bennett, Sherman handed Johnston a telegram bearing word of Lincoln's assassination. Perspiration beaded on Johnston's forehead as he read. He knew this potentially changed everything. "Mr. Lincoln was peculiarly endeared to the soldiers," Sherman observed, and he feared that the news might unleash the worst among his troops. Johnston nodded, admitting that the situation was "extremely delicate."[22]

In language reminiscent of Grant's exchange with Lee, Sherman explained that he wanted to spare the South any further devastation. With Johnston's army outnumbered and Lee's surrendered, the Federal commander observed that capitulation would be honorable. He would therefore offer the same terms Grant had extended to Lee. Johnston demurred. While the Appomattox terms were generous, his army was not surrounded. The two armies were separated by more than four days' march. Instead, reminding Sherman of Davis's correspondence, Johnston suggested that rather than a partial suspension of hostilities, perhaps they might "arrange the terms of a permanent peace."[23]

Such terms would reach far beyond what Grant had offered Lee at Appomattox. Grant had overseen only the surrender of a single army, recognizing that peace negotiations belonged firmly under the control of civil authorities. But Sherman increasingly believed that military commanders rather than politicians would be better equipped to end the war. He told Johnston he would have to think on such terms. The Confederate general agreed but observed that he would have to consult Davis (now somewhere near Salisbury pushing south toward Charlotte). Shaking hands, the generals stood and agreed to reconvene at noon the next day.[24]

Returning to his field headquarters, Sherman sat down to write to his chief of staff, Bvt. Maj. Gen. Joseph Webster, back in New Bern. He had enjoyed a "full and frank exchange of opinions" with Johnston, he relayed, but the Confederate general needed to discuss the terms with Davis and his cabinet. Sherman assured Webster that the delay would not cost them anything. In fact, the roads were drying up, so if negotiations failed and he needed to pursue the Confederates once more, his army would make better speed. But chief on Sherman's mind was the consequence of Johnston's army disbanding with no peace settlement. "There is great danger that the Confederate armies will dissolve and fill the whole land with robbers and assassins," he observed, "and I think this is one of the difficulties that Johnston labors under. The assassination of Mr. Lincoln shows one of the elements in the rebel army, which will be almost as difficult to deal with as the main armies," he warned. Asking Webster to share these thoughts with Grant, Sherman also requested the general-in-chief to alert him if Maj. Gen. Philip Sheridan and his cavalry were on their way south from Virginia to intercept the rebels. "I don't want Johnston's army to break up in fragments," he concluded.[25]

Johnston's army was not Sherman's only worry. Returning to Raleigh by train, he discovered that word of Lincoln's murder had reached his men. Enraged soldiers gathered at the depot, shouting, "Don't let Johnston surrender!" and "Don't let the Rebels surrender!" In the confines of his diary that evening, Maj. Charles Wills of the 103rd Illinois conceded that the "army is crazy for vengeance. If we make another campaign it will be an awful one." He had heard that Sherman was to meet Johnston again that day, but he hoped the Confederate general would not surrender. He wanted one more fight in which the rebels would be thoroughly vanquished. Whatever happened, Wills believed a harsh reality awaited the errant rebels. "God pity this country if he retreats or fights us," Wills vowed.[26]

Hoping to calm his men, that evening Sherman issued Special Field Orders No. 56 officially announcing Lincoln's death. "It seems that our enemy, despairing of meeting us in open, manly warfare, begins to resort to the assassin's tools," he declared. While Sherman believed the great mass of Confederates scorned such atrocities, he nevertheless issued a stern warning to the nation's enemies: "We have met every phase which this war has assumed, and must now be prepared for it in its worst shape, that of assassins and guerrillas; but *woe* unto the people who seek to expend their wild passions in such a manner, for there is but one dread result."[27]

Sherman had long worried about irregular warfare. On April 9, even as Grant and Lee were meeting, Sherman had written of his fears about guerrillas to his wife, Ellen. While he believed the vast majority of Confederates would not wage war again if peace should come, there was a "class of young men who will never live at Peace." "Long after Lees and Johnstons Armies are beaten & scattered," he predicted, "they will band together as Highwaymen and Keep the Country in a fever, begetting a Guerrilla War."[28] News of Lincoln's assassination only exacerbated his fears.

Sherman's dread of young men at the helm of continued resistance was not unfounded. Although he had no way of knowing as much, most of those who had absconded from Appomattox and vowed to continue the fight were thirty or younger. The vast majority of Army of Northern Virginia soldiers had been born after 1836, meaning it was overwhelmingly a young man's fight.[29] But it was not the gray-haired officers who held an unshakable faith in the Confederate cause in the face of Lee's surrender, nor was it the more middling-class or impoverished farmers who remained resolute. It was those such as Thomas Rosser, Ham Chamberlayne, David McIntosh, James Albright, Charles Friend, Harry Townsend, and Gordon McCabe, who were young, were overwhelmingly of the slaveholding elite, and had come of age during the sectional crisis of the 1850s. The only world they had ever known was one of political fury revolving around slavery, of intense sectional discord and vitriol. Well-educated at institutions such as the University of Virginia or South Carolina College, they had been among the loudest proponents of secession, including Chamberlayne, who decried that the "old men were wrong" in opposing secession. "Show me a white head & a boy of twenty," he had declared in December 1860, "& I will trust the boy!"

When the war came, these young men had enlisted early, and many served as second-echelon officers.[30]

Among the ranks of the diehards in April 1865 stood John Dooley, an officer in the famed 1st Virginia. The son of an Irish immigrant and one of Richmond's richest families, Dooley enlisted in August 1862, taking his body servant with him to war. He fought at Second Manassas, Antietam, and Gettysburg, where he was wounded during Pickett's charge and captured. He spent the next nineteen months in Union prison camps, first at Fort McHenry and then Johnson's Island, where he tracked the fortunes of Lee's army. Released from prison in late February 1865, he returned to a besieged Richmond before heading to visit a fellow prisoner near Lynchburg. When he learned that Richmond had fallen and Lee surrendered, like Chamberlayne and the others he headed south to find the Confederate government and offer his services once more. "As long as I am an officer in the C[onfederate] States army I feel honour bound to follow the fortunes of Confederacy until its cause is hopeless or its hopes of success revive."[31]

Although they did not call for guerrilla war (as Sherman feared), with Confederate defeat seemingly imminent, it was the younger generation who maintained a resolve to continue the struggle.

Approaching the Bennett House with his personal staff and several of his generals on April 18, Sherman discovered that Johnston had not yet arrived. Around 2:00, Johnston finally rode up, and the generals resumed their talks. Johnston stated that he had authority to surrender all remaining Confederates in the field, but he needed some assurance that their political rights would be protected. Sherman reminded him that Lincoln's December 1863 proclamation of amnesty, which offered any soldier below the rank of colonel a complete pardon if he surrendered and took an oath of loyalty, was still in effect. Grant's terms at Appomattox had extended this offer to all officers, including Lee. This, Sherman explained, would restore their rights of citizenship. Johnston remained unsatisfied and noted that Breckinridge had ridden with him that day and was close at hand. When Sherman protested that he could negotiate only with military figures, not political ones, Johnston insisted that Breckinridge was acting only in his capacity as a general, not as the Confederate secretary of war. The Federal commander dropped his objections and sent a staff officer to find Breckinridge back near the picket line.[32]

In the confines of the small cabin, the conference continued. Negotiating for far more than Lee had dared, Johnston and Breckinridge insisted that both officers and men remained uneasy about their political status. As such, they had brought a memorandum produced by Postmaster John Reagan proposing the disbandment of all Confederate forces and a recognition of U.S. authority on condition of numerous political guarantees.[33] They all agreed that slavery was dead. There was no need to discuss that further. But the Confederates needed some promise of political rights. Sherman looked over the terms and then called for his saddlebags, from which he produced a bottle of whiskey. Breckinridge, too, poured a glass and after a short time began extolling the virtues of Reagan's terms. No, Sherman declared, they were inadmissible. Instead, thinking back to his conversation with Lincoln at City Point in March, he took pen in hand and began to write.[34]

The terms proved more than the Confederates might have hoped— and much more expansive than those offered by Grant at Appomattox. The Confederate armies "now in existence" would march to their respective state capitals where they would deposit their arms and public property in the state arsenal; existing state governments would be recognized by the executive of the United States; federal courts would be reestablished in several states; political rights would be guaranteed; and the U.S. government promised "not to disturb any of the people by reason of the late war, so long as they live in peace and quiet, abstain from acts of armed hostility, and obey the laws in existence at the place of their residences." Fully aware that he had exceeded his authority by including political provisions, Sherman concluded the memorandum of agreement with a pledge to seek the approval of "our respective principals" before the terms went into effect. The two armies would thus maintain their status quo for forty-eight hours until such authority could be attained.[35] After signing the agreement, the two commanders shook hands and departed for their respective headquarters.

Both contemporaries and historians have long speculated as to why Sherman offered political terms that exceeded his authority as a military commander. After all, he had repeatedly assured Grant that he would offer the same terms as those given at Appomattox, and he had promised his father-in-law that he would avoid political matters. Some have suggested that he wanted the glory of ending the war "by one single stroke of the pen." Others have surmised that he believed he was fulfilling Lincoln's desires for a conciliatory stance that would restore order to the South as quickly as possible through a general amnesty and the resumption of civil governments. Sherman had recently learned that Lincoln had sanctioned Maj. Gen. Godfrey Weitzel's call to allow the Virginia legislature to reconvene, even as Richmond remained occupied by Union forces. Lincoln, he believed, wished to restore home rule to the South immediately. An antebellum Whig and devoted Unionist, Sherman similarly held that the quickest way to reunite the nation was to trust the South's leaders to accept the war's results.[36]

All of these factors likely influenced Sherman. But the one he discussed the most—before the firestorm of criticism erupted from Washington condemning his terms—centered on the prospect of a continued guerrilla war. Arriving back at his headquarters that evening, Sherman sat down to write Grant and Halleck. He enclosed a copy of the agreement that he believed would "produce Peace from the Potomac to the Rio Grande" and asked that they have the new president, Andrew Johnson, endorse the copy so that he might carry out the terms. As he had done in his message to Grant the previous day, he couched his explanation in the context of irregular war. "The point to which I attach most importance," he explained, "is that the dispersion and disbandment of these armies is done in Such a manner as to prevent their breaking up into Guerilla Bands." He had agreed to the "mode and manner of the surrender of arms set forth, as it gives the States the means of repressing Guerillas which we could not expect them to do if we stript them of all arms." While he believed that most men in the South sincerely desired peace and would not resort to war again during the century, he could not help but fear the repercussions of irregular warfare. Only a few days later from his headquarters in Raleigh he repeated the same concerns to Ellen. "There is great danger of the Confederate armies breaking up into Guerillas and that is what I most fear."[37]

If the specter of guerrilla warfare motivated Grant's generous parole policy in the wake of Appomattox, it drove Sherman to offer the Confederates far more than they might have dared to expect.

David McIntosh and Ham Chamberlayne did not consider themselves guerrillas. In fact, they remained concerned that their status as officers in the Confederate army still held. On April 16, Chamberlayne had asked Col. Archer Anderson to introduce him to Breckinridge. In the retreat from Petersburg, Chamberlayne's baggage had burned and with it his captain's commission. He now sought assurance that his status as an officer would not be in dispute.[38] Several days later, McIntosh penned a letter to Jefferson Davis explaining that he had escaped on the morning of April 9 "prior to any official announcement that a surrender would be made." His reason for writing was to ensure that his standing as an officer would not be affected. Even as Johnston and Sherman were meeting at Durham Station to discuss surrender terms for the Army of Tennessee, the South Carolinian remained committed to the cause. He wanted a guarantee from the president, a man likewise on the run, that his behavior at Appomattox would not jeopardize any future promotions within the Confederate ranks. McIntosh simply could not fathom that the Confederacy was collapsing around him.[39] Instead, he and Chamberlayne rested while their horses were shod before climbing back in their saddles and turning south yet again, this time bound for Charlotte to find Davis and the remnants of the Confederate government.[40]

If McIntosh and Chamberlayne considered themselves legitimate, regular soldiers, both homebound Confederates and those poised to continue the fight recognized the threat of deserters. In Patrick County, Virginia, locals warned Harry Townsend and his party of Richmond Howitzers to be on guard for a band of deserters who had attacked both citizens and passing soldiers. "We were cautioned to be careful in our actions and language while passing through the country in which their camp was situated," he wrote on April 23.[41] The situation was no better in North Carolina. While sleeping in a grove of beech trees outside of Greensboro, the shadow of a man startled John Dooley. Jolting up, Dooley realized the night prowler was none other than a Confederate straggler. The shadow figure advanced slowly, then offered to sell him a pair of shoes. Chasing the skulker away, Dooley awoke the next morning to discover that one of his messmates had lost a leather bag containing all of his worldly possessions. "Of course I couldn't swear to the fact," Dooley conceded, "but the impression must forever remain indelibly fixed in my mind that the shoe trader of an hour previous must have been the thief. And I think I may safely defy any of your Yankees to rob more adroitly than that skulking vagabond." Dooley and other Confederates recognized that plenty of less-than-desirable characters had filled the ranks of their armies. And now that they had been set loose from any formal military control, their outrages might know no bounds, making the journey southward perilous — "perilous," Dooley explained, "because the counties through which we are to pass are said to be infested with swarms of bushwhackers who are sworn enemies of the Confederacy, being nearly all deserters from the army and living on plunder."[42] Although different from guerrillas who waged war on the United States, deserters and skulkers were likewise among those whom Sherman and Grant feared — men unbridled by the dissolution of Confederate armies who, if left unchecked, might terrorize the region and prevent the true promise of peace.

Riding into Charlotte on an unseasonably warm April 19, McIntosh and Chamberlayne sought out Brig. Gen. Martin W. Gary, then serving as

Davis's escort, to learn what the future course might hold. Having received McIntosh's query regarding his escape from Appomattox, Davis assured the artillery captain that he had the right to extricate his command at Appomattox. In fact, Davis declared, "had you been surrendered you would have been at liberty to refuse to give a parole." McIntosh and his men were "fully entitled to make your escape before being surrendered," Davis observed. Moreover, McIntosh could serve in any assignment made by a Confederate officer still in the field.[43] Although Davis and his party were bound for Augusta, Georgia, McIntosh was to report to Brig. Gen. John Echols, commanding in Charlotte.[44]

McIntosh would obey orders from his commander in chief, but first he planned to visit his Society Hill, South Carolina, home. Chamberlayne, however, would head farther south, having received official orders from General Gary, who had likewise escaped from Appomattox. Chamberlayne was to report to Secretary of War Breckinridge in Augusta. Leaving McIntosh without a goodbye, he swung up in the saddle once more, now accompanied by quartermaster Maj. Jonathan Maynard, bound for Georgia, where he would determine his next course of action on behalf of the Confederacy.[45]

Loyal Territory

Leaving Appomattox astride a dilapidated gray horse he had found after receiving his parole, Thomas Jefferson Murray Jr. had ridden north. Bound for their northern Virginia homes, he and several others from his former unit, the 17th Virginia, had survived a harrowing ferry crossing of the James River before passing through Fluvanna County and into Orange County. For some days, the dark-haired twenty-two-year-old lieutenant and his traveling companions traversed muddy roads, forded swollen streams, and camped in bushes along the roadside when no houses could be found. But soon they would shed their muddy and powder-grime-encrusted uniforms. Soon the days of marching, drilling, and sleeping in tents would be behind them. If the horse Tom Murray had acquired was any indication, perhaps his luck had improved.

But only a day's ride from home, his fortunes turned for the worse. Though he had been warned by his comrades to avoid the Federal outpost in Fauquier County, Murray felt certain that his parole papers offered protection and passage through Union lines to reach his home in Fairfax County. Grant had promised as much. But as the manhunt for Lincoln's murderers continued, the Union soldiers stationed just south of the Washington defenses thought otherwise. They immediately placed Murray under guard and escorted him to the provost marshal's office. There, debates ensued as to whether to detain him in the local jail. Pleading that he had just learned of his father's death in Fairfax County and needed desperately to attend to his family, Murray begged to go home. Two sympathetic members of the provost guard relented, but they told Murray that he remained a prisoner. He would be escorted to his home and allowed to spend one evening with his grieving mother. The following morning, U.S. soldiers returned, carting Murray off on a bumpy and jarring ride in a lumber wagon along the corduroy road to Fairfax Station, where they placed him alongside other captured Confederates all bound for Alexandria.

More bad news awaited Murray upon his arrival. Despite his parole, he and the others were hauled before acting provost marshal Capt. William Winship, where their names were recorded. From there, Union guards marched them to a large, empty room and confined them alongside some 200 or 300 other Confederates, many of them members of the 17th Virginia — local men who had likewise tried to return home. As his eyes adjusted to the darkness, Murray realized they had been taken to a military prison in the former Price, Birch & Co. slave jail on Duke Street. The son of a Fairfax attorney who had owned seven slaves in 1860, Murray and his fellow Confederates could not have escaped the indignity: men who had gone to war to protect their slave-holding nation now found themselves confined in the very pens where they previously traded in flesh.[1]

Later that evening, those prisoners with parole passes in hand (a large number had not yet been paroled) were marched back to Captain Winship. Again, Union officials recorded the prisoners' names and instructed them to hand over their passes from Appomattox. Scarcely believing their eyes, the Confederates watched as the Federals ripped apart the Appomattox paroles and began to insert their names on new blank passes. Outraged, they refused to accept the passes, one of the men declaring, "If Gen. Grant's parole is not sufficient to protect us we don't want any of your d——d safe conducts!" Ignoring their protests, the provost marshal ordered all of the commissioned officers to arrange themselves in a line then directed a sergeant to step forward with a pair of scissors. One by one, he snipped first the brass buttons from their uniforms, then the bars and stars on their collars. "This is a d——d hateful job to me," Murray claimed the sergeant whispered, "but I can't help it." Stripped of their rank and the proof that they had remained with Lee's army until the bitter end, Murray and his comrades were released into the streets with orders to return the next morning. "We were treated with a brutality and lack of manliness that we could not but contrast unfavorably with the conduct of the men to whose prowess we had been compelled to surrender." Finally, Winship released Murray and the others, sending them to their homes — under guard.[2]

The mix of paroled and unparoled rebels moving south through the Confederacy proved unsettling enough to the Union high command. But those heading north into loyal territory — especially in the wake of Lincoln's

Loyal Territory

Photograph showing a Union army guard and other men in front of a building designated Price, Birch & Co., "dealers in slaves," at 1315 Duke St., Alexandria, Virginia. The Union army used the former slave jail to house Confederate prisoners both during the war and after Appomattox, including Thomas Murray. Library of Congress Prints and Photographs Division, LC-DIG-ppmsca-11746.

assassination—generated a host of new anxieties. Chief among them were the potential legal and political consequences of Grant's magnanimous terms. Maj. Gen. Winfield Scott Hancock had first raised the issue on April 16 regarding Mosby's men. But the Union high command as well as local communities in the border North soon realized the problem extended far beyond the Gray Ghost. What was to be done with Confederates from loyal states such as Maryland and Kentucky? Should they be allowed to return to communities that considered their actions treasonous? Would they also have to take the oath of allegiance to return home? If they refused, what would happen to them? The degree to which Grant's terms would serve to ease the defeated Confederates back into civilian life and protect them from charges of treason remained woefully unclear.

Maj. Gen. E. O. C. Ord's decision to send paroled Confederates from Richmond to the North in the days immediately following the surrender had only exacerbated an already tense atmosphere near the outskirts of Washington. Some of Lee's men who arrived in D.C. and Maryland had resided in the region before casting their lot with the Confederacy. Still others had traveled north, eager to catch railroads to their homes in West Virginia, Tennessee, Texas, and other locales in the southern states.[3] In communities still reeling from Lincoln's assassination, both loyal citizens and Union officials in the capital region were increasingly aggravated by the large number of rebel prisoners who were arriving daily—most still in uniform.

In Washington, the mood remained both somber and tense. Throngs of men and women donning black tearfully waited their turn to pass by the president's body lying in state at the White House while Union troops patrolled the city. "The streets swarmed like beehives," Brig. Gen. Porter Alexander wrote upon arriving in the city from Virginia. "The passion & excitement of the crowds were so great that anyone on the street, recognized merely as a Confederate, would have been instantly mobbed & lynched." Thankfully, Alexander had purchased a civilian coat and pants in Richmond along with a U.S. army private's overcoat, dyed black instead of blue. "But, to a close observer, such a coat would seem particularly suspicious," he admitted. Already in the city, he went immediately to the Brazilian minister, who said he had no authority to send anyone directly to Brazil, which remained the last slaveholding nation. Instead, Alexander would have to travel to New York to speak with the consul. "He said that," the artillerist observed, "I am sure, just to get rid of me. He seemed to be actually afraid lest my being in his house might bring a mob on him." After securing a pass to travel north from none other than Grant's headquarters, Alexander worried that his dyed overcoat had given him away. Convinced that he was being tailed by a detective, he headed for the Baltimore & Ohio station, where he boarded a train to New York, arriving on Wednesday, April 19, still bent on making his way to Brazil.[4]

Alexander's ability to navigate the streets of Washington without consequence proved exceptional. In the days after the assassination, hundreds of Lee's soldiers in and around Washington—including those just across the Potomac River in Virginia—found themselves imprisoned. On April 18, the provost marshal for the Defenses North of the Potomac issued orders that all paroled prisoners of war desiring transportation, as well as those held in Alexandria (which was within Union lines) but claiming residence in Baltimore, should be sent to department headquarters for "safe keeping." Paroled or not, having joined the Confederate army, these men could not "claim protection from the government and must be returned south" beyond Union lines. During subsequent days, U.S. officers forwarded hundreds of Lee's men to prisons in and around the District of Columbia. Some proved to be unparoled rebels who surrendered themselves in the hopes of acquiring the parole that had so freely been given elsewhere in Virginia. On April 17, Capt. William A. Barnes and five of his men from the 17th Virginia arrived at Fairfax Court House seeking paroles. Immediately, the Union officer in command sent them to a jail in Alexandria, either the Cotton Factory or the old slave pen, before they were forwarded once more to Washington. Perhaps most ironic, with them traveled John Brown, listed as a "colored servant" by a U.S. provost marshal. Brown, too, would be held indefinitely.[5]

If those who had not been paroled might have expected to be detained upon entering Union lines, like Tom Murray, those who had surrendered at Appomattox were shocked to realize how little their passes guaranteed. Capt. Oscar Hinrichs, an engineer from Lt. Gen. Jubal A. Early's command, had received his parole at Appomattox. Arriving in Washington via a steamship from City Point on the morning of April 18, Hinrichs borrowed money to purchase clean underwear and a civilian suit before proceeding to the provost marshal, where he expected merely to register his name. From there, he planned to travel by train to Baltimore and then on to his family in New York City. Instead, Hinrichs found himself delayed "against all expectations" before being sent to the Soldiers' Rest, a waystation for Union soldiers near the Baltimore & Ohio station. On the nineteenth, he could only marvel that his parole had not lived up to its promise. "Remain in prison today," he scribbled in his pocket diary. "In the afternoon a whole negro regiment arrives, which embellishes our situation," he wrote.[6]

Lt. Channing M. Smith of the 1st Battalion Virginia Infantry likewise headed to prison rather than to his home. Bound for his Parkersburg, West Virginia, residence, he made his way first from Appomattox to Richmond, where he registered with the provost marshal on April 15. From there, he headed to City Point and then to Fort Monroe, boarding a steamer to Washington, where he planned to take the train west. Upon arriving in Washington, like Hinrichs, he again registered with the provost marshal, but from there he, too, was detained at Soldiers' Rest, which he described as "an awful place." The following morning, April 25, he and a group of others were placed on railroad cars along with "a very strong guard" and shipped to Alexandria, Virginia, where Union guards held them at the former Mount Vernon Cotton Mill, now the Washington Street Prison. This was a far cry from his experience upon leaving Appomattox, when soldiers from the Army of the James had shared their rations. Now detained in a room with seventeen officers from the South, Smith marveled at how his situation had changed since April 12. "Who ever heard of 'Paroled Prisoners' being confined in prison & not allowed to go to their houses," he wondered in his journal. Throughout late April and into early May, at least 385 other Army of Northern Virginia soldiers would find themselves detained at the Washington Street Prison, some for days, some for weeks. The only way these paroled rebels would be allowed to leave was to take the oath of allegiance to the United States. Refusing to disavow his loyalty to the Confederacy, Smith remained imprisoned.[7]

Still, Union forces continued to hunt Confederates who had not yet willingly surrendered. On April 20, Union troops tracked down James Dickey of the 8th Virginia Cavalry at his home in Vienna and arrested him. That same evening, members of the 13th New York Cavalry found Capt. J. Owen Berry of the 8th Virginia Infantry at his Fairfax home. Having refused to seek a parole of his own accord, the provost marshal sent Berry to the prison at Johnson's Island. Perhaps local Unionists had informed the cavalrymen of the rebels' whereabouts, or maybe scouting parties were searching homes of known Confederates. Regardless of the circumstances, the efforts to find and detain any of Lee's men who refused to willingly surrender underscored the urgent concern that any future uprising be prevented.[8]

Each day, more and more rebels filed off the steamers at Baltimore's harbor, increasing Bvt. Brig. Gen. William W. Morris's anxiety. He remained at a loss as to what to do with their ever-mounting presence — and their demands for free transportation along railroads to their homes in Kentucky, Tennessee, and states farther south. Dashing off a telegram to the War Department on April 18, he requested orders, uncertain about how to proceed.[9]

The problem, however, soon fell upon Maj. Gen. Lew Wallace, who resumed command of the Middle Department (part of Hancock's Middle Military Division) later that day. Sailing into the harbor, Wallace became outraged at the sight of so many rebels who clearly had ignored Morris's April 15 instructions about wearing their uniforms. "The number is increasing rapidly," he fumed to a member of Hancock's staff, "and their presence is exceedingly obnoxious to the loyal citizens." On top of this, rumors of secret meetings among rebel officers and soldiers abounded — rumors that had to be taken seriously in the wake of Lincoln's murder.[10]

An incensed Wallace pleaded with Grant to provide answers to the seemingly inescapable problem. He had learned of secret meetings throughout the city and other portions of the Middle Department "relative to the rebel officer's [sic] and soldiers, who have returned to their homes under the terms of Lee's surrender." Wallace proved especially primed to take a firm stance against their perceived threat. As a lawyer and Republican politician from Indiana, what he lacked in professional military training he made up for with his argumentative nature, which had sparked conflicts with Grant, Maj. Gen. Henry Halleck, Secretary of War Edwin Stanton, and even Indiana governor Oliver Morton, making him an unlikely candidate for further field command after the summer of 1862. But Lincoln understood both the need to appease Hoosiers and Wallace's political savvy, and in March 1864 he had appointed Wallace to take control of the Middle Department headquartered in Baltimore, where Wallace quickly realized that the department was swarming with rebel sympathizers and spies. By July, his wife concurred, noting that the "city is rebel to the core."[11]

That fall, Maryland voters had prepared to vote on a new constitution that would abolish slavery and disenfranchise Confederate sympathizers. "Henceforth, Maryland is to be ruled by her loyal citizens alone," declared a Cumberland newspaper. "The rights of citizenship, which [rebels] have betrayed, the privileges which they have abused, will be stripped from them today," the paper continued, "and in all future time they will stand forth as monuments of the punishment which a loyal people inflicts upon its enemies and betrayers." With every intention of aiding the loyal Marylanders, Wallace ordered investigations and arrests of suspicious persons and expelled those he deemed disloyal, including an alleged female spy and her children.[12] With Wallace's successful management of the election, voters approved the constitution by a thin margin, 30,174 to 29,799 (50.31 percent to 49.69 percent). But only those who would take an oath of loyalty were permitted to cast ballots. Confederate sympathizers argued they had been unconstitutionally disqualified and within days challenged the results in court. Both the Maryland Court of Appeals and the Superior Court promptly dismissed the petitions.[13]

With this in mind, Wallace turned to several Maryland judges for legal guidance in April 1865. Had a citizen of Maryland who left the state and joined the rebel army forfeited his residency?, he asked.[14] Judge Robert N. Martin of the Superior Court responded in the affirmative. "Without a particle of doubt," Martin wrote, "one who was formerly a citizen of Maryland, lost his residence in Maryland and was to be treated as a non resident by connecting himself with the Rebel Army." Although a dubious interpretation of the law, this was all Wallace needed. He forwarded the opinion to Grant. Invoking his legal training, Wallace stated that he could "see nothing under the law" which "precludes the state authorities from prohibitory action against returning rebels and soldiers." He proposed asking Maryland governor Augustus Bradford to issue a proclamation forbidding rebel soldiers and officers from returning, under penalty of prosecution for treason against the state. "Such a mode," he explained, "cannot be constructed as a molestation of the paroled men by the U.S. authorities." Grant would not be breaking his promise to Lee, he assured the general-in-chief.[15]

With similar inquiries pouring in from subordinates in the Shenandoah Valley and Nashville, coupled with the situation at Richmond and Fort Monroe, Grant grew increasingly frustrated. His terms had intended to get the rebel soldiers home as quickly as possible, but it was becoming ever more apparent that the terms had generated more questions than answers.[16]

Grant turned to Hancock's query regarding paroled men *from* the loyal states.[17] On April 17, he had concluded that it was better to have Mosby's and Col. Elijah White's men in Maryland "as paroled prisoners of war than at large as guerillas." But now, even as Wallace was gathering legal opinions to make his case, Grant changed course. In a telegram to Hancock on April 19, he informed the general whose command straddled the states of Virginia, West Virginia, and Maryland that "all who claim homes in states that never passed ordinances of secession have [for]feited them and can only return on compliance with the Amnesty proclamation." To be sure his subordinate understood, he put it more explicitly: "Maryland, Kentucky, Delaware, and Missouri are such states. They may return to West Va. on their paroles." Rushing to ensure that all knew of Grant's decision, Hancock ordered his adjutant to distribute copies of the order to his subordinates throughout the Middle Military Division.[18]

Grant offered no explanation as to how or why he had come to his conclusion that paroled rebels from the loyal states could no longer claim to be residents—and by extension, citizens—of these states. But it complimented his orders prohibiting paroled rebels of the so-called Confederacy from traveling through loyal states. Combined, these orders intended to keep Confederate sympathizers out of loyal territory—a problem Grant had not considered at Appomattox. Equally important, the orders would not violate the terms of surrender that allowed rebels to return to their homes. As rebels, they had relinquished claim to their homes in these loyal states.

In Baltimore, Wallace wasted no time in implementing Grant's directives—and he added a few of his own for good measure. Elaborating on General Morris's April 15 declaration, Wallace observed that the gray uniform worn by "certain young men, said to be students, has become so offensive to loyal soldiers and civilians, that it is prohibited in this Department."[19] In addition to refusing Confederates passage through Maryland, he forbade provost marshals from issuing passes for anyone (loyal or disloyal) to travel to Richmond.[20] But did Grant's new conditions apply to members of Lee's army who had surrendered and already returned home to loyal states? Wallace asked his superior, Hancock, if he could he remove such men from the Middle Department. No, Hancock replied. He was not to interfere with them. Hancock could not withdraw the terms he had offered them. State authorities, though, he observed, might make different decisions.[21]

While Union generals attempted to prevent rebels from returning to loyal regions, Unionist civilians proved just as desirous of knowing who among them harbored Confederate sympathies. By the third week of April, local newspapers began publishing lists of returning prisoners. Among the twenty-seven names published on April 24 was Thomas Murray—recently released from the old slave pen in Alexandria.[22] Yet some newspapers went beyond merely publishing names. A Washington paper reported that among the paroled prisoners who had returned was Dr. Cornelius Boyle. "He is said, while in the rebel army, to have shown uniformly great bitterness if not positive cruelty towards Washingtonians captured by the rebels." Confederates— even paroled ones—would not be easily welcomed back into the fold.[23]

If he was not already increasingly frustrated with the situation, a little after four o'clock on Friday, April 21, Grant received Sherman's letter detailing the terms he had offered General Johnston. Just that morning, Lincoln's funeral train had departed Washington on its long journey back to Springfield, Illinois, and now Grant held in his hand terms that proved terribly troubling, especially in light of the assassination. He would have to speak to Secretary Stanton at once.[24]

At seven o'clock that evening, Grant and Stanton met at the War Department and immediately decided that the entire cabinet must be called. Within the hour, all but Secretary of State William H. Seward, who still lay grievously wounded from the April 14 attack, had arrived, along with President Andrew Johnson. An irate Stanton asked Grant to read Sherman's terms to the group. When Grant finished, Stanton, barely containing his rage, rattled off a flurry of objections. Sherman, he intoned, had no authority to enter into such an agreement and conceded as much when he sent his terms to Washington for endorsement (Grant had done no such thing at Appomattox). The document, Stanton insisted, was "a practical acknowledgment of the rebel government." It would enable the rebels to reestablish slavery and reclaim their confiscated lands, perhaps even relieve the rebels of all "pains and penalties" for their crimes. Foreshadowing concerns that would grow in the coming days, Stanton feared that Sherman's agreement might call into question the existence of loyal state governments, most notably that of West Virginia. Above all, and underscoring Stanton's and others' fear of continued warfare, the secretary pointed out that Sherman's agreement "placed arms and munitions of war in the hands of the rebels at their respective capitols [*sic*], which might be used as soon as the armies of the United States were disbanded and used to conquer and subdue the loyal states." The terms were "no basis of true and lasting peace" but instead "relieved rebels from the pressure of our victories and left them in condition to renew their efforts to overthrow the United States government."[25] Even in the wake of Appomattox, the threat of war still loomed.

Stanton's fear that the Sherman-Johnston agreement was "a practical acknowledgment of the rebel government" struck at one of the most fundamental legal question of the war: had the eleven seceded states engaged in war, or in insurrection? Or put another way, had the Confederacy become a separate nation, as it claimed?[26] Were Confederates to be treated as enemy belligerents—as foreigners waging war against the United States? If so, they were subject to international laws of war, and individuals could not be prosecuted for treason. If not, then Confederates were still citizens protected by the Constitution and immune from seizure of property under the Confiscation Acts. Perhaps most importantly, they would be considered insurrectionists and therefore were eligible for the death penalty.[27] Sherman's terms might settle the question in the South's favor, thereby undermining the legality of emancipation and confiscation of land. And more so than Grant's terms, which promised that Lee's *soldiers* would be left alone so long as they observed the law of the land, Sherman's agreement might prevent *any* rebel from being held accountable for crimes against the United States.

After Stanton finished his diatribe, the cabinet agreed that Grant should inform Sherman that the terms had not been approved and that hostilities should resume at the earliest moment. Not content to wire instructions, President Johnson ordered Grant to proceed immediately to Sherman's headquarters and take command. At 10:30 that evening, Grant dictated a message to Sherman informing him Johnson had rejected the agreement. As Stanton had commanded, Grant included a copy of the March 3 telegram from Lincoln, which had instructed Grant not "to decide, discuss, or confer upon any political question" in his dealings with Lee. "The rebels know well the terms upon which they can have peace and just where negociations [sic] can commence, namely: when they lay down their Arms and submit to the laws of the United States," Grant reminded him. Sherman's job was not to adjudicate such political terms but to force a military capitulation. After dispatching his response, at midnight Grant boarded a steamer bound for North Carolina.[28]

The swift response by Johnson's cabinet served as a reminder that generals in the field were but an arm of the executive; they had no authority to decide on political and civil questions.[29] Not content to lambaste the general in private, Stanton publicly rebuked Sherman in a memorandum he fired off to the *New York Times* detailing the cabinet's objections and implying that the general's actions had amounted to insubordination and perhaps even treason.[30]

The next morning, April 22, Stanton remained irate. Even as he sent Grant south to demand Sherman offer the same terms extended to Lee at Appomattox, Stanton began to question Grant's terms. Would they—should they—be upheld? Turning to Attorney General James Speed, he implored Speed to examine the terms of capitulation between Grant and Lee. A successful trial lawyer before the war, Stanton wondered about the limits of the terms. He asked Speed to address three questions. First, could former residents of Washington who left to serve the Confederacy as rebel officers return to their homes in the city? Second, could former residents who served in the Confederate civil service return to Washington? Finally, were Confederate officers who appeared in public in the loyal states while wearing their rebel uniforms engaging in a "fresh act of hostility on their part to the United States," and if so, could the United States treat them as "avowed enemies of the government"?[31]

Stanton had asked Speed for an official opinion that all government officials, military and civilian, would be compelled to enforce. As members of the executive branch, attorneys general provided the legal justification for presidential initiatives while simultaneously acting as impartial guardians of basic law. By the spring of 1865, previous attorneys general had concluded that their opinions were quasi-judicial and "binding upon all other members of the government." Any government official who went against a ruling would be charged with disregarding officially pronounced law.[32]

Answering the secretary later that same day, Speed offered his official opinion. He began by explaining that the president performed two functions of the government—as commander in chief of the military and as a civilian

Attorney General James Speed. Brady-Handy Photograph Collection, Library of Congress Prints and Photographs Division, LC-DIG-cwpbh-00969.

leader. It was only as the government's civil head that the president possessed the power of pardon—a power that could not be delegated. Grant had acted by Lincoln's authority, but only as it related to military matters. He had no authority from the president to confer amnesty to surrendered soldiers. Grant's authority extended only to military issues, Speed observed, a "fact to be well known" to the Confederates with whom he made the agreement.[33]

Given this limited scope of authority, the legal question was not whether Grant *could* approve paroles that would allow rebels to return and reside in loyal communities; rather, the question was whether the general *had* granted such permission. Citing the *Prize Cases* (1863), which had established the president's authority to proclaim a blockade against the Confederacy, Speed explained that the Supreme Court had ruled that rebels were belligerents within a clearly defined territory. The Confederacy was not a "loose, unorganized insurrection, without defined boundary," but had clearly defined boundaries, marked as they were "by lines of bayonets, which can only be crossed by force." Persons residing south of those lines were to be treated as enemies (under this interpretation, no Unionists lived in the Confederate states). More importantly, Speed maintained, the same held true for residents of the loyal states who crossed this boundary and offered their services to the Confederate armies. In becoming belligerents, they had forfeited their homes in loyal states. If the Supreme Court's decision was not enough, Speed turned next to the laws of war. Citing Emmerich de Vattel, he explained that Appomattox had witnessed the capitulation of Lee's army, not merely a truce. In a truce, sovereigns might prevent enemies from entering their territory. It followed, then, that the rights under a capitulation should prove no less stringent. Again, he reiterated that all persons within enemy boundaries had forfeited their residences in loyal territory. Therefore, when Grant gave Lee's paroled soldiers permission to return to their homes, it did not include homes in loyal states.[34]

Speed's response to Stanton's next question followed the same logic. Individuals in the civil service of the rebellion were not embraced by the terms of the surrender of Lee's army (and therefore could not return to their homes in Washington). To Stanton's final question, Speed referenced the first: if rebel officers and soldiers could not return to loyal states, they certainly had no right to wear their uniforms in any of the loyal states. "They have as much right to bear the traitors' flag through the streets of a loyal city as to wear a traitor's garb," he observed. Those who dared do so were violating their paroles and therefore could be arrested and detained.[35] Prohibiting the rebel uniform offered one small measure aiming to make visual displays of disloyalty a crime.

Secretary Stanton promptly sent Speed's opinion to every department and district commander as General Orders No. 73. Speed's legal opinion now stood as a military order. The U.S. Army would be charged with enforcing the measures.[36]

But it was not enough to convey the policy only to Union forces. Just as Stanton had publicly shamed Sherman in leaking to the press the surrender terms the general had offered Johnston, the secretary now made sure that the entire nation was aware of Speed's opinion. On April 24, the opinion appeared in newspapers from coast to coast. Washington's *Evening Star* heartily endorsed Speed's interpretation. Even prior to the attorney general's opinion, the paper had maintained that the "ex-Washingtonians," as it styled them, were "apostates having voluntarily disfranchised themselves here." The paper rejoiced that the decision would relieve loyal citizens "from a dangerous element in our midst," thereby "averting the danger of such serious breaches of the peace as were threatened had these fellows appeared here again wearing their old plantation airs of insolence and swagger."[37]

Union generals rushed to enforce the order. In Norfolk, Maj. Gen. George H. Gordon immediately ordered provost marshals in the District of Eastern Virginia to arrest any rebel still wearing his gray uniform. This "badge of rebellious service," Gordon later wrote, "was so offensive to the eyes of Union men, that I felt constrained to suppress it upon its first appearance."[38] From his headquarters in Baltimore, General Wallace wasted no time in applying the policy to the Middle Department. He had already detained approximately 100 rebel officers and enlisted men, all of whom had previously been paroled. Holding them under guard, he sought permission to ship them back south to Fort Monroe.[39] Next, he turned his attention to any Maryland rebels who had returned to their homes, ordering their immediate arrest and detainment. He directed his officers "to carefully and rigorously execute" these orders in respect to "all Rebel officers, soldiers and citizens discovered in their department." But he was not content to sit and wait for Confederates to turn themselves in; rather, he issued a circular appealing for information from "loyal citizens in ferreting out offenders," a practice that proved a "prolific source of blackmailing" as informants were frequently bought off.[40]

Accounts coming from Virginia of violence and destruction committed by Lee's men in former Confederate territory exacerbated Marylanders' fears. On April 21, the schooner *Ocean Wave* anchored along the Warwick

River about eighteen miles from Fort Monroe went up in flames. A Washington newspaper reported that paroled soldiers from Lee's army were presumed to be the culprits. Having been sent to their homes in counties bordering the James, Elizabeth, and Nansemond Rivers, they were said to be "prowling around in squads, intent upon some mischief." But it was not local men alone presumed to be committing these acts. Despite the best efforts by military authorities, the paper noted that "large numbers of these prisoners, unable to go North by reason of an order recently issued by the Secretary of War, are scattered all over Old Point," committing "acts of violence and desperation."[41]

The southern Maryland counties of Prince George's, Charles, and St. Mary's were of particular concern to Unionists. Rumor had it that Lincoln's assassins had been harbored there by Confederate sympathizers, and rebel soldiers had reportedly murdered a Captain Watkins in St. Mary's. Fearing that the locals might continue to harbor both rebel soldiers and guerrillas, the Union army established posts in each of the counties to prevent any more disloyal demonstrations.[42] Across the Chesapeake Bay, citizens of Talbot County had no problem in voicing their animosity toward the rebels. "They return with an air as defiant and pompous as though they were perfect heroes and had the heads of the Government under their immediate control," observed a local newspaper. "We cannot expect that outlaws, murderers and freebooters have any self-respect, consequently," the paper continued; they needed to be taught "that they have been conquered." Echoing the language of jurists and Union military officials, the paper declared that "they have no 'rights' here; that word belongs entirely to rebels [in] rebel States. This is not their residence."[43] Just as Grant and Speed had formally declared, the loyal citizens of Maryland maintained that the Appomattox terms did not apply within their state lines.

Some civilians turned to the federal government to prevent Lee's men from returning to their communities. On April 24, the Baltimore City Council requested that General Wallace close "disloyal churches" and formally protested the homecoming of any Confederates—paroled or not—"believing, as we do, their presence in our midst will be a constant source of irritation, fraught with the deadliest mischief."[44] Twenty citizens of Frederick turned to President Johnson. If the "scoundrels" of Lee's army who had "thrice invaded their native State to pillage, burn, and devastate property" were allowed to return and "impose their hated presence on the loyal men of Maryland," there would be "anything but peace." The previous year, Jubal Early's forces had threatened to raze the city if the residents failed to pay a ransom. But they had endured other atrocities of war: their horses and cattle had been stolen, their fields had been laid to waste, and dwellings and barns had been burned, reducing hundreds of loyal residents to poverty. "For these reasons," they wrote, "it is utterly impossible for us at present to tolerate these returning, but unrepentant traitors." To prevent public disorder, they asked the president to issue a general order prohibiting all rebels from returning. If he did not, they warned, "violence and mob law will be the only resources of an exasperated people."[45]

Not waiting for a response from Johnson, the Frederick Unionists took matters into their own hands, forming a committee to purge their communities of traitors. Groups of Unionists in Harford County and the Eastern Shore county of Talbot followed suit, as did those in Carroll County, where a formerly enslaved man named Menellis Gassaway declared that there were so many Union men "that it was dangerous for whites in some places to say they were Rebels."[46] On April 25, the "loyal citizens of Cumberland" in Allegany County formed a "committee of vigilance and safety" of twenty-five members pledging to arrest any returning rebel soldiers and turn them over to the authorities.[47]

Vigilance committees drew from the precedent of resistance to royal authority in the 1770s. But they had more immediate predecessors in the 1850s and the war. In the wake of the Fugitive Slave Act, abolitionists had organized vigilance committees to prevent slaveholders in their quest to capture and return runaway slaves. They legitimized their efforts to resist federal laws by invoking the language of "preserving law and liberty." Maintaining order, abolitionists had insisted, was a justifiable reason to thwart unjust laws compelling northerners to participate in the capture and return of absconded slaves.[48]

Such groups, however, did not confine themselves to the free states. In the wake of John Brown's 1859 raid, communities throughout the South formed committees of vigilance in response to the "recent lawless aggression at Harper's Ferry by a band of deluded and fanatical abolitionists." In Amherst County, Virginia, participants in a public meeting instructed the committee to watch for and expel "from the borders of our county all strange persons who may come amongst us under suspicious circumstances," including "emissaries" plotting "similar outrages in our midst."[49] In the weeks prior to the 1860 presidential election, former governor Henry Wise implicitly invoked the Revolution in his call for the creation of committees of safety replete with "minutemen" in every Virginia county should Lincoln be elected. Following the election, vigilance committees outside Richmond scrutinized

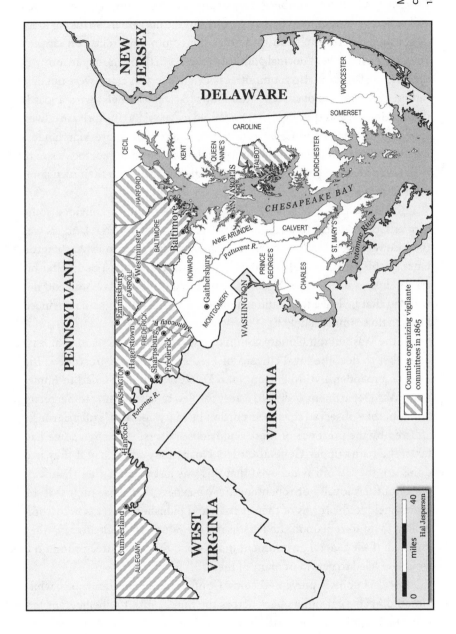

Maryland
counties,
1865.

Counties organizing vigilante
committees in 1865

miles

Hal Jespersen

passersby for strangers, detaining those whose identity proved questionable. Throughout the spring of 1861, towns and cities from Virginia to Alabama organized committees of public safety, charged with appointing home guards and policing communities in search of "disloyal" individuals. Invoking long-established Anglo-American traditions, the committees relied on citizens who might circumvent normal political processes in the name of patriotism.[50]

The post-Appomattox committees of vigilance, therefore, were not new but the continuation of citizens attempting to establish their own standards of behavior.[51] It was this logic that took hold in Maryland in April 1865. Even though both Speed and Grant now agreed that Confederate Marylanders who had not taken the oath of loyalty could not return home, the desire to maintain order compelled Unionists strongholds to look to their own communities for protection.

The mere threat of such groups could be enough to convince some former Confederates to abandon hopes of returning to Maryland, as was the case with Bob Heck. A onetime resident of Boonsboro in Washington County, the paroled rebel returned to the town on April 25. Soon after his arrival, however, the local vigilance committee came to his home and demanded that he leave within fifteen minutes. Whatever was said convinced Heck to do so immediately.[52]

If the Washington County committee succeeded in persuading at least one rebel to flee, the loyal citizens of Frederick remained frustrated. The local commander, Bvt. Maj. Gen. John D. Stevenson, had failed to implement War Department orders to arrest paroled rebels. Writing to Secretary Stanton, they observed that their portion of Maryland was "still grievously afflicted by the presence of these obnoxious traitors." Although some had taken the oath (under General Orders No. 73 they could stay if they had done so), the Unionists believed that this was just a ruse rather than "evidence of their loyalty or repentance." "We expect that these men shall be strictly held to the terms of their paroles and punished for treason by compelling them to remain in the Paradise of the Southern Confederacy," they quipped. If the federal government did not act, the committee promised it would be "glad to get rid of many of them."[53]

Local Unionists prevented some Confederates from returning, while Union officers sent others back across the border into the belligerent territory of Virginia. At least a handful of rebels experienced harsher reprisals. On April 24, Noble J. Thomas reported to the D.C. provost marshal's office and registered as a paroled prisoner. Four days later, the local police arrested him near the Baltimore Street Depot. The charge: treason. Prior to the war,

Thomas served as a lieutenant in the metropolitan police before joining the Confederate army as a captain and assistant quartermaster in Wise's Brigade. He had surrendered with the remainder of Lee's army at Appomattox and returned to Washington. When some of his former colleagues heard of his arrival, they sought his arrest. Thomas proved not just any rebel. At a hearing before a justice of the peace (not military authorities), witnesses testified that he had acted as a spy and an informer, pointing out Union men to Confederate authorities in Alexandria prior to its occupation by Union troops. One witness charged that Thomas had incited a crowd to hang him. The testimony proved enough for the justice to remand Thomas to jail to await his sentence.[54]

While Thomas found himself at the mercy of civil courts, Lewis Webb of the 1st Maryland Light Artillery was held by military officials. Webb had been paroled at Appomattox and detained by the provost marshal of Alexandria for several days. Upon his release he had reached his mother's Baltimore home on April 21 and promptly registered with the Middle Department as required. But he arrived in the harbor city as Wallace's frustration continued to mount. On April 25, Wallace issued General Orders No. 87, fully implementing Speed's opinion as military order within his lines. "All rebel officers, soldiers and citizens discovered in this Department in violation of any of the provisions of said General Orders must be immediately arrested and held in confinement," Wallace commanded. The next day, Union soldiers swept the city. Among those hauled in was Webb.[55]

These instances underscored the degree to which the paroles failed to provide the protection that Lee and his soldiers expected — an expectation without precedent in the long history of paroles. Never before had a parole been interpreted in such sweeping terms. But Grant's addition of the phrase "not to be disturbed by United States authority" had led Confederates and many U.S. officers to understand the paroles as a blanket amnesty.[56] Grant's changing orders, Speed's opinion, and the actions of local communities, however, all challenged the extent to which paroling ensured that the federal government would not interfere in Confederates' lives so long as they went home and broke no laws.

Just as Grant's Appomattox terms had led to unforeseen problems, applying Speed's opinion presented a host of new quandaries. The same day Union soldiers arrested Webb, General Wallace wrote to Washington inquiring as to what he should do with all the detained rebels. Because Baltimore was under martial law, the men could be held indefinitely without charges. But this meant feeding them. To send them away required transportation, for which he had no authority to order. Nor did he know whether he was to send them south to a point in the Confederate lines or let them go north. Some desired to take the oath of allegiance under Lincoln's amnesty proclamation — the one act that ostensibly allowed them to travel anywhere. But was this permissible? Or even advisable? "The feeling here against returning rebels is so bitter that to avoid collisions & bloodshed I am compelled to act continuously and arrest rather than let them loose," he wrote. Given the hostility and the ever-mounting problem of dealing with the returning rebels, he pleaded with the War Department to prevent any more from coming into Maryland, a problem that might well grow if the men of Johnston's army likewise put down their arms.[57]

10

Men on Parole Are
Bound in Honor

On April 24, Grant arrived in Raleigh to oversee Johnston's surrender. While there, he wrote his wife, Julia, describing the North Carolina capital as "a very beautiful place" where nothing had been destroyed and locals desperately desired peace. Elsewhere on the journey, he had witnessed grim devastation. "The suffering that must exist in the South the next year, even with the war ending now will be beyond conception," he wrote. He agreed that some of the slaveholding political leaders should be punished, but he hoped the bloodshed might soon end. "People who talk now of further retaliation and punishment, except of the political leaders, either do not conceive of the suffering endured already or they are heartless and unfeeling."[1] Grant had vacillated between elation, rage, and empathy in the past two weeks. But what he desired more than anything was peace.

Determined not to overshadow his trusted subordinate and in spite of Secretary of War Stanton's demands, Grant refused to meet with Johnston. Instead, he gave Sherman strict instructions to end the truce and demand Johnston surrender in accordance with the terms offered at Appomattox. Johnston, however, pushed back, observing that the Appomattox terms had proven inadequate. "The disbanding of General Lee's army has afflicted this country with numerous bands having no means of subsistence but robbery," he replied. Sherman received Johnston's message early on the morning of April 26, but given Grant's and Stanton's response, he knew he could offer nothing more. For a third time in a week, he boarded a train to Durham Station prepared to deny the Confederate general's request.[2]

As the two met again in Bennett's farmhouse, Johnston persisted in his objections. His men needed to be able to protect themselves on their way home—and to get home. Unable to reach agreement, Sherman summoned Maj. Gen. John Schofield for advice. The primary surrender document should be identical to the Appomattox terms, Schofield observed. But they could draft a separate document specifying Johnston's supplemental terms. The six additional terms included several of the provisions that Grant had offered Lee on the morning of April 10 (including those of Special Field Orders No. 73): soldiers could retain their private horses, and field transportation would be loaned to Confederates. But several were either more specific or went beyond Grant's provisions because of the experiences related by Lee's men as they passed through Johnston's camps. Most of Johnston's men hailed from western states and faced a long journey home. The second article, therefore, allowed each Confederate brigade to retain one-seventh of its small arms while its troops marched to their respective state capitals to deposit their arms. The fourth article specified troops from Arkansas and Texas (ostensibly those farthest from their homes) would be transported by water from Mobile or New Orleans. After discussing these terms, Sherman turned over the proceedings to Schofield and departed.[3]

Remarkably, authorities in Washington did not object to the provision allowing Confederate brigades to retain one-seventh of their small arms.[4] It is likely that Grant had not read the supplemental terms when he telegraphed Halleck at 10:00 P.M. on April 26 announcing that Johnston had surrendered "on the basis agreed upon between Lee and myself for the Army of Northern Virginia."[5] Perhaps more surprising is the fact that no element of Attorney General Speed's opinion appeared in the Durham Station terms. Why was there no provision forbidding the paroled men from traveling through the loyal states to reach their homes? Why no provision prohibiting men from loyal states from returning to their homes? (Several units from Kentucky and Maryland served in the Army of Tennessee.) Grant certainly knew about the attorney general's opinion by the time he arrived in Raleigh. Sherman should have likewise received a copy of Stanton's General Orders No. 73 implementing Speed's opinion. But the general order applied regardless of the surrender terms. Sherman did not have to include such provisions. They were already in force.

Johnston's men were not the only Confederate soldiers in North Carolina. Those from Lee's army who had escaped Appomattox had gathered in

Men on Parole Are Bound in Honor

Greensboro and the surrounding area hoping to offer their services to the Army of Tennessee. Turned away by Johnston and Beauregard, soldiers such as James W. Albright finally decided to seek out paroles.[6] Having done so, Albright approached a Federal commander and asked permission to reopen his printing office of Sterling, Campbell, & Albright. The next day, the Union officer returned, agreeing that Albright could reopen the shop, but not the bookstore, on the condition that Albright print parole passes for Johnston's men. Supplied with paper, Albright and his brother Bob set to work.[7] A more unlikely scenario seems hard to imagine: two Confederate brothers, one having escaped from Appomattox and the other having surrendered there, tasked with printing the parole passes for nearly 37,000 Confederates in the Army of Tennessee.[8]

Now men from both Johnston's and Lee's armies drifted across the North Carolina piedmont. Like Sherman, Governor Zebulon D. Vance worried that the disbanding of the Confederacy's two largest armies might unleash bands of soldiers "disposed to do violence to persons and property" in his state. Even before Johnston's army had been paroled, Confederate soldiers had looted warehouses in Greensboro. In an effort to curtail any further destruction, he issued an order on April 28 commanding all soldiers passing through North Carolina to "abstain from any and all acts of lawlessness." He cautioned them against "assembling together in towns and cities" and urged all to return to their homes as quickly as possible. But should they encounter any "lawless or unprincipled men" committing acts of desperation, he appealed to those from North Carolina, "whether they have been surrendered and paroled, or otherwise, to unite themselves together in sufficient numbers" under the supervision of civil authorities to quell the violence. Such would not be a violation of their parole, he assured them.[9] Disbanded Confederate soldiers, it appeared, could be both the problem and the solution.

As Johnston's men began their journeys home from North Carolina, many of Lee's men still found themselves detained within Virginia's boundaries. As provost marshal for the Department of Virginia, Bvt. Maj. Gen. Marsena R. Patrick, had worried that Grant's prohibitions on rebels traveling through loyal states might cause more harm than good. So had Lee. On April 21, Lee summoned Patrick to his home on Franklin Street in Richmond. "We had a very full and free interchange of opinions and views," Patrick recalled, "and he seemed to me, as much gratified in Seeing me, as any one I have met with."

But more than reminiscing about their days in the Old Army, Lee wanted to discuss the travel restrictions placed upon his men. Privately, Patrick worried. "On the whole," he confided in his journal, "I almost feel that our troubles are to come."[10]

Patrick need not have worried about those Confederates who agreed to take an oath of allegiance to the United States. They would be allowed to travel wherever they pleased. Lee's adjutant general Charles Marshall agreed to take the oath in late April so that he might leave Union-occupied Alexandria.[11] Edward Roach of the 33rd Virginia had been paroled at Lynchburg before traveling to Fort Monroe, where he took the oath on April 23 and boarded a ship for New York. Others who took the oath embarked on steamers to Boston, Philadelphia, Washington, and even Baltimore.[12]

But those who refused to take the oath would receive no such accommodations. Instead, they would be detained by U.S. authorities. Among Lee's men held at Fort Monroe was Capt. Andrew Hero of New Orleans's Washington Artillery. Sustaining a fracture to his left knee during the evacuation of Petersburg on April 2, he had been apprehended by Union troops during the retreat. He should have been sent to a northern prisoner-of-war camp, because his capture predated the surrender. But for unknown reasons— perhaps because of his wound or a misunderstanding among Union officials—Hero remained in Virginia. Writing to his mother on U.S. Christian Commission stationery from Burkeville, he assured her that his wound was healing and that he would seek a parole and return to New Orleans (adding that he lacked any underclothing and desperately needed money). On April 12, the provost marshal in Burkeville granted his parole. But by April 26 he had reached only Fort Monroe. Penning yet another letter to his mother, he praised the officers for providing comfortable lodging. But his parole seemed to be in name only. He would be allowed to travel to Halifax or Europe, but if he did not take an oath of allegiance to the U.S. government, he would not be allowed to sail to his home in New Orleans. "This is what little dependence is to be placed upon contracts entered into with them," he declared.[13]

Hero's reference to Halifax or Europe came directly from the Union high command. On April 22, General Halleck, commanding the Military Division of the James, had authorized "paroled officers of the insurgent army"—not enlisted men—passports and free passage to Halifax (by May 2, at least six Confederate officers had taken this offer).[14] But upon learning of the order, Secretary Stanton flew into another of his rages and ordered Halleck to rescind the order. Just as Ord had balked at Grant's demands that he cease sending paroled rebels north, Halleck, now in Richmond and seeing for him-

Men on Parole Are Bound in Honor

self the ever-mounting problem of detained Confederates, objected. Firing back at Washington, he reminded Stanton that this was the secretary's idea. Moreover, he lamented the large numbers of paroled men. "If retained here we must support them or they will resort to highway robbery," he observed, sounding a great deal like General Wallace in Baltimore. "Every one we get rid of is a clear gain." Within a few hours, Stanton responded. Although there had been discussions of sending Confederate officers out of the country, he had never authorized furnishing transportation at the government's expense.[15]

Conversely, Stanton *had* authorized sending paroled mechanics and their families to Philadelphia, New York, or Boston.[16] Although the Union armies might soon be demobilized, northern cities remained in desperate need of manual laborers. If these men were willing to take the oath of allegiance, they would be heartily welcomed in the North. Still, the question of who could travel where and on what conditions loomed large. But believing that his parole should have been sufficient, Hero refused to take the oath and was forced to remain at Fort Monroe.

Despite the arrest of John Wilkes Booth's alleged conspirators, the principal assassin still remained on the run. With his whereabouts unknown, rebels planning to travel through the loyal states found themselves stranded. Union officials had forbidden former quartermaster Maj. Alexander W. Vick of Heth's Division and eight of his comrades from Tennessee from leaving Fort Monroe. After surrendering at Appomattox, the men had made their way to the fort hoping to attain transport aboard a steamer to Baltimore, where they planned to take the railroad to Cincinnati, Louisville, and ultimately Nashville. But upon reaching the Union post, they had been detained and informed of Wallace's order that no paroled prisoners should pass through the Middle Department. With no clothes except their Confederate uniforms, no money, and no kin or business connections in that section of Virginia, they turned to their former commander.[17]

Upon receiving their letter, Lee picked up his pen to write Grant.[18] He informed the Union commander that he had heard numerous complaints from officers of rank and had hoped that such obstacles would be removed as quickly as possible. But the plea from Vick, coupled with the orders issued by commanders in both Norfolk and Baltimore requiring oaths of paroled soldiers before allowing them to proceed home, had led him to write the general-in-chief. Had not the paroles at Appomattox been sufficient? "Officers and men on parole are bound in honor to conform to the obligations they have assumed," Lee wrote, adding that this obligation could not be "strengthened by any additional form or oath, nor is it customary to exact them." In requiring paroled soldiers of the Army of Northern Virginia to take a loyalty oath, Lee believed Grant was revoking the terms of surrender.[19]

Even as Lee wrote to Grant inquiring on behalf of his men, the former Confederate leader came under attack. Since returning from Appomattox, Lee had kept a low profile with the exception of an interview he gave to Thomas Cook of the *New York Herald* on April 24 in which he took special pains to note that he was a paroled prisoner and described Lincoln's assassination as deplorable. A few days later, an image of Lee "with members of his late staff in the toggery of the bastard Confederacy" appeared at a New York gallery (most likely the photograph taken by Mathew Brady in Richmond on Easter Sunday). His demeanor, observed the *New York Times*, did not reflect one "professing at once a ready submission to the fate of war."[20]

But it was Lee's farewell order to his troops that proved particularly galling. On April 27, the *New York Times* published the order "so that our readers may see what encouragement paroled rebel officers have had from their chief, to bear themselves insolently and defiantly, on their release." Unionists responded with fury. The address had been "dictated by a spirit of defiance to the supreme authority of the government; to have been at once the index and inspiration of a contemptuous, sullen, and persistent disregard of any obligation of loyalty." In the order, Lee had boasted that he surrendered only because of overwhelming Union resources and praised his men for "devotion to *their* country." Given his words, it was no surprise that the paroled rebel soldiers arriving in northern cities proved "more insolent, obtrusive, and defiant," foisting themselves "into the society of loyal men, parading the insignia of their treason," and boasting that if Lincoln had been assassinated ten days sooner, they might be parading through the streets of Washington as the victorious army. In view of this "rampant spirit of treasonable insolence," the paper urged Secretary Stanton to apply the strictest legal standards to the surrender terms. Grant's terms should not allow "foul-mouthed treason" to "stalk abroad unrebuked and unpunished."[21]

Unionists had to look no further than the halls of Congress for evidence that treason still stalked the nation. Reports had surfaced that Democratic congressman Benjamin G. Harris of Maryland had paid two paroled Confederates to continue making war against the United States. Such charges against Harris might have been expected. Representing the Fifth District of Maryland, Harris, like many of his constituents, had long been critical of the war.

Men on Parole Are Bound in Honor

Robert E. Lee, son G. W. Custis Lee (*standing, left*), and staff officer Walter Taylor, April 1865. Photograph taken by Mathew Brady in the basement below the back porch of Lee's Franklin Street residence in Richmond. Library of Congress Prints and Photographs Division, LC-DIG-cwpb-06233.

Upon his election to Congress in 1863, he cast dissenting votes against war appropriations, and the following year the House censured him for treasonable utterances after he prayed for southern victory on the floor.[22] This would not to be his last such offense.

Bound for Baltimore, Sgt. Richard Chapman and Pvt. William H. Reed would soon learn crossing into Maryland brought new challenges, including finding lodging within a loyal state. Both men had served in Company K of the 32nd Virginia, Corse's Brigade, Pickett's Division, and seen their last action on the morning of April 6, deployed along an open field above Sailor's Creek before Sheridan shattered their lines. Most of the division had been captured, but a fair number—including Chapman and Reed—broke and ran.[23] Chapman soon learned he had lost more than his division. During the evacuation of Richmond and Petersburg, five of his brothers had been killed, two at Amelia Court House and three at Rice's Station. With little more to lose, he would go home. Sometime between April 14 and 17, Reed had wandered into Burkeville and received a parole. By April 22, the two men had managed to reconnect and decided to head north through Northumberland County to the banks of the Potomac. Looking across the muddy river, Chapman pulled out a blank parole he had obtained along the way and filled it in: Sgt. Chapman, Co. K, 32nd Virginia.[24]

On the morning of April 26, they crossed the Potomac into St. Mary's County, Maryland. As they meandered down the dusty road, they soon spotted Harris in the field overseeing African American field hands. Wearing a filthy captain's coat and pulling out his forged parole pass, Chapman explained that they were returning from Lee's army, but somewhere along the trip Reed had lost his parole. Harris took Chapman's pass in his hand and nodded. Chapman could go anywhere with this pass, he observed, but Reed would have to prove he had been paroled. The two men needed to travel to Leonardtown and check in with a Captain Willoughby at the provost marshal's headquarters. He pointed toward the road and instructed them to go down one hill and up another toward the town.[25]

Trudging into Leonardtown at dusk, Chapman and Reed found the provost marshal's office in a hotel. Chapman again removed his parole and explained that Reed had lost his at some point in the past week. Maj. John M. Waite, commander of the local post, wrote out a pass for Reed but told the men they would need to take the oath of allegiance before returning to a loyal state. Waite explained he was not authorized to give the oath, so Chapman and Reed would have to go to Washington. He urged them to wait until the next day and sent them three miles outside of town to a Mr. Clark's resi-

Men on Parole Are Bound in Honor

dence, where they might spend the evening. With darkness encroaching as they headed down the dirt road, Chapman and Reed agreed that they would instead stop at Harris's home. He had been generous in his earlier advice. Perhaps he would allow them to spend the evening with him.[26]

Unbeknownst to the rebels, they had just requested to stay with a U.S. congressman. Standing at the gate, Harris glanced back toward his house before shaking his head. No, he said, the "Yankees had their eyes on him." He could not allow them to stay there. Instead he pointed the way back to Leonardtown and offered each a dollar in federal scrip for a hotel and breakfast. But he counseled the men that they should go home if they liked. When they protested that they had learned of Grant's order barring rebels from returning to the loyal states unless they had taken the oath, Harris balked. "The general-in-chief is a damned rascal," he spat before launching into a tirade that seemingly relished Lincoln's death and declared the southern cause a just one. He then advised the two Confederates not to take the oath of allegiance but to be exchanged and "go back and fight them again."[27]

The next morning, Chapman and Reed returned to Leonardtown, where a Union sergeant approached them. Whether he had intentionally been following Harris is unclear; regardless, the sergeant had overheard the rebels' conversation with the congressman and reported it to Major Waite. At once, Waite ordered the sergeant and a guard of six men sent to Harris's home to arrest the congressmen under the fifty-sixth article of war: relieving the enemy with money, punishable by death. The two rebels would be detained as well—as witnesses for the U.S. government.[28]

April ended with as much uncertainty as it had begun. The men of Lee's army who had started the month together in the works of Petersburg and Richmond now found themselves scattered from New York to New Orleans. Some had made it home, such as Caldwell Calhoun Buckner of the 7th Virginia Cavalry. By April 26 he had returned to his Orange County, Virginia, farm, "Island View," where he set about clearing the peach orchard and plowing fields. Whatever his reasons for initially absconding with General Rosser and others at Appomattox, by late April he had turned his attentions to harrowing and clearing weeds, planting his fields, and rebuilding fences.[29]

Even as Buckner returned to his prewar labors, some of his comrades found themselves detained in Union guardhouses. In addition to those confined in Alexandria, Baltimore, and Washington, paroled soldiers ended up in the city jail at Norfolk. The provost marshal charged some of these men with drunkenness or using disloyal language. But more often, Union soldiers arrested men such as J. Chivers, who had been "going around the city with uniform." It did not help that Chivers appeared to be intoxicated.[30]

Thousands more continued their journeys. Those who filled the decks of steamers finally sailing south toward Savannah and other ports or jostled along on westward-bound railcars found themselves accompanied by Union guard. Such was the case for the 750 paroled men from Lee's army who arrived aboard the steamer *Atlanta* in New Orleans on April 29. Sarah Morgan observed that they were "the sole survivors of ten regiments who left four years ago so full of hope and determination."[31] Men who had marched off to war under the Confederate banner now returned under the Stars and Stripes. Even more importantly, they returned as prisoners of war. Upon arriving in New Orleans, Union authorities required that the paroled rebels report to the nearest provost marshal and register their name, rank, regiment, place of residence, and date and location of their parole. They would not be allowed to bear arms or wear their Confederate gray or any article from the Union uniform. They were not entitled to participate in civil affairs or enter into business pursuits. Those who failed to abide by these rules, warned Maj. Gen. Nathaniel Banks, would forfeit the rights conferred by the parole and face imprisonment.[32]

Even with such restrictions, desperation rather than military order compelled some Confederates to seek out U.S. troops. Having relied on his parole pass to secure transportation to Atlanta, T. H. Jones once again pulled the now wrinkled and creased paper from his pocket on April 24. In return, he received three pairs of pants along with the same number of shirts, drawers, and pairs of socks. With a fresh wardrobe (and two extra sets to spare), he set off on the final leg of his journey to Augusta, Georgia.[33]

To the north, cavalry general Thomas Rosser had gathered nearly 500 men at Swope's Depot, ten miles west of Staunton.[34] Even though a great many of his troopers had voluntarily sought out paroles, upon learning that Johnston had surrendered his army, Rosser issued a second proclamation on April 28. In what he declared as General Orders No. 4, Rosser urged his men "to continue the struggle for Liberty as long as there is hope of success." He directed "all true men who are determined to never abandon our sacred cause" to meet him at Staunton on May 10 for the purpose of reenlisting, reorganizing, and heading west to join whatever forces might still be in the field.[35] Having issued his order, Rosser mounted his horse and galloped off to the southwest in the company of William Lowther Jackson, a cavalry brigade commander in Lomax's Division.[36] Riding into Staunton on April 29,

Men on Parole Are Bound in Honor

Col. Horatio B. Reed of the 22nd New York Cavalry dismissed rumors that Rosser might manage to reunite his command. The Confederate general had enjoyed "little success," Reed observed, "the men refusing to join him." Even the locals, he claimed, were "opposed to his operations."[37]

Colonel Reed seemed more attuned to the shifting southern sentiment than did Rosser. On the same day that Rosser issued his second call to continue the fight, fellow cavalry officer Thomas Munford ordered members of his brigade to return to their homes. Upon visiting his Botetourt County home, Munford had learned that Col. Gus Dorsey's band of 1st Maryland Cavalry was advancing up the Shenandoah Valley in response to his April 21 call. Like so many other cavalrymen, approximately 100 of the Maryland troopers had voluntarily sought out paroles in the Valley. But nearly 100 more remained committed to the cause. Munford, however, conceded that the time had come to capitulate. Writing to Dorsey, Munford explained that they could not reach Johnston's army in North Carolina, and there was nothing left to do but "abide our time and be ready to strike." He praised the Marylanders' devotion to the cause, observing that "you who struck the first blow in Baltimore, and the last in Virginia, have done all that could be asked of you." And although never referencing Speed's opinion or General Orders No. 73 directly, Munford told Dorsey that his men should make Virginia — not Maryland — their home "until an opportunity offers for us to strike again."

Munford's admonition to the 1st Maryland, however, was no acquiescence. He made no acknowledgment of the magnanimous surrender terms, no concession that the war had reached its conclusion. "I believe the battle is yet to be fought, for we can never submit to Yankee rule," he wrote. "My hope is that the Yankees will oppress us so heavily that the people will soon rise again."[38] With such sentiments still on the tongues of rebels, it is little wonder that Confederates like Marylander Lewis Webb remained locked up in Union holding cells.

11

Southbound

Even as David McIntosh, Gordon McCabe, Ham Chamberlayne, and other young officers pushed south toward Charlotte in late April determined to continue the fight, thousands of Lee's paroled men who had left Appomattox persisted in their journeys home. Throughout the Carolinas and into Georgia and beyond, they clambered onto railroad cars, some so crowded that the men were forced to ride on the tops. Even when they managed to find passage, with tracks demolished throughout the region, railroad travel proved sporadic and unpredictable at best. Men might catch a freight train in Greensboro or Salisbury only to find that they must disembark where the tracks had been destroyed and hoof it to the next station. After learning that the rickety train on which he rode was packed with ammunition, a North Carolina soldier admitted that only his exhaustion compelled him to continue on such a dangerous ride.[1] Even among those who rode the rails for a portion of the trip, a substantial amount of time was spent walking.[2]

A significant number of soldiers from the Deep South had first gone to City Point and Fort Monroe, Virginia, hoping to sail south. After traveling by train from Burkeville to Fort Monroe, 450 parolees from several Alabama and Georgia regiments climbed aboard the *Admiral Dupont*. The 200-foot side-wheel steamer had begun the war as a Confederate blockade runner, but now it sailed south to Savannah filled with prisoners of war instead of precious commodities. On the evening of April 19, the men disembarked from the great iron ship before marching to the Camp of Distribution near the Central Railroad grounds to await the trains.[3] Several days later, a guard of twenty-two men from the 3rd Pennsylvania Artillery accompanied more than 500 paroled rebels aboard the steamer *Kingfisher* into Savannah's harbor. But this homecoming was marked by an additional sorrow. During the trip, twenty-two-year-old Pvt. Richard Cribb of the 10th Georgia Battalion succumbed to the chronic illness that had plagued him throughout the war. So close to his Dooley County home, he died at sea, his comrades committing his body to a watery grave.[4]

Although the brigades and regiments splintered more as they moved south, men continued to travel in small groups rather than alone. Sgt. Maj. Lewis H. Andrews of the 8th Georgia had been among the approximately 250 men of Anderson's Brigade who had marched away from Appomattox. Yet within a few days, Andrews and five others had struck out on their own. Even with their smaller party, finding food remained almost as challenging as securing transportation. At Salisbury, Andrews and his comrades waited hours at a Union post for "eatables," only to learn that none would be forthcoming. With no food in their stomachs, they left in disgust, marching another nine miles before finding a pile of straw in which to sleep. The train that arrived the next morning proved equally packed, "on top and everywhere else," so the men designated as foragers set out to find something— anything—to eat. Returning with only two canteens of milk, they hatched a plan to capture a chicken roost. After another restless night in the straw, they began marching again before sunrise. Midmorning, still desperate for something to eat, half the party set out for a nearby commissary store, where they drew one day's rations, while the rest of the men readied a fire to cook whatever provisions might be found. Marching toward Charlotte the following day, their luck improved when a civilian supplied them with a lunch of bread, butter, pie, and milk. A few days later, still ravenous, two of the men literally ate crow. When they pronounced the meal "fine," Andrews quipped he was willing to take their word for it.[5]

Soldiers passing through familiar regions often sought out friends, family, and even acquaintances along the journey. Just across the Virginia border near Warrenton, North Carolina, several members of the 30th North Carolina stopped at their former quartermaster's plantation, where they enjoyed supper and a room in which to sleep.[6] At Lyon's Mill on the Tar River, a different group of men from the same regiment was grateful to find a former comrade—home for unknown reasons—who invited them to his father's residence, where they consumed "as much corn whiskey as we wanted." After several rounds, the men concluded they should probably camp there for the evening.[7]

But the homeward-bound trip could prove perilous beyond the quest for food and transportation. Having made their way well into North Carolina,

Gus Dean and fourteen of his comrades of the 2nd South Carolina Rifles rejoiced when they stumbled upon an unoccupied shed after a long day's march. The structure consisted of large posts driven into the ground, topped by logs and then rails, and covered with straw. Such a find offered a great deal of relief on a terribly rainy night. But the good fortune proved short-lived. During a particularly heavy downpour, the shed collapsed on the sleeping men. One of the largest logs came crashing down on William McClinton, crushing his head and chest, killing him instantly. A piece of scantling landed on Dean's head and hip, pinning him under the debris for more than an hour before his companions managed to pull him out. Having survived the war and witnessed the deadly arsenal explosion at Danville, Dean and his comrades feared their luck was running out.[8]

Others encountered unexpected detentions by Union forces. Lewis Andrews and his traveling companions arrived in Greensboro on April 19 through a combination of riding the rails and marching. But that evening, as Johnston and Sherman awaited approval of the surrender terms, Union troops forced Andrews and his comrades into a parole camp. In a town rife with rumors — that Lincoln had been killed, that Secretary of State Seward had been wounded, that Jefferson Davis had been captured, and that an armistice of ten days was in effect — the parole camp offered the safest respite for the night. And rations. They might have been detained for the evening, but at least they would not go hungry.[9]

In Montgomery, Alabama, the Federal provost marshal assigned members of Hood's Texas Brigade to quarters near the city's artesian well. For a week, the men bivouacked in the two-story building as more of the brigade drifted into the town and their commanders, Capt. W. T. Hill and Maj. W. H. "Howdy" Martin, attempted to secure passage to Mobile. As a reminder that they were prisoners of war passing through Union lines, the provost marshal ordered the men to have their paroles countersigned before boarding a steamer bound for Mobile. Reaching New Orleans several days later, the Texans again found themselves assigned to quarters in a large cotton shed — this time under guard — while they waited more than nine days to make the next leg of their journey.[10]

With each passing day, more and more men arrived home. On Thursday, April 20, a sick and filthy Henry Bahnson stumbled up to his father's door in Salem, North Carolina. Since receiving his parole at Farmville, he had ridden on a train to Danville, where he participated in the raid on the commissary before riding the rails again to Greensboro and then walking the remaining distance to Salem. Opening the door to see an emaciated figure, Bahnson's father stared in disbelief. Could this be his son? The son whose own company had reported his death and buried a body, marking a headboard with Bahnson's name? Gaunt and dirty, his appearance soon dispelled all "the glamor and illusions of the pomp and pride and circumstances of glorious war." Rushing him into the house, his mother drew a hot bath while the young private stripped off the underclothes he had worn continuously for more than seven weeks. The vestiges of martial life would likewise be discarded. Once more, he sat in a chair, ate with a fork, drank from a glass, and slept in a bed.[11]

Those still on the road sought out Confederate-sympathizing civilians willing to provide food and lodging. Most were individuals or families, such as the Stileses near Asheboro, North Carolina, who prepared a "big mess of chicken for the crowd" of soldiers passing their home on April 21.[12] Indicative of what had changed as much as what had not, in countless instances paroled men found themselves waited on by men and women who remained in bondage despite Lee's surrender. Each day soldiers filled the backyard and kitchen of Eliza Andrews's Georgia home. To accommodate the hundreds, perhaps thousands, of men, her mother had kept two enslaved women "hard at work, cooking for them."[13] In other instances, entire communities worked to assist the soldiers, such as the ladies of Augusta, Georgia, who organized a food and clothing drive for soldiers passing through the city, or the town of Edgefield, South Carolina, which held a "grand barbecue" of mutton, shoat, hams, turkeys, chickens, cakes, and custards to show their gratitude for the "toilsome and dangerous service these brave men have rendered." Looking more like the homecoming of a triumphant army rather than a defeated one, the "gray coats and brass buttons and tinsel braidery . . . and brave, manly, young hearts were in full force."[14]

Whether opening up their homes to small groups of men or hosting the remnants of entire brigades on their lawns, many of the civilians who aided the men on their journey home expressed a deep and continuing devotion to the Confederacy—and its soldiers. Witnessing squads of unarmed men passing through Chapel Hill, North Carolina, Cornelia Phillips Spencer wanted desperately to run after them, call them into her home, shake their rough hands, spread a warm meal before them, and thank them. "God bless you all," she would say; "we are just as proud of you, and thank you just as much as if it had turned out differently." Restraining herself, she settled on opening her home to them.[15] Catherine Edmondston of Halifax County, North Carolina, concurred. When one of Lee's paroled soldiers arrived at her home, she noted that "our sympathies are such with those of that noble band" that "any of them are welcome to our house & we consider it a privilege to do all we can for them."[16] If the government could no longer shelter and feed the men who had fought for southern independence, then Confederate-sympathizing civilians would do the best they could.

Such sentiments allowed them to forgive some returning soldiers for their transgressions. Eliza Andrews watched as soldiers seized horses in broad daylight in a Georgia town. When one veteran caught her staring at him as he led a mule away from its owner, the soldier called out, "A man that's going to Texas must have a mule to ride, don't you think so, lady?" Although she offered no reply, Andrews conceded in her diary that the Texan had so far to go that the temptation for him to take another man's mule was great.[17] On May 1, in a scene reminiscent of those that had taken place at Danville, Virginia, and Greensboro, North Carolina, a mob of Confederate soldiers ransacked Augusta, Georgia, looting government stores and pillaging a locally owned tobacco shop. Yet the city paper tried to rationalize their actions. Using the same logic as that applied by Confederate officers who believed the men were due government goods as compensation for their service, the paper observed that "the sacking of government stores would have been proper enough had there been anything like fairness in the plunder of the property." Instead, it proved "an unequal distribution . . . and the parties engaged have done great injury to their fellow soldiers who have not yet arrived." The paper declared the pillage of the tobacco shop "the most heinous part of the affair" because it affected private individuals. But, the editors insisted, "we do not believe that many of those implicated were of Lee's or Johnston's armies, if so, they were instigated by shameless parties." Still, the paper urged no more destruction of private property. "No true defender of his country should tarnish the glorious record of the past four years by a moment's rashness and for so insignificant a profit."[18]

According to some civilians and editors, mobs of Confederate soldiers raiding government warehouses could be explained if not condoned (while the looting of private stores was not) because of defeat. Echoing Lee's farewell address at Appomattox in which he had praised the loyalty, valor, and "unsurpassed courage and fortitude" of "the brave survivors of so many hard-fought battles," newspapers and civilians alike reasoned that Confederate soldiers had fought valiantly and bravely only to be overwhelmed by superior northern resources. Of course, they should not engage in looting and plundering. But many Confederate sympathizers believed it could be forgiven as part of the social contract that implied soldiers, especially those who had given their all, were entitled to be fed.[19]

Although the vast majority of the white southern population had supported the Confederate war effort, most people recognized that there were those who did not.[20] As the Army of Northern Virginia dispersed across the countryside, soldiers encountered both devoted Unionists as well as folks who had grown weary of Confederate impressment agents and refused to give any more for a cause that was most certainly lost. Near Thomasville, North Carolina, a soaked and exhausted John Dooley and his comrades could find no place to dry their clothes or a morsel to eat. "The people in this vicinity seem rather unfavorable towards Confederate soldiers and are very distant and inhospitable," he complained. "Most of them are of that persuasion call[ed] 'Dunkers' or 'Friends' who find their religion very convenient when war arises."[21] Farther south in North Carolina, Ranson J. Lightsey and his comrades stopped in the neighborhood of "some strong Unionists," one of whom informed the Mississippians that "he was glad that the Yankees whipped us."[22]

Others found the prospect of passing through Unionist strongholds more than just insulting. Still bound for Lincolnton, Harry Townsend and his small band of Richmond Howitzers were warned to be careful upon crossing the border from Virginia into Stokes County, North Carolina. "The people are Tories or Union men in sentiment and are much greater lovers of the Yankees than of the Confederates," Townsend observed. "They often attack Confederate soldiers who may be passing through this country and strip them of their valuables." With no weapons to defend themselves, Townsend and his men remained on high alert. But whether deterred by the group's size or intimidated by the tenacity of Confederates bold enough to march through the region that had so long been a terror to all travelers, the Unionist threat failed to materialize.[23]

In the pro-Union mountains of eastern Tennessee, Capt. William Harder and his large group of paroled men were not so fortunate. Arriving in Sullivan County on April 23, the men were in desperate straits, "all nearly starved . . . naked and befuddled." The locals refused to feed the Confederates, but they did offer a warning. "We were told that every Confederate that went through or attempted to go through eastern Tennessee were killed and that we would meet the same fate," Harder explained. Still, the men pressed on to Greeneville, the home of President Johnson. In the winter of 1863, Lt. Gen. James Longstreet had wintered his corps in the valley at the foothills of the Appalachians. But a Union post now occupied the town. With the U.S. troops either unwilling or unable to provide rations, the paroled men traded Confederate scrip to Federals for crackers and meat.[24]

But tensions remained high. When Harder and two other officers reported to the local provost marshal for passes to board a train to Knoxville, a captain from an Ohio command began to harass and curse the Confederates. Harder explained that they were paroled prisoners of war desiring to go home on the terms offered by Grant, but the Ohioan continued his rant. "He abused the Confederates with ugly epithets," Harder recorded that evening, "and cursed me violently and told me to go home to my negro wife and bastard mulattos." Accusing Harder of race-mixing proved to be the final straw. Paroled soldier or not, Harder drew his sword and lunged toward the Union soldier's breast. One of Harder's men caught his arm, pulling him back just as forty or fifty Ohioans drew and cocked their pistols only to be joined by two more Confederates drawing their sidearms. For several brief moments, silence filled the office. Finally, another Federal officer pushed through with pistol in hand ordering all arms lowered. Amid the overlapping and complicated loyalties of a border state, the officer proved to be a Union man from Tennessee who informed the Ohioans that "with his life he would defend those paroled Tennesseans." Regardless of the cause for which they had fought, now that his brethren had laid down their guns, he would guarantee them peace. Relieved that the situation had passed without any blood, the provost marshal quickly scribbled out passes, and the Confederates hurried aboard the train to Knoxville.[25] As those heading home to West Virginia, Kentucky, and Maryland would likewise discover, the lines between friend and foe, government and civilian, would prove incredibly murky for Confederates from Unionist territory.

Yet even in regions sympathetic to the Confederacy, the refusal or inability of civilians to provide food led some soldiers to resort to violence and plundering—just as Union and Confederate authorities had feared. Georgian lieutenant David Champion and his traveling companions became outraged when an older man in the Carolinas refused to accept Confederate money for corn and bacon. "Seeing it was useless to try to trade with him," Champion explained, "I ordered the boys to go to his corn crib and smokehouse and get the corn and bacon we needed. We carried the corn to a mill nearby on the creek and ground it and borrowed his washpot to cook the meat in." Not only did they take enough to satiate themselves in the moment, but they filled their haversacks before departing.[26] At Griffin, Georgia, members of Hood's Texas Brigade planned an assault against two Confederate commissaries, one filled with bacon, the other with flour. Assisting them was a squadron of fifty well-armed Confederate cavalrymen detailed to protect the warehouses. Determined to outmaneuver the managers who denied them access to the food, the men "divided their forces and attacked the two warehouses at the same time," employing railroad irons as battering rams. Within minutes, the two squads had secured hams, bacon, and flour. Not deterred by the Texans' behavior, the women of the town promptly boiled the ham and baked the men bread.[27]

Foraging, both sanctioned and not, had been a common occurrence within both Union and Confederate armies, often leaving those on the home front wanting. That had not changed in the wake of surrender. As one North Carolina soldier explained, taking food to prevent starvation could not be considered "stealing": "I know no old soldier would, and no risk of punishment of danger ever stopped their 'foraging.'" He had witnessed soldiers crawl up to cows and funnel milk into their canteens, kill pigs in sight of a farmhouse, and bait chickens or ducks with a pin on a string. He had participated in absconding with a hive of honey and, in one of his last acts as a soldier, taken part in the raid on the commissary in Danville. "I don't believe any sane man would be fool enough to starve if he could steal anything to eat," he rationalized.[28]

Such a sentiment held by the time Lee's men reached Charlotte. As in Danville and Greensboro, a mob of Confederate soldiers raided Confederate warehouses. Frank Mixson and Jim Diamond, who had already enjoyed their share of loot in Danville, encountered a large crowd of Lee's paroled men taking whatever they could shove into their pockets and makeshift haversacks. "But as we had plenty to eat we didn't take much hand in it," Mixson maintained. The two did, however, abscond with "a bolt of real good jeans."[29]

As Charlotte erupted in chaos, John Dooley, a paroled prisoner from Johnson's Island who had headed south along with many of Lee's men vowing to continue the fight, now contemplated his options. Charlotte was rapidly filling with stragglers, officers, and government officials, including Jefferson Davis and his cabinet, all of whom remained determined to push into the Trans-Mississippi. Each hour, hundreds more arrived along the railroad from Salisbury, North Carolina. But with no resources and no place to stay, should Dooley return to Virginia? Although he feared that all there would be beggars like himself, he deemed it "madness to go farther South." Moreover, news of Lincoln's assassination troubled him. While he was glad that the "tyrant" and "monster" had fallen, he worried about the larger repercussions for the South. Lincoln's death by an assassin's bullet had left "the taint of suspicion upon Southern men." Moreover, he observed, the notion of "ridding society of obnoxious individuals cannot but awake feelings of terror and distrust in the breast of well disposed citizens who may well fear lest the practice become of frequent occurrence and the stealthy blow of the assassin take the place of free speech."[30] If Union officials worried about the anarchy that Lincoln's murder might foreshadow, Confederates did likewise. Dooley would remain in Charlotte a few more days before deciding his course.

While he waited, others continued on their southward journeys into South Carolina. Crossing the border to the west of Charlotte, a surgeon of the 16th Georgia and his small mounted party found themselves in Union-controlled territory where their parole passes proved useful. At the Catawba River, they met troopers from the 12th Ohio Cavalry who escorted them through the lines before stopping in Yorkville (present-day York), where they again showed their passes to obtain U.S. rations. If the Yankees proved willing to assist the paroled Confederates, locals did not. Close to the Georgia border, the surgeon complained that the South Carolinians had proven especially inhospitable, refusing them at all but two houses along the way. "Would to compare S. C. with either N. C. or Virginia t'would be odious," he scribbled in his diary. "There is no comparison both states being so far ahead of 'little' S. C. in generosity and hospitality."[31]

As they continued their trek, in scenes repeated from Virginia to Texas and every place in between, Lee's men began to reach their homes. For a steady three weeks after the surrender and "for two years off and on somebody come along going home," remembered an enslaved man in Louisiana.[32]

The first priority for many of these soldiers hoping to resume their civilian lives was a bath or even a haircut. For men who had endured filth a good portion of their soldiering career, cleaning themselves up offered one more step in the process of becoming a civilian. After walking more than 200 miles, on April 20 Robert Crumpler and his comrades from the 30th North Carolina halted to wash and shave in the hopes of making themselves "as presentable as possible" before venturing on to their Sampson County homes.[33] Others had been unable to wash their clothing, shave, or bathe before arriving home and therefore divested themselves of their filthy, tattered uniforms and cleaned themselves as quickly upon arrival as they could. Surgeon Spencer Welch of the 13th South Carolina had spooned with four of his companions each night and ridden astride his small mule for more than three weeks. Upon reaching his father's home in Newberry, he shed his dirty, vermin-infested rags for "clean, whole clothes" and crawled into a real bed. These simple acts did more than anything to restore him. "I feel greatly refreshed," he wrote his wife.[34] And though overjoyed to see his loved ones, the teenage Frank Mixson's arrival home prompted an immediate trip to the outhouse, where his family instructed him to wash and change into fresh clothing. His tattered and reeking Confederate uniform, however, was to be buried.[35]

Whether settled back at their homes or still on the road, Confederates moving across the South in the days and weeks after Appomattox witnessed a world far removed from the slaveholding society they had pledged to defend in 1861. So did African Americans. On farms and plantations, cities and towns, enslaved men and women bore witness to the change the war had wrought. "I seen our 'Federates go off laughin' an' gay," remembered an ex-slave from Alabama. They had departed for war singing "Dixie," certain they were going to win, but now they returned skin and bones, their eyes hollow and their clothes ragged. "De sperrit dey lef wid jus been done whupped out of dem," he observed. In occupied Charleston, a member of the 54th Massachusetts took notice as well. "From the paroled armies of the defunct Confederacy came large numbers of soldiers in dilapidated garments and emaciated physical condition." Their destitution was so great, the veteran noted, "they were glad to share the rations of our colored soldiers." At least some enslaved men who had been attached to Lee's army returned alongside their former masters, anxious to be reunited with their own *free* families. Edwin Bogan of North Carolina was one such man who traveled home with his former owner to his wife and young son. But newly freed men and women also joined the rebel soldiers on the roads crisscrossing the region, underscoring all that had been done and undone during four years of war.[36]

Nowhere was the new order more apparent than in Confederate soldiers' encounters with U.S. Colored Troops. On April 26, the *Wilmington* steamed into the Savannah port with 690 paroled rebels, including David L. Geer and other members of Finegan's Florida Brigade, those who claimed to have killed two USCT soldiers back in Virginia.[37] In Georgia, their deadly retaliation continued. While awaiting a ship to Jacksonville, a Black sentinel had reportedly stomped out the Floridians' campfire. Enraged, they plotted his execution: using a surgeon's knife, they slashed the Black soldier's throat, then tossed him and all evidence of the crime in the river. When white officers grew suspicious about the missing sentinel and threatened to send the Confederates to prison on the Dry Tortugas, Geer and sixty-three other Florida soldiers still awaiting steamers fled in the middle of the night, traveling overland rather than risk further inquiries. For a third time since leaving Appomattox, they had killed Black soldiers — and gotten away with it.[38]

Other interactions with Black soldiers proved less deadly but no less revealing of how much the social order had changed. At Selma, Alabama, U.S. officers ordered members of Hood's Texas Brigade to disembark a train so that a USCT regiment might travel to Mobile. "We protested, of course, and bitterly, against what some of our men denounced as a regular 'Yankee trick,'" wrote Capt. W. T. Hill of the 5th Texas, "but our protest was unheeded, and we had to wait at Selma until the next day." Several days later at New Orleans, the Texans found themselves guarded by a USCT company— a slight Hill believed to be intentionally demeaning. More humiliating for the Confederates, the Black soldiers had taken to cutting the rebels' buttons off their coats. "The Texans were quick to 'catch on,'" Hill observed, "and by cutting off their brass buttons themselves, denied the negroes the great satisfaction of doing so."[39] In the wake of surrender, Black soldiers guarding paroled Confederates, cutting buttons off rebel coats, or taking precedence in travel embodied the world turned upside down. The presence of Black men in uniforms, perhaps more than the surrender itself, represented the death of the Confederacy and a new racial order.[40]

Yet some Confederates proved unready to acquiesce to such a reality. From Greensboro on April 25, Gordon McCabe wrote his future wife, Jane. He had arrived in the city on the seventeenth, and since that time he had received no word from Virginia. "Everybody here asked eagerly, 'What is Virginia going to do?'" Fight, he told them. A handful of young Virginians had made their way to the railroad town hoping to join Johnston's forces. Both Ham Chamberlayne and David McIntosh had continued southward toward South Carolina, he told her. But others remained in North Carolina weighing their options. "There are a great many Va. officers here, who are forming themselves into a Battalion, — a sort of *Corps d'Elite*," he explained. "Where we are going, of course, I do not know; to Trans-Miss., I suppose, if we can elude Sherman." But a thread of realism ran through him. "If God spares my life, and this Army should be surrendered," he continued, "I propose to return to Virginia before going abroad, unless France and the United States get to fighting, when we may probably get something to do in the service of H. S. H. Napoleon III."[41] He would go to Mexico and fight for the French. But he would not — could not — live under Yankee rule.

Capt. William Frederic Pendleton of the 50th Georgia concurred. Having avoided Appomattox, he had made his way to Charlotte by April 18. There, he received orders from Maj. Gen. A. R Wright to proceed immediately to Ware County, Georgia, "for the purpose of collecting & forwarding" all officers and men belonging to Lee's army who may have been on furlough at the time of the surrender or who had dropped out of the ranks.[42]

During the last week of April, Harry Townsend and his fellow artillerists finally reached their destination of Lincolnton, North Carolina. Perched on a high bluff above the South Fork of the Catawba River, the town had been the rallying point for those who had escaped Appomattox and hoped to continue the struggle. Here they found residents handing out provisions at the courthouse for both paroled and unparoled soldiers as well as offering beds in several local hotels and residences. But they found very little news. "We had expected to gain some definite information at this point which could guide our future course, but found no orders awaiting us, nor any officer in command," Townsend recorded in his diary. Instead, they spoke with a paroled lieutenant who informed them that Secretary of War Breckinridge had refused the service of officers and men from Lee's army and had bid them to return to their homes, as no Confederate government now existed east of the Mississippi River. Sympathetic to their aims, however, the lieutenant advised them to go to Charlotte, where they might learn something more definitive. Bidding adieu to Lincolnton, Townsend and his comrades started for the Queen City.[43]

For McCabe, Pendleton, Townsend, and others who remained committed to the cause, the Army of Northern Virginia had not yet been thoroughly vanquished. For Confederates determined to return home to loyal Union states, the story would prove much different.

12

Disgraceful to Live and
Associate with Rebels

Unionists from Georgia to Maine remained well aware that Confederate sympathies had not been quelled by the surrender or disbanding of the rebel armies. Among those who felt this most keenly were residents of the border states, and chief among them residents of West Virginia. On April 26, the same day Sherman finally accepted Johnston's surrender and John Wilkes Booth found himself surrounded by Union troops on Virginia's Northern Neck, the citizens of Clarksburg, West Virginia, met to write President Johnson about the impending return of rebels.

Situated in Harrison County along the Northwest Turnpike, Clarksburg had long held divided loyalties. Only weeks after Lincoln's 1860 election, western Virginia politicians gathered in the town to condemn secession and urge the state not to hold a convention on the subject. When their efforts failed and eastern Virginia seceded in April 1861, the local militia company, the Harrison Rifles, splintered between the Unionists and the secessionists. Even as they parted ways, tensions flared in the town. In July 1861, the sheriff arrested some fifteen to twenty secessionists, a move that the local paper observed "almost rids the place of rebels." Over the next four years, approximately 350 young men marched off to join the Confederate forces, while nearly 800 committed themselves to the U.S. army. Although the town remained overwhelmingly loyal and under Union control throughout the war (serving as a large quartermaster depot for Maj. Gen. George B. McClellan's army during 1861), it retained enthusiastic support for the Confederacy — including the intimidation of and threats against Unionists. As one Union soldier explained in the fall of 1861, "The Rebels called on me to fight for the South as I was a Southern man. I told them nay. They made me leave my home, then I enlisted. They then burnt my house and I am now in the service of the United States."[1]

In the spring of 1865, the residents of Harrison County needed only to look to their southeast to see evidence that such atrocities against Unionists continued. On April 24, a group of Confederates slipped into Barbour County, where they ransacked the home of Sanford Nestor, a Union private in the Home Guard. Under the command of Michael Haller, the Home Guardsmen followed the culprits to a farm skirting Teter's Creek only to be ambushed by the rebels. In the fray, Haller was wounded and taken prisoner alongside two of his men. The rebels executed all three, allegedly after making the Union men "kneel and pray for the Confederacy."[2]

In light of such continued attacks, some of Clarksburg's most influential residents wrote to Johnson. Recalling the president's condemnation of treason as "the highest crime," they worried that the "men who went from our midst breathing threatenings and death against us" are now returning. Endorsing the letter, Robert S. Northcott, a local newspaper editor, explained that "the class of rebels alluded to rendered themselves so obnoxious before leaving that I fear that in some instances people will resort to Judge Lynch's Court if they are permitted to return. In many communities vigilance committees have already been appointed for the purpose of ejecting these traitors, and if your Excellency can interpose some means of preventing their return here or of having them prosecuted immediately upon their return, it will add much to the future harmony of our State." The loyal men of Harrison County hoped that the Federal courts might step in to prevent a resort to lynch mob violence.[3]

Other communities had no qualms with forming vigilance committees to hunt down and forcefully evict returning rebels. As many as 15,000 men from West Virginia had joined the Confederate army, and loyal residents feared what their return might mean. Lincoln's assassination only escalated their anxiety. On April 16, the citizens of Wheeling promptly formed a committee of thirty-six men to prevent the return of anyone who had left the city to support the rebellion. A little more than a week later, even after learning of Attorney General Speed's directive that rebels could return to West Virginia, Unionists in Preston County declared that rebels "had better not return amongst us, as we disown them as citizens, and look upon them as our enemies who would destroy us and the government if they could." Meeting on April 29, the loyal citizens of Tyler County described the rebellion as "the cause of the devil" and likewise resolved that any who had served in the Confederacy were forbidden from returning to their homes within the county. "We consider it disgraceful to live and associate with rebels or rebel sympathizers," they wrote, "and we earnestly request all such, for their own safety and peace of mind, to sell their property and remove from amongst us," adding that "when they leave for other parts, we conjure them to build up for themselves new characters and rid themselves of the foul disgrace which now attaches to them." From Brooke County, tucked between the Ohio and Pennsylvania borders, veterans of the 2nd West Virginia formed a committee vowing to prevent traitors from coming back. "When they re-belled against the government," the committee insisted, "they gave up all claim to citizenship with us." In the capital of Charleston, the local group harkened back to the Revolution in casting itself as a "committee of safety" composed of thirteen members.[4] Within a matter of weeks, no fewer than twelve locales in West Virginia had passed similar resolutions or formed vigilance committees like those in Maryland.[5]

This was no idle talk. When three "renegade rebels" rode into Ritchie County dressed in full uniform and addressed their former acquaintances as if the war had never happened, the town of Harrisville erupted. More than fifty people spilled into the streets, surrounding the mounted Confederates and threatening their lives. The men escaped, but barely.[6] Other rebels found themselves hunted down. After rumors surfaced that two Confederate brothers had attempted to return to their home near Fairmont, a squad of Home Guard visited the men's mother. She assured them that her sons had not returned and that she knew nothing of their whereabouts. Not trusting a rebel sympathizer, the Home Guard searched the area and found the two rebels concealed in the woods. As the Confederates attempted to flee, a flurry of gunshots echoed through the mountains, killing one brother and wounding the other.[7]

Other returning rebels readied themselves for a renewed fight. In 1861, Samuel Woods had voted for secession as Barbour County's delegate to the convention and subsequently joined a Virginia regiment. Promoted to captain in the Quartermaster's Department, he found himself in charge of army stores in Staunton. His wife and six children had initially remained in the fiercely divided community of Philippi, but by the summer of 1862 anti-Confederate sympathy in the town had reached such a fevered pitch that she and the children sought refuge in Waynesboro, Virginia, to be near her husband. In the spring of 1865, Woods was returning to Philippi with his son Frank when he was intercepted by a group of seven men, all former Union

Disgraceful to Live and Associate with Rebels

West Virginia counties, 1865.

Counties organizing vigilante committees in 1865

soldiers from the area. With revolvers clearly visible in his side pockets, Woods furnished the parole he had signed at Charlottesville and insisted he had a right to return home. The Union soldiers warned him against going back, but armed, Woods continued on his way to Philippi without incident.[8]

Despite Woods's bravado, even those who had taken the oath of allegiance had reason to worry. John Rundle, the former editor of the *Kanawha Valley Star*, had joined the Confederacy in June 1861. As a member of the 36th Virginia, he had seen action in both the western and eastern theaters, disbanding with his unit after Lt. Gen. Jubal Early's rout at Waynesboro in March 1865. Like many of his comrades, he made his way home to the Kanawha Valley, where he turned himself in to the provost marshal at Charleston and took the oath on April 22. He knew, even after taking the oath, he was unwelcome. Yet rather than return humbly and quietly, he issued a notice to the Union people of Kanawha Valley: "If you (the Union men) will treat us right and not insult us, we will keep quiet; but if you don't, these hills will be filled with sharpshooters."[9]

Perhaps such threats led one Unionist to suggest that the U.S. army send the county's soldiers home. "They can and will do more, as *citizens*, to protect the loyal people from depredations and secure quiet submission to the State and Federal authority than twice their number of soldiers from other sections of the country," he wrote a Wheeling newspaper. "Their accurate knowledge of the topography of the places where [rebels] reside will enable them to pursue predatory bands with better success than can be done by any military organization."[10] If the Union army would not protect loyal West Virginians from returning rebels, the local men would do so.

All of these instances served as evidence that Grant's orders allowing Confederates to return to West Virginia were misguided at best. And they infuriated Governor Arthur Boreman. Firing off a letter to Secretary of War Stanton on May 5, the governor asked that the full meaning of Attorney General Speed's opinion be implemented. West Virginia had *not passed* an ordinance of secession, he pointed out, and had been loyal from the beginning. The state had been exempted by Lincoln's proclamation delineating what constituted insurrectionary territory in the Congressional Claims Payment Act of July 1864 and had furnished its share of troops. Why should Speed's opinion not apply to West Virginia?, he asked. More important, Boreman explained West Virginia's peculiar circumstances. "Situated on the border, very many went from here into the rebel army, and now they return, wearing their rebel uniforms, and many of them with as much impudence and insolence as when they went away," he noted. "The loyal people here feel themselves in-

Disgraceful to Live and Associate with Rebels

sulted by the conduct of these rebels, and are only restrained from decided action by their love of law and order."[11]

Unionists from West Virginia were as desirous as Marylanders that acts of rebellion would cease. Lincoln's assassination proved the most devastating. But there were at least two other concerns motivating them. First, even before West Virginia gained statehood, the region had split along Union and Confederate lines, becoming a fiercely partisan battleground where reprisals by bushwhackers and guerrillas were not uncommon. For four long years, rebel guerrillas had attempted to squelch Union support not only by attacking individuals and their property but also by "destroying post offices and county courthouses, waylaying sheriffs and tax collectors, and threatening the operation of law courts."[12] Many wondered if Lee's surrender would mean anything to those who had tried for so long to thwart Union authority. Second, although West Virginia had been admitted to the Union in 1863, a great deal of fear remained concerning the legality of dismembering the state of Virginia. Recognizing that almost a quarter of the counties exhibited pro-Confederate behavior and at least two (Jefferson and Berkeley) refused to recognize their inclusion within its borders, Unionists worried that the state and its boundaries might be challenged after the war by thousands of paroled Confederates returning to a state they had been trying to annihilate. If rebels returned and voted, they would potentially outnumber Unionists, and the state might revert to Virginia.[13]

Grant, however, refused to rescind his order. Any paroled rebel from West Virginia would be allowed to remain at home so long as he respected his parole and the local laws, and returning Confederates were not to be driven from their homes by citizens without proof that a crime had been committed. Proceedings such as those in Parkersburg and elsewhere that had ordered all paroled men to leave the place were to cease at once.[14]

To the southwest, loyal Kentuckians had also begun to feel the effects of returning rebels from both Lee's and Johnston's armies. Union veteran Samuel McKee wrote to President Johnson in desperation. More than 1,200 rebels had been "turned loose" in Mount Sterling—the same men who had engaged in a wicked attempt to overthrow the government and who had carried out murder and plunder, wreaking devastation across the state. Now, McKee explained, they walked the streets in their Confederate uniforms with pistols belted around them. He wanted to see them stripped of their "traitor garb" and their arms handed over to the Union army. "I cannot see why a Paroled Prisoner of war is allowed privileges here, that are denied him in other states," he intoned. But more importantly, he feared what the future might bring. If allowed to return, the men would surely band together during the coming August election for members of Congress. "Rebel Sympathising Citizens here openly boast that the Rebels have the power and will control Elections in the State," he noted. Federal authorities must aid them, or Kentucky would fall to Confederates *after* the battlefield fighting had ended.[15]

Loyal citizens of Washington, D.C., worried as well. Despite Speed's opinion, Grant had not directly addressed those rebels who hailed from the nation's capital. But like citizens of Maryland and West Virginia, Washington's residents decried returning rebels, using a city council meeting to admonish those who had left their homes to not return to the city. Those who had "defied the national government, and engaged in the horrid work of treason," were not welcome.[16]

More problematic were those Confederates who hailed from northern Virginia—from those communities directly across the Potomac River from Washington. Hundreds of paroled rebels such as Tom Murray had been imprisoned upon arriving at their Fairfax County and Alexandria homes. But under Speed's opinion and War Department orders, they should not have been detained. Despite the fact that the area had been controlled by the Union since very early in the war, like West Virginians, they had been residents of a state that held a secession convention. Release them, Grant instructed on May 6. As with any other Virginia—or West Virginia— Confederate, they had a right to return to their homes and remain there so long as they observed the laws in force where they resided.[17]

In Maryland, Grant's order forbidding the return of rebels remained in effect. Yet defiant and pompous Confederates continued to strut through the streets of Baltimore.[18] Frustrated with the continual presence of rebels in a city whose reputation had now been forever infamously linked to Lincoln's assassination, General Wallace—in Washington, where he now served on the military commission to try the suspects in the president's assassination— issued stern orders to would-be traitors. He wrote that "the sale of portraits of any rebel officer or soldier, or of J. Wilkes Booth, the murderer of President Lincoln, is forbidden hereafter in this department. All commanding officers and provost-marshals are hereby ordered to take possession of such pictures wherever found exposed for sale, and report the names of the parties so offending, who will be liable to arrest and imprisonment if again guilty of a violation of this order."[19] For Wallace and others, the need to quell the Confederate spirit had grown rather than diminished since Lee's surrender.

From the headquarters of the Military District of Patuxent at Port To-

Disgraceful to Live and Associate with Rebels

bacco, Maryland, came orders on May 1 again prohibiting Confederates from donning their uniforms and insignia of rank as well as displaying—or even having in their possession—rebel flags. Anyone who dared utter a disloyal sentiment or question, "by word or deed," the authority of the United States would be detained. All officers, soldiers, and citizens sympathetic to the rebel cause who had not taken the oath of allegiance—including anyone who gave aid to or even had information on Booth's flight through the state—would be arrested and detained by military authorities. The state of anxiety proved so high in southern Maryland that the provost marshal ordered every person residing in Prince George's, Charles, and St. Mary's Counties to take an oath of allegiance in order to conduct any business. Moreover, the oath would state that it had been taken voluntarily, "without mental reservation," and would be "accompanied by consistent conduct and loyal acts." The fear of rebels taking a coerced oath proved immense. If these requirements did not prove stringent enough, the order instructed "truly loyal persons" to inform military officials if they knew of anyone who failed to cooperate.[20]

Those who had taken the oath, however, were free to go as they pleased. And Grant insisted that military authorities honor this pledge. In early May, a Baltimore man wrote Grant that his son, Joseph D. Sullivan, had served in the Baltimore Light Artillery—a unit surrendered with Lee's army. The twenty-four-year-old Sullivan had escaped Appomattox but sought a parole at Winchester on April 26, where he took the oath that same day before reporting to the provost marshal in Baltimore. But upon doing so, he had been ordered north of Philadelphia (rather than south, into the former Confederacy). Why, his father asked the general-in-chief, was his son not permitted to remain in Baltimore? Grant wondered the same thing and demanded that General Wallace explain his actions.[21]

Sullivan had been sent north, Wallace replied, by Col. John Woolley, provost marshal, under the old orders relating to deserters and refugees. Sullivan had been captured in the Shenandoah Valley during the fall of 1864 and sent to the prisoner-of-war camp at Point Lookout. Only days before Lee began his retreat from the trenches of Petersburg, Sullivan had been paroled. Less than a month later, he sought a second parole. And this time, he was sent north because Woolley did not deem Baltimore a safe place for this die-hard rebel. Wallace agreed with Grant that this had been a mistake.[22]

But Wallace remained unclear as to the reach of Speed's opinion. Would rebels from loyal states be permitted to take the oath?, he asked Grant. And if so, what effect would taking the oath have on the question of residence?

He had allowed those who had taken the oath and desired to leave to do so. But what of those who wanted to stay in Baltimore?[23] Speed's opinion had not discussed those who took the oath. But the same terms that had existed since Lincoln's 1863 amnesty proclamation remained in effect: any rebel who voluntarily took the oath of allegiance would be permitted to stay. They had declared themselves loyal to the Union once more. Grant ordered Wallace to release Sullivan immediately and allow him to return to his Baltimore home.[24]

Sullivan would not be the only rebel sent home under Grant's orders that day—including some who had not taken the oath. Having responded to Wallace, Grant next turned his attention to the letter he had received from Lee a few days prior. Lee had questioned why some of his paroled soldiers had been detained at Fort Monroe and denied passage through Baltimore unless they took the oath. The general-in-chief concurred. As the sun dipped beneath the horizon on May 1, Grant telegraphed the commanding officer at Fort Monroe and ordered passes issued to Major Alexander W. Vick and his comrades so that they might travel through Baltimore to their Tennessee homes. "The same privilege may be extended to any other prisoners you may have who want to pass by the North," he directed. As U.S. forces looked to begin their own process of demobilization, it remained in the army's best interest to clear out all the paroled prisoners from the garrison as quickly as possible. But Grant cautioned that no more rebels were to be received for the purpose of traveling north. Ensuring such an order was executed on the ground would prove far more difficult.[25]

Early May found provost marshals throughout Virginia exceedingly busy. Lee's soldiers continued to arrive at Union posts in Farmville, Charlottesville, Louisa, Beaver Dam, Ashland, Columbia, Richmond, and up and down the Shenandoah Valley. They trickled into headquarters at Bowling Green, King George County, Westmoreland County, Northumberland County, and Fairfax Court House. And they sought paroles beyond the borders of Virginia. Singly and in small bands, they ambled into provost marshal offices in Cumberland, Maryland; in Clarksburg as well as both Charleston and Charles Town, West Virginia; in Washington, D.C.; and even farther afield in North Carolina. By the month's end, no less than 6,616 men from the Army of Northern Virginia had been added to the parole lists, bringing the total of those paroled after Appomattox to more than 15,000.[26]

Some local men had made their way home sometime between February and mid-April but only recently decided to surrender.[27] In the Shenandoah Valley, Lt. Gen. Stonewall Jackson's famed mapmaker, Jedidiah Hotchkiss,

Disgraceful to Live and Associate with Rebels

finally decided to surrender himself. "I went to Staunton to-day and got my-self paroled as a prisoner of war, with permission to remain at home," he re-corded in his diary. "There was a large crowd at Staunton, more than could be paroled," he observed on May 1. Still more would arrive. Over the course of the month, nearly 1,200 of Lee's men would be granted parole in the Val-ley city. Yet Confederate soldiers were not the only ones seeking out Fed-eral troops. Just as enslaved men and women had sought out Federal camps during the fighting, they now gathered at posts such as Staunton seeking rations and protection from Confederates who refused to recognize eman-cipation.[28]

Despite the opportunities afforded to them, some rebels still refused to surrender. On Saturday, April 29, Col. Horatio B. Reed of the 22nd New York Cavalry had ridden into Staunton with more than 600 troopers. Shortly after setting up his headquarters, he received a flag of truce from Col. W. P. Thompson of the 19th Virginia Cavalry inquiring as to the terms of surren-der. Reed informed him that he could surrender upon the same terms offered to the Army of Northern Virginia, to which he belonged. By the following day, the rebels still had not surrendered. After sending out a scout, Reed learned that Thompson's 100 or so men had scattered to the mountains and were not yet ready to acquiesce. Convinced that more Federal troops might help bring them to their senses, Maj. Gen. Winfield Scott Hancock ordered Maj. Gen. Alfred T. A. Torbert to send yet another brigade to Staunton to continue the paroling. As had been the case, Hancock remained concerned about the threat posed by guerrillas. Torbert was to post circulars, similar to those published throughout the lower Valley on April 10, warning of the dire consequences that would fall on those who refused to surrender and on those on the home front who harbored them.[29]

There was one bit of good news. On May 4, General Rosser sent word to U.S. authorities that his men would gather in Staunton on May 10 to sign paroles and turn over their arms.[30]

While Union forces continued to parole Lee's men in the Valley and be-yond, provost marshals now found themselves also administering the oath of allegiance. Contrary to Lee's admonition to Grant that the parole should be enough—that the terms of the surrender had said as much—numerous Union commanders continued to require the oath for any number of practi-cal matters. Taking the oath was necessary for those confined within Union lines in places such as Washington Street Prison in Alexandria who wished to be released. Those who sought transportation aboard government-operated steamers had to take the oath, as did those who wished to return to their homes in loyal states. As distasteful as many rebels found it, they recognized the need to comply, leading to long lines of paroled prisoners awaiting their turn to pledge their loyalty to the United States.[31]

From Washington to the smallest Union post, federal officials implemented policies that defied both logic and law in the name of quelling the rebellion. Grant and Speed had repeatedly maintained in the weeks since April 9 that the parole was a military status marking Lee's soldiers as prisoners of war. If this was the case, the rebels held the status of alien enemies and therefore had no rights of citizenship. The oath, not the parole, proved necessary to restore to Confederates their rights as citizens.[32] Yet even as the federal government demanded that rebels take an oath of allegiance, many loyal northerners continued to debate whether the paroles precluded Confederate soldiers from prosecution for treason. How could both be necessary? Only citizens could commit treason. If the oath was required to *restore* one's citizenship, logic held one had not been a citizen (and therefore could not commit treason). The confusion of dual status theory, treating Confederates as belligerents under the laws of war but as traitors under domestic law, confounded efforts to end the war, just as it had efforts to prosecute the war.[33]

Even with such uncertainty, by early May, more than 5,000 Confederates had pledged an oath of loyalty in Richmond alone. Writing to Grant, General Halleck explained that demand necessitated opening four offices in Richmond for that purpose, all of which proved densely crowded each day. Among those flocking in were "many of Lee's paroled officers." "The rebel feeling in Virginia is utterly dead," Halleck assured Grant, "and, with proper management, can never be revived."[34] Halleck failed to note, however, that oath-taking was a requirement for almost every aspect of life. Both soldiers and civilians — no distinction was made — had to take the oath in order to import goods, practice law or any other profession that required a license, make a claim for restoration of private property, or acquire a marriage license. Even clergymen would be required to take the oath in order to officiate. Any person violating these orders would be arrested.[35]

Coercing loyalty — or pledges of loyalty — was not new. Throughout the war, Union military officials and provost marshals in occupied regions had required the oath for provisions or licenses to practice professions.[36] Guerrilla warfare, especially in border state regions, made declarations of loyalty even more pressing. In the summer of 1862, the U.S. government mandated that all citizens in the Department of Southwest Missouri take an oath of loyalty, for which they would be given a certificate, in order to vote and serve as witnesses or jurors in trials.[37]

If oaths were used as a stick, they could likewise serve as the carrot. Lincoln's Ten Percent Plan of December 1863 offered the opportunity for states to rejoin the Union once 10 percent of their voting population had taken the amnesty oath. Unlike the ironclad oath, in which an individual pledged he or she had never supported the Confederacy, or an oath of allegiance, which promised future loyalty, the amnesty oath conferred a general pardon to an entire class rather than to a single person. But Lincoln excluded several categories from the amnesty, including U.S. congressmen who had left office to join the rebellion, U.S. naval and army officers who had resigned their commission to join the Confederacy, officials and agents of the Confederate government, and high-ranking Confederate officers.[38] This offer continued to exist in April and May 1865. Indeed, instructions had gone out to military commanders in mid-April that any Confederate — soldier or civilian — who desired to take the amnesty oath would be allowed to do so.

But *which* oath a Confederate should take became a source of debate. On May 4, General Ord had authorized the provost marshal in Richmond to administer the amnesty oath to "all persons in the civil or military service of the late rebel Government without regard to their rank or employment." Writing to Grant, Ord's superior, Halleck, explained that "all classes are offering to take the amnesty oath" and that "those excluded from its benefit are nevertheless taking it and making petitions for pardon." Halleck noted that many of Lee's officers had come forward to take the oath, while rumors abounded that the rebel chieftain might follow suit. "Should he do this the whole population with few exceptions will follow his example," he maintained. In short, Halleck believed "it would be unfortunate to check by unnecessary arrests this general desire for amnesty."[39]

After considering Halleck's suggestion, Grant agreed. "Although it would meet with opposition in the North to allow Lee the benefit of Amnesty," he conceded, "I think it would have the best possible effect towards restoring good feeling and peace in the South." Unlike the parole, which offered only questionable protection against any treason charges, amnesty would provide absolution. It would forgive Lee for any crime he may have committed in waging war against the United States. If Lee were to seek amnesty, the great majority of Confederates would be guided by his example.[40]

Not yet aware of the generals' communications about Lee, on May 7 President Johnson informed Halleck that administering the amnesty oath was not acceptable. Confederate men and women were eligible to take an oath of allegiance as prescribed by Congress in 1861, but not the amnesty oath of December 1863. Johnson reminded Halleck that the amnesty oath could be administered only to those who applied for amnesty. Moreover, it excluded most Confederate officers and officeholders.[41]

Halleck insisted that the president had misunderstood. The oath of allegiance, administered to U.S. officeholders and federal employees who promised to uphold the Constitution, did not seem applicable to rebels. Only those who had given no aid to the rebellion could take the ordinary oath. Those who had given such aid took the amnesty oath. Moreover, Confederates excluded under the amnesty proclamation had been informed that they "could only be purged of treason by pardon from the President." The U.S. army would not forward such petitions to Johnson until rebels had taken the amnesty oath. This preliminary step, Halleck maintained, conferred no rights but was merely "a prerequisite to having their petitions considered." Halleck maintained that this method was already producing good results.[42]

Indeed, it appeared to Richmond resident Elizabeth Munford that "every one is taking the oath." Writing her husband from the former Confederate capital, she observed that "it is not forced upon you, and the form is so much modified that any one who is bound to live in the United States can take it without perjury." Even as her son continued to rally his cavalrymen in the Valley, Munford explained that taking the oath was "rendered absolutely necessary, unless you leave your families to starve." But "it is a bitter pill to all, after every thing we have suffered and endured for the last 4 years," she conceded.[43] Necessity and fear, not loyalty or contrition, compelled both Confederate soldiers and civilians to seek the oath.

At least some African Americans condemned the ease with which less-than-contrite rebels might pledge their loyalty to the nation they had been trying to destroy. "Since these traitors have defied the powers of the Government to the extent of their endurance, a little discrimination ought to be exercised to ascertain who are worthy to be readmitted to the privileges of American citizens," observed war correspondent Thomas Morris Chester from Richmond. He had overheard numerous rebels remark that following Lee's surrender, they were willing to take the oath, but he urged caution. "They refused, with scorn, to heed the mercy of the Government," he noted; "now let them experience its justice as a warning to treason in the future."[44]

Chester might well have been appalled by such dubious claims of loyalty had he read the letters from Lewis Webb's mother to Grant. Having been detained twice since surrendering at Appomattox, first at Alexandria

Disgraceful to Live and Associate with Rebels

and then in Baltimore, on May 6 Webb took the oath and was released to head north. But in the days prior to his discharge, his mother had turned to Grant in desperation. Describing herself and her husband as "loyal parents" (a status Union officials readily denied), she recounted how her son had returned home only to be incarcerated with the threat that he would be banished from his home state. "Were ours the only hearts crushed, and bleeding, by the rescession [recension] of your order, and the terms of surrender to Genl Lee — I should be constrained to bear it in silence — but as so many households (rejoicing like ourselves) at the return of prodigal sons — after years of absence — have been lacerated by it — I cannot but feel, Genl, judging from your noble course of late — but that you will pardon me for calling your attention to circumstances as they exist."[45]

Setting down the letter, Grant fumed. From his Washington office, he fired off a telegram to Col. John Woolley, the provost marshal in Baltimore. Why had Webb — a paroled soldier who had taken the oath — been sent north? This was a direct violation of orders. "Constant complaints are made against you for banishing men who have taken the oath of allegiance much to my annoyance and consuming in addition much time," Grant added. Indeed, only a week earlier, Grant had considered relieving Woolley from duty. But in his reply to the general-in-chief, Woolley coolly explained the situation. Webb had been released on May 6, two days prior to Grant's order allowing paroled Confederates to return to their homes in loyal states if they had taken the oath. Woolley maintained that he had not violated any orders. But he was wrong.[46]

The orders to which he referred were issued by the Headquarters of the Army on May 8. In them, Grant directed that all paroled officers and men of late rebel armies who hailed from states that had never participated in the rebellion "and who *are not exempted from the President's amnesty proclamation*" upon "taking the oath" be permitted to "return to their former homes in those states."[47] Contrary to Woolley's justification, Grant's order was not new. It did not represent a change in course. Rather, Grant was reiterating the same position he had held since April 17: *paroled rebels* from Maryland, Missouri, Kentucky, Delaware, and the District of Columbia *could* return to their homes *if* they took the oath. Frustrated that his officers in the field proved inconsistent at best and insubordinate at worst, Grant had been compelled to issue yet another order.

But Grant's officers sometimes interpreted orders differently, depending on their own experience and the situation on the ground. Most were not intentionally ignoring his orders. They were doing the best they could on a day-by-day basis. Most remained as dedicated as Grant to ending the war as swiftly as possible.

Accordingly, that same day, the War Department had ordered the release of all prisoners of war, except officers above the rank of colonel, detained in northern prisons who had been captured *before the fall of Richmond*. If these men took the oath, transportation would be furnished to send them home. Grant likewise personally instructed that all paroled rebels detained at Alexandria's Washington Street Prison be sent home. Those who were from states that had never been in rebellion would be required to take the oath of amnesty. Those from Virginia and other Confederate states would not be required to do so if they returned to their homes.[48] On the outskirts of Washington, the order went out again: send all paroled rebels from seceding states who were confined in Alexandria to their homes. Only those exempted from the amnesty proclamation were to be detained.

On the morning of May 9, precisely one month after he had surrendered with the 1st Battalion Virginia Infantry, Channing Smith finally walked out of the prison gates. After taking the oath (which he was not technically required to do as a West Virginian), he headed toward his Parkersburg home.[49] Channing recognized that returning home could be a terrifying—and potentially deadly—prospect, because many West Virginia Unionists still refused to support Grant's orders. Writing to a local newspaper, an unnamed citizen from Marion County vowed that Unionists intended to carry out their resolutions regarding returning rebels, no matter what Grant or any authority said. Another aggrieved Unionist offered a more pointed reaction: "anything short of extermination or banishment, and confiscation of their property would be misplaced mercy."[50] On the evening of May 16, loyal citizens from Wheeling met again to pass more resolutions barring returning rebels. Why should men who had murdered civilians, stolen property, and starved Union prisoners of war be allowed to return "to plot anew treason in our midst?" Taking the oath meant nothing to men who were traitors. If the U.S. government insisted that the terms of surrender protected these men, the governor of the state needed to act. They beseeched Governor Boreman to yet again lobby Washington to place West Virginia on the list of states that had not supported secession. In the meantime, they reiterated their demand that all returning rebels immediately depart.[51]

Even some of Grant's high command had trouble obeying the orders. In Baltimore, General Wallace pushed his authority to its limits. Always suspicious of rebel sentiment in the city, he instructed Woolley to remain vigi-

Disgraceful to Live and Associate with Rebels

lant. The provost marshal was to post guards at all landings and depots, on the lookout for paroled Confederates. All who arrived were to be taken into custody and were required to provide "satisfactory evidence" of their status as paroled soldiers. Only then would they be allowed to take the oath of allegiance. Any who failed to produce the required evidence or were unwilling to take the oath would be held as prisoners. For those who desired to take the oath, Woolley was to remind them of "the feeling existing amongst citizens, and cautioning them to beware of personal difficulties and danger." If, after such notice was given, they still desired to remain in Baltimore, Woolley would permit them to do so. But Wallace hoped to convince them to leave.[52]

Such command decisions at the local level continued to contribute to confusion and inconsistency. On the morning of May 6, yet another ship carrying paroled Confederates was set to push off from the docks at Fort Monroe. Hoping to convince those Confederate from other states still lingering in Virginia that they should head home, Union officials published notice that all those traveling toward Charleston, Savannah, Pensacola, Mobile, and New Orleans could find passage — free of charge. Only those from Texas, where Gen. Kirby Smith had refused to surrender, were denied transportation.[53] But what of those heading through loyal territory? At Fort Monroe, Capt. A. Gilchrist remained uncertain. In addition to those from Lee's army, paroled prisoners from Johnston's army had begun arriving, desiring transportation to their homes in Tennessee and Kentucky, accessible most readily via trains from Baltimore. "Is the order prohibiting them from going north of this point still in force?" he asked Provost Marshal Marsena Patrick, pointing out that officers were mostly in citizen dress and wished to travel at their own expense.[54] Were they allowed to do so — without taking an oath of loyalty?

13

Enemies or Insurgents

Even as Grant ordered more and more rebels back into and through Maryland, one resident proved unable to escape charges of disloyalty. Throughout the first two weeks of May, Congressman Benjamin G. Harris faced a court-martial trial before a military commission for breaking the laws of war. Perhaps ironically, the key witnesses to Harris's treasonous behavior were none other than two rebel soldiers.[1]

Like so many others from the ranks of Lee's army, Richard Chapman and William Reed found themselves confined in a Union prison only weeks after Appomattox—but for reasons far different from those of their comrades. They had been sent to the Old Capitol Prison in Washington with instructions that they "be treated as kindly as circumstances will permit as they are only to be used as witnesses." At Harris's court-martial they took center stage, answering questions posed by the judge advocate general regarding the congressman's loyalty. Both recounted their conversation with the congressman, explaining that he had refused to accommodate them on the night of April 26 but instead offered them each a dollar to seek lodging in Leonardtown. Equally as damning, they both testified that Harris had decried Grant as a "damned rascal" and told them they could go home on their paroles without taking the oath of allegiance—in fact urged them not to take the oath but to go back and "fight them again."[2]

Throughout the eight-day trial, the focus centered not on Harris's loyalty but rather on the status of the paroled rebels, Chapman and Reed. Harris, after all, believed that under the terms offered by Grant at Appomattox, the rebels *did not* have to take the oath in order to return home. Indeed, he pointed to the conditions of capitulation between Grant and Lee as evi-

dence that paroled prisoners "should be allowed to return to their homes."
As a U.S. congressman, Harris had read Speed's April 22 opinion forbidding
rebels from returning to the loyal states but disagreed with it. Equally important, Harris believed that Grant had changed the terms of capitulation
offered at Appomattox in demanding rebels pledge an oath of loyalty to the
United States before returning to Maryland. This, Harris maintained, made
the general a "damned rascal."

If Harris's demeaning words evoked the ire of Union authorities, he was
charged only with violating the fifty-sixth article of war, specifically relieving enemies of the United States with money and harboring and protecting them by helping them to procure food and lodging. In his defense, Harris first argued that because Chapman and Reed were *paroled*, he could not
be found guilty of aiding an enemy. "When the article speaks of the enemy,
does it mean prisoners of war, the captives of your arms and subjects of your
power?" he queried. "Does it mean paroled prisoners, whose hostility to your
country is suspended during the continuance of the parole?" As paroled prisoners, Chapman and Reed were no longer enemies, he insisted.[3]

In another line of defense, one that ran contrary to the last, Harris argued that Chapman and Reed were not paroled. Harris therefore asked the
court to summon Bvt. Maj. Gen. George H. Sharpe, provost marshal for the
Army of the Potomac, as a witness and requested the general bring with him
the duplicate roll of the 32nd Virginia containing the names of those surrendered at Appomattox. Harris hoped to prove that the roll *did not* contain the
names of Chapman or Reed. If the rebels had not been paroled, he argued,
they were enemies of the state and therefore could not testify against a citizen. On May 11, Sharpe appeared before the court-martial with the 32nd Virginia roll and observed that it did not contain the name of either Chapman
or Reed. But, he cautioned, this did not mean the men had not been paroled.[4]

In painstaking detail, Sharpe explained. By the time Lee's army reached
Appomattox, the commands had disintegrated into chaos and confusion.
With the loss of commanders such as Lt. Gen. Richard S. Ewell, officers
and men did not know to which command they belonged. Pickett's Division, which included the 32nd Virginia, proved a particular mess, because
a considerable portion of the division had been captured at Sailor's Creek.
Moreover, a large number of Lee's men had left the army before the surrender — some to find food, others to escape — and for several days after April 9
thousands had drifted back into the camps hoping to secure the benefits of
surrendering. But upon returning, many found that their own commands
had already been paroled and had departed, while others discovered that

their officers had fled the field, leaving them to seek out other commands for the purpose of being paroled. As such, a man from the 32nd Virginia might find himself listed with some other regiment. But this was not the only reason for the inconsistent lists. "A large number of men of General Lee's army were not paroled at Appomattox Court House at all," Sharpe testified. The written convention signed by the commissioners on April 10 had allowed for the paroling of men far beyond Appomattox, so they had gone to Lynchburg, Farmville, and myriad other places. Chapman and Reed might not appear on the roll of the 32nd Virginia — or on the Appomattox rolls at all — but that did not mean their names were not listed with another brigade or that they had not sought out paroles elsewhere.[5]

After Harris presented his case, W. W. Winthrop, major and judge advocate, countered each of the congressman's objections. The testimony of enemies would not be rejected; instead, it would be received with caution. Indeed, in this case, the testimony of the two rebels had been corroborated by loyal Union soldiers. More important, the paroled status of the men did not matter. Even if they had been paroled, this in no way modified their status as enemies of the state. Referring back to the *Prize Cases*, Winthrop reminded the panel that all persons engaged in the rebellion were enemies. And they were no less enemies simply because they had been paroled. The parole had not formally discharged them from service in the Confederate army. They were liable at any moment to be exchanged, even without their knowledge. The effect of the parole, Winthrop observed, was "simply to exempt them from capture or attack by our own forces till exchanged." The parole, he argued, did not relieve a man from his responsibility as a soldier.[6]

Nor did the terms of capitulation extended by Grant at Appomattox modify their status as enemies. Harris had pointed to Grant's Special Field Orders No. 73 issued on April 10 allowing paroled rebels to pass through Union lines to reach their homes, but Winthrop dismissed this as well. Relying heavily on Speed's April 22 opinion on the terms of capitulation and invoking international law theorists Emmerich de Vattel and Henry Wheaton, Winthrop concurred that rebels who had not taken the oath could not return to the loyal states. "All the authorities, indeed, hold that prisoners of war may be permitted upon their parole to reside unmolested in *the territory of their own government*, but no more than this." Grant had cleared up his meaning in a series of telegraphs to Ord on April 18–20 observing that "it was no part of the agreement that we should furnish homes, subsistence, or transportation to Lee's army." Harris could not justify his actions as complying with Grant's order.[7]

The proceedings concluded on May 11, just as another military commission prepared to hear testimony in the presidential assassins' tribunal. The following day, the court-martial found Harris guilty. Although the crime carried a death sentence, the court ordered him forever disqualified from holding any office in the United States and sentenced him to three years in the penitentiary.[8] Chapman and Reed fared much better, despite the fact that they had been repeatedly described as enemies. Even before the trial concluded, both men took the oath of allegiance, on May 9 — as Grant instructed they be allowed to do. Chapman set sail to Jersey City, New Jersey, while Reed boarded a steamer bound for New York City.[9] After testifying on behalf of the United States, perhaps both men thought their interests better served by heading north rather than south or even back to Baltimore.

As Harris's trial ended, yet another military commission convened in Martinsburg, West Virginia. Again, a military court would question the limits and protections afforded by the Appomattox surrender, but this time, paroled Confederate major and assistant adjutant general Henry Kyd Douglas stood trial.

Douglas had grown up near Sharpsburg, Maryland, and was on his way to his father's home when he learned that his parole would not allow him to cross the Potomac River into loyal territory. Instead, he stopped just south of the river in the hamlet of Shepherdstown, West Virginia, where he boarded with a friend. Informed that he must not be seen in public in his Confederate uniform, the twenty-six-year-old staff officer sold his mule and used the proceeds to purchase a change of clothing. Even so, local Unionists became increasingly suspicious of the rebel in their midst. "It was soon understood at all neighboring posts that I was a dangerous character to be unconfined," Douglas later wrote. Rumors ran wild through town, and soon the young staff officer found himself under increased scrutiny. "The espionage," he observed, "soon accomplished results."[10]

Despite such foreboding signs, when a local lady proposed that Douglas have his photograph taken wearing his Confederate uniform, he agreed. "It seemed a harmless suggestion and I adopted it," he later explained. On Friday, May 5, he donned a citizen's coat and the military pants of his Confederate uniform and accompanied the woman to Thomas L. Darnell's studio, where he posed both with her and alone. But after their likeness had been taken, the gallery and antechamber had been filled with "ladies and little girls," and he insisted it would have been inappropriate for him to change.

Confederate officer Henry Kyd Douglas faced a court-martial for donning his rebel uniform in Shepherdstown, West Virginia, in May 1865. National Park Service.

He therefore departed in his full uniform, replete with a major's star on the collar. As the Confederate officer walked through the streets, onlookers took notice and reported the offense to military authorities stationed at Martinsburg. The next morning, a company of cavalry under the command of Capt. William H. Seidenstricker galloped into Shepherdstown, arrested Douglas, and confiscated the negative from the photographer's studio. Wounded by a shot to his left scapula and captured at Gettysburg, Douglas had already spent ten months imprisoned at Johnson's Island before being exchanged and returning to Lee's army. Now he found himself held in solitary confinement in the basement of a Catholic church in Martinsburg.[11]

The military commander in the region, Bvt. Maj. Gen. John D. Stevenson, charged Douglas with three counts: violating his parole by appearing in public in a Confederate uniform — "a badge of treason and rebellion and as such marking his hostility to the Government of the United States and intended and designed to encourage and incite rebellion"; violating General Orders No. 28 issued by the Military District of Harpers Ferry on April 26,

Enemies or Insurgents

which prohibited wearing a Confederate uniform in public; and treason in that Douglas "did take up arms and attempt to overthrow the government of the United States" and subsequently appeared in the public streets in uniform with an intent "to weaken and destroy the United States and to incite treason."[12] In Norfolk and other locales, Confederates had been arrested for wearing their uniforms.[13] But this would be the first court-martial for such an offense.

On May 10, the military commission convened in an improvised courthouse in Martinsburg's public square. Douglas, admitted to the bar a year before the war began, represented himself but to no avail. The commission found him guilty on the first two charges but acquitted him of the treason charge before sentencing him to confinement at Fort Delaware for two months. Reviewing the case on May 16, Stevenson explained why the seemingly innocent act of wearing a rebel uniform warranted such a punishment: "The purposes of the Government, and the whole purposes of the war, are to utterly eradicate such feelings in the country. Acts savoring of treason, of themselves, cannot be palliated—This is one of that class."[14]

Union commanders far from West Virginia and Maryland reiterated Secretary Stanton's General Orders No. 73 forbidding rebels to appear in public wearing a Confederate uniform. Officers in particular were warned against displaying any badges, insignia, or uniforms denoting their rank. From the Headquarters of the District of East Tennessee came a stern warning—any who did so would "be considered guilty of an act of hostility toward the United States government" and therefore "subject himself to arrest and imprisonment."[15] In Richmond, where Ord remained reluctant to enforce the prohibition against uniforms, rebel uniform jackets were auctioned off by the boxful for ten cents each. "This may be regarded as an evidence of the respect which the people here have for the colors in which traitors delighted to shoot down patriots," declared Black correspondent Thomas Morris Chester.[16]

A few days after Douglas's conviction, a Union guard marched him to the train station accompanied by the beat of martial music. After a night spent in a Harpers Ferry jail amid bounty jumpers, horse thieves, and deserters, Douglas boarded the train again. But rumors had reached Union officials that Douglas might know something about Lincoln's assassination. He was to be sent directly to Washington. On the very day that Sherman's army made its grand entry into the capital, the Union guard hauled Douglas to the provost marshal's office, from which he was sent to the Old Capitol Prison. Hundreds of other paroled Confederates had been released from its

walls only days earlier by Grant's order. Now Douglas found himself confined once again, this time in a cell next Mary Surratt, one of the accused
assassins.[17]

A month and a half after Appomattox, Douglas and other Confederates
wondered just how much protection Grant's terms and the paroling process
offered them. Both Confederate officers and enlisted men interpreted the
parole as a blanket amnesty, and many Union officers concurred. But all were
quickly learning otherwise. Their paroles might be ignored, and if they were,
the rebels would not be safe from prosecutions for treason.[18]

Some white northerners continued to see Lee's men as potentially threatening even in defeat. From Alexandria, where Union officials still routinely
detained returning rebels, abolitionist Julia Wilbur worried that Grant's liberal terms might result in more, not less, turmoil. "The rebels are scattered
all over the country and will make a great deal of trouble yet," she predicted.
"There will be conspiracies to burn cities no doubt & do all manner of mischief." She worried that the leading rebels would escape and agreed with
others that it was "absurd to spare Lee & punish others, when he is the guil-
tiest traitor of all."[19]

Such concerns renewed the wartime debate on the intersection of belligerent status and the domestic law of treason. Had Grant's terms *really*
recognized Confederates as belligerents, thereby precluding treason prosecutions?[20] Speed's opinion had declared that paroles affected only military
actions and did not confer amnesty from civil prosecution. Others concurred, including the lawyer turned general Benjamin Butler. Several days
after Lee's surrender, the major general despised in the South for his contra-
band policy at Fort Monroe and his order threatening to treat New Orleans
women as prostitutes delivered an address in Washington. He pointed out
that Lee had been educated at the public expense, advanced to dignity in
the U.S. army, married into George Washington's family before committing
one of the most overt cases of treason in leading the rebel forces. "We are
not ready to receive such men back to take part with us, or to be of us," he
thundered.[21]

After hearing of the impassioned speech, President Johnson asked the
general (hardly an international law expert) for his thoughts on punishing
the rebels. Butler responded immediately, drafting a lengthy missive arguing for the criminal liability of Lee and his soldiers. He explained that paroling was but a relatively recent phenomenon in world history, which served

Enemies or Insurgents

as a method of "restraining prisoners of war, before exchange[,] from being again found in arms." In other words, it acted as a method of imprisonment in which the pledge of the individual stood as a substitute for guards and prison. "The parole," he noted, "confers no *rights* upon the prisoner, but only the privilege of partial liberty, instead of close confinement." The surrender of Lee's army was a purely military convention. "It could not and did not alter in any way or any degree the civil rights or criminal liabilities of the captives either in persons or property as a treaty of peace might have done."[22] This was key—there had been no peace treaty, only the surrender of an army and its soldiers.

A correspondent for the *New York Times* likewise assured its readers that Grant's terms were not nearly as lenient as many presumed. Simply put, the punishment for breaking one's parole (which included breaking any law, including now wearing one's Confederate uniform) was death. Many worried that the rebels would simply be exchanged and sent home under no penalty. "Of course they will not be exchanged," observed another newspaper, "and they are therefore bound, under penalty of death, to refrain from hostilities against the government." *If* the U.S. government decided to exchange and release the soldiers from their paroles, however, they would become ordinary citizens subject to civil authorities. Perhaps more importantly, when the war was declared over, they would no longer be protected as prisoners of war. As Butler explained to Johnson, "The war is virtually at an end, and Lee's men can hardly be said to be prisoners of war even without the action of the Government." In his estimation, the terms of surrender did not prevent Lee's troops from being punished for treason.[23]

Not content with editorials, the *New York Times* called on Columbia University law and political science professor Francis Lieber to elaborate on the legal status afforded by the paroles.[24] "Does the cartel which admits him as a paroled prisoner of war clothe him with immunity as a citizen? Is he protected against trial while prisoner of war, and unexchanged, for any and every crime he may have committed while in arms against the United States?" asked the newspaper.[25] At least a handful of rebels could testify that it did not including men such as James Buckley, a paroled rebel, hauled in by a Baltimore provost marshal for disloyalty.[26] Even as far west as Nashville, guards arrested paroled prisoner D. H. Smith for using disloyal language.[27]

In early May, the jurist and author of the Lieber Code offered a lengthy explanation to the public in his article "The Status of Rebel Prisoners of War." He observed that a belligerent was not a criminal, and by extension, a prisoner of war was not a convict. Like Speed, he maintained that the parole was military in character; it said nothing about citizens' rights. A parole did not imply pardon for any offenses committed prior to the surrender; as such, prisoners of war remained responsible for any penal crimes they had committed before their capture (such as in the case of Noble Thomas of Washington, who had been charged with treason as a spy and informer). In a rebellion, a surrender implied only that "the act of appearing in arms against the other contracting party, shall not be viewed as a crime." Moreover, breaking the parole was punishable by death when the person breaking the parole was captured again.

This aside, Lieber believed that recognizing the Confederacy as a belligerent power was a mistake. The United States had applied the laws of war to the Confederacy out of humanity, but that should not shield rebels from criminal liability for treason under domestic law. The laws of war were "made for the intercourse of warring parties who commit no crime by warring with one another," he observed, whereas the Confederates "prove that they commit a crime—i.e. treason or armed rebellion against their lawful government."[28] The paroles *should not* protect rebel soldiers from charges of treason.

But two of Lieber's points proved especially important. First, he reasoned that those who had served as soldiers could not enjoy greater immunities than the civilians who had joined the rebellion. Second, as soon as the rebellion was at an end, the power of the parole ceased "and the paroled person becomes again simply a citizen."[29] Echoing others, he observed that paroles were restricted to wartime. Once the rebellion was declared at an end, the paroles would offer no protection, thereby opening the possibility of trying at least top-level generals.[30]

While theorists, journalists, and lawmakers in New York and Washington debated the status of paroled rebels, the effects of disbanding Confederate armies shaped the daily lives of those on the home front. Scouts from Fredericksburg, Virginia, reported that disbanded officers and soldiers from Lee's army were marauding the provisions and property of locals. "Young men belonging to respectable families, who have been in the army, swear they will not work for a living, and devote themselves to plunder," remarked one newspaper. To the northwest in Loudoun County, residents likewise related constant incursions by paroled rebel soldiers into Maryland "who drive off horses, cattle, etc. and tear down and destroy every American flag displayed in that neighborhood." With each passing day, the accounts seemed to multiply. Accounts of pillaging and robbery poured into Union headquarters from Kentucky, the panhandle of West Virginia, southwest Virginia, and along the Atlantic coast.[31]

Commanding the Department of West Virginia, Bvt. Maj. Gen. William H. Emory wondered whether he was to treat former Confederate soldiers like combatant enemies or as citizens committing crimes. In the vast mountainous region between the Ohio River and the Shenandoah Valley, rebel soldiers had taken to stealing horses, saddles, pistols, and arms as well as plundering their neighbors before hiding in the hills to avoid Union forces. "The citizens are bringing such allegations in the civil courts," Emory reported, but the rebels asserted that the acts were committed under orders from their officers. Refusing to concede defeat, they claimed that they were acting in their capacity as soldiers—as belligerents—and therefore should be afforded the protection of the United States. The rebels were relying on the laws of war to protect them. As citizens they might be prosecuted in civil courts. As belligerent soldiers, they claimed, they could not. Although Lieber and others disputed this rationale, Emory acknowledged that it left him in a legal quandary. "Many of the acts complained of were no doubt committed by order of the rebel authorities," he noted, "while it is equally certain that the other, were committed in a spirit of wantonness and plunder for individual gain."[32]

Union forces in the Shenandoah Valley and northern Virginia faced similar problems of paroled soldiers marauding and stealing horses. Unlike Emory, Torbert, commanding the Army of the Shenandoah, had no doubts as to the appropriate response, directing his subordinate to send him the names of five officers who might constitute a commission. He would order a trial of the offenders at Staunton for violation of their paroles.[33] From the Middle Military Division, Hancock endorsed this action, as did Halleck from the headquarters of the Military Division of the James in Richmond. Paroled soldiers or citizens found marauding were not entitled to any quarter; rather, they were to be taken prisoner, promptly tried by a military commission, "and punished with death or otherwise less severely, according to the circumstances of the case."[34] Replying to Col. E. V. Sumner in Fredericksburg, General Ord wasted no time calling for a trial. He simply ordered the cavalry to "shoot guerrillas, horse thieves, or marauders." From his headquarters in Danville, Maj. Gen. Horatio Wright likewise ordered all guerrillas and paroled prisoners who broke their paroles to be hanged at once.[35]

The Union high command was thinking in part of two men: John S. Mosby and Thomas Rosser. In mid-April, Colonel Mosby had twice led

Hancock and others to believe that he would surrender. Instead, he had disbanded his command on April 21. Most of his men had sought out paroles that next evening in Winchester, but the Gray Ghost had not appeared. Frustrated with Mosby's impertinence, on May 3, at Grant's suggestion, Hancock increased the award offered for the "apprehension and delivery at any military post" of the colonel from $2,000 to $5,000.[36] Whether inspired by the bounty on Mosby's head or simply believing the time had come to give up the fight, the next day, Major General Rosser promised Union authorities he would gather the men of his command and surrender them as a unit in Staunton. Yet rumors continued to swirl that the cavalry general, now accompanied by Maj. Gen. Lunsford Lomax, had instead begun readying his men for a raid with 3,000 to 5,000 men on Union lines near Philippi, West Virginia. After the strike, the men would disband and disappear—not surrender.[37] Such reports only fanned the flames of resistance and retribution in West Virginia.

In Washington, Grant likewise heard rumors, albeit ones that claimed Rosser had been captured near Richmond. Telegraphing Halleck on May 9, Grant ordered that Rosser be brought to Washington "to be tried for deserting his command after it had been surrendered."[38] There would be no lenient terms for those who had absconded. Both newspaper accounts and Rosser insisted that he had been apprehended by Union troops at Hanover Court House while visiting his wife, but Halleck reassured Grant that Rosser had come voluntarily within Union lines at Richmond. "He was not captured," Halleck informed Grant, "but surrendered himself on the terms of Lee's capitulation, and promised that his entire command should lay down their arms."[39]

Rather than rallying at Staunton on May 10, as his last general order had instructed, Rosser would gather his men in the valley town to surrender. Most of his men had either turned themselves in already or dispersed into the countryside. Yet in small detachments or as individuals, they arrived over the next few weeks at provost marshal stations throughout the Shenandoah Valley and at locales as distant as Charleston and Norfolk. There would be no single paroling of his command. Moreover, Rosser admitted that he had concealed thirteen artillery pieces between Staunton and Lexington as well as another eight near Pittsylvania Court House and had buried small arms near Charlottesville.[40] The hiding of arms and dispersal of small bands of men into the countryside was precisely what Grant and others had feared most as Union forces finally ground down the Confederate armies. But in the wake

Enemies or Insurgents

of Lincoln's assassination, many Union officials remained especially wary of lawless and marauding bands of soldiers unleashed from the laws of war who might disappear into the civilian population only to materialize again. The prospect of continued guerrilla-style warfare, the kind waged so effectively by Mosby, remained a threat.

As the hunt for Mosby continued, the process of ending the war continued in Washington as much as it did on the field of battle. In an executive order of May 9, President Johnson declared the acts and proceedings of the Confederacy null and void, carefully reserving the right to prosecute those responsible for treason. The following day, even as Union cavalry surrounded Jefferson Davis in Georgia, Johnson observed that "armed resistance . . . may be regarded as virtually at an end." Piecemeal though it may have been, the United States was dismantling the Confederacy such that it "disappeared as a political and legal entity."[41] Grant followed up these legal declarations with several military orders that intensified expectations of peace. Following the surrender of Lt. Gen. Richard Taylor's army at Citronelle, Alabama, on May 4 and the subsequent disbanding of all forces east of the Mississippi, including that of Lt. Gen. Nathan Bedford Forrest, Grant declared that as of June 1, any persons found in arms against the United States east of the Mississippi River would be regarded as guerrillas and punished by execution.[42] While Union provost marshals would continue issuing paroles to Confederates who surrendered themselves, as of May 11, Union soldiers were no longer authorized to search the countryside for those who had not surrendered. Finally, in perhaps the greatest signal the war was coming to a close, Grant endorsed plans for the demobilization of Union armies.[43]

Still, the Union army wanted Mosby. After leaving Salem, Virginia, on April 21, Mosby and several of his men had ridden south to the outskirts of Richmond. Upon learning that Johnston had surrendered, Mosby disbanded what remained of his command. At least two of the men who had stayed with him, his brother William as well as Ben Palmer, sought out paroles in Winchester on May 15.[44] But Mosby assumed that his refusal to surrender to Hancock had negated his opportunity to do the same. Instead, he rode on to the foothills of the Blue Ridge near his boyhood home, seeking shelter with his uncle John Mosby in Nelson County. There he remained for nearly two months, with occasional excursions to Lynchburg to visit his parents. At some point in early May, Mosby sent Palmer's father to ask Lee if he might help. For a second time, Lee interceded on behalf of one of his men. In Richmond, Lee turned to Provost Marshal Patrick to inquire as to whether

Mosby might yet still be eligible for parole. Patrick did not know. He would have to consult the general-in-chief. In the meantime, Mosby would lay low. Despite the $5,000 price on his head, he refused to seek exile.[45]

Even as he delayed answering Lee's query about Mosby, Grant began to relax his position on sending rebels home to the loyal states. The question had become more pronounced with the surrender of Johnston and Taylor's armies. Taylor's force alone included more than 1,000 men from Missouri, now prohibited from returning if they refused to take the oath. What would become of these men? Would they turn to banditry and highway robbery? Grant feared as much. "I do not see half the objection to having whipped rebels, bound by [their paroles] to observe the laws prevailing upon where they may be . . . going into loyal communities," he wrote Secretary Stanton on May 18, "that I do to retaining in those communities disloyal men, as we are doing, who are bound by no oath and who have suffered nothing from the war." In Grant's estimation, paroled soldiers could be trusted more than disloyal civilians. Rather than preventing them from returning to their homes, oath or not, he advised the secretary to authorize all paroled prisoners, from any state, to return to their antebellum residences. If, however, state authorities prevented rebels from returning, the U.S. military would not interfere.[46]

As the Union Army of the Potomac and Sherman's force gathered in Washington for the Grand Review, Confederate soldiers from all three field armies east of the Mississippi River continued to fan out from their respective surrender sites. Still traveling to their homes in Georgia, Alabama, Mississippi, Louisiana, and Texas, men such as Lewis H. Andrews reached into pockets for passes in order to draw rations from Union posts.[47] Upon arriving in the port of New Orleans, paroled Confederates reported to the local provost marshal, as military orders commanded, where their paroles would be stamped.[48] At Mobile, Capt. W. T. Hill and others of Hood's Brigade handed over their Appomattox paroles for inspection before receiving rations.[49] Fellow Texan G. S. Qualls reported to the provost marshal's post in Montgomery on May 9 in order to receive two rations.[50] Every time Lee's men handed over that slip of paper, they were reminded that they remained prisoners of war, prisoners bound by the conditions of the surrender.

Yet proximity to home reminded them that they would soon be among friends and family, not just other soldiers. Upon reaching the Texas state line, Sgt. D. H. Hamilton and others in Hood's Brigade decided the time had come to boil their clothes and rid themselves of the remaining members of

Enemies or Insurgents

the "Royal Irish Brigade, still secreted under the seams of our clothing." Borrowing pots, tubs, and homemade soap from a local family, the men gathered along a small stream where they scrubbed the "cooties" from their clothing and bodies. "We did not think that it was just the proper thing to do to take these veterans home and introduce them into polite society," Hamilton admitted.[51]

While members of Hood's Brigade finally reached the Texas border, paroling of Lee's men continued back east. Some surrendered themselves beyond the borders of the Old Dominion. In West Virginia, no fewer than 768 men sought paroles at posts in Charleston, Clarksburg, Romney, Moorfield, and New Creek. At least 1,483 men from the Army of Northern Virginia turned themselves in to provost marshals in North Carolina, including Clayton Wilson. Heading home to Alabama on horseback, he made it to Bladen County, North Carolina, on April 23, when he discovered that his horse's back was in no shape to continue. He decided to rest for a week for the animal to heal, but a month later he remained in North Carolina. Finally, on May 22 he could wait no longer and decided to sign a parole so that he might catch a steamer out of Wilmington and draw rations.[52] Still others received paroles farther south. Ham Chamberlayne had held out for more than a month in the hope that the Confederacy might yet keep fighting. But having tendered his services to the Army of Tennessee (which Johnston declined) and attempted to report to Secretary of War John C. Breckinridge in Augusta, Georgia, the artillerist finally signed a parole in Atlanta on May 12. Rather than returning to his beloved Virginia, he headed west to Hinds County, Mississippi. He would remain there with his refugee mother and her brother, mulling over his future plans.[53]

The great majority of those who sought paroles in May did so in Virginia. After learning of Rosser's capitulation and hearing threats that the Union army intended to "burn and destroy everything he had," on May 20 Thomas Munford and two of his staff officers surrendered at Lynchburg.[54] Artillerist captain John J. Shoemaker had returned from North Carolina in April after Johnston refused to receive any of Lee's men. But it was not until May 22 that he sought a parole in his hometown of Lynchburg.[55] Gordon McCabe remained in North Carolina until mid-May, when he finally gave up the fight and resolved to go home. Having seen the U.S. army's order forbidding Confederates from donning their uniforms, he had thought it best to travel first to Richmond, where he hoped to get money and clothes from his father's family before venturing to his residence in Petersburg. Presumably after acquiring civilian clothing, on May 22 he, too, turned himself in at the

Pvt. A. S. Dorman, Company I, 10th Georgia Infantry—known as the "Fayette Rifle Grays"—had been on detached duty at Drewry's Bluff in March 1865. He failed to surrender at Appomattox but was captured and paroled at Athens, Georgia, on May 8, 1865. PA0294, John L. Nau III Collection, Small Special Collections, University of Virginia.

local provost marshal's office and signed his parole.[56] During May, the Union army had paroled an additional 4,000 Army of Northern Virginia soldiers in the Old Dominion.[57]

As the days grew longer and warmer with the approach of summer, it became ever more apparent to loyal West Virginians that Grant's orders would continue to protect returning rebels. Still, many pressed Governor Boreman to do more—to enforce Speed's opinion in a state born out of an objection to secession. Yet despite his pleadings with Washington, and even more so given Grant's new stance toward allowing *all* rebels to return home to any state without taking the oath, Boreman resigned himself to the situation.

On May 26, he issued an address to the people of West Virginia. "The rebellion has proven a failure," he began; "in all its proportions as an organized resistance to the authority of the Government, it is ended." While no one would forget who had initiated the bloodletting nor the devastation suffered by those who had remained loyal, he urged his state to move forward. The loyal population was rightfully angry that Grant and Speed had permitted the return of rebels, and he assured them that he had endeavored to

Enemies or Insurgents

have the orders revoked without any success. "You have the right to protest against them and petition for the revocation," he observed. But he cautioned, while the orders remained in force, it was the duty of law-abiding citizens to respect them. If, however, anyone guilty of treason, a felony, or another offense arrived in their communities, the loyal citizenry of West Virginia should bring that person before the courts. Fearful of widespread civil strife, the governor urged Unionists to observe the law rather than take matters into their own hands. The loyal citizens of West Virginia needed to respect the rule of law and abide by the authority of the United States.[58]

If loyal, white West Virginians feared the return of Lee's men, freed-people throughout the South found even more reason for concern. Arriving in Savannah on May 6, Assistant Surgeon Robert Pooler Myers of the 16th Georgia reflected on his new status as a "paroled prisoner of war." What worried him most was what life would bring now that Georgia was "under Yankee rule and guarded by *Negroes.*"[59] Even though the Thirteenth Amendment had yet to be ratified, the Union army's presence ensured that the social and political order of the slaveholding South had been upended. From Albemarle County, Virginia, Robert Garlick Kean, head of the Confederate Bureau of War, decried "the abolition of slavery immediately, and by a military order," as "the marked feature of this conquest of the South." Throughout Virginia he had witnessed the immediate results of emancipation. "Great numbers of negroes quit work and flocked to Richmond and other garrisoned towns, where they had to be supported by the issue of rations," he observed. But, according to Kean, even the U.S. army had become frustrated, ordering "that the negroes should remain on the plantations and work." He had heard reports that in Appomattox and Buckingham Counties, Union soldiers had shot and "unmercifully whipped" African Americans. From his residence in Albemarle on June 1, he could only conclude that former Confederates were waiting "for the US military authorities to take some order for reorganizing society and establishing a definite basis upon which such reorganization was to proceed."[60]

Other Confederates refused to wait for Union authorities. In late May, the Freedmen's Bureau commissioner in Alabama reported that a group of recently returned Confederates "took some Freedmen and cut off their ears" in an attempt to terrorize them into submission and returning to the fields. Others had been "inhumanely bruised and hacked."[61] Murders of Black soldiers continued as well. In the small town of Kinston, North Carolina, Sgt. Norman B. Sterrett of the 39th USCT reported that the presence of his regiment had infuriated the white citizens. "I heard them calling in all manner of names that were never applied to the Deity, to deliver them from the hands of the *smoked Yankees*," he wrote. "The next thing they saw was the *smoked Yankees* marching some of their fellow citizens to jail at the point of the bayonet." Perhaps it was this incident that provoked the killing of Sterrett's comrade David C. Bracker by a "notorious rebel."[62] Exasperating the situation were false reports reprinted in northern Democratic papers claiming that soldiers of the USCT in Memphis had plotted to kill paroled rebel soldiers in revenge for the Fort Pillow massacre.[63]

More than six weeks had passed since Appomattox, and yet the post-surrender world remained more uncertain than ever.

14

Pardon and Amnesty

At the end of May 1865, Andrew Johnson initiated his plan to reunite the divided the nation. Johnson had become convinced that Lincoln's 1863 amnesty proclamation would not suffice once hostilities ceased and asked Attorney General Speed to advise him on the president's power to pardon. On May 8, Speed offered his formal opinion observing that the president alone had a constitutional right to grant reprieves and pardons. No act of Congress was necessary. The attorney general argued that extending such benevolence and clemency would be invaluable in ending the insurrection. Indeed, the pardon's purpose was "to soothe and heal, not to keep alive or to initiate the rebellious and malignant passions that induced, precipitated, and sustained the insurrection." While the Constitution had not defined amnesty or pardon, Speed observed that amnesty was an act of oblivion or forgetfulness, while a pardon served as a remission of guilt. "There can be no pardon where there is no actual or imputed guilt," he maintained. In other words, "the acceptance of a pardon is a confession of guilt."[1]

For nearly three weeks the president conferred with Speed, Secretary of War Stanton, and other members of his cabinet on the topic. Finally, on May 29, he issued his first proclamation of pardon and amnesty, which conferred amnesty "with restoration of all rights and property, except as to slaves," to all participants in the rebellion who took an oath promising to support and defend the Constitution and to support all laws concerning the emancipation of slaves. Once an individual took the amnesty oath, his or her citizenship would be restored.[2]

As with earlier amnesty offers, not every rebel was eligible to receive Johnson's offer. Fourteen classes were excluded and would have to apply for individual pardons, including former rebels with taxable property worth more than $20,000 or anyone who vacated a judicial position or seat in Congress in order to support the rebellion. Alongside these categories stood those directly tied to the Confederate military effort: individuals who had attended West Point or the Naval Academy, resigned a commission in the U.S. army or navy, or tortured prisoners; all Confederate officers above the rank of colonel in the army (and lieutenant in the navy); and all persons currently confined as prisoners of war. Finally — and perhaps most often overlooked — in keeping with Speed's April 22 opinion and General Orders No. 73, the proclamation exempted "all persons who left their homes within the jurisdiction and protection of the United States and passed beyond the Federal military lines into the so-called Confederate States, for the purpose of aiding the rebellion." All of these individuals would have to submit individual applications for pardon to Johnson.[3] But the vast majority of Lee's men — of all Confederate soldiers — would be pardoned by the simple act of taking the amnesty oath.[4]

The proclamation simultaneously afforded a great deal of protection to the rank and file of Lee's army, closed the doors for prosecuting Confederates who had been pardoned, and set in motion a host of new legal and constitutional questions about reunion. Most importantly, Johnson's focus on personal pardon and amnesty proved a legal act that was unsuited to address the attachment to the Confederate nation that still burned bright mere weeks after Appomattox. As countless rebels would claim both in the summer of 1865 and decades later, taking an oath or applying for a pardon was not an admission of guilt. Instead, they remained firm in their conviction that the Confederate cause had been righteous.[5]

Restoring the Union proved to be both a legal and theoretical problem driven by two questions: first, how to treat the state governments that claimed to have left the Union to form the Confederacy, and second, how to address the individuals who had joined the rebellion (both civilians and soldiers). For Johnson, who believed that the states had never left the Union, the second question proved to be of utmost importance. Where Lincoln had utilized the pardon as a war measure meant to induce rebels back into the Union and undermine the rebellion, Johnson saw the pardon as an instrument — perhaps *the* instrument — of reconstruction. Reestablishing individual loyalty to the Union proved his greatest concern. In Johnson's estimation, reunion and reconstruction rested on the pardoning power.[6]

Rebs Taking the Oath at Richmond, 1865, sketch by Alfred R. Waud. Library of Congress Prints and Photographs Division, LC-DIG-ppmsca-21252.

As Congressional Republicans would come to realize, pardons conferred a great deal of protection to former rebels. Unlike the parole, by definition a pardon guaranteed immunity for prosecution of treason and absolved individuals of guilt for a crime. Pardons enabled individuals to conduct business and to make contracts, and, perhaps most frightening for Unionists in border states, pardons could potentially restore political privileges. Pardons remained distinct from taking the oath, as Lt. Gen. James Longstreet quickly discovered. In late May, the provost marshal in Campbell County, Virginia, had administered the oath to the rebel general, but that did not absolve him of crime. He would receive no such benefit until pardoned by the president. But once a person was pardoned, that status could not be revoked.[7] Because only the president could grant pardons, he wielded enormous power and influence over the direction of postwar politics.[8]

Outside of Washington, jurists and northern civilians likewise acknowledged that the rebellion had left two unresolved questions: how to treat individual rebels and how to restore the states to the Union. On the first question, New York lawyer Charles P. Kirkland fell into the camp that sought to forgive the masses of Confederates because they had been duped by the South's slaveholding aristocrats. In a pamphlet soon making its way across the North, Kirkland observed that the "millions of whites, whom they have so long held in subordination," had "grievously erred," but they had received "an equally grievous punishment" and should be offered amnesty. A small number of leaders, however, should be indicted for the crime of treason. Among them Kirkland counted Davis, Breckinridge, former U.S. congressmen and senators, and those who tortured Union prisoners.

Lee, however, presented a more difficult case. He had violated his oath of office to the U.S. military and "aided the Rebellion more effectively than any other single individual." More problematically for Kirkland, Lee remained "an unrepentant impudent rebel ... notwithstanding all the kindness and magnanimity shown him in the surrender terms." The chief evidence of this was the farewell order Lee had issued to his disbanding army on the field at Appomattox. When Lee told his soldiers that their conduct had endeared them to their "countrymen" and praised his men's devotion to their "country," he had failed to repudiate the Confederacy as a nation. "Instantly, on the issuing of this order, the man should have been arrested for *violation of his parole* in its spirit if not in its letter," Kirkland argued, "for if the sentiments put forth in that document were adopted and acted on by those to whom it was addressed, they never would have become in reality 'Citizens of the Republic.'" Rather than submitting, Lee had stoked the fires of hatred toward the Union. Kirkland hoped the U.S. government would take Lee's actions seriously and decide whether he might "be subjected to a traitor's doom."[9]

Such bombastic language seemed to embolden rather than quell rebels' attachment to the Confederacy. From his Lexington, Virginia, home, Lee's artillery chief, William Pendleton, admitted that a great deal of uncertainty surrounded Johnson's proclamation: Confederate officers and others excluded from the general amnesty wondered if the president might yet confiscate their property, banish them from the Union, or inflict some other final humiliation. "But the fact is," he wrote his daughter in mid-June, "I do not believe the shrewd Andy will violate Grant's parole, notwithstanding the blood-and-thunder announcement of malignant judges, charging grand juries, etc." Grant had pledged to uphold the paroles, and although "some wretches affect to regard this as mere military arrangement," Pendleton insisted they would not venture to harm Lee or any other Confederate soldier. "I am not particularly anxious about my own destiny," he assured his daughter, "satisfied as I am that duty in the sight of God has been my aim, and that our cause is and has always been a righteous one."[10]

Pardon and Amnesty

While those who had stayed with Lee's army to the end wound their way home by foot, ship, and railroad car, many of their comrades who had been captured in battle days and even years prior to Appomattox remained in northern prisons. From within their confines they had followed the course of the war — of Richmond's fall, Lee's surrender, and Lincoln's assassination. They knew that their brethren in Lee's ranks had been sent home on parole, and many had heard that Grant had ordered those captured before the fall of Richmond (excepting officers above the rank of colonel) released.[11] By mid-May many had taken to writing to none other than Grant asking for reprieve. From Fort Delaware, Lt. H. Coffee of the 1st Texas Legion, Capt. John Humphrys of the 50th Virginia, and forty-seven others beseeched the general-in-chief to release them on taking the oath of allegiance. Many had been imprisoned since Gettysburg. Others were crippled for life. Invoking the domestic world that depended upon their return, they observed that all had "either wives or children or mothers and sisters" who needed them home. Equally desirous of returning the men home, Grant recommended that they be released at once and provided transportation to their respective states. And still more petitions flowed into Grant, one promising that if permitted to return to their homes, "we will use our utmost endeavors to speedily restore the Union." Grant believed they would. "I hope early means may be devised for clearing our prisons as far as possible," he informed Secretary Stanton.[12]

On June 6, President Johnson ordered the discharge of most remaining rebel prisoners of war. All enlisted men and officers not exceeding the rank of captain would be released upon taking the oath of allegiance (although those who wished to take the oath of amnesty would be permitted to do so after their release). Commanders of the various prisons would discharge approximately 50 prisoners each day, beginning with those who had been confined the longest. With more than 50,000 men still detained in seventeen different prisons, it would take two months to empty the camps. Officers of higher rank and those who had graduated from West Point or Annapolis would be discharged after all others had been processed. Finally, he commanded the Quartermaster's Department to furnish the rebels transportation to their homes. Only those standing trial for Lincoln's assassination, those captured with Jefferson Davis, or those within another special category (such as Henry Kyd Douglas and Congressman Benjamin Harris) were to be detained.[13]

Some of these men experienced a process that proved even more formal than that undertaken at Appomattox.[14] At Point Lookout in Maryland, which contained more than 18,000 Confederate prisoners in early June, the process was exceptionally lengthy, according to Samuel Pickens, an Alabamian captured in the trenches of Petersburg on April 1. In mid-June, Pickens noted that he and a comrade "bundled up early & went down to the house where the ceremonies are performed — i.e. the machine where U.S. citizens are made out of rebel soldiers." After waiting for several hours, Pickens and his squad stepped forward two at a time to give their name, rank, company, regiment, location of capture, and other identifying information, such as height, complexion, and eye color. When all had been registered, the men formed three sides of a hollow square under the canopy of a large U.S. flag, placed their hands on the Bible, and swore an oath of loyalty to the Union before being required to kiss the Bible. The men subsequently collected their parole passes, after which they again had to fill out yet another register listing their prewar residence and occupation. Only then could they board steamers and sail south to their homes in Virginia, North Carolina, and beyond. "With all this form & ceremony," Pickens observed, "I don't wonder at their only getting out 700 a day."[15]

Even as Confederate prisoners swore an oath of loyalty to the United States, a district judge in Virginia remained committed to trying leading rebels for treason. A New Yorker by birth, John C. Underwood moved to Clarke County, Virginia, in the 1840s, where he wed a local woman. By the 1850s, he had become an outspoken member of the new Republican Party. But after a mob attacked him for his antislavery sympathies and support of John C. Frémont's bid for the presidency, he left his wife and children behind and went back to New York. Not until the Civil War did he return south, when he was appointed to the federal court in the occupied and loyal Virginia territory composed of Alexandria and Norfolk. As an increasingly radical Republican, his convictions that rebels must be punished for treason had only grown during the war. Within ten days of Lincoln's assassination, Underwood traveled to Washington along with a delegation of Unionist Virginians to meet with the new president. Returning to Norfolk, he wrote Johnson that he was "encouraged by your recent declarations in favor of the punishment of the leading rebels" and prepared to summon a grand jury to indict the leaders. "The returning rebels now swarming in our towns are so defiant in their conduct,"

Underwood observed, "that the condition of loyal men in this State will be not only uncomfortable but extremely unsafe unless the power of the Government to punish treason shall be fully demonstrated."[16]

With Johnson's approval, two days after the president presented his amnesty proclamation, Underwood delivered an impassioned charge to the grand jury in the U.S. Circuit Court for the District of Virginia at Norfolk. In fiery language, he demanded the trials of "the authors and conductors of the most gigantic, bloody, and unprovoked crimes that ever cursed our world." Rebels, Underwood intoned, had "murdered tens of thousands of the flower of our youth and manhood, by slaughter on our battlefields and by starvation in the most loathsome dungeons." But their greatest crime was treason, as defined in Article 3, Section 3, of the Constitution. Invoking the arguments used by Lincoln and others, Underwood argued that a universal prosecution of the hundreds of thousands who had supported the rebellion was both unreasonable and impossible (excusing their behavior in part on the grounds of poor education). The rebel leaders, however, must be punished. "The grand instigators and most responsible and intelligent principals of this great conspiracy, with hands dripping with the blood of our slaughtered innocents and martyred President, are still at large unwhipped of justice."[17]

In the final paragraph of the charge, Underwood laid out his position on the paroles. They did not, he observed, afford any protection from prosecution for treason. Invoking Attorney General Speed's opinion on pardoning power, he informed the grand jury that the paroles were "merely a military arrangement, and can have no influence upon civil rights or the status of the persons interested." The Confederates were to be treated under domestic law, not as enemy belligerents.[18]

Other Unionists agreed. In the wake of Lincoln's assassination, Union soldiers, civilians, and ministers had called on the government to show no mercy to arch-traitors. While the masses might be pardoned, the slave oligarchy deserved to swing from ropes. From Brooklyn, Reverend Samuel Spear informed his congregation he would "keep hanging the leading rebels till justice in this form had fully met the demands and wants of the public safety." "If I represented the authority of this nation," he observed, "I should not treat them with rose-water and soothing syrup, but with the just severities of righteous law."[19] Reverend Henry Martyn Dexter recommended that "every rebel who was registered as colonel, or as of higher rank, in the Confederate army, or was of corresponding prominence in the civil service," be tried, condemned, and executed for treason.[20] And some pointed to Lee, in particular. "General Lee may be a Christian gentleman," observed one north-erner, "yet he is a traitor to his country, who richly deserves to be hung for his crimes."[21]

Attitudes had nevertheless softened among many northerners by early June, with Democrats and moderate Republicans increasingly endorsing Grant's position that magnanimity would serve to disarm Confederate ideology and draw wayward rebels back to the Union. Some abolitionists and Radical Republicans likewise began to defend this calculus, including editor Horace Greeley, Congressman Thaddeus Stevens, Senator Charles Sumner, and Chief Justice Salmon P. Chase. Responding directly to Francis Lieber, the radical abolitionist Gerrit Smith took up the topic of prosecuting rebels in a speech at New York's Cooper Institute on June 8. By treating rebels as enemy belligerents under the laws of war, Smith maintained, the Union had implicitly agreed not to seek retribution. "The government has neither the legal nor the moral right to try the rebels," he argued, and "the way to a sure and enduring peace lies not through perfidy and vengeance but through justice and love." Like Grant, he believed that Confederates may have committed treason, but the "safety of the North" could be secured only by ending "the clamor for blood."[22]

Still, many loyal northerners demanded that rebel leaders at least be prosecuted for treason. Among the most vocal were the editors of the *New York Times*. Only days after Underwood issued instructions to the grand jury impaneled to indict rebel leaders, the *Times* railed that it was "absurd" to conclude that Grant's terms had exempted any rebel from civil procedure. Channeling Speed's May 8 opinion, the paper reminded readers that only the president could confer amnesty and pardon. The surrender terms were military in nature and shielded "Lee and his armed followers as prisoners of war; but not at all as traitors to the government. It gives them military, but not civil immunity." For the *Times*, the central question revolved not around the dual legal status of individual rebels but around the Union's supremacy — the priorities of state versus national allegiance. Lee's contention that he had drawn his sword only to defend Virginia was no defense for treason. "The paramount and indefeasible obligation of every American citizen to the Federal constitution of the United States, is the only basis of our civil security, and cannot be reestablished by sanctions too signal or solemn," the paper declared. Lee, in particular, deserved punishment as a warning to any future would-be traitor. Whether he should be executed for his crime was a separate question. That could be settled *after* the authority of the federal government — of the Union — had been "vindicated by arraignment, a trial, and a sentence."[23]

On June 7, the grand jury composed of Black and white Unionists concurred, prompting U.S. district attorney Lucius Chandler to issue indictments against Lee and thirty-six other Confederate leaders for treason.[24] The list included civil office holders, such as former Virginia governors William "Extra Billy" Smith and John Letcher. But the indictments likewise named sixteen officers from the Army of Northern Virginia, including three lieutenant generals (James Longstreet, Jubal A. Early, and Richard S. Ewell); four major generals (W. H. F. "Rooney" Lee and G. W. Custis Lee [Robert E. Lee's sons], Fitzhugh Lee [Lee's nephew], and William Mahone); and four brigadier generals (William H. F. Payne [captured by Federal forces on April 15 and released from Johnson's Island on June 2], Henry Wise, Eppa Hunton [captured at Sailor's Creek], and Roger Pryor [who had resigned his commission in 1863 and was captured in November 1864 as a spy and released]). Finally, alongside his adjutant, Walter H. Taylor, Lee found himself indicted.[25]

In many ways, the list made little sense. At least two of the accused, Ewell and Hunton, remained confined in northern prisons and as such had not been paroled (and therefore were not protected by the surrender terms). And having not returned to the field, after being released just before Appomattox, Pryor had not been paroled. But all of the other field generals had been paroled.[26] Then there were those not indicted, including the other two ranking members of the high command, artillery chief William N. Pendleton and Second Corps commander John B. Gordon. Likewise absent was George Pickett (a West Point graduate accused of war crimes for executing twenty-one Union soldiers in North Carolina) along with Thomas L. Rosser and John S. Mosby (both of whom had initially refused to surrender). It remains unclear why the grand jury included some Army of Northern Virginia officers but not others.

Mass-printed with blanks to allow the insertion of specific details for each individual, the indictments accused the given individual with "being moved and seduced by the instigation of the devil, wickedly devising and intending the peace and tranquility of the said United States of America to disturb, and the Government of the said United States of America to subvert, move and incite rebellion and war against the United States." For those from the Army of Northern Virginia, the date of the offense was listed as April 1, 1865, in the county of Dinwiddie, where the army had been entrenched prior to the fall of Petersburg, a location well within the court's jurisdiction. Along with a "great multitude of persons," including upward of 500 men, the indictment charged that each officer had "arrayed in a warlike manner ... with cannon, muskets, pistols, swords, dirks, and other warlike weapons" against the United States. As was required by the Constitution, each indictment carried the name of two individuals who served as witnesses.[27] Satisfied with the results, Underwood headed to Washington to confer with Speed about the impending trials.

Notice of the indictments rippled out from Norfolk, filling national newspapers as well as those on the other side of the Atlantic. Some commended the grand jury's decision, noting that Lee would "learn that treason is the highest crime known to the law," advising that he seek "repentance." Others rebuked the indictments. One London paper wondered whether such a stance might not be in the United States' best interest. In consideration of the parole terms offered by Grant, the indictments "might be regarded by the public and by foreign nations in a light highly unfavorable to the honor of the Government."[28]

Closer to home, William Pendleton was nearly apoplectic with rage. Although not included among the indicted, he had heard that "a creature named Underwood," a "tool of tyranny," had summoned a number of officers to testify against Lee and others. As one of the Appomattox commissioners, Pendleton had helped draft the final terms of surrender and believed beyond any doubt that they afforded protection from prosecution for treason. He immediately turned to General Gibbon, one of the Union commissioners, to remind him of the solemn compact that paroled Confederates would remain "unmolested by Federal authorities." He admonished Gibbon to remember that Lee's men would have never laid down their arms "however great the odds stacked against them" had they supposed that the paroles would be disregarded. If Gibbon was a man of any honor, he would ensure that the paroles were upheld.[29]

Lee was not nearly so confident. When Maj. Gen. George Gordon Meade had visited his Richmond home in early May and urged him to take the oath of allegiance, Lee responded that he had no objections to the oath and intended to submit to the Constitution and laws of the land. But he reminded Meade that at present he was a prisoner of war and did not want to forgo "that status until he could form some idea of what the policy of the Government was going to be towards the people of the South." After learning of President Johnson's proclamation, however, Lee had finally decided to pursue the pardon.[30]

Lee was not so bold as to believe that the terms agreed on at Appomattox could not be overturned. Rather, news of the indictments accelerated his quest and spurred Lee to seek help from his Old Army network. He

Pardon and Amnesty

wanted affirmation that Grant would endorse any such application he submitted and sought out advice from Senator Reverdy Johnson of Maryland. Lee turned next to General Ord, still in Richmond, for advice. If Lee took the oath and sought a pardon, he asked Ord, would Grant support him? Still bent on promoting reconciliation, Ord quietly contacted Brig. Gen. Rufus Ingalls, chief quartermaster of the army and a classmate of Grant's at West Point. With Grant away in New York, Ingalls sought out Grant's chief of staff, John Rawlins, who assured him that "General Grant will cheerfully advise the President to grant it." With added guarantees from some of Johnson's closest advisers, Ingalls reported back to Ord, encouraging Lee to send his papers through Ord to Grant immediately. "If successful there will be great benefits following to all concerned," Ingalls observed on June 10.[31]

With assurances from several Union generals, on June 13 Lee took up his pen to write Grant. As he had done in his previous letter to the general-in-chief, he expressed his belief that the surrender terms had offered protection to all those who had been paroled. "I am ready to meet any charges that may be preferred against me, and do not wish to avoid trial," he wrote, "but, if I am correct as to the protection granted by my parole, and am not to be prosecuted, I desire to comply with the provisions of the President's proclamation, and therefore enclose the required application." Although he maintained that the surrender terms afforded him protection from prosecution, Lee nevertheless sought the president's exoneration via pardon.[32]

Four days later, Lee expressed similar sentiments to Walter Taylor, likewise among the indicted. He assured his former adjutant that he would let U.S. authorities pursue their course, repeating his insistence that he had no wish to avoid a trial. But he would not — could not — flee the country. Recognizing that that the only punishment for treason was execution, some of those listed on the indictments had elected to expatriate themselves, including Jubal Early, who was bound for Texas and ultimately Mexico. Lee would not leave. Instead, he stood fast in his insistence that Virginia needed the support and aid of "her sons to sustain and recuperate her." They should seek the president's pardon and "put themselves in a position to take part in her Government, and not be deterred by obstacles in their way."[33]

In Washington, Grant again interceded on behalf of the rebels. Upon receiving Lee's letter on June 16, Grant endorsed his petition, forwarding it to Secretary Stanton and recommending that pardon be granted and Underwood ordered to "quash all indictments found against paroled prisoners of war."[34] Grant explained that, in his opinion, Lee and others could not be tried for treason so long as they observed the terms of their parole. Rather than arguing that the paroles served as a blanket immunity, (perhaps unknowingly) Grant was invoking international law: in treating the rebels as paroled prisoners of war, and therefore as enemy belligerents rather than insurrectionary civilians, they could not be prosecuted for the civil crime of treason. But in reality, Grant was not concerned with legal arguments so much as with the practical implementation of peace and reconciliation. As he explained, "Good faith, as well as true policy, dictates that we should observe the conditions of that convention." Alternatively, subjecting officers to treason trials might dispose Confederate soldiers to "regard such an infraction of terms by the Government as an entire release from all obligations on their part." In other words, war might continue. Battles might rage again. With the Union armies already undergoing a rapid demobilization, Grant feared that the war might never end if treason trials ensued.[35]

After forwarding the endorsement to Stanton, Grant headed to the White House to speak to Johnson in person. Convinced by Maj. Gen. Benjamin Butler's argument that the paroles protected Confederates only while they remained prisoners of war (and by extension, so long as the nation remained in a state of war), Johnson asked Grant when the Confederates might be tried. "Never," Grant quipped, "unless they violate their paroles." He reiterated the position he had outlined in his letter to Stanton. In order to secure Lee's surrender, he had vowed the Confederate soldiers would not face reprisals. Moreover, Lincoln had endorsed the terms. And Johnson had done as much when he insisted that Sherman extend the same terms to Johnston at Durham Station. How could the government possibly rescind such promises? Moreover, failure to uphold the surrender terms might unleash bands of outlaws and bushwhackers, thus continuing the war "in a way that we could make very little progress with, having no organized armies to meet." Alongside his fervent belief in upholding the honor of his word, an imminent fear of guerrilla warfare continued to shape Grant's policies and actions.[36]

But Johnson refused to drop the issue. Whatever his position toward pardons for the rank and file, he wanted rebel leaders punished. At a cabinet meeting, a frustrated Grant reiterated his position maintaining that both his personal honor and that of the country rested on upholding the surrender terms. Still, Johnson pressed. Why, he asked Grant, did "any military commander have the right to protect an arch-traitor from the laws?" Angry and speaking plainly to the president, Grant observed that as a general it was none of his business what Johnson or Congress did respecting political rights or the confiscation of property. But as a general, it was his duty to deal with the enemy in front of him, to "either kill him, capture him, or

Pardon and Amnesty

parole him." Becoming increasingly impassioned, Grant reminded the president that he had offered Lee a set of terms to compel the surrender. If he had informed Lee that he and his soldiers were "open to arrest, trial, and execution for treason, Lee would have never surrendered, and we should have lost many lives in destroying him." They had surrendered on terms that spared their lives — terms that promised them protection and exemption from punishment for actions acceptable under the rules of civilized warfare. Grant maintained he had acted according to military law, and so long as Lee and his officers observed the terms, they should not be subject to arrest. Secretary of State Seward alone nodded in agreement. Still, Johnson refused to yield. Exasperated, Grant invoked his most powerful political weapon: he would resign his commission if the government pursued the treason charges. Returning to his office in the War Department, a fuming Grant put his staff on notice. "I will not stay in the army if they break the pledges that I made."[37]

Johnson relented. The new president could not afford to lose the Union's most prominent and beloved hero. Instead, on June 20, he directed Attorney General Speed to instruct U.S. district attorney Lucius Chandler not to issue warrants of arrest against Lee or any of the others listed on the indictments until further orders. Grant then composed a response to Lee. Enclosing a copy of his June 16 letter to the War Department, Grant informed Lee that his position had been endorsed. The paroles were to be observed.[38]

Despite newspaper reports to the contrary, Speed's instructions to Chandler had not demanded that he issue a *nolle prosequi*—a formal notice that a prosecutor had dropped the charges.[39] Although Grant believed the indictments should be "quashed," that had not formally happened. Grant may simply have convinced Johnson that Lee and the others could not be tried until an end of the war had been officially declared. In fact, only days before Grant received Lee's letter, an assistant attorney general informed a New Orleans sheriff that Speed maintained that "officers who are at large and under the capitulations of Generals Lee and John[t]son ought not to be tried or arrested by the Courts of the United States for treason until the President has officially proclaimed the suppression of the rebellion and announced the war is at an end." When such a proclamation had been issued, the surrender terms would no longer protect Confederates from prosecution by the federal government.[40] While everyone desired a state of peace and an end to the bloodshed, a formal, legal end of the *state of war* could potentially have dire consequences for some of the leading rebels.[41] For now, their paroles would protect them, a fact made all the more apparent with the imprisonment of political leaders, including several governors, members of the Confederate cabinet, Confederate vice president Alexander Stephens, and Jefferson Davis.

Grant, however, believed the indictment dispute settled and therefore turned to drafting his official report of military operations since becoming general-in-chief on March 4, 1864. Overwhelmingly, it explained how the army carried out his strategy of exhausting Confederate resources and morale. But the report emphasized making peace as much as making war. For Grant, Lee deserved a great deal of credit on this front. "No matter what Gen. Lee's offenses may have been against the offended dignity of the Nation, great consideration is due him for his manly course and bearing in his surrender at Appomattox," Grant submitted. Although struck out in the final version of the report, Grant initially observed that if Lee had been "persuaded that he was to be tried for treason and pursued as a traitor, the surrender never would have taken place." Repeating a common refrain, Grant insisted that Lee and his men would have scattered across the South, "with arms in hands, causing infinite trouble." But thanks in large part to Lee's influence, the Confederate armies had laid down their guns and gone home "desiring peace and quiet." While Grant agreed that the political leaders should "reap the reward of their offence," he continued to maintain that disbanding the Confederate armies and sending the soldiers home on parole was key to peace.[42] With the impending threat of war in Mexico with the French, Grant wanted the rebellion quelled as quickly as possible.[43]

But even with Grant's intercession, the indictments had convinced at least some Confederates that they were no longer safe from prosecution in the United States. In the wake of Appomattox, rebel men and women such as Sarah Morgan had scribbled impassioned diary passages threatening to abandon their native land. Despite opposition by Lee, for many these were not idle threats. Determined not to bear the humiliation and horror they were sure would accompany treason trials, "Yankee subjugation," or the presence of newly emancipated African Americans, thousands fled the country.[44] Belligerent and bitter, several families from the Lower South states fled to Brazil, by 1865 the only slaveholding nation in the Western Hemisphere, when Emperor Dom Pedro II held out the offer of subsidies and tax breaks in an effort to improve his nation's cotton production.[45] For Confederate leaders, however, the stakes were much higher. In the wake of the indictments and arrests of officeholders, many rightfully feared that they would be subjected to trials for treason.

Rank-and-file Confederates had little reason to fear punishment for treason, but the conditions of their paroles would remain in place until President Johnson declared the war ended, limiting their mobility and requiring that they routinely report their whereabouts to Union officials. Having spent more than a month laboring for the Union army, printing passes for the men of Johnston's army in Greensboro, in early June James Albright headed north toward Norfolk on foot hoping to be reunited with his fiancée. Reaching Suffolk and then Portsmouth, he did what all paroled Confederates remained compelled to do: register with the provost marshal. By mid-June he had arrived at Mattie Purvis's home, and within days a Baptist minister married the couple before a gathering of nearly fifty guests. The next morning, the newlyweds departed for Greensboro. Traveling first to Richmond, Albright again registered with the local provost marshal, but this time he would be required to take the amnesty oath before the couple boarded a train for their North Carolina home, where he would introduce his new wife to his seven-year-old son, George.[46]

Even with such strictures, Lee's men recognized that failing to receive a parole made them subject to arrest and imprisonment. Throughout June, provost marshals in Virginia, West Virginia, North Carolina, and beyond continued to accept the surrender of Army of Northern Virginia soldiers. The numbers proved much smaller than in late April and early May, but still they came. In Virginia, 83 turned themselves in at Staunton, 65 at Gordonsville, and 43 at Winchester. Another 21 surrendered at Moorfield, West Virginia. Farther from Appomattox, Lee's soldiers sought paroles at Greensboro, Charlotte, and Macon. Whether these men were conscious of the legal protections the parole still afforded as long as the war remained a legal reality is unclear, but at least 241 soldiers from the Army of Northern Virginia sought out paroles in June, even after Johnson's amnesty proclamation ostensibly made them unnecessary.[47]

At least some white southerners had begun to wonder about the number of Confederates who continued to arrive at paroling stations. In Georgia, one man observed that the daily crowds at Macon's provost marshal office seemed to exceed the entire active force of the Confederate armies. Where had they come from?, he asked, to which another quipped, "Why, don't you see from the mud on their sleeves and breeches, that they are just out of the swamp!" Although a newspaper described this comment as "facetious," perhaps it was closer to the truth than many former Confederates cared to ac-

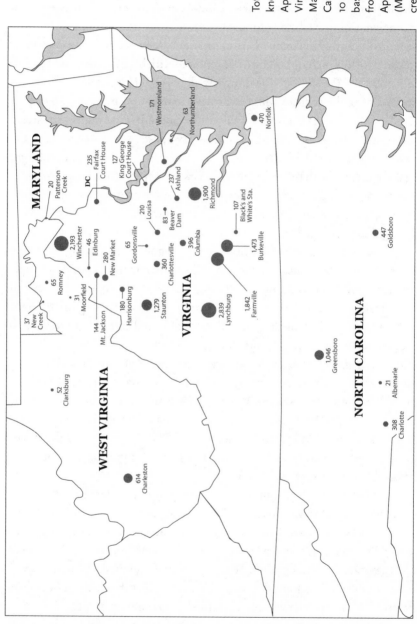

Total number of known paroles beyond Appomattox in Virginia, West Virginia, Maryland, and North Carolina between April 10 and July 15, 1865, based on material from author's Beyond Appomattox database. (Matt Weisenfluh, created in Tableau)

knowledge. The paper continued, "When a full return of all Confederates who have been paroled since the surrenders of General Lee and Johnston shall be made, it will present some curious statistics, more flattering, perhaps, to the numerical strength than the moral heroism of the Southern people. We shall then be able to learn, not what was the available, but the unavailable force of the South."[48]

The fact that so many Confederates had sought out paroles after Appomattox—as many as 15,744 by the end of June—confounded the portrait of soldiers' commitment to the cause.[49] On the one hand, it suggested that a significant number of men had dropped out of the ranks during the march west from Richmond and Petersburg. Perhaps they had not been as dedicated as their comrades who surrendered at Appomattox. On the other hand, some of those who had not yet been paroled had been die-hard rebels determined to continue the fight, men who had fled south toward Johnston's lines or west to await calls from Rosser and Munford. The question remained, if the diehards had stayed until the end, might Lee have broken out of Appomattox?

Among those still refusing to surrender rode David G. McIntosh. After escaping the field at Appomattox, the artillery officer had headed south alongside other members of his artillery battalion. After Johnston's surrender, most of his comrades had admitted their cause was lost and returned to Virginia. But McIntosh declined to do so, seeking out the fleeing Jefferson Davis along the South Carolina–Georgia border. Traveling with the Confederate president for two days, he realized that he would be most effective in continuing to wage war if he headed west to the Trans-Mississippi Department to join Gen. Kirby Smith's fight. Only when McIntosh learned of Smith's surrender did he concede that his fight had ended. But unlike the vast majority of soldiers in Lee's army, he would never seek a parole and never ask for a pardon.[50]

Other diehards conceded that they had no other choice but to surrender. In May, John S. Mosby had asked Lee to intercede on his behalf and determine whether he might still be eligible for a parole. But as of June 6, even before Grant took up the issue of Lee's indictment, Johnson and his cabinet were still debating the merits of paroling Mosby. In the meantime, Provost Marshal Sharpe advised that Mosby should seek amnesty under Johnson's May 29 proclamation.[51] Perhaps the indictments against Lee and others convinced him that the time had come to surrender himself. Twice in early June, Mosby sent his brother William to the provost marshal's office in Lynchburg to ask if the colonel might be paroled upon surrendering to authorities. The local captain was not convinced he possessed the authority to grant a parole to a rebel with a $5,000 price tag on his head and would have to seek approval from Halleck in Richmond. After confirming with the War Department, Halleck agreed to sanction a parole, so long as Mosby came in of his own accord. If he did not, Union forces were to arrest the guerrilla and report to Richmond. But the provost marshal in Lynchburg had not yet received the orders when Mosby rode into town on June 13. Still waiting on Halleck's response, the provost guard instructed Mosby to leave town immediately lest he be arrested before official word arrived from Washington.[52]

More than two months after Appomattox, on June 17, Mosby walked out of the Lynchburg provost marshal's office with a parole in hand. The Gray Ghost had finally surrendered. Yet his specter continued to haunt the U.S. cavalry. When Mosby rode into Charlottesville five days later, the local commander could scarcely believe that the guerrilla who had menaced Union forces and civilians was walking free. Doubting the authenticity of Mosby's pass, he detained him before firing off a telegram to Col. Albert Ordway, the new provost marshal general in the Department of Virginia. This could not possibly be true, he pressed. From Lynchburg came a succinct response: "Col. Mosby has been paroled."[53] Paroled, but not yet pardoned.

In June, the restored legislatures of several southern states renewed the voting rights of white men who had taken the oath or received a presidential pardon, but the prohibition against donning rebel uniforms remained in place throughout both the North and South.[54] In Clark County, Georgia, a Union captain ordered any person found in the streets or any public place dressed in the uniform of a Confederate officer to be arrested and tried before the provost court. Acknowledging the poverty of some soldiers, the captain added that "those who cannot obtain citizens clothes must take from the gray cloth all military buttons, trimmings or insignia of rank." In Staunton, Virginia, Union soldiers stood along street corners with shears, cutting off brass buttons and stripping Confederates of their gray coats. When one young Confederate rode into town wearing his military coat, four or five Union troops advanced upon him immediately. Even Black men wearing discarded Confederate jackets lost their buttons. The hunt to remove every vestige of rebel gray prompted one local to liken the act to the British policy outlawing the Highland plaid after the Jacobin rebellion in 1745. "The miserable Yankees are only intensifying and perpetuating sectional hate," he declared.[55]

Those daring enough to flout the law soon found themselves facing more

Pardon and Amnesty

than the loss of their buttons. From Richmond, General Ord finally issued an order prohibiting the rebel uniform, but he did not limit his directive to officers. Observing that a sufficient time had elapsed since the surrender for all such forces to secure apparel other than uniforms, Ord promised that any rebel appearing in public wearing insignia of rank after June 15 would be liable for arrest. Those arrested were sent to Libby Prison, where provost marshals removed their buttons, stripes, braids, or any other insignia of rank before detaining the men overnight. The lone exception was to be made for those returning from northern prison camps. Patrols were instructed not to molest them in any way. Commanding the Department of West Virginia, General Emory made no such exceptions. Any person found wearing a rebel uniform as well as any paroled prisoner found carrying a firearm would be arrested and detained.[56]

Former rebels, however, were not the only ones facing detention. On June 12, Bvt. Maj. Gen. John W. Turner ordered provost marshals throughout the District of Henrico to conduct daily mounted patrols to ensure that African Americans had passes from their employers. All Black men without employment were to be sent to Chimborazo Hospital, while Black women would be sent to the alms house. "The object of the Patrols and duties of the Provost Marshal in this respect is to see that idle negroes do not congregate in crowds in the streets, creating rows and disturbances," Turner instructed. "The negroes as well as the white people must be made to keep the peace."[57] The presence of the Union army had been necessary to enforce emancipation (and would continue to be essential in the years to come), but even this freedom would carry many of the markers of enslavement, conferred by passes and tied to employment.[58]

Despite some increasing restrictions on both rebels and freedmen, loyal residents of the border states continued to worry. Some Marylanders initially took solace in the fact that Johnson's amnesty proclamation had exempted those who had left loyal regions to join the rebellion. Confederate soldiers from Maryland, Kentucky, Missouri, Delaware, and the District of Columbia would have to apply individually to Johnson for pardon in order to return. "If those paroled return they violate their paroles, which only gives them freedom of movement, within the states that seceded," observed a Hagerstown newspaper in late June. If they returned to Maryland, military authorities could ostensibly remove them. But seldom did this prove the case. Instead, the influx of paroled rebels from Lee's army continued unabated throughout June. Moreover, the rebels arrived openly, reporting to the local provost marshal's office, where they took the oath. Within days, their names appeared in local newspapers.[59] Few applied personally to Johnson for a pardon.[60]

Yet again, the dictates of military orders and reality diverged, leaving locals to resort to their own means. When John Wakenight returned to his Boonsboro, Maryland, home, he found he was no longer welcome. A private in the 23rd Virginia Cavalry captured in early March and released from Fort Delaware on June 21, Wakenight had made it back to the small village only to be threatened by the local vigilante committee. Within days, the town newspaper boasted that he had been forced to leave. A similar incident unfolded in Harford County, where locals lashed a board to the back of a returned rebel emblazoned with the word "traitor" before marching him through the town. After enduring the type of humiliation Lee's soldiers had feared before the surrender, the townsfolk placed the rebel on a train and dared him to return. At Emmitsburg, Unionists could hardly believe the irony of rebels seeking protection from the U.S. military. Ordered to evacuate the town within twenty-four hours by several discharged Union soldiers, seven returning rebels made a hasty flight out of town and to provost marshal Capt. H. C. Neill in Frederick, where they were "safely ensconced behind a hedge of 'hated Yankee bayonets.'" Bound by Brig. Gen. John D. Stevenson's orders not to molest paroled Confederates, the captain urged the Union veterans to observe the law. Concurring, they returned home, but lest the traitors attempt to sneak back into Emmitsburg, the local paper published their names: Joseph Shorb, George Rider, Robert Miles, Hanson Webb, Hugh Vincent Barry, Thomas McBride, and —— Shorb.[61] While the federal government might not enforce its own promise to prevent rebels from returning, local communities would use whatever means necessary to keep the traitors from their midst.

Unlike those from Maryland, Kentucky, and Missouri, Johnson had not exempted West Virginia Confederates from his amnesty proclamation. Rather than restoring peace, the president's leniency had aggravated tensions. In the northern and northeastern portions of the state, returning rebels encountered mounting resistance. Many found their names published in local papers — a public shaming and warning against their return.[62] Others found their families intimidated, including Samuel Woods, who had brandished his parole pass and firearm to get back to his Philippi home. Throughout the summer, Unionists threatened his wife and children, hoping to intimidate the rebels into leaving, including one incident in which a man rode his horse through the side door, into their home, and back into the street. On another occasion, fifty or more men, some of whom were Union veterans dressed in uniform, paraded through the town demanding the whereabouts of any known rebel. With tensions mounting rather than dissipating, Woods rode to Clarksburg seeking protection from U.S. forces, which he immediately received. For more than a week, a troop of Union soldiers camped in the middle of Philippi to discourage any more threats. As had been the case in Maryland, the tables had now turned, with Confederates seeking protection from U.S. troops.[63]

Some loyal West Virginians counseled against efforts to "drive out" returning Confederates, observing that such men would bear the stigma of "rebel" for the remainder of their lives. But others continued to insist on legal means of removing the secesh. In mid-June, a Wheeling newspaper pointed out that a recent opinion from Attorney General Speed offered a remedy under civil law. Citing rebels charged with robbery during Brig. Gen. John Hunt Morgan's 1863 raid into Kentucky, Speed declared that the federal government should not prevent or interfere with state courts regarding the arrest of paroled rebel prisoners charged and indicted under state law for crimes such as robbery.[64] Dismissing individual Confederates' wartime status as belligerents, Speed offered the possibility that state courts—not the federal courts—could prosecute them for crimes committed prior to the summer of 1865, regardless of whether the men had been paroled.

Border state Unionists took note. By late July, courts in West Virginia had begun leveling charges against returning rebels. Among them stood Charles A. Swann, Robert V. Gustin, George W. Way, James C. West, and William Wilson. In late June, the Morgan County court issued an indictment against each man, "a rebel in the rebel army," for "aiding and assisting the enemies of this State in the late rebellion." The men, however, might have expected such a charge upon their return. A year earlier, in May 1864, Governor Arthur Boreman had issued a proclamation listing thirty-three Morgan County residents (including at least one woman) who had "deserted their homes and actively engaged" in the rebellion. He declared that each would be considered an enemy of the state unless he (or she) returned within sixty days and took an oath of allegiance to the United States. Swann and the other four listed in 1865 had failed to do so. Upon their arrival back in the county, the court ordered them to appear on the first day of October to show cause as to why their personal and real estate should not be possessed and sold. Their status as paroled prisoners of war mattered not in Morgan County, West Virginia.[65]

15

Rebels Still

On Tuesday evening, June 27, a volley of six rifle shots rang out near New Market, Virginia. When the smoke cleared, two Confederate cavalrymen lay dead: twenty-two-year-old Capt. George W. Summers and twenty-year-old Sgt. Isaac Newton Koontz both of Company D, 7th Virginia Cavalry.

More than two months earlier, Summers and Koontz had ridden west from Appomattox, alongside other members of Rosser's command. When Col. Elijah White disbanded their brigade at Lynchburg, it is unclear whether Summers and Koontz attempted to join up with Johnston's army in North Carolina or elected to start home immediately. Whatever decision they made in early April, they had returned to their Page County homes by late May. On the twenty-second of that month, they had crossed Massanutten Mountain into Shenandoah County alongside Koontz's cousin Jacob and Andrew Jackson Kite, likewise members of the 7th Virginia Cavalry. Their families would later claim that the four men had been bound for Winchester, where they hoped to be paroled. Regardless of the circumstances that brought them over the gap in the mountain, as they headed north along the Valley Pike they encountered six troopers of the 22nd New York Cavalry, a portion of the guard carrying ex-governor John Letcher north to prison. Drawing their revolvers, the rebels demanded the Union horses and some greenbacks, then proceeded back over the Massanutten to Page County.[1]

When George Summers arrived at home, his father was livid. What was his son thinking? The four young Confederates — none of whom had been paroled — had committed robbery against the Federal government. Surely the Union authorities would retaliate. The next morning, the elder Summers enlisted neighbors to accompany him across the mountain to the camp of the 192nd Ohio at Rude's Hill, where they spoke with the commander, Col. Francis W. Butterfield. If they returned the property, Butterfield informed him, the boys "should not be molested nor disturbed." Thanking the colonel for his generosity, Summers crossed the mountain once more and informed his son of the promise. The horses along with "a dollar and half in money" were promptly returned to the 192nd Ohio and the issue seemingly resolved.[2]

But as with so many other aspects of life in the summer of 1865, the incident had not reached its conclusion. Animosities and fears generated by the war had not been extinguished. Indeed, many seemed to flare up just at the moment when peace seemed within reach. Almost exactly a month later, Jacob Koontz and several other former Confederates got into a heated argument with a local Unionist. Incensed, the Unionist accused Koontz of being a horse thief and threatened to speak to Union authorities. The details of this conversation with the Union troops are unknown, but on Monday, June 26, Col. Cyrus Hussey, replacing Butterfield, who was on leave, ordered Capt. Lycurgus D. Lusk of the 22nd New York Cavalry to proceed to the Luray Valley "and there arrest and execute severally and all without delay whatsoever, the following named men who have been guilty of attacking U.S. troops and stealing horses since the surrender." Listed and underlined in red were the names of George Summers, Isaac Newton Koontz, Jacob Koontz, and Andrew Kite. The next morning, Hussey informed the adjutant general's office that these four men "constituted the gang that attacked, robbed, and drew arms upon the party of cavalry at the narrow pass below here on or about the 22nd day of last month."[3]

As rebels had dispersed across the countryside, reports of horse thievery proved increasingly common. In early May, Union cavalry had scouted the vicinity of Columbia Furnace in Shenandoah County after hearing that approximately twenty-five members of the 7th Virginia Cavalry were harassing locals and stealing horses.[4] But reports of horse thieves also poured into U.S. posts from the counties of Fairfax, Prince William, Loudoun, and beyond. Many speculated they were guerrillas or outlaws, but in other instances, paroled soldiers were implicated. Outside of Harpers Ferry, Union cavalry hunted down Edward S. Wright, a paroled soldier from White's Battalion, after reports that he and a Black man named James Brooks had stolen two mares, which they took to Albemarle County and sold. Whether his accomplice was a former slave coerced into aiding him remained unclear. But accused of a crime that constituted breaking his parole, Wright faced a military commission in late June, where he was found guilty and sentenced to five years in prison.[5] The local commander in the Shenandoah Valley, however,

George Summers.
Courtesy of Linda Flowers
private collection.

elected to send a sterner message. Horse thieves would not face merely the prospect of prison.

In the twilight of June 27, Captain Lusk's company rode along the South Fork of the Shenandoah River toward the homes of Summers and Koontz. From his rocker on the front porch, Jacob Koontz's father could hear the clomping of hooves crossing the nearby bridge and rushed to warn his son and nephew that the Federals were indeed on their way. Jacob managed to escape, but Newton had not roused from bed when the Union cavalrymen arrived to arrest him. Granted permission to write a letter to his fiancée, Newton guessed he would be taken to Mount Jackson and put on trial (presumably a military tribunal, although he did not say). "The Lieutenant and men appear to be gentlemen," he assured her, before adding that he had acted as a "gentleman in returning the horses." Several miles away, another party of Union troopers surrounded George Summers's home, with orders to arrest his son. The elder Summers protested, pointing out that the horses had been returned and Colonel Butterfield had vowed there would be no further trouble. But the Union captain would hear none of it. After bidding his mother and father farewell, George climbed into a saddle and headed west back through the gap in the mountain alongside Koontz.

When the Union cavalrymen reached Shenandoah County that afternoon, they informed the two rebels that they would be executed. There would be no trial. Despite pleas from both men that the execution be delayed until the next day, there was no chance for goodbyes with loved ones. The only concession would be allowing the men to write letters to their families. With a trembling hand, Summers scrawled out his farewell. "Would to God that I had died upon the battlefield in the defense of my dear native South," he wrote, "but it has been otherwise ordered." At the foot of Rude's Hill, only yards from the Union camp, the infantry formed a firing squad as the two men were blindfolded, bound, and forced to kneel. At 7:30 P.M., shots echoed across the valley.[6]

Within days, accounts of the execution appeared in newspapers from Ohio to Louisiana. Most described it as a "Tragedy," observing that there was no justifiable defense for the attack upon the Union cavalry and horse thievery, even as they expected a far less severe punishment. Others decried it as "Murder in Cold Blood."[7] But the context in which the executions had occurred cannot be overlooked. Grant, Sherman, and others of the Union high command had long worried about guerrilla warfare — before but especially in the wake of Appomattox and Lincoln's assassination. Even the surrender of Mosby had not quelled the fears or realities of bushwhackers. Well into late June, reports continued to flow into the War Department from across Virginia of assaults against loyal people, especially freedmen and freedwomen, along with the accounts of horse stealing and robbery by returned rebel soldiers and guerrillas. With the local courts closed and no civil authority to prevent or punish such acts, Union officers felt they had little ability to preserve good order.[8] If local matters fostered an atmosphere of angst, the ongoing trial of the Lincoln conspirators in Washington only heightened tensions.

The executions at Rude's Hill were both exceptional and predictable. In part, the reaction of the Union troops in the Valley may have been a product of circumstances in their own camps. The victims of the horse thieves, the men of the 22nd New York Cavalry, had proven dysfunctional throughout May. Their commander, Col. Horatio B. Reed, had finally ordered several insubordinate troopers gagged and forced to "carry a twenty pound log for two hours as a punishment." When one of the men refused to do so, the colonel suspended him by his hands before seventeen of his company "armed with carbines loaded and capped" cut him down. Within minutes, the men were disarmed and forwarded to the provost marshal. But the conditions were getting out of control. Frustrated with the unruly behavior, Reed threatened to disarm the entire regiment. The 192nd Ohio remained equally problematic. Its constant state of dirty camps, filthy uniforms, and inability to maintain soldierly appearances had frustrated army leadership.[9]

By June 1865, the demobilization of the Union armies was underway with thousands of men arriving home each day, but those forces who remained in the field to end the war were not the same units that had won the war. Many had seen far less time in the ranks, including the 22nd New York Cavalry, mustered into service in March 1864, and the 192nd Ohio, which had formed only in March 1865. Moreover, as volunteer units, many believed their duty to quell the rebellion had ended, and they were anxious to get home.[10] Yet these green and undisciplined troops had been among the few Union soldiers stationed in the Shenandoah Valley between Winchester and Staunton, tasked with helping to subdue any rebel activity.

As had been the case since April, local commanders continued to make decisions that sometimes failed to accord with Grant's terms and military policy. "In order to secure the protection of life and property over so large a territory, the punishments for crime were necessarily more severe and summary," members of the 192nd Ohio later explained of the executions. All offenders had been allowed trial and counsel, with one exception: "a party of four guerrillas who attacked the forces after the surrender of the Rebels, two of whom, a Rebel Captain and Sergeant, were arrested and summarily executed."[11]

The punishment proved far harsher than perhaps fit the crime. But Union commanders had given numerous warnings. In April, General Hancock had cautioned those harboring guerrillas that "every outrage committed by them will be followed by the severest infliction."[12] This position had not changed. Given the intense desire to end all guerrilla warfare — and the fact that unparoled rebel soldiers had held Union troopers at gunpoint and stolen their horses — perhaps the executions should not have come as such a surprise.

And yet they did. Returning from his furlough, Colonel Butterfield realized that the executions had inflamed rather than dampened anxieties. On July 19, he issued a statement to the citizens of Shenandoah and adjoining counties in which he attempted to dispel rumors that anyone involved in bushwhacking or other "similar actions" against Federal forces during the war was to be hunted down and summarily punished. Such stories had already caused many citizens to flee their homes and take refuge in the mountains, but Butterfield insisted this would not be the case. "No citizen," he promised, "will be held accountable or be molested for . . . offenses committed *prior* to the surrender of Gen. Lee's army." But, he cautioned, "where parties who are guilty of the cool-blooded murder of Union people, or of crimes committed *since* the surrender of Lee's army, are apprehended, they shall in all cases in future have a fair and impartial trial, and when found guilty be punished as the crime merits."[13]

For Butterfield, Appomattox would be a line in the sand. Without using the legal rhetoric, he had effectively declared that April 9 served as a demarcating line between rebels' status as enemy combatants and as traitorous citizens. He had assured rebel civilians (not just soldiers) that they would not be arrested or tried for civil crimes committed prior to April 9 — with the exception of murdering a Unionist in cold blood. Although his announcement had no legal authority, it only further muddied the waters. Had the war ended? To many, what constituted the end seemed a moving target.

As the days grew longer and the humidity mounted in Washington, the growing piles of individual applications brought limited clarity. By late June, the attorney general's office had received more than 300 petitions from both soldiers and civilians. But President Johnson expected to review each one, so he proceeded with a great deal of caution, granting very few in those early summer months.[14]

Johnson had not required applicants to repudiate secession or justify their willingness to take an oath to the United States. But many soldier petitioners used the opportunity to explain their reasons for joining the Confederate forces as well as their renewed loyalty to the United States.[15] Thomas L. Rosser's June 20, 1865, application proved typical. In a letter addressed to the president, he explained that he had entered West Point in 1856, where he had watched the gathering storms of war, remaining quietly at school and not wishing to act in haste. But when southern congressmen left for their homes "declaring war at hand" and calling on southern men to rise in defense of their homes, Rosser tendered his resignation. He insisted that in resigning from West Point he had withdrawn his allegiance from the United States, because his duty rested with his home state of Texas. Believing it "cowardly and unmanly to refuse his services," he had accepted a commission in the Confederate army and had acted under "patriotic motives and a firm conviction of right." As a Confederate officer, Rosser had "endeavored to do my whole duty," sustained several wounds, and been rewarded for his service by promotion to major general. "In the performance of my duties my only desire was to serve my country," he insisted. Like so many of his comrades, Rosser concluded by invoking the language of trial by battle. "All questions of difference and difficulty have been settled by the war and I take this decision as final," he declared, "and what I now desire is peace and liberty and the rights of an American citizen."[16] Omitted in the application was his self-promotion to lieutenant general after Appomattox as well as his refusal to surrender until mid-May. Nevertheless, Virginia governor Francis Pierpont approved the petition and forwarded it to Johnson on June 21.[17]

Several of those included in the June 7 treason indictments likewise applied for pardon that month, offering explanations for their past and future loyalties. Captured at Sailor's Creek, Lt. Gen. Richard "Dick" Ewell forwarded an oath and petition from the confines of Fort Warren. "This oath is the strongest proof I can give of my wishes to become a loyal citizen," he informed Johnson, and "to do my duty to the country." Upon receipt on June 19, Grant endorsed Ewell's petition, but Secretary of War Stanton was not so sure. With the indictment issue still unsettled, the secretary marked the application as postponed for further consideration in the cabinet.[18] After his release from Johnson's Island, Brig. Gen. William H. Payne, too, would apply for pardon in mid-June. Like others, he implicitly invoked the protection of the parole in his application, pointing out that his only connection to the war had been through the military. "I never held a political office in my life," he wrote. "I gave my heart entirely to what I honestly believed to be the service of *my country* and I claim that in this loyalty, mistaken though it may be, the U.S. Government will find the best element for valuable citizenship."[19] As with Ewell, his application was filed in Washington, but no decision would be made just yet. William Mahone, Eppa Hunton, Roger Pryor, Fitzhugh Lee, and one of Lee's sons, Rooney—all charged by the grand jury for treason—would likewise file applications. All would be left to wonder whether they would be granted a pardon or continue to face charges.

Still awaiting word on his pardon application, Robert E. Lee made plans to move his family out of Richmond. The constant stream of visitors to his home on Franklin Street had convinced him to look for a place in the countryside. Yet conscious that he was a paroled soldier, he sought the permission of the U.S. army before departing. On June 21, he wrote to Col. Albert Ordway notifying the provost marshal general that he planned to relocate his family to Cartersville in Cumberland County, along the James River canal. "My son, G. W. Custis Lee, a paroled prisoner like myself, will accompany me," he wrote. Ordway's predecessor, Marsena Patrick, had informed Lee that no passport would be necessary, but with the looming indictment, he would take no chances. He wanted to be sure his departure would not be construed as breaking his parole or otherwise committing an offense.[20]

Even as Lee remained keenly aware of the restrictions placed on him as a paroled prisoner of war, Grant continued in his efforts to send every rebel

Rebels Still

home. On June 27, the general-in-chief recommended that all officers still detained at Fort Delaware be discharged as swiftly as possible. Doing so not only would diminish expenses but would allow the Union's soldiers to go home as well.[21]

In an effort to continue the process of dismantling the great war machine, in early July Grant proposed two more courses of action to Secretary Stanton to be issued by a general order. First, Grant recommended that all paroled prisoners of war who had voluntarily taken the oath of allegiance be permitted to leave their homes and seek employment elsewhere. No longer would the restrictions of the paroles mandate they remain at home. Second, Grant suggested that all restraints placed upon Confederate soldiers, paroled or not, be lifted. In effect this meant that those from loyal states such as Maryland and Kentucky should be allowed to return their homes. But— Grant added— "their taking the oath of allegiance will not restore them to citizenship."[22]

Stanton declined to approve such an order.[23] Grant's stipulation that the oath would not restore citizenship conflicted with the president's amnesty proclamation. With the exception of fourteen excluded classes, taking the amnesty oath *did* restore citizenship. Yet again, military goals and the law ran counter to one another. This time, however, it did not matter. There had been no declaration of a cessation of hostilities, and therefore the paroles would remain in effect.

Well into late June and early July, the men of Lee's army remained reliant upon their parole passes for sustenance, transportation, and protection. From their pockets or haversacks, rebels presented their folded scraps of paper in return for rations at Union posts in towns such as Lynchburg. Some had only recently been released from northern camps and were passing through on their way to North Carolina, Georgia, Alabama, and Tennessee. Others had finally recovered enough from illness and wounds to travel south. With their passes in hand, they could attain enough rations to help them on their way.[24] Some had been paroled at Appomattox but were only reaching their Deep South homes by midsummer, including Thomas G. Wallingford of the 4th Texas, who reported to the provost marshal in New Orleans on June 26. Upon presenting his pass, he climbed aboard a steamer bound for Texas. Arriving in Houston on July 3, he was relieved to learn that his pass meant the army would furnish transportation all the way to his home in Hempstead. William F. Wharton of the 1st Maryland Cavalry had likewise surrendered at Appomattox. But more than two months later, military orders mandated that he report to the Baltimore provost marshal en route to his Prince George's County, Maryland, home.[25]

In some southern locales, Confederate women attempted to mitigate the humiliation of paroled soldiers begging their victors for food. Transforming their soldiers' relief society into a *paroled* soldiers' relief society, the women of Petersburg beseeched residents to send any food or contributions that might help alleviate the suffering of returning Confederates. Soon donations of canned meats, bread, flour, butter, dried fruits, and vegetables filled their coffers while nearly fifty young men and women staged an entertainment at the city's Phoenix Hall, raising more than $230 for the society. In the next few months, they provided aid to more than 12,000 parolees. At Memphis, the ladies' relief society voted to donate a substantial portion of its funds to destitute paroled soldiers. When this was deemed insufficient to care for all who needed it, the organization held a grand concert as well as a production of *The Lady of Lyons* for the soldiers' benefit. "The paroled soldiers are most deeply grateful for the kind efforts in their behalf," a local paper reported, and "declare that they will never forget the angel women of Memphis." The Ladies' Soldiers Aid Society of Richmond cared for wounded Confederate soldiers still lingering in hospitals and furnished means for them to reach their homes. Foreshadowing the Ladies' Memorial Associations that would organize in the coming year, these women took up an obligation to care for soldiers, a duty that would have fallen to the Confederate government had it still existed. In doing so, like many of the returning soldiers, they refused to relinquish their attachment and dedication to the Confederacy — even in the wake of surrender.[26]

In late June, John Richard Dennett, a correspondent for *The Nation*, embarked on a tour of the defeated South. Traveling aboard a steamer toward Richmond, he spoke with several rebel soldiers. "While ready enough to admit themselves conquered," he reported, they "still declare that it is only because their country has been subjugated that they now pay obedience to the United States." A young rebel elaborated, arguing that "half the Northern army was made of up of foreigners and bought men, to say nothing of" the USCT. Near the old battlefield at Manassas, another veteran offered northern writer John Trowbridge a similar justification, insisting that the Confederate armies had never been whipped, only overpowered with the help of Black soldiers.[27] Here, in the summer of 1865, one of the central tenets of the Lost Cause had been given full voice: Confederate soldiers had not been defeated fairly but simply overwhelmed by Union armies packed with unworthy foes.

Some captured Confederate officers remained in the northern camps, including Eppa Hunton, apprehended at Sailor's Creek a mere two days prior to Appomattox. "I think the President A. J. is waiting for the country to quiet down before turning loose the Genl. Officers," he wrote his wife from Fort Warren. But like others, he believed "their presence at home under parole would tend very much to pacify the country." He could not, however, complain about his current conditions. Although New York afforded the "coldest and wettest climate" he had ever seen, he had never been without a fire or blankets to keep warm. During the day he was free to roam the ramparts of the fort, as the sprig of grass and wild flowers included with the letter proved. And yet still he waited. The days passed, bringing more warmth and sunshine with them. The cold had entirely dissipated by the time Hunton was released on July 25 in the wake of Johnson's order releasing all remaining prisoners of war belonging to the rebel army or navy after they took the oath of allegiance.[28]

All, that is, except those captured with Jefferson Davis on May 10 and those in a handful of exempted categories. Maj. Henry Kyd Douglas, for example, would remain at Fort Delaware until August 23 for donning his uniform while under parole. So, too, would political prisoners such as Confederate vice president Alexander Stephens and Confederate senator Clement Clay. Yet most others would walk free, including some political prisoners such as Governors John Letcher and Zebulon Vance and former senator R. M. T. Hunter.[29]

Still, Lee worried about the indictment against him. Near Cartersville with his wife and two daughters, he busied himself planting corn in what had become an excessively hot summer. In late July, Lee wrote to Senator Reverdy Johnson of Maryland and thanked him for interceding on his behalf regarding the indictment and pardon. But Lee pointed out that the indictment was still pending against him. As such, he had not made Grant's letter of June 20 public, only shared it with other officers in the Army of Northern Virginia in the same condition. He supposed that if Grant had wanted it made public, he would have done so. Now Senator Johnson wished to ask Grant for permission to publicize the correspondence. "Should he consent to your request," Lee replied, "I, of course, have no objection. But should he not, I request that you use it in the manner I have above indicated."[30]

Grant would not consent. He had gone beyond what was proper in furnishing Lee a copy of his letter to President Johnson supporting the rebel general's pardon application. In admitting as much, Grant tacitly acknowledged that he had verged on pushing the issue too far with the president.[31]

As much as his own welfare, Lee agonized about that of his sons. Writing to Rooney at month's end, Lee said he hoped that others would not be prosecuted. He expected the federal government to both procrastinate and continue with its "denunciatory threats." In the meantime he advised patience. "As soon as I can ascertain their intention toward me, if not prevented, I shall endeavor to procure some humble, but quiet, abode for your mother and sisters, where I hope they can be happy." When officials from Washington College arrived beseeching Lee to accept the presidency of the Lexington institution, with no word on his pardon application, the possibility that he might still be arrested and tried for treason loomed large.[32]

Despite President Johnson's demand that paroled prisoners from Maryland, Missouri, Kentucky, and Delaware apply personally for a pardon, by early August few had done so. And yet the rebels continued to return to those states. Once more, commanders on the ground were left to deal with the ambiguity. On August 1 from his Baltimore headquarters, General Hancock again ordered all unpardoned rebels in the Middle Department to report to the local provost marshal and register.[33] If any wished to leave their homes and visit other places, they would need approval from their local district headquarters. Non-Maryland residents were forbidden from entering the state unless they had been granted special permission from Hancock or someone of higher authority (such as Grant or Secretary Stanton). Passes or consent issued by provost marshals or commanders in former Confederates states would not be recognized, and persons bearing such would be sent back south. Finally, any Maryland Confederate who failed to report and be registered would be arrested and imprisoned.[34] The prohibitions against returning Confederates set forth by Attorney General Speed's April 22 opinion and General Orders No. 73 continued. Until they were pardoned, rebel soldiers remained paroled prisoners of war. They were not free to come and go as they wished but were required to alert Union authorities of their whereabouts at all times.

The same held true in former Confederate territory. From Lynchburg, Virginia, Bvt. Maj. Gen. John Irvin Gregg reminded rebels that the privileges granted by their paroles hinged upon their good behavior. "When a paroled prisoner insults any officer of the Government *which grants him the parole*," Gregg observed, "he forfeits all its benefits and becomes a prisoner of war liable to be confined at the will of the captor, or punished as the Military Commission may direct." He subsequently ordered all paroled men in

This iconic photograph is often misidentified as Union troops at the Appomattox Court House in April 1865, but it actually depicts the 188th Pennsylvania on provost guard duty at Appomattox in either August or September 1865. Library of Congress Prints and Photographs Division, LC-DIG-ppmsca-35136.

Lynchburg to report to headquarters within twenty-four hours. Along with their residences, the men were to provide information about their means of living.[35] This had not been a condition of their paroles, yet it served as one more reminder that so long as a legal state of war existed, they remained prisoners of war.

Still, the audacity of rebels who refused to seek pardons infuriated some loyal northerners. Writing to Senator Charles Sumner in early August, Francis Lieber fumed, "What will you do with the traitors who do not apply for pardon or who decline in accepting it?" In Europe, a culprit could not decline a pardon. But in the United States, accepting a pardon implied acknowledgment of guilt and thus could not be forced upon someone. "What is to be done with men of the worst kind who do not apply for pardon?" Lieber wondered. Concerned primarily about political leaders such as former U.S. senator R. M. T. Hunter, his trepidation extended to military leaders as well.[36]

Without pardons, rebel soldiers were without rights. Any who wished to participate in the upcoming state elections would have to seek pardons, as would those who had any hope of reclaiming property that had been claimed by the federal government. Lee counted himself among those whose property had been seized, namely his home at Arlington. But he was not alone. Former Virginia governor and major general Henry A. Wise remained under indictment in August and had yet to apply for pardon. Upon returning to his Princess Anne County property, "Rolleston," after Appomattox, he discovered that it had been occupied by the Freedmen's Bureau. Irate and spewing obscenities, Wise fired off a letter to the military authorities at Norfolk. "I find my home occupied by a considerable number of *freedmen* and others, who hinder and disturb my possession, and molest the premises thereof, and I am unable to return." He requested that "said negroes" be removed and that he be allowed to return to his home and remain there under the condition of his parole. Union military officials promptly rejected his application, finding no reason why he should take possession of the property until he had been pardoned by the president. "Even then," Bvt. Brig. Gen. Orrin L. Mann observed, "it may be necessary for Mr. Wise to prove ownership." Moreover, he had abandoned the property in 1861 in order to move farther from Union lines. "Though he wishes to go to his former home," the general observed, "he does not abandon his status as a 'so-called' officer; but in fact, makes his claim specifically in that capacity, and as he does so (neglecting to seek pardon and restoration of right), he must be treated as a rebel prisoner of war, with no rights that we are bound to respect." It was hard to escape the irony of a freedmen's school on the property of the man who had ordered John Brown's execution fewer than six years earlier—a former governor, major general, and now prisoner of war.[37] Like so many others, Wise's status as a prisoner of war continued to both hamper and protect him.

Mosby learned the same lesson. On the afternoon of August 9, the Gray Ghost rode into Alexandria. In a town long occupied by Unionists and the Union army, it did not take long for word of the famed guerrilla's presence to spread. Near George Harper's tailor shop, a crowd of both admirers and enemies swelled, forcing Mosby to take refuge in the home of a local woman on St. Asaph Street. But still the people came, shouting and yelling, causing such a stir that Alexandria's provost marshal, Bvt. Brig. Gen. Henry H. Wells, ordered Mosby's arrest. Infuriated, Mosby demanded to know the cause of his detainment. He insisted that having been paroled and having taken the amnesty oath, he had the right to enter Alexandria, where he hoped to be readmitted to the Virginia bar. Wells was not so confident this was the case and wired the War Department for clarification. In the meantime, Mosby would remain behind bars—for his own safety as much as for the peace of the town. More than thirty Union men, Wells explained, had entered complaints against the "highway robber, plunderer, and common horse thief."

Hearing the guerrilla was in town, they had vowed to shoot him at first sight. In yet another instance of local commanders offering their own interpretation of the laws, Wells declared that the amnesty oath was meant to "cover men who had engaged in honorable warfare, and not such as him, whose whole military life for the past four years was a violation of the laws of war."[38]

News of Mosby's arrest blared from headlines across the nation—even across the Atlantic. For a brief moment, some Unionists took solace that perhaps "Mosby, the guerrilla," would not simply be allowed to walk free. But the next day, word from the War Department revealed otherwise. Secretary Stanton ordered Mosby released with the understanding that he was to return to his Fauquier County home (per the terms of his parole) and was forbidden from setting foot within Alexandria or Washington, D.C. Mosby accepted and departed for Warrenton.[39]

August marked four months since Grant had extended his generous terms of surrender to Lee's army. In those months, everything had changed—and yet much had not. Almost all of Lee's men had returned to their homes, fields, and shops. Most who had not been paroled at Appomattox turned themselves in to provost marshals from Maryland to Georgia. Those held in northern prison camps had been released. Still, the future remained uncertain. Those not pardoned under President Johnson's general amnesty wondered if their paroles would continue to protect them. Would they be prosecuted for treason? If not, would their status as citizens—with the rights and protections afforded by the U.S. Constitution, a constitution they had forsaken—be restored? What of the border region Confederates? Would they be returned to their antebellum status as citizens of their respective states? Perhaps most importantly, how would emancipation and African Americans, some of whom served as Union soldiers, reshape the social and racial world of the South?

Amid all of this uncertainty—perhaps because of it—the audacity and unrepentant sentiments of many Confederates had not vanished. Mosby and Wise offered proof of such bombastic attitudes. But so, too, did a gang of rebel soldiers who disguised themselves in Union uniforms in occupied Norfolk where they "attacked negroes wherever they happened to meet them."[40] From Mississippi came reports that returned rebels were waging attacks against African Americans with a new hellishness. Rebel soldiers paced the streets of Natchez in uniform as policemen while former slaves were forcibly carried out of town and left to starve or return to their former owners. From

Vicksburg came accounts that "the colored people were being killed, their entrails cut out . . . by those prowling exasperated renegades of mankind called surrendered rebels." "The surrender of the rebels is interpreting itself into the surrender of the colored men into the hand of the rebels," reported P. Houston Murray. "The returned rebels have commenced to actually re-enact the crimes, the barbarous, the fiendish deeds they have always been guilty of, but with increased force of savageness," he wrote. Black soldiers had fought to save the Union, but now the government appeared to be abandoning them in their hour of greatest need. "As slaves we had some protection from our masters," Murray observed, "as freemen, we have none."[41] Disbanding the rebel armies had not only failed to enforce emancipation or protect the lives of African Americans, it had also made life more dangerous for them.

With each passing day, former rebels seemed to become more emboldened. In August, artillery captain Ham Chamberlayne finally returned to Virginia from his uncle's Mississippi home. The journey had given him time to ponder the war's objects, causes, and failure. "The failure is such, that not one of the huge losses in its prosecution ever appeals to me; they are but parts of the whole," he wrote. But lest such sentiments suggest acquiescence, Chamberlayne offered a dire promise. "That whole, I hope and trust, will be too hard for us to bear, & will not be borne. And besides every drop of blood of ours that was spilled is, I believe, as a seed on the ground, whence will spring wrath and armed men."[42]

Even as the last waves of summer heat gave way to crisper autumn days, the uncertainty remained. By September 1865 Johnson had begun doling out pardons to individual Confederates—eventually more than 15,000— in order to keep his Reconstruction plan solvent. Yet news columns once more rang out with word that yet another Confederate soldier had been indicted for treason. The grand jury of the U.S. District Court in Baltimore had handed down indictments against five men, including Bradley T. Johnson, a former Maryland resident and brigadier general in the Army of Northern Virginia. Johnson had been attached to Johnston's army in April and had taken the amnesty oath and applied for pardon in early July, claiming that he did not fall under the exemption of those from the loyal states as he had abandoned his Maryland residence in 1861 and chosen to make North Carolina his new home. Even with the endorsement of several Raleigh politicians, however, like most other Confederate officers, he had not yet received word from the president. Instead, he was charged with levying war against the

United States in the summer of 1863, when he had invaded Maryland as part of the Gettysburg campaign.

When Chief Justice Samuel Chase endorsed a bench warrant for Bradley Johnson's arrest on December 1, the former general sought out the provisional governor of North Carolina for assistance. The governor beseeched the president to pardon Johnson, and the state's legislature followed suit, petitioning the president for clemency. Bradley Johnson's mother-in-law, too, took up her pen and wrote to the president, explaining that her daughter and grandchild had been forced to seek medical treatment in Milwaukee, Wisconsin, while Johnson's parole had kept him from joining them. "You, Mr. President, are a husband and a father and cannot but feel for those so deeply concerned," she wrote. But even such pleas could not stir Andrew Johnson. He refused to grant the pardon.[43]

In the months that followed, Bradley Johnson remained in North Carolina and managed to evade arrest. But in February 1866, when his wife turned dangerously ill while still in Milwaukee, he wrote to the president on his own behalf. He explained that he had been included in the convention between Sherman and Johnston, but as a citizen of Maryland, he had been forbidden by Speed's opinion from returning to his native state, hence his decision to settle in Raleigh. Now his wife needed him, prompting his request for an extension of his parole (if not a pardon) that would permit him to travel anywhere in the United States, including the loyal state of Wisconsin. His ill wife likewise implored the president to issue her husband a pardon. Whether the president ever saw the missives is unclear, but fortunately for the rebel general, his letter landed on Grant's desk. Even as Congress's Joint Committee on Reconstruction listened to a flood of new testimony describing unrepentant rebels and the horrors committed against southern African Americans, Grant stood by his surrender terms. He could not grant a pardon — that was a power reserved for the president — but he could issue a second parole. On March 10, 1866, he issued a pass permitting the rebel general to move freely throughout the United States. Within days, Bradley Johnson had boarded a train and headed to Milwaukee.[44]

On the morning of March 27, while lodging with his family at Barnum's Hotel in Baltimore, a U.S. deputy marshal took Johnson into custody and hauled him before Maryland district court judge William Giles. Johnson's counsel argued that the former general was not subject to arrest by reason of his parole received at Durham Station the previous April and extended by Grant on March 10. Judge Giles was not so convinced and believed the matter should be heard before a full bench of the circuit court. In the meantime, Bradley Johnson's bail would be set at the staggering sum of $20,000, and the case would be heard during the court's next term in late April. Johnson and his lawyer paid the bail and awaited the hearing.[45]

The question before the court was whether the military paroles should continue to protect rebels such as Johnson. But the court would not have a chance to adjudicate it. Instead, on March 30, 1866, Grant interceded once again. Writing to President Johnson, Grant asked that Bradley Johnson be released from his bonds. "There is nothing clearer in my mind than that the terms of the paroles given by officers and soldiers who were arrayed against the authority of the General Government of the United States prior to their surrender exempts them from trial or punishment for acts of legal warfare so long as they observe the conditions of their parole," Grant wrote. Again, the president questioned the protection afforded by the paroles. When Attorney General Speed pushed even more, Grant snapped: "I will be drawn and quartered before they shall be violated." At that, the president yielded once more to Grant's wishes and directed Speed to order Johnson's release and instruct authorities that the former general was not to be arrested again unless upon instructions from his office. On April 5, 1866, Judge Giles ordered that the bail be returned and Johnson discharged from the arrest. One month later, the president approved his pardon.[46]

Yet Grant refused to intervene when matters fell outside of the bounds of the Appomattox surrender paroles — especially when it involved the treatment of Union prisoners of war. When Joseph E. Johnston reached out to Grant for help in early 1866 in the case of John H. Gee, former commandant of Salisbury Prison court-martialed in North Carolina for war crimes, Grant drew a line. While the paroles protected those for "past offences, so far as these offenses consisted in making war against the Government of the United States," he informed Johnston that they did not protect rebels from charges of war crimes. "Gee is charged with willfully starving to death prisoners of War . . . [and] otherwise maltreating them to such an extent as constitute Murder in a very aggravated form."[47]

Grant's influence with the president was likewise of little use in obtaining pardons. In early November 1865, James Longstreet traveled to Washington to meet with his old friend Grant. He had not yet applied for a pardon, he explained, because he did not believe he was guilty of any offense. But when Grant offered to support his application, Longstreet accepted. The following day, the general-in-chief informed the former rebel general he had met with Stanton and Johnson and recommended a pardon as "a personal favor."

But Johnson refused. Meeting with Longstreet at the White House, the president bluntly informed him that "there are three persons of the South who can never receive amnesty, Mr. Davis, General Lee, and yourself. You have given the Union cause too much trouble." Encouraged by Grant not to give up hope, Longstreet returned south and once more pleaded his case to the president in writing. Still, no pardon appeared. In December, just as Congress was returning to session, Grant explained to Longstreet that it remained politically inexpedient for the president to extend a pardon at that time. But Longstreet should rest assured that Johnson would treat him *as if* he had received amnesty. "You need have no concern but that it will eventually be granted," Grant promised.[48]

Grant's insistence that the military paroles be enforced, combined with Johnson's amnesty proclamation, would ultimately protect Confederate soldiers, if not civilians such as Jefferson Davis, from prosecution for treason.[49] But in the fall of 1865 and into the spring of 1866, this was not yet certain. In the border regions Unionists held out hope that the rebels might still be punished. For example, nearly 2,000 cases appeared on the docket in eastern Tennessee for treason or giving aid to the enemy. In Maryland, Unionists sought to prosecute any resident who had left the state to join the Confederacy. The military authorities submitted more than 4,000 names to the grand jury, but only the most prominent rebels—men like Bradley T. Johnson— would face indictments.[50]

For those who had not yet been pardoned, the paroles and their conditions remained in place. Such was the case for former brigadier general William H. Payne, who had been captured after Lincoln's assassination, detained at Johnson's Island, and indicted alongside Lee and others. Like thousands of others excluded from Johnson's amnesty proclamation, he had applied personally for a pardon in mid-June, but he had yet to receive word from the president. Residing in Warrenton with his brother, Payne still suffered from wounds received at Petersburg and hoped to visit Baltimore for surgery. Per the conditions of his parole, in August 1865 he asked the local provost marshal for permission to visit the Maryland city. But his request was denied. As Maj. Gen. Andrew A. Humphreys observed, "Good medical treatment can be had in Virginia." Still, Payne persisted, writing in September to the War Department. This time his request would be granted, but only for a period of ten days. After that, he would have to return to Virginia.[51]

Even Robert E. Lee and his sons remained bound by the conditions of their paroles. Upon assuming the presidency of Washington College in Lexington, Virginia, in October 1865, Lee had taken the oath of allegiance and forwarded it to Johnson. But the president still refused to pardon him. Even though Johnson had declared the insurrection at an end in April 1866, which ostensibly should have lifted conditions of parole, for Lee both the limitations and the protections remained in place. In July 1866, Lee's son Custis wrote Grant. As a paroled officer, he recognized that he was bound to limit himself to his home state. But he and his brother Rooney desired to travel to Warren County, North Carolina, for the dedication of a tomb over the remains of their sister Ann, who had died during the war. Although Lee's sons had not requested that their father travel with them, Grant's adjutant Adam Badeau, responded directly to the senior Lee, granting him a permit to attend the ceremony. The document read, "Robert E. Lee, a paroled officer of the late Confederate Army is exempt from arrest by military authorities unless directed by the President of the United States, the Secy of War, or from these Headquarters so long as he observes the conditions of his parole. The restriction requiring paroled officers to remain at their homes is removed *in this case* and Mr. Robert. E. Lee will be allowed to travel unmolested throughout the United States." A grateful Lee thanked Grant but pointed out that he would be unable to attend the ceremony, although both Custis and Rooney would do so.[52] For all of Grant's generosity, in the fall of 1866 Lee legally remained a prisoner of war under indictment.

Yet Johnson continued to dole out pardons to those excluded from his May 1865 proclamation. In January 1867, he sent Congress a partial list of prominent officers and elected officials who had been pardoned, among them Bradley T. Johnson. By December that list had grown to include individuals such as Longstreet.[53] In retaliation for Congressional Reconstruction and declaring once more that the insurrection had ended, Johnson announced a second amnesty in September 1867, which opened the door for all former soldiers to seek pardon, and the following July he offered a third.[54] This proclamation excluded only Davis, who had been released on bail in May 1867 but remained under indictment.[55]

The ratification of the Fourteenth Amendment in 1868, however, posed a problem for the federal government—and a loophole for Confederates. Section 3 of the amendment held that any Confederate who had formerly taken an oath to uphold the Constitution but "had engaged in insurrection or rebellion" against the United States would be prevented from holding any office, civil or military, state or federal. According to Chief Justice Salmon P. Chase's interpretation, the clause might exonerate former Confederates from any punishment other than holding public office. It is unclear why Chase offered such an unlikely interpretation of the amendment. But in doing so, he gave Davis's attorneys an argument for quashing the indictment against the Confederate president.[56]

With the possibility that the Supreme Court might entertain the defense's motion, Johnson acted to prevent the Davis case from going to trial. On Christmas Day 1868, the president issued a final amnesty proclamation declaring "a full pardon and amnesty for the offense of treason against the United States," including those under indictment, thereby forestalling Davis's motion. On February 11, 1869, less than a month before Grant was to be sworn in as president, Johnson's attorney general, William Evarts, entered a *nolle prosequi* for all thirty-seven indictments found against the rebel leaders in Virginia. Davis, Lee, Longstreet, and the others no longer faced prosecution. "Who would have thought, five years ago, such a result possible?" asked a New York newspaper.[57] Though challenged for nearly four years after Appomattox, Grant's terms of surrender had been upheld.

Long before all of this unfolded, some Unionists claimed that Confederates had been so thoroughly defeated and subjugated at Appomattox that they were willing to acquiesce to any terms of peace. Testifying before the Joint Committee on Reconstruction in January 1866, the sheriff of Fairfax County, Virginia, concluded that the rebels "seemed to be perfectly satisfied with everything. So as they only got home they were glad enough to submit to anything." As soon as they got their pardons, however, it all changed. An Alabama Unionist concurred, observing that "the people then would have accepted any terms and every term," including the enfranchisement of African Americans.[58] The president's lenient amnesty and pardon proclamations had welcomed rebels back into the nation as citizens (albeit in many instances without voting rights). Once pardoned, they could no longer be charged with treason. Emboldened, many Unionists claimed, former Confederates turned to restoring as much of their antebellum society as possible. They elected former Confederate leaders to Congress and crafted new means of controlling the labor and bodies of freedpeople through Black Codes.[59]

Others blamed Grant for the state of affairs, observing that the root of all problems lay in the surrender terms. According to E. L. Godkin's *The Nation*, Grant should have "stipulated unconditional surrender." Instead, the Union general-in-chief's "unfortunately and unskillfully worded" terms had served to protect Lee's soldiers from any charges. "What was still more unfortunate," the columnist continued, "was that after this convention such haste should have been made in concluding similar ones with the other rebel commanders, so that at last the parole has been made to cover with immunity such persons as [Nathan Bedford] Forrest and [Raphael] Semmes." In rapidly setting his terms to paper, Grant had set a precedent with legal and political ramifications that might undo all that the Union army had achieved.[60]

Such finger-pointing failed to acknowledge that the ends of war came through the piecemeal surrenders of Confederate armies rather than a peace treaty that clearly defined the fruits of victory and the penalties for defeat. But a treaty would have recognized the Confederacy as a sovereign nation. It was a double-edged sword. Constrained by both the Constitution and politics, Grant had compelled the surrender of Lee's army in the way he thought most likely to achieve reunion. Even a year after Appomattox, he remained guided by the same principles that had shaped his terms. It was not some chivalric honor that compelled him to uphold the paroles. Rather, he remained committed to ending the war as quickly and peacefully as possible. He wanted every rebel to surrender himself. He wanted to prevent guerrilla action and avoid the prospect of defeated Confederates rushing south to Mexico, where they might join forces with the French.[61]

All of these elements motivated Grant's actions and explain why he encouraged the paroling of nearly 16,000 men from Lee's army in the weeks and months after Appomattox.[62] Moreover, his decisions were accompanied by those made at the local level by subordinate officers in far-flung departments and districts, by civilians, and by paroled Confederates. In many of these instances, army officials and local communities were not worried about the constitutionality of their orders and actions. Nor were they necessarily considering the long-term consequences. They were trying to do what seemed best in that moment and in that place, however events might have unfolded, however misguided they may seem in hindsight.

Epilogue

In 1886, speaking to a crowd of Maryland Confederate veterans at Gettysburg, Bradley T. Johnson observed that Grant's surrender terms had permitted Confederate soldiers to return to their homes and to retain their swords—"the emblem of our right and the outward mark of the respect which we had won." Without such a concession on Grant's behalf, Johnson boldly insisted, "no surrender would have been made by either Lee or Johnston." Confederates had laid down their weapons but retained "our reserved right of self-defense, of our honor, of our property and our institutions." Ignoring the fact that Confederates had waged their war for independence in the name of slaveholding, Johnson intoned that "the cause of the Confederate States was the cause of civil liberty" and insisted "that cause will never be a 'lost cause.'"[1] For Johnson, the Confederate cause not only had survived the surrenders but was vindicated by their terms.

The seeds of Lost Cause orthodoxy had been planted during the war itself. But as Johnson suggested, the nature of the war's ending had further enshrined Confederates' belief in southern superiority and a war waged for constitutional principles.[2] In the decades after 1865, veterans who carried a parole pass from Appomattox could count themselves among those Lee had described as the "brave survivors of so many hard-fought battles." Echoing his farewell address, Lee's men insisted they had been vastly outnumbered and overwhelmed by superior Union resources, but not defeated in battle. Confederates had been heroic even though destined to fail against the mighty United States war machine.

Many boasted that they had never been forced to capitulate. Benjamin Washington Jones, who had escaped across the James River on April 9, remained fiercely proud that he and several of his comrades never endured the "humiliation of a surrender." "We were not paroled," he defiantly proclaimed, "and some have never assented to the 'oath of allegiance.'"[3] When asked years later what the greatest moment of his military career had been, Thomas Rosser responded "without hesitation" that it was his successful charge at Appomattox, after which he "left that fatal field in triumph, refusing to surrender either myself or my command to the enemy."[4] The ends of the war had been marked by resistance and defiance as much as by surrender.

Confederate soldiers did not march away from Appomattox victorious, but they did come home unconquered.[5] As they pushed west from the trenches of Petersburg and Richmond, most had refused to give up hope that their cause might yet prevail. Many who surrendered at Appomattox marched home more like soldiers than the prisoners of war they were. Carrying with them the words of Lee's farewell order, they admitted that they had been whipped on the battlefield and compelled to yield to overwhelming Union resources, but that had not meant that their cause had been unjust.

The refusal to accept defeat was more than just the rhetoric of defiance. Those who escaped the surrender and rode south to join Johnston or west to the Shenandoah Valley clung to the cause. Individuals and groups who murdered soldiers of the USCT or forced newly freed men and women to assist them refused to concede that slavery had ended or that the Confederate war to protect slavery had resulted in emancipation. Those who eventually sought out paroles in Virginia and beyond continued to insist that their cause had been legally and morally just. Even among those compelled to seek individual pardons from President Johnson, many defended the constitutionality of their actions.

Nothing had quelled their belief in the righteousness of the Confederacy. There had been no "golden moment" when Lee's starving and desperate soldiers had been so thoroughly subjugated that they were willing to accept any conditions. If anything, the humiliation of registering at provost marshal offices, the ban on rebel uniforms, the perils faced by border region Confederates, the indictments of rebel leaders, the struggles to return home, and the presence of both white and Black Union occupying troops emboldened their claims of southern virtue and northern barbarity. The quest for an independent Confederate nation may have ended in the spring of 1865, but an attachment to and defense of the Confederate cause would continue to flourish.

The disbanding of the Army of Northern Virginia had not marked the end of the nation's division. It was only the beginning, foreshadowing much of what would play out in the decades to come: retaliation against African Americans, defiance of meddlesome federal agents, and the election of Confederate leaders to state and national offices, all couched in the Lost Cause veneration of Lee and his soldiers as righteous and invincible — even in defeat.

Acknowledgments

There are many aspects I especially enjoy about writing books: the exhilarating moments of uncovering a detail in the archives, the outlining and re-outlining of chapters, and the feeling of triumph when a chapter finally clicks are just a few. But perhaps what I cherish most is the journey along the way that is shaped by so many colleagues, friends, and family members.

Throughout the process, no one has been more supportive and encouraging than my editor and friend Mark Simpson-Vos. He has endured more conversations about this project than I'm sure he would like to recall, and he has always answered my queries with wisdom and patience. His attention to detail, narrative, and argument is without parallel. Others at the University of North Carolina Press have been critical in shepherding this book into existence, including Julie Bush, Dominique Moore, Jay Mazzocchi, Liz Orange, and the anonymous readers whose suggestions were invaluable. I met Hal Jespersen many years ago at a University of Virginia Civil War conference and am delighted to have his maps included here.

I've spent a good portion of the past six years visiting archives and locations throughout Washington, D.C., Virginia, and North Carolina, trying to trace the story of the Civil War's last days. At each of these locales, historians and archivists helped guide me through a tangle of sources and pointed me in new directions, including John McClure (at the Virginia Museum of History and Culture) and Mike Musick (formerly of the National Archives). For sharing their knowledge and expertise, I would like to thank the staff of the Albert and Shirley Small Special Collections Library and Interlibrary Loan at Alderman Library, University of Virginia. I wish to extend my deep appreciation to the always patient Sally Anne Schmidt for her assistance with documents and images from the John L. Nau III Collection now housed at UVA. Trevor Plante at the National Archives has been tremendous; I would never have located some of the essential records that I relied upon for much of the book without his help and keen insight. John Coski, now at the American Civil War Museum in Richmond, has been a dear friend since I began research on my first book. His generosity is without comparison.

I likewise would have been at a loss without friends and historians in the National Park Service. At Appomattox Court House National Historical Park, Patrick Schroeder not only shared the Going Home Research Files that launched me on this project but also took time to show me and my nephew, Conner, around the battlefield, helping me to better understand all that unfolded in early April 1865. Equally as important, he generously read several early versions of chapters and saved me from a number of missteps. Ernie Price (formerly of Appomattox and now superintendent at Camp Nelson National Monument) spoke to me extensively early on in the research, as did Bert Dunkerly (Richmond National Battlefield Park). Keith Snyder (Antietam National Battlefield) helped me locate images and provided a wonderful private tour of the field for me and my husband, Spencer Lucas. I began my history career in the National Park Service and know the depths of devotion and commitment of those on the front lines. I am grateful for all they do.

I have had the wonderful fortune to have friends and colleagues of astonishing goodwill and scholarly guidance. Keith Bohannon ranks among the most generous and has always kept a steady stream of sources pouring into my inbox over the years. Jim Broomall, Rick Eiserman, Robert K. Krick, Josh Rothman, and Susannah J. Ural likewise shared research materials. Megan Bever, Peter Carmichael, Steve Cushman, Cynthia Nicoletti, Aaron Sheehan-Dean, Katy Shively, Amy Murrell Taylor, and Joan Waugh lent their wisdom. Bill Blair invited me to present an early chapter to his graduate students at Penn State, which, along with our many conversations about his own book manuscript, helped steer my project toward a better path. I am deeply grateful to Liz Varon and Jim Marten, both of whom read the entire manuscript and offered exceptional advice. As always, I owe a special debt to Gary Gallagher for never failing in his generosity and wisdom.

My students continue to be a source of inspiration. At Purdue, I was privileged to have several stellar undergraduate research assistants, including Emma Gaier, Allison Kraft, and Sam Opsahl. Graduate student Zachary Elledge worked tirelessly to transcribe and input data into my Beyond Appomattox database, and Molly Mersmann has assisted me on her many research expeditions. Omkar Patil, a graduate student in computer science, was instrumental in helping me build the first version of a digital project on the paroles beyond Appomattox. At UVA, undergraduates Cole Davidson, Geneva Weidhaas, and Matt Weisenfluh have continued to edit and build the database as interns through the Nau Center. Graduate student Jesse George-Nichol helped find materials when I was still in Indiana, while Daniele Celano tracked down several important legal cases. Kevin Caprice has assisted me on countless research projects, from transcriptions to sleuthing for sources.

I began this project while at Purdue University, and returning to UVA meant saying goodbye to a history department and university that had been incredibly supportive. I may no longer be able to call Dave Atkinson and Katie Brownell colleagues, but they remain the dearest of friends. Michele Buzon, Cole Jones, Wendy Kline, and Randy Roberts are likewise much missed. At UVA, Liz Varon and Will Kurtz immediately made the Nau Center feel like home. I am beyond grateful for all of their guidance and collegiality. In particular, Will has spent a great deal of time helping to refashion my parole data so that it might become a real website, along with guidance from Worthy Martin of the Institute for Advanced Technology in the Humanities. I thank John Nau for his unyielding support of the center, and I am especially indebted to Claudrena Harold, the Corcoran Department of History Chair, for her leadership and friendship.

Nothing has made returning to Virginia sweeter than family. My parents, Robert and Sharon Janney, remain my biggest champions and my inspiration. My brothers, Andrew and Marc; sister-in-law, Monica; nephew, Conner; and nieces, Isa and Addie, add laughter, love, and support. My husband, Spencer, continues to keep me grounded, reminding me that there is more to life than history and work (even as he builds more and more bookshelves). And then there is Campbell. I began this book not long after he was born. In the time that I have spent researching, writing, and rewriting, he has grown into the most incredible, inquisitive, and witty child we could be blessed to have. I love you to the moon and back, Campbell.

Notes

ABBREVIATIONS

APCO	Appomattox Court House National Historical Park, Va.
CMLS	Confederate Memorial Literary Society Collection, Virginia Museum of History and Culture, Richmond
CSR	Compiled Service Record from National Archives accessed through Fold3.com
CV	*Confederate Veteran*
DU	Perkins Library, Special Collections Library, Duke University, Durham, N.C.
GPL	Ulysses S. Grant Presidential Library, Starkville, Miss.
HSP	Historical Society of Pennsylvania, Philadelphia
NARA	National Archives and Records Administration, Washington, D.C., and College Park, Md.
NCDAH	North Carolina Division of Archives and History, Raleigh
OR	*War of the Rebellion: The Official Records of the Union and Confederate Armies.* 128 vols. Washington, D.C.: GPO, 1880–1901
PAJ	*Papers of Andrew Johnson*, edited by LeRoy P. Graf and Ralph W. Haskins, 16 vols. (Knoxville: University of Tennessee Press, 1967–2000)
PM	Provost Marshal
PUSG	*Papers of Ulysses S. Grant*, edited by John Y. Simon et al., 32 vols. (Carbondale: Southern Illinois University Press, 1967–2012)
RG	Record Group
SHC	Southern Historical Collection, Wilson Library, University of North Carolina at Chapel Hill
SHSP	*Southern Historical Society Papers*, edited by J. William Jones et al., 52 vols. (Richmond: Southern Historical Society, 1876–1959)
TSLA	Tennessee State Library and Archives, Nashville

UVA   Small Special Collections, University of Virginia, Charlottesville

VMHC   Virginia Museum of History and Culture, Richmond

INTRODUCTION

1. Marvel, *Lee's Last Retreat*, 161–67; McIntosh Diary, April 9, 1865, David Gregg McIntosh Diary and Papers, VMHC; "Last Colonel of the Artillery, A.N.V.," *CV* 25 (May 1917): 224–26. As Jason Phillips points out, McIntosh's account was most likely penned from memory when he returned home rather than in the field (*Diehard Rebels*, 227n47).

2. McIntosh Diary, April 9, 1865, VMHC; Gallagher, "An End and a New Beginning," 65–66; Calkins, *Appomattox Campaign*, 159–64.

3. McIntosh Diary, April 9, 1865, VMHC.

4. McIntosh Diary, April 9, 1865, VMHC.

5. McIntosh Diary, April 9–13, 1865, VMHC.

6. Most books on the war either stop with Appomattox or understand it as a postscript. On Lee's army, see Glatthaar, *General Lee's Army*; and Powers, *Lee's Miserables*. There are several books on the Appomattox campaign, but these tend to begin with the collapse of the siege at Petersburg and end with the surrender. See, for example, Marvel, *A Place Called Appomattox*; Marvel, *Lee's Last Retreat*; Calkins, *Appomattox Campaign*; Calkins, *Battles of Appomattox*; and B. Davis, *To Appomattox*. For historians who describe it as a smooth transition to peace, see Catton, *Stillness at Appomattox*; and Winik, *April 1865*. For the argument that Appomattox was a harbinger of reconciliation, see Blight, *Race and Reunion*, 214, 356. For historians who have challenged the notion that Appomattox represented an "easy" peace or an agreement to forget the meaning of the war for either side, see Janney, *Remembering the Civil War*; and Varon, *Appomattox*. For a discussion of the multiple negotiated settlements that helped end the war, see Silkenat, *Raising the White Flag*; and Dunkerly, *To the Bitter End*.

7. See, for example, Noe, "'Disturbers of the Peace'"; Earle and Burke, *Bleeding Kansas*; Emberton, *Beyond Redemption*; Grimsley, "Wars for the American South"; and Marrs, *Nineteenth-Century American Literature*. Others have more specifically argued that a legal *state* of war (if not an extension of the war itself) lasted until early 1871 including G. Downs, *After Appomattox*; and Neff, *Justice in Blue and Gray*. This book aims to strike a middle ground in this debate, reminding the reader that the lived experience often does not offer such clear markers of periodization. What individuals and groups perceived as the "end of the war" shifted and changed, often multiple times.

8. Blight, "Civil War Isn't Over."

9. Gallagher, *Confederate War*.

10. *Wheeling (W.Va.) Daily Intelligencer*, May 13, 1865. Bvt. Maj. Gen. George H. Sharpe had served as the Chief of the Bureau of Information (organized military intelligence) between February 11, 1863, and March 16, 1865.

11. Confederate troop strength is very difficult to determine, especially because so many of the records were destroyed during the final campaign. My numbers are based on a close reading of the *OR* along with the work of other historians. Grant estimated that at the beginning of the campaign, Lee had 70,000 men (C. A. Dana to Stanton, April 12, 1865, Grant Papers, Series 3, Unpublished Materials, box 26, GPL). Gary W. Gallagher argues that on April 2, "the Army of Northern Virginia and miscellaneous units from the

Richmond defenses (including a battalion of sailors) almost certainly approached, and perhaps exceeded, 60,000 men of all arms" ("An End and a New Beginning," 42, 56). Chris M. Calkins estimates Lee's strength at 58,400 at the beginning of the Appomattox campaign (*Final Bivouac*, 208). Finally, William Marvel states that "between 51,200 and 57,200 men should have begun the retreat." He observes that thousands deserted during the evacuation but that when Lee united the Confederate units that had occupied the defenses around Petersburg and Richmond at Amelia Court House, "he probably collected about 45,000 men . . . not counting the naval battalion that joined him there." These numbers do not include detached units such as Mosby's. For an in-depth analysis of Lee's troop strength, see Marvel, *Lee's Last Retreat*, 201–6. For the 11,530 Confederate casualties between Sutherland Station (April 2) and the final battle at Appomattox Court House (April 9), see Calkins, *Appomattox Campaign*, 201–2. Although the numbers on both sides were often exaggerated, a *New York Times* report on April 30, 1865, observed that a "full twenty thousand" of Lee's men had deserted him in the last forty-eight hours before the surrender. Finally, it is unclear precisely how many men Union authorities paroled at Appomattox. The numbers range from 26,000 to 28,231 (*OR*, ser. 1, 46 [3]: 851–53, 1279).

12. Beyond Appomattox database created by author. Through an extensive survey of RG 109, entry 212, NARA, as of December 2020, I have compiled a database of 16,997 soldiers from the Army of Northern Virginia who were paroled at sites beyond Appomattox between April 10 and July 15, 1865. A handful of these soldiers may have been paroled more than once. This database has been a community effort, including invaluable assistance from graduate and undergraduate students at Purdue and the University of Virginia: Zachary Elledge, Emma Gaier, Allison Kraft, Sam Opsahl, Geneva Weidhaas, and Matt Weisenfluh. At Purdue, computer science graduate student Omkar Patil was instrumental in helping me create a digital map of this data, which I plan to revise and make public with the help of the Nau Center's Will Kurtz and the University of Virginia's Institute for Advanced Technology in the Humanities.

13. Blair, "Finding the Ending of America's Civil War"; G. Downs, *After Appomattox*; Neff, *Justice in Blue and Gray*, 204.

14. G. Downs, *After Appomattox*, 2–3.

CHAPTER 1

1. Curran, *John Dooley's Civil War*, 358–61; Longstreet, *From Manassas to Appomattox*, 620; *OR*, ser. 1, 46 (3): 529; Acken, *Blue Blooded Cavalryman*, 238; Sternhell, *Routes of War*, 163.

2. J. E. Whitehorne Diary, April 4, 1865, SHC; Calkins, "Final March to Appomattox," 236–37; Whitehorne CSR. In addition to the diary held by the SHC, there is a privately published account: J. E. Whitehorne and Fletcher L. Elmore, *Diary of J. E. Whitehorne, 1st Sergt, Co. "F," 12th Va. Infantry, A. P. Hill's 3rd Corps. A.N.Va.* (Louisville, Ky: F. L. Elmore, Jr., 1995). But a comparison with the typescript held by the SHC reveals that the published account has been heavily edited, perhaps interspersed with letters.

3. E. Augustus Klipstein to My Dear Wife, February 10, 1865, John L. Nau III Collection, UVA.

4. Lowell W. Haven to My Dear Mother, February 22, 1865, and Edmund P. French to Friend Willie, March 5, 1865, Nau Collection, UVA. Emphasis in original.

5. *OR*, ser. 1, 46 (3): 1357.

6. *OR*, ser. 1, 46 (3): 529.

7. Joseph H. Prime to Darling, April 8, 1865, item DL1247, Nau Collection, UVA.

8. Benjamin Sims Journal, April 1–2, 7, 1865, NCDAH; William Andrew Mauney, "A Diary of the War between the States" transcript, entries April 3–23, 1865, VMHC. Historian William Marvel likewise notes that "Virginia units lost an average of 75.4 percent of their aggregate present from March 1 until the last volley at Appomattox" (*Lee's Last Retreat*, 205–6).

9. Nevins, *Diary of Battle*, 520, diary entries April 6–7, 1865; H. C. Metzger to Father, April 14, 1865, Nau Collection, UVA; *OR*, ser. 1, 46 (3): 545; John Rumsey Brincklé Papers, diary entry April 4, 1865, Library of Congress, A People at War Collection (microfilm). Lee assumed command of what he christened the Army of Northern Virginia in June 1862.

10. Albright Reminiscences, April 6, 1865, James W. Albright Diary and Reminiscences, SHC. This collection includes typescripts of a diary kept by Albright between April 1864 and April 1865 and typescripts of reminiscences compiled at a later date that add more details.

11. Albright, *Greensboro*, 17, 78; U.S. Bureau of the Census, *Eighth Census of the United States*, 1860 (hereafter 1860 U.S. Census).

12. Albright, *Greensboro*, 79; *Greensboro (N.C.) Times*, November 12, 1857, September 28, 1861; Albright CSR; Reminiscences of Mrs. James W. (Martha Sarah Purvis) Albright (North Carolina Digital Collections), State Archives of North Carolina, Raleigh.

13. Gallagher, "An End and a New Beginning," 54–57; Calkins, *Appomattox Campaign*, 97–111; Dunkerly, *To the Bitter End*, 5–6; Varon, *Appomattox*, 15.

14. Coffman and Graham, *To Honor These Men*, 420–21.

15. Albright Reminiscences, April 6, 1865, SHC.

16. Sheridan, *Personal Memoirs*, 2:180; Haley, *Rebel Yell and the Yankee Hurrah*, 261.

17. Stewart, *History of the One Hundred and Fortieth Regiment*, 266.

18. *Richmond Whig* reprinted in the *Daily Constitutionalist* (Augusta, Ga.), April 27, 1865.

19. Catton, *A Stillness at Appomattox*, 369–80; McPherson, *Battle Cry*, 847–48; Gallagher, "An End and a New Beginning," 60–61; R. White, *American Ulysses*, 404.

20. Longstreet, *From Manassas to Appomattox*, 619; Wert, *Longstreet*. Longstreet had been born in South Carolina.

21. Whitehorne Diary, April 8, 1865, SHC; Gordon McCabe to Mary W. Cabell, care of Dr. Clifford Cabell (Buckingham County), April 7, 1865, Early Family Papers, section 17, VMHC; A. Gordon, *Memories and Memorials*, 1:292 (letter dated April 11, 1865).

22. Longstreet, *From Manassas to Appomattox*, 620; Hinson, "Diary," entry April 8, 1865; Gallagher, "An End and a New Beginning," 63.

23. For more precise details on the route of Walker's men, see Calkins, *Battles of Appomattox*, 5–6.

24. Albright Reminiscences, April 8, 1865, SHC; Personal Diary of John Willis Council, April 8, 1865, NCDAH; Calkins, *Battles of Appomattox*, 17–19, 26, 29; Marvel, *Lee's Last Retreat*, 146; Varon, *Appomattox*, 33.

25. Calkins, *Battles of Appomattox*, 39–40, 144; A. Gordon, *Memories and Memorials*, 1:291; Albright Reminiscences, April 8, 1865, SHC.

26. Gallagher, "An End and a New Beginning," 65; Longstreet, *From Manassas to Appomattox*, 623–24; *OR*, ser. 1, 46 (1): 1303–4; Longacre, *Fitz Lee*, 185.

27. Thomas, *Three Years with Grant*, 318–20; Grant, *Personal Memoirs*, 717.

28. John W. Bone, "Record of a Soldier in the Late War," 47, Lowery Shuford Collection, NCDAH; Alexander, *Fighting for the Confederacy*, 530–31.

29. Alexander, *Fighting for the Confederacy*, 530–33.

30. Alexander, 534–35; Gallagher, "An End and a New Beginning," 68; Marshall, *Aide-de-Camp*, 263.

31. Moore, *Story of a Cannoneer*, 302–7.

32. Julia Wilbur Diary, April 9, 1865, transcription by Alexandria Archaeology; E. A. Klipstein CSR; E. Augustus Klipstein to My Dear Wife, February 10, 1865, John L Nau III Collection, UVA.

33. Calkins, *Battles of Appomattox*, 145; Marvel, *Lee's Last Retreat*, 165; A. Gordon, *Memories and Memorials*, 1:291, diary entry April 9, 1865; Townsend, "From Petersburg," diary entry April 9, 1865, 105; Charles C. Richardson, "A Few Reminiscences of My Experience in the Civil War, as a Confederate Soldier and Member of the Surry Light Brigade," Going Home Research Files, APCO; Charles Friend, "Last Fight of First Richmond Howitzers," Going Home Research Files, APCO. The men of the 1st Company of the Richmond Howitzers were among those who were separated from the main body of Lee's army on April 8 and headed north toward Red Oak Baptist Church. The 2nd and 3rd Companies surrendered with Lee on April 9. George Bernard of the 12th Virginia Infantry, away from the army on furlough and trying to reconnect, also heard these rumors about Lincolnton sometime around April 9 (Bernard, *War Talks*, 280).

34. Longacre, *Lee's Cavalrymen*, 332–33.

35. Munford, "Last Days of Fitz Lee's Confederacy," 21–22, VMHC; Calkins, *Battles of Appomattox*, 121–23.

36. David S. Grimsley to John W. Daniel, February 2, 1905, Papers of John W. Daniel and the Daniel Family, UVA.

37. Marvel, *Lee's Last Retreat*, 177–78; Longacre, *Lee's Cavalrymen*, 332–33; Munford, "Last Days of Fitz Lee's Confederacy," 23, VMHC; Driver, *First & Second Maryland Cavalry*, 123. Brig. Gen. William H. F. Payne was wounded on March 30. His command included the 5th, 6th, and 8th Virginia Cavalry along with the 36th Virginia Cavalry Battalion. Munford's old brigade included the 1st, 2nd, 3rd, and 4th Virginia Cavalry.

38. Freeman, *R. E. Lee*, 4:130; Marvel, *Lee's Last Retreat*, 178–79. This included repatriated prisoners who were especially fearful of returning to the Union prisons should the parole terms not hold.

39. Personal Diary of John Willis Council, April 9, 1865, NCDAH.

40. Lewis T. Nunnelee, Postwar Memoir and Diary, entries April 9–20, 1865, CMLS. Shoemaker's Battery was also known as the Beauregard Rifles, Lynchburg Beauregards, and Virginia Horse Artillery.

41. Harwell, *Confederate Diary*, April 9, 1865, 17.

CHAPTER 2

1. J. E. Whitehorne Diary, April 9, 1865, SHC.

2. Marshall, "Appomattox Courthouse," 357; Catton, *Never Call Retreat*, 454; Calkins, *Appomattox Campaign*, 170–71; Cauble, *Surrender Proceedings*, 44–47; Gallagher, "An End and a New Beginning," 70. Grant's aides were Orville E. Babcock and Lt. William McKee Dunn. Lee also asked Walter H. Taylor to accompany him to the surrender conference, but Taylor demurred.

3. Sheridan, *Personal Memoirs*, 2:200–201; Grant, *Personal Memoirs*, 2:629–30; Marshall, *Aide-de-Camp*, 269–70.

4. Marshall, "Appomattox Courthouse," 358; Grant, *Personal Memoirs*, 2:630–31. Several of Grant's staff remained, including Babcock, Asst. Adj. Gen. Col. Thomas S. Bowers, and Parker (Varon, *Appomattox*, 55). Sheridan later claimed he was not present (Styple, *Generals in Bronze*, 25).

5. *OR*, ser. 1, 46 (3): 665. Marshall recalled that Grant first wrote the terms in pencil before having Lee examine them. Once Lee approved, Grant asked Colonel Parker to make a copy in ink (Marshall, "Appomattox Courthouse," 358).

6. Grant, *Personal Memoirs*, 2:631; Waugh, "'I Only Knew What Was in My Mind.'"

7. Clipping of Badeau, "Grant at Appomattox," *Chicago Tribune*, June 15, 1896, in Appomattox Subject File, GPL.

8. T. Jones, *Captives of Liberty*, 213–38; Witt, *Lincoln's Code*, 16–19; Dilbeck, *More Civil War*, 88.

9. Vattel, *Law of Nations*; R. White, *American Ulysses*, 32; Witt, *Lincoln's Code*, 71, 83–86, 137; Skelton, *American Profession of Arms*, 171–72; Morrison, "Best School in the World," 87–125; Reardon, *With a Sword in One Hand*, 8.

10. Greenberg, *Wicked War*, 126–29; Silkenat, *Raising the White Flag*, 12–14; J. Davis, *Papers of Jefferson Davis*, 3:24; R. White, *American Ulysses*, 80–84; Grant, *Personal Memoirs*, 1:73. Greenberg explains that Taylor's decision made sense — the American troops "were exhausted, hungry, and low on ammunition. They were in no state to continue the grueling hand-to-hand combat that would be required to secure the city. Taylor was also fairly sure the war was now over. . . . Had the war been about the Mexico-Texas boundary, it would have been over" (128).

11. Greenberg, *Wicked War*, 169–71; Grant, *Personal Memoirs*, 1:78–80; Henderson, *Glorious Defeat*, 165.

12. Waugh, *U. S. Grant*, 53–55; Silkenat, *Raising the White Flag*, 65–68; Brinton, *Personal Memoirs*, 133; Richardson, *A Personal History of Ulysses S. Grant*, 221, 228. Silkenat notes that Grant never discussed the origins of his demand for unconditional surrender, but there is evidence that it might have come from Gen. Charles F. Smith, Grant's instructor at West Point. For a wonderful overview of surrenders during the Civil War from individual soldiers to entire armies, see Silkenat, *Raising the White Flag*.

13. Silkenat, *Raising the White Flag*, 67–68.

14. *OR*, ser. 1, 24 (1): 59–60; Clampitt, *Occupied Vicksburg*, 16–17; Silkenat, *Raising the White Flag*, 145–51.

15. *OR*, ser. 1, 24 (1): 60–61; *OR*, ser. 1, 24 (3): 479; Clampitt, *Occupied Vicksburg*, 17–18; Silkenat, *Raising the White Flag*, 145–51. For the wording of the Vicksburg parole, see Davis and Tremmel, *Parole, Pardon, Pass*, 145.

16. Silkenat, *Raising the White Flag*, 94; Varon, *Appomattox*, 30–31; G. Brown, "Prisoner of War Parole"; Witt, *Lincoln's Code*, 230, 255–56, 389–90; Grant, *Personal Memoirs*, 2:306–8. For more on the breakdown of the prisoner exchange system, see Silkenat, *Raising the White Flag*, 93–100.

17. For more on how precedent shaped Grant's terms, see Varon, *Appomattox*, 30–31; Waugh, *U. S. Grant*, 65; Waugh, "'I Only Knew What Was In My Mind,'" 307–18; and Silkenat, *Raising the White Flag*, 189.

18. Witt, *Lincoln's Code*, 285–86.

19. Varon, *Appomattox*, 31–33.

20. Sherman, *Memoirs*, 2:840; "Admiral Porter's Account of the Interview with Mr. Lincoln," in Sherman, *Memoirs*, 2:328–30. For more on Lincoln's Proclamation of Amnesty and Reconstruction, or Ten Percent Plan, see Blair, *With Malice toward Some*, 91, 196–97.

21. Basler, *Collected Works of Abraham Lincoln*, 8:330–31. In late February, while discussing prisoners under a flag of truce, Maj. Gen. E. O. C. Ord and Longstreet discussed how the war might be brought to a close. Ord subsequently conveyed a confidential message to Grant from Longstreet on the topic, which likely led to Lee seeking the interview (Ord to Grant, February 27, 1865, Ord Subject File, GPL; W. Davis, "Confederate Peacemakers," 148).

22. Lee to Grant, March 2, 1865, in Dowdey and Manarin, *Wartime Papers*, 911–12; Grant to Lee, March 4, 1865, *PUSG* 14:98–99n; Grant to Stanton, March 4, 1865, *PUSG* 14:100. For more on Confederate efforts to negotiate peace ahead of Appomattox, see W. Davis, "Confederate Peacemakers."

23. *OR*, ser. 1, 24 (1): 60–61; *OR*, ser. 1, 24 (3): 478–79; Clampitt, *Occupied Vicksburg*, 51–58.

24. On emancipation as military necessity, see Gallagher, *Union War*. On emancipation as a process, see Levine, *Fall of the House of Dixie*; Oakes, *Freedom National*; and G. Downs, *After Appomattox*.

25. Authored by jurist Francis Lieber, Lincoln issued General Orders No. 100 to all Union forces in the spring of 1863, which laid out the rules for just conduct in war. Lieber's vision of a moral war did provide protections for prisoners. Included in the code's 157 articles were several provisions concerning paroles and capitulation. As legal historian Cynthia Nicoletti has pointed out, the code bound the Union army "by virtue of the president's order, but it did not embody widely agreed upon, unexceptional principles of international law as it was customarily understood" (Nicoletti, *Secession on Trial*, 254, 259; Witt, *Lincoln's Code*, 232, 389–90; Dilbeck, *More Civil War*, 86–97).

26. Neff, *Justice in Blue and Gray*, 5, 15, 19. For examples of paroles before Appomattox, see Davis and Tremmel, *Parole, Pardon, Pass*, 144–45.

27. Among those who have emphasized Appomattox as a moment that helped forge a smooth transition from war to peace are Catton, *Stillness at Appomattox*; and Winik, *April 1865*. For the argument that Appomattox helped establish a reconciliation between former slaveholders and the white North that came at the expense of African Americans, see Blight, *Race and Reunion*.

28. G. Downs, *After Appomattox*, 13; Witt, *Lincoln's Code*, 286.

29. Varon, *Appomattox*, 58; Longstreet, *From Manassas to Appomattox*, 624.

30. Silkenat, *Raising the White Flag*, 206. Varon points out that Colonel Marshall did not see Lee as a "passive recipient of Grant's leniency" (*Appomattox*, 67).

31. Silkenat, *Raising the White Flag*, 206–7; Marshall, *Aide-de-Camp*, 269–70; McPherson, *Battle Cry*, 848–50; Catton, *Never Call Retreat*, 454.

32. *OR*, ser. 1, 46 (3): 666–68; McPherson, *Battle Cry*, 848–50; Grant to Maj. Gen. George Meade, April 9, 1865, *PUSG* 14:377–78; Silkenat, *Raising the White Flag*, 207. They also discussed exchanging the 1,000–1,500 Union prisoners the Confederates still held.

33. Gibbon, *Personal Recollections*, 321; John Rumsey Brincklé Papers, diary entry April 9, 1865, and letter to his brother April 14, 1865, Library of Congress, A People at War Collection (microfilm); Haley, *Rebel Yell*, 265, diary entry April 9, 1865; Gibbon, *Personal Recollections*, 321; Sgt. John C. Doty diary, April 10, 1865, railsplitter.com, accessed June 13, 2017. On the seven USCT regiments at Appomattox, see Varon, *Appomattox*, 93–101.

34. Nevins, *Diary of Battle*, 520–21, diary entry April 9, 1865; John Rumsey Brincklé Papers, letter to sister April 18, 1865, Library of Congress, A People at War Collection (microfilm).

35. Diary of John Wilson Warr, April 9, 1865, Going Home Research Files, APCO.

36. Hinson, "Diary" entry April 9, 1865, 119.

37. Whitehorne Diary, April 9, 1865, SHC; Diary of Edward Valentine Jones, April 9, 1865, Going Home Research Files, APCO.

38. Julia Wilbur Diary, April 9, 1865, transcription by Alexandria Archaeology. *Civilian and Telegraph* (Cumberland, Md.), April 13, 1865; *OR*, ser. 1, 46 (3): 683. Grant endorsed plans for demobilizing the Union forces on May 11, 1865.

39. Draft of letter from R. E. Lee to U. S. Grant, April 10, 1865, item 462, R. E. Lee Headquarters Papers, Call No. Mss3 L515a, VMHC. Thanks to Keith Bohannon for sharing this citation.

40. Grant, *Personal Memoirs*, 2:633. There are different accounts as to the weather on the morning of April 10, some suggesting it was raining lightly and others describing it as a clear morning (Marshall, *Aide-de-Camp*, 254; Thomas, *Three Years with Grant*, 316–17).

41. Grant, *Personal Memoirs*, 2:634.

42. Gibbon, *Personal Recollections*, 326–28; Grant, *Personal Memoirs*, 2:632–34.

43. *OR*, ser. 1, 46 (3): 686.

44. *OR*, ser. 1, 46 (3): 687.

45. *OR*, ser. 1, 46 (3): 685–86.

46. "From R. A. (Bob) Gray to his cousin, Isabell S. Buzzett," in Georgia Division of the United Daughters of the Confederacy, *Confederate Reminiscences*, 1:129; Eppa Hunton to his wife, April 22, 1865, Hunton Family Papers, VMHC; Hunton, *Autobiography*, 123–39.

47. Gibbon, *Personal Recollections*, 329–31; *OR*, ser. 1, 46 (3): 685–86.

48. *PUSG* 14:380; *OR*, ser. 1, 46 (3): 685–86.

CHAPTER 3

1. Calkins, *Battles of Appomattox*, 144–46; Shoemaker, *Shoemaker's Battery*, 49; Lewis T. Nunnelee, Postwar Memoir and Diary, entries April 9–20, 1865, CMLS. Shoemaker's Battery was also known as the Beauregard Rifles, Lynchburg Beauregards, and Virginia Horse Artillery.

2. Albright Reminiscences, April 8–10, 1865, SHC; Morris and Foutz, *Lynchburg in the Civil War*, 54–56.

3. Tripp, *Yankee Town*, 159; Diary of Mary Washington Cabell (later Early), entries April 9–10, 1865, Early Family Papers, VMHC.

4. Stonebraker, *Rebel of '61*, 102; Morris and Foutz, *Lynchburg in the Civil War*, 54–55.

5. F. Summers, *Borderland Confederate*, 106, diary entry April 9, 1865; Sommerville quoted in Tripp, *Yankee Town*, 160.

6. Bushong and Bushong, *Fightin' Tom Rosser*; Akers, "Colonel Thomas T. Munford," 25, 122.

7. The feud between Rosser and Munford grew in the postwar years, especially after the publication of an article by Rosser in an 1884 column of the *Philadelphia Weekly Times*.

8. Akers, "Colonel Thomas T. Munford," 110; Stonebraker, *Rebel of '61*, 103.

9. Hotchkiss, *Make Me a Map*, 265, diary entries April 8 and 9, 1865; Tripp, *Yankee*

Town, 159; Albright Reminiscences, April 8–9, 1865, SHC; *OR*, ser. 1, vol. 46 (1): 1303–4; F. Summers, *Borderland Confederate*, 105–6, diary entry April 9, 1865.

10. Bernard, *War Talks*, 283; Morris and Foutz, *Lynchburg in the Civil War*, 55.

11. David S. Grimsley to John W. Daniel, February 2, 1905, John Moncure Daniel Papers, 1853–1920, accession #4802, UVA.

12. Hewett and others, eds., *Supplement to the Official Records*, pt. 1, 7:742–43.

13. Diary of Caldwell Calhoun Buckner, April 9–May 16, 1865, in Papers Chiefly Pertaining to Virginia, 1803–1904, accession #8995, UVA; Armstrong, *7th Virginia Cavalry*, 120. Buckner's diary indicates he had decided to take the oath of allegiance to the United States on May 16, and his papers show that he did so on May 31.

14. My observation that the vast majority of those who did not surrender at Appomattox went home is borne out by my Beyond Appomattox database.

15. Albright Reminiscences, April 8–10, 1865, SHC.

16. Charles Friend, "Last Fight of First Richmond Howitzers," Going Home Research Files, APCO; *Morning Post* (Raleigh, N.C.), April 9, 1905.

17. Townsend, "From Petersburg," 105–6; Henry Townsend CSR; 1860 U.S. Census. He is listed as "Henry Townsend" in the CSR but wrote under the name Harry C. Townsend.

18. Townsend only mentions a "Col. Walker" in his diary, which is likely Edward Thomas Walker, the only Confederate colonel who resided in Bedford County. Krick, *Lee's Colonels*, 357. On the Confederate army's role in protecting slavery, see Woodward, *Marching Masters*.

19. Townsend, "From Petersburg," 106–7.

20. Townsend, 108.

21. A. Gordon, *Memories and Memorials*, 1:292 (letter dated April 11, 1865).

22. *Philadelphia Inquirer*, April 15, 1865.

23. *OR*, ser. 1, 46 (3): 699.

24. *Daily National Republican* (Washington, D.C.), April 14, 1865; Duncan, *Beleaguered Winchester*, 252; "Diary and Recollections of I. Norval Baker," in Quarles, *Diaries*, 122.

25. *OR*, ser. 1, 46 (3): 699.

26. *OR*, ser. 1, 46 (3): 699.

27. Sutherland, *Savage Conflict*, 166, 238–39, 242–45; Mosby, *Memoirs*, 149–50.

28. Sheehan-Dean, *Calculus*, 328–29; Mosby, *Memoirs*, 284; New England soldier quoted in Sutherland, *Savage Conflict*, 243.

29. *OR*, ser. 1, 43 (1): 811; Ramage, *Gray Ghost*, 193.

30. Sheehan-Dean, *Calculus*, 330–33; *OR*, ser. 1, 43 (2): 920; Sutherland, *Savage Conflict*, 242–45; Ramage, *Gray Ghost*, 185–200, 228–42. Only four of the seven men Mosby selected to be executed died. Sheehan-Dean describes Mosby's execution orders as a "proportional response" that "hewed more closely to the practice of justice retaliation" than revenge.

31. Ramage, *Gray Ghost*, 232–367, 259–61.

32. *OR*, ser. 1, 46 (3): 685.

33. Grant, *Personal Memoirs*, 2:634.

34. *OR*, ser. 1, 46 (3): 701.

35. RG 393, part 1, entry 2407, NARA (p. 136); Ramage, *Gray Ghost*, 263; *OR* ser. 1, 46 (3): 750, 753–54.

36. Maj. Thomas J. Rowland Letters, April 12 and 28, 1865, CMLS.

37. Chamberlayne and Chamberlayne, *Ham Chamberlayne*, 320–22. Chamberlayne

wrote two letters to his brother and sister on April 12. They are slightly different but contain similar sentiments. Both are quoted here.

38. Chamberlayne and Chamberlayne, 322–23; Lucy Parke Bagby to John J. Reeve, April 15, 1865; Lelian Cook diary, April 10–17, 1865, reprinted in the *Richmond News Leader*, April 3, 1935. For more on Confederate women's faith even in defeat, see Janney, *Burying the Dead*, chap. 1.

39. Bushong and Bushong, *Fightin' Tom Rosser*, 182.

40. Silkenat, *Raising the White Flag*, 93–97.

41. Thomas Rosser to Veterans of the Old Dominion broadside, April 12, 1865, Scrapbook of Betty Winston Rosser, Thomas L. Rosser Papers, accession #1171, a-b, box 2, UVA; Bushong and Bushong, *Fightin' Tom Rosser*, 182–83; Rosser, *Riding with Rosser*, 73–74; Hotchkiss, *Make Me a Map*, 265, diary entry April 10, 1865.

42. Sutherland, *A Savage Conflict*, 237–38; *OR*, ser. 1, 43:1081–82.

43. Alexander, *Fighting for the Confederacy*, 531–32.

44. On die-hard rebels, see Phillips, *Diehard Rebels*.

45. Albright Reminiscences, April 11, 1865, SHC.

46. Harwell, *Confederate Diary*, April 12, 1865, 19.

47. B. Jones, *Under the Stars and Bars*, 266–72.

48. B. Jones, 266–72; George C. Holmes CSR. Holmes would not be released until July 1, 1865.

49. Charles C. Richardson, "A Few Reminiscences of My Experience in the Civil War, as a Confederate Soldier and Member of the Surry Light Brigade," Going Home Research Files, APCO. On the morning of April 19, 1865, the men were paroled and allowed to continue on their way home.

50. B. Jones, *Under the Stars and Bars*, 274–76. On the importance of slavery to Confederate armies, see Woodward, *Marching Masters*.

51. At least 12,445 soldiers that had been part of the Army of Northern Virginia, even if on detached service, sought paroles between April 18 and July 14, 1865 (Beyond Appomattox database).

CHAPTER 4

1. Kena King Chapman Diary (1049-z), April 10, 1865, SHC; Kena King Chapman CSR.

2. J. E. Whitehorne Diary, April 9, 1865, SHC. Numerous contemporary accounts claim there were approximately 8,000 to 10,000 "infantry with arms." See, for example, Robert E. Lee's report in *OR*, ser. 1, 46 (1): 1266–67; and Kena King Chapman Diary (1049-z), April 9, 1865, SHC. These numbers, however, were only speculation and would offer a foundation for the Lost Cause argument that Lee's army was overwhelmed by superior Union resources rather than defeated. The important point, however, is that numerous individuals offered similar numbers in their wartime diaries and letters.

3. Glatthaar, "Tale of Two Armies," 339. For another discussion of how those who remained assessed stragglers, see Varon, *Appomattox*, 106–7.

4. Marshall, "Appomattox Courthouse," 360; Stone, *Wandering to Glory*, 244. Robertson incorrectly states the date of the 23rd South Carolina's arrival as April 7 rather than April 9.

5. Walters, *Norfolk Blues*, 224, diary entry April 9, 1865. For more on Confederate soldiers anticipating the major themes of Lee's farewell address, see Varon, *Appomattox*, 103.

6. Potts, *Death of the Confederacy*, 5.

7. *PUSG* 14:385; "Paroles of the Army of Northern Virginia," 386–87; Gibbon, *Personal Recollections*, 339–40.

8. "Paroles of the Army of Northern Virginia," 386–88; W. P. Roberts CSR; Thomas Munford, "Last Days of Fitz Lee's Confederacy," 29, VMHC.

9. *SHSP* 15:448–49.

10. Varon, *Appomattox*, 102; Diary of Edward Valentine Jones, April 9, 1865, Going Home Research Files, APCO.

11. Among those who have emphasized Appomattox as a moment that helped forge a smooth transition from war to peace are Catton, *Stillness at Appomattox*, and Winik, *April 1865*. For the argument that Appomattox helped establish a reconciliation between former slaveholders and the white North that came at the expense of African Americans, see Blight, *Race and Reunion*. For a counterargument, see Janney, *Remembering the Civil War*.

12. Marshall, *Aide-de-Camp*, 277–78. According to Freeman, the language of the original draft is unknown. Freeman, *R. E. Lee*, 4:153–55.

13. Dowdey and Manarin, *Wartime Papers*, 934–35; Marvel, *Lee's Last Retreat*, 189; Lightsey, *Veteran's Story*, 44; Polley, *Hood's Texas Brigade*, 278. For an extensive discussion of the various versions of the address, see Cauble, *Surrender Proceedings*, 86–89.

14. Varon, *Appomattox*, 68–70.

15. Gallagher, *Confederate War*, 12; Woodward, *Marching Masters*, 185.

16. Levy quoted in Cauble, *Proceedings Connected with the Surrender*, 151. According to Cauble, Levy was captured at Appomattox Station on April 8 and paroled at Farmville on the 14th. It is unclear when and how he got a copy of Lee's farewell address (167).

17. Calkins, *Final Bivouac*, 4.

18. Nine and Wilson, *Appomattox Paroles*, 4; *OR*, ser. 1, 46 (3): 694.

19. Chamberlain, *Bayonet!*, 153.

20. *OR*, ser. 1, 46 (3): 685.

21. Alexander, *Fighting for the Confederacy*, 541; John Gibbon to Mama [wife, Fannie], April 11, 1865, John Gibbon Papers, HSP; Gibbon, *At Gettysburg and Elsewhere*, 256; *OR*, ser. 1, 46 (3): 696.

22. Hinson, "Diary," 119; Walters, *Norfolk Blues*, 224, diary entry April 10, 1865. Officially, 1,559 Confederate cavalry troopers were paroled at Appomattox. But as Chris M. Calkins observes, there were not that many involved in the ceremony as many on the official list had left the area (*Final Bivouac*, 9).

23. Charles Bickem Fields Diary, April 11, 1865, mss5:1 F4655:1, VMHC; Gibbon, *Personal Recollections*, 332; Walters, *Norfolk Blues*, 225, diary entry April 11, 1865.

24. Whitehorne Diary, April 10–11, 1865, SHC; William D. Alexander Diary, #2478-z, April 11, 1865, SHC.

25. John Gibbon to Mama [wife, Fannie], April 11, 1865, John Gibbon Papers, HSP; Gibbon, *At Gettysburg and Elsewhere*, 256; Gibbon, *Personal Recollections*, 332.

26. Cauble, *Surrender Proceedings*, 90–91.

27. Blair, *With Malice toward Some*, 100–27. Blair points out that the position of home front provost marshals was created by the Conscription Act of 1863. Under this system, the provost marshal for each state appointed men from civil life to enforce the draft. Blair provides an excellent explanation of the provost marshals and their role in enforcing loyalty.

28. *Wheeling Daily Intelligencer*, May 13, 1865.

29. *OR*, ser.1, 46 (3): 851–53; *Wheeling Daily Intelligencer*, May 13, 1865.

30. D. L. Geer, "Memories of the War," *Florida Index* (Lake City), March 9, 1906.

31. *Wheeling Daily Intelligencer*, May 13, 1865; *SHSP* 15:4–7, 453–58.

32. Royce Gordon Shingleton notes that "many soldiers might have been counted as surrendered who had already begun the trek homeward" ("South from Appomattox," n. 8).

33. Benson, *Berry Benson's Civil War Book*, 200–203; Berry Benson and Blackwood Benson CSR; Berry Benson Papers, #2636, SHC, journal entries for Berry and Blackwood, April 9–15, 1865.

34. *OR*, ser.1, 46 (3): 851–53, 1279.

35. John Crawford Anderson to David Anderson, April 11, 1865, in Craig, *Upcountry South Carolina Goes to War*, 163.

36. Haley, *Rebel Yell*, 265, diary entry April 10, 1865.

37. John Crawford Anderson to David Anderson, April 11, 1865, in Craig, *Upcountry South Carolina Goes to War*, 163; Kena King Chapman Diary (1049-z), April 10, 1865, SHC; Power, *Lee's Miserables*, 283.

38. Henry J. Millard to Sister Hattie, April 26, 1865, Henry J. Millard Letters, Massachusetts Historical Society, Boston.

39. Quoted in Marvel, *Lee's Last Retreat*, 185.

40. Pearce, *Diary of Captain Henry A. Chambers*, 262, diary entry April 9, 1865.

41. Typescript Diary of Unknown Soldier, Library Files, APCO. Capt. Oscar Hinrichs described Gordon's speech as "in even poorer taste" than the speech he gave on April 9. Williams, *Stonewall's Prussian Mapmaker*, 268.

42. Marvel, *Lee's Last Retreat*, 185.

43. Glatthaar, *General Lee's Army*, 309–14; Levine, *Confederate Emancipation*, 63; McCarthy, *Detailed Minutiae*, 19; Alexander, *Fighting for the Confederacy*, 76, 507–8.

44. *Journal of the Congress of the Confederate States of America*, 1st Cong., 2nd Sess., 1:45, 118, 152, and 5:262.

45. Frederick CSR.

46. Glatthaar, *General Lee's Army*, 309–14; Martinez, *Confederate Slave Impressment*; Levine, *Confederate Emancipation*, 62.

47. *SHSP* 15:45, 62–63, 487; Scipio Africanus CSR; Joe Parkman CSR.

48. Cutrer, *Longstreet's Aide*, 143–52; transcript of Civil War diary of Giles Buckner Cooke, diary entry April 8, 1865, Lewis and Latane Family Papers, accession #1525-a, UVA.

49. Douglas, *I Rode with Stonewall*, 333–36. In his postwar account, Douglas later claimed that, unbeknownst to him, Buck had taken his horse and papers to Lexington for protection. It is unclear whether this "faithful slave" account has any validity.

50. William M. Abernathy, "Our Mess: Southern Army Gallantry and Privations, 1861–1865," 1902, Mississippi Department of Archives and History, Jackson.

51. Thomas P. Devereux, "From Petersburg to Appomattox," 1912, Thomas Pollock Devereux Papers, SHC.

52. John Crawford Anderson to David Anderson, April 11, 1865, in Craig, *Upcountry South Carolina Goes to War*, 163.

53. Blackett, *Thomas Morris Chester*, 302–3; Harrison interview in Arkansas narratives, vol. 2, part 3, 185–86, Federal Writers' Project, *Born in Slavery*, Library of Congress. For more on African Americans' understanding of Appomattox as the end of slavery, see Varon, "Last Hour."

54. Varon, *Appomattox*, 95–97, 169–73, Clement quote p. 170–71; Berry interview in Rawick et al., *American Slave*, vol. 16, 5–6.

55. Calkins, *Final Bivouac*, 11–12. The 1st Division of the Twenty-Fourth Corps remained at Appomattox Court House.

56. Arnold, *Fourth Massachusetts Cavalry*, 31–32; S. Buck, "With Lee after Appomattox"; W. Taylor, *General Lee*, 296–97; W. Taylor, *Four Years with General Lee*, 154.

57. Arnold, *Fourth Massachusetts Cavalry*, 32.

58. Chamberlain, "Appomattox."

59. Quoted in U.S. National Park Service, *Appomattox Court House*, 80.

60. *New York Times*, April 19, 1865.

61. Whitehorne Diary, April 12, 1865, SHC.

62. J. Smith, *Antietam to Appomattox*, 596; Stewart, *History of the One Hundred and Fortieth*, 273–74. Stewart reported that fewer than 8,000 men had arms to deposit during the appointed ceremony, although Gibbon's final report would claim 10,000 small arms had been surrendered (*PUSG* 14:384).

63. Whitehorne Diary, April 9, 1865, SHC; *SHSP* 15:351. The dashes are in the typescript of the diary held by the SHC.

64. Lieber to Sumner, April 11, 1865, in Lieber, *Life and Letters*, 357.

CHAPTER 5

1. William Henry Harder Memoir, April 13, 1865, TSLA; William H. Harder CSR. His memoir is based on extensive notes he took and thus includes dates like a diary. He observes that there were sixty-three men left with the regiment on April 9, but this number differs from the *SHSP* listing of paroles, which lists fifty-two men and four officers (pp. 290–91).

2. William Henry Harder Memoir, April 13, 1865, TSLA; William H. Harder CSR; Phillips, *Diehard Rebels*, 178–79. On Confederate demobilization, see Tarbell, "Disbanding the Confederate Army"; Holberton, *Homeward Bound*, 87–96; Cimbala, *Veterans North and South*, 13–17; and Cimbala, *Soldiers North and South*, 197–204.

3. Mixson, *Reminiscences of a Private*, 121.

4. Hodijah Baylies Meade, "Memoirs of a Confederate Surgeon in the Army of Northern Virginia," UVA.

5. J. E. Whitehorne Diary, April 13, 1865, SHC.

6. Scholars and popular culture have long described the dispersal from Appomattox as one of straggling men heading home singly or in pairs. For example, see P. Buck, *Road to Reunion*, 30–31. For examples of some of the smaller parties that left, see Owen, *In Camp and Battle with the Washington Artillery*, 393; Lightsey, *Veteran's Story*, 45; and John W. Bone, "Record of a Soldier in the Late War," 50, Lowery Shuford Collection, NCDAH.

7. "Civil War Reminisces of Nathaniel Burwell Johnston," A Contribution to the 1972 Appomattox Civil War Institute by J. Ambler Johnston, Richmond, Virginia, Going Home Research Files, APCO.

8. Diary of Edward Valentine Jones, April 11–12, 1865, Going Home Research Files, APCO.

9. Caldwell, *History of a Brigade of South Carolinians*, 244; Coker, *History of Company G*, 182 (account by E. L. Wilkins); William Joseph Miller, "My Experience as a Soldier in

the Confederate Army," in South Carolina Division of the United Daughters of the Confederacy, *Recollections and Reminiscences*, 5:224; Montgomery, *Appomattox and the Return Home*, 10.

10. A. C. Jones, "Third Arkansas Regiment at Appomattox," *CV* 23 (July 1915): 314; H. Simpson, *Hood's Texas Brigade*, 468–69; Powers, *Lee's Miserables*, 284; Dunkerly, *To the Bitter End*, 33–34; N. C. Denson Memoirs, Greg Coco Research Files, APCO. On the numbers of Hood's Brigade surrendered, see Polley, *Hood's Texas Brigade*, 278–79.

11. Historians have tended to describe Appomattox as the moment when Lee's army "ceased to exist" (Powers, *Lee's Miserables*, 284; Glatthaar, *General Lee's Army*, 471). Others argue that the army disintegrated even before reaching Appomattox. Yael Sternhell writes, "Once the army set out on the road, it came apart. The most seasoned veterans could not withstand the power of retreat to break down an organized military body" (*Routes of War*, 163). Jason Phillips acknowledges that many in Lee's army and other Confederate armies marched home as units (*Diehard Rebels*, 178–81).

12. Nine and Wilson, *Appomattox Paroles*, 28; Abner Cox CSR.

13. *Resolutions Adopted by Bratton's Brigade.*

14. Shingleton, "South from Appomattox," 240–42, diary entries April 12–13, 1865.

15. On the war as a period of unrelenting movement, see J. Downs, *Sick from Freedom*; Sternhell, *Routes of War*; and Foote, *Yankee Plague*.

16. For example, see Personal Diary of Thomas E. Plowden, April 12, 1865, Going Home Research Files, APCO; I. G. Bradwell, "Last Days of the Confederacy," *CV* 29 (1921): 56–58; William D. Alexander Diary, April 20, 1865, SHA; and Shingleton, "South from Appomattox," 242.

17. Murray, "Going Home from Surrender."

18. Stanfield, *Confederate Diaries and Letters*, diary entry April 13, 1865 (no page numbers).

19. Bernard, *War Talks*, 284.

20. Daniel T. Nelson Journal, April 17–19, 1865, and Nelson to Sarah Nelson, April 20, 1865, Daniel T. Nelson Papers, VMHC.

21. Henry C. Metzger to Father, April 14, 1865, John L. Nau III Collection, UVA. For more on Union soldiers rejecting the idea of occupation, see Lang, *In the Wake of War*, 182–209.

22. Albert G. Harrison to Parents, April 17, 1865, John L. Nau III Collection, UVA.

23. From the Twenty-Fourth Corps Headquarters on April 10, Gibbon issued General Orders No. 43, stating that "all guards, patrols, officers, and soldiers of the U. S. forces will respect such certificates, allow free passage to the holders thereof, and observe in good faith the provisions of the surrender, that the holders shall remain unmolested in every respect" (*OR*, ser. 1, 46 [3]: 709–10).

24. McCarthy, *Detailed Minutiae*, 161.

25. Claims 202071 and 202079, RG 92, entry 225, NARA. U.S. surgeon Daniel T. Nelson observed in his journal on April 19 that near Burkeville "paroled prisoners violated their parole & are hung" (Daniel T. Nelson Papers, VMHC). As Elizabeth Varon observes, "The notion that the parole certificates conferred protection on their bearers gained immediate currency among the Confederate troops" (*Appomattox*, 73).

26. Graves, *History of the Bedford Light Artillery*, 65.

27. Whitehorne Diary, April 14, 1865, SHC.

28. Quoted in Trudeau, *Out of the Storm*, 151–52.

29. Walters, *Norfolk Blues*, 226–28, diary entries April 12–14, 1865; D. L. Geer, "Memories of the War," *Florida Index*, March 16, 1906.

30. Daniel T. Nelson to Sarah Nelson, April 20, 1865, Daniel T. Nelson Papers, VMHC; Walters, *Norfolk Blues*, 227–28, diary entries April 13 and 14, 1865; Stanfield, *Confederate Diaries and Letters*, diary entry April 14, 1865 (no page numbers); Channing M. Smith Diary, April 12, 1865, VMHC.

31. Under the Confederacy, the South Side Railroad was 5-foot gauge, but the U.S. military rolling stock ran on a width of 4 feet 8½ inches. In order to more efficiently move supplies to the front, the Ninth Corps had been readjusting the gauge. By April 9, the line had been opened to Burkeville (Calkins, *Final Bivouac*, 65).

32. Alexander, *Fighting for the Confederacy*, 545.

33. Parole Passes and POW Collection Series, CMLS Collection under the management of the VMHC; "Richmond and the Rebellion," *New York Evangelist*, April 27, 1865; *Bedford (Pa.) Enquirer*, May 12, 1865.

34. Oldham quoted in Neely, *Southern Rights*, 3.

35. Camp, *Closer to Freedom*, 13, 20; R. Mitchell, *Civil War Soldiers*, 58; Savage, *Standing Soldiers*, 169.

36. Diary of Edward Valentine Jones, April 14–15, 1865, Going Home Research Files, APCO.

37. William Joseph Miller, "My Experience as a Soldier in the Confederate Army," in South Carolina Division of the United Daughters of the Confederacy, *Recollections and Reminiscences*, 5:224.

38. Coker, *History of Company G*, 182 (account by E. L. Wilkins). Gus Dean, of the 2nd South Carolina Rifles, Bratton's Brigade, noted that his regiment marched together for two days (Augustus Dean Memories).

39. Mixson, *Reminiscences of a Private*, 123–24; Shingleton, "South from Appomattox," 241–42, diary entries for April 14–18, 1865.

40. Clark, *Histories of the Several Regiments*, 4:216.

41. Coski, "We Are All to Be Paroled."

42. Shingelton, "South from Appomattox," 241, diary entry April 14, 1865.

43. Cutrer, *Longstreet's Aide*, 143–52; Clark, *Histories of the Several Regiments*, 4:214–18.

44. Fulton, *War Reminiscences*, 147.

45. For examples of African Americans who left Appomattox on their own, see Capt. Henry Carter Lee Pocket Diary, April 11, 1865, CMLS; Charles Crowley to Edward Porter Alexander, February 19, 1884, Edward Porter Alexander Papers, box 4, SHC; and Alexander, *Fighting for the Confederacy*, 545.

46. Capt. Henry Carter Lee Pocket Diary, April 11, 1865, CMLS.

47. Charles Crowley to Edward Porter Alexander, February 19, 1884, Edward Porter Alexander Papers, box 4, SHC; Alexander, *Fighting for the Confederacy*, 545. In Alexander's memoir, he notes that "Charley was very anxious to accompany me" to Washington, "but I gave him ten dollars in gold which his accumulated hire had bought."

48. *PUSG*, 14:384.

49. Claiborne, *Seventy-Five Years in Old Virginia*, 300; Hubard, *Civil War Memoirs*, 220 (describes activities on April 11, 1865).

50. Douglas, *I Rode with Stonewall*, 335.

51. Glatthaar, *Forged in Battle*, 201.

52. Diary of Edward Valentine Jones, April 14, 1865, Going Home Research Files, APCO.

53. Wiatt, *Confederate Chaplain*, 240, diary entries April 17–18, 1865.

54. D. L. Geer, "Memories of the War," *Florida Index*, March 16, 1906; Waters and Edmonds, *Small but Spartan Band*, 183. Some of the account can be verified, including that the *Wilmington* departed City Point on April 17 for Fort Monroe before sailing to Savannah on April 22. Numerous members of Finegan's Brigade were among the 690 paroles aboard the ship (*Savannah Daily Herald*, April 26, 1865). David F. Geer likewise appears on the list of those paroled at Appomattox (David F. Geer CSR).

55. Blackett, *Thomas Morris Chester*, 320; *Beverly and Tom Lowry Database of Civil War Courts-Martial*. Nance's sentence was commuted.

56. On reenslavement, see Newhall, "Under the Rebel Leash."

57. Glatthaar, *Forged in Battle*, 155–58, 201–2; Trudeau, *Like Men of War*, 61–62; Ural, *Hood's Texas Brigade*, 223–24; Carmichael, *War for the Common Soldier*, 258.

58. RG 393, part 4, entry 1465—Register of Prisoners, November 1862–September 1865, vols. 370–71, NARA. Butler was finally freed on June 1, 1865, when he was sent to Soldiers' Rest in Washington to rejoin his regiment.

59. Carmichael, *War for the Common Soldier*, 201; cavalryman quoted in Krick, *9th Virginia Cavalry*, 34.

60. Not all of the victims of Confederate wrath during the war were part of the USCT. During the Gettysburg campaign, Lee's soldiers had captured free African Americans in Pennsylvania and sent them south to be sold into slavery (Ayers, *Thin Light of Freedom*, 46, 49).

61. Alexander, *Fighting for the Confederacy*, 462.

62. William J. Pegram to his sister, Jenny (Virginia Johnson Pegram McIntosh), Petersburg, August 1, 1864, section 1, folder 2, Pegram-Johnson-McIntosh Papers, VMHC. Lee likely knew of the atrocities committed by his men at the Crater (S. Lee, *Memoirs of William Nelson Pendleton*, 358–59).

63. Personal diary of John Wilson Warr, April 14–16, 1865, Going Home Research Files, APCO.

64. Journal of T. B. Swann, April 14, 1865, Going Home Research Files, APCO.

65. William Henry Harder Memoir, April 15, 1865, TSLA.

66. McCarthy, *Detailed Minutiae*, 162.

67. Murray, "Going Home from Surrender." The Black Horse Cavalry was Company H, 4th Virginia Cavalry.

68. Thomas P. Devereux, "From Petersburg to Appomattox," 1912, Thomas Pollock Devereux Papers, SHC.

69. Hurt, *Agriculture in the Confederacy*, 248; Blair, *Virginia's Private War*, 119–20.

70. Thomas P. Devereux, "From Petersburg to Appomattox," 1912, Thomas Pollock Devereux Papers, SHC.

71. John W. Bone, "Record of a Soldier in the Late War," 50, Lowery Shuford Collection, NCDAH.

72. See, for example, Asst. Surgeon Robert Pooler Myers, Diary/Letter Copy Book, April 16, 1865, CMLS; and Clayton Wilson, Diary of Clayton Wilson, Going Home Research Files, APCO.

73. Fulton, *War Reminiscences*, 140.

74. Personal Diary of John Willis Council, April 9–27, 1865, NCDAH.

75. Owen, *In Camp and Battle with the Washington Artillery*, 393; C. C. McMillan, "Record and Experiences of an Old Confederate Soldier," in South Carolina Division

of the United Daughters of the Confederacy, *Recollections and Reminiscences*, 12:433; Lewis H. Andrews, "After the War Was Over," *Atlanta Journal*, May 21, 1904.

76. See, for example, Personal Diary of John Willis Council, April 9–27, 1865, NCDAH.

77. For examples of women on the home front discussing sending letters with homeward-bound Confederate soldiers, see Mother [Mary Penn] to My Dear Eliza [Elizabeth Penn Hairston], April 16, 1865, and Sarah R. [Hay] to dear Sister [Eliza Penn Hairston], May 23, 1865, both in box 1, folder 7, Elizabeth Seawell Hairston Papers, SHC.

78. P. W. Watkins to Sam, April 15, 1865, box 1, folder 6, and Mother [Mary Penn] to My Dear Eliza [Elizabeth Penn Hairston], box 1, folder 7, Elizabeth Seawell Hairston Papers, SHC.

79. McFall, *Danville in the Civil War*, 102. James I. Robertson suggests that the plundering began as early as April 11 and was instigated by "women and children of all ages" who were soon joined by "hundreds of paroled and demoralized soldiers" ("Danville under Military Occupation," 331).

80. McFall, *Danville in the Civil War*, 103; J. Robertson, "Danville under Military Occupation, 332–33; I. G. Bradwell, "Making our Way Home from Appomattox," *CV* 29 (1921): 102–3. No one ever determined what caused the explosion as none of the eyewitnesses survived.

81. Shingleton, "South from Appomattox," 242; McFall, *Danville in the Civil War*, 105. Danville remained in Confederate hands until April 27.

82. Whitehorne Diary, April 16, 1865, SHC.

83. Whitehorne Diary, April 22, 1865, SHC.

CHAPTER 6

1. *PUSG* 14:384.

2. For more on troop strength, see note 12 in the introduction.

3. Burrage, *History of the Thirty-Sixth Regiment*, 297; Hopkins and Peck, *Seventh Regiment*, 265; *History of the Thirty-Fifth Regiment*, 397–98; Burrell, *A History of Prince Edward County*, 182–83.

4. Henry T. Bahnson Papers, folders 1 and 3, SHC; Henry T. Bahnson CSR.

5. RG 109, entry 212, box 42, Farmville folder, NARA; S. S. Keeling CSR. For an example of a hospital patient, see Wm. Gaston Lewis CSR.

6. RG 109, entry 212, box 42, Farmville folder, NARA; Beyond Appomattox database; Calkins, *Final Bivouac*, 208. A member of the 36th Massachusetts observed that 1,742 men were paroled "from the field at Appomattox." But it is unclear whether he knew precisely how many had been paroled from the hospitals rather than directly from the field (Burrage, *History of the Thirty-Sixth Regiment*, 297).

7. Frank Lobrano Diary, April 11–12, 1865, Louisiana Historical Association Collection, Howard-Tilton Memorial Special Collections, Tulane University, New Orleans; *OR*, ser. 1, 46 (1): 1246, 1249; Gibbon, *Personal Recollections*, 338–39.

8. *OR*, ser. 1, 46 (1): 1216, 1246, 1256; *PUSG* 14:383; *Rockingham Register* (Harrisonburg, Va.), April 28, 1865; Gibbon, *Personal Recollections*, 340–41; Arthur Stone to Mother, April 14, 1865, John L. Nau III Collection, UVA.

9. *Rockingham Register*, April 28, 1865; Tripp, *Yankee Town*, 161.

10. *OR*, ser. 1, 46 (3): 796; *OR*, ser. 1, 46 (1): 1216. Although Turner reported 5,000 paroles, I have located only 2,839 parolees from Lynchburg between April 12 and April 17,

at least 1,085 of whom were able-bodied men — more than an entire regiment even in the earliest days of the war (RG 109, entry 212, box 43, Lynchburg folder, NARA).

11. *OR*, ser. 1, 46 (1): 1246.

12. RG 109, entry 212, box 43, Lynchburg folder, NARA; *SHSP* 15:56–57; Frank Lobrano Diary, April 12–13, 1865, Louisiana Historical Association Collection. In the month of April, out of the nearly 8,500 soldiers who sought paroles, more than 5,000 were Virginians (Beyond Appomattox database).

13. Gibbon, *Personal Recollections*, 340–41. For more on James Holcombe as a commissioner to Canada, see Mayers, *Dixie and the Dominion*, 35.

14. Wert, *Longstreet*, 406; Cutrer, *Longstreet's Aide*, 143.

15. RG 109, entry 212, boxes 42–43, NARA; Beyond Appomattox database. Several examples include Clayton Aubrey, who served with the 2nd and 14th Kentucky Cavalry until captured at Buffington, Ohio, in 1863, and 1st Lt. Robert Vandiver of Merrick's Missouri Regiment. Clayton Aubrey CSR; Robert Vandiver CSR; John D. Murtaugh CSR.

16. Robert Emmett Curran observes that John Dooley, a former prisoner from Johnson's Island, met at least eight fellow parolees between Lynchburg and Danville, most of whom were not from the region. Curran speculates that this was "more than happenstance" (*John Dooley's Civil War*, 491n22).

17. Frank Lobrano Diary, April 13–14, 1865, Louisiana Historical Association Collection.

18. Wiatt, *Confederate Chaplain*, April 14, 1865, 239.

19. *OR*, ser. 1, 46 (3): 746.

20. RG 109, entry 212, box 41, Burkeville folder, NARA.

21. Frank Lobrano Diary, April 13–14, 1865, Louisiana Historical Association Collection.

22. Gibbon, *Personal Recollections*, 343–45.

23. Daniel T. Nelson to Sarah Nelson, April 16, 1865, Daniel T. Nelson Papers, VMHC.

24. Albert G. Harrison to Parents, April 17, 1865, John L. Nau III Collection, UVA.

25. John Rumsey Brincklé Papers, diary entry April 16, 1865, Library of Congress, A People at War Collection (microfilm).

26. Calkins, *Final Bivouac*, 64.

27. Hubbs, *Voices from Company D*, 572, diary entry April 15, 1865; Diary of Annie G. Dudley Davis, April 15, 1865, Huntington Library, San Marino, Calif.

28. Rebecca to cousin Jeanie, April 18, 1865, Jane Norton Wigglesworth Grew Correspondence, Massachusetts Historical Society, Boston.

29. Lane, *Soldier's Diary*, 261–62, diary entry April 19, 1865.

30. Lynch, *Civil War Diary*, 150, diary entry April 20, 1865.

31. Manley Ebenezer Rice to Elizabeth Jane Day Rice, General Hospital, Fort Gaines, Alabama, April 30, 1865, Manley Ebenezer Rice Papers, Huntington Library, San Marino, Calif.

32. Bvt. Brig. Gen. William W. Morris to Grant, April 12, 1865, *OR*, ser. 1, 46 (3): 727.

33. Myers, *Self-Reconstruction of Maryland*, 24; *OR*, ser. 1, 46 (3): 776–78.

34. *OR* ser. 1, 46 (3): 778, 800, 818, 867; General Orders No. 6, April 15, 1865, RG 393, part 2, vol. 124, NARA; General Orders No. 7, April 17, 1865, RG 393, part 2, vol. 124, NARA; *Evening Star* (Washington, D.C.), April 22, 1865; RG 393, part 4, entry 1458 — Letters Received and Endorsements Sent, Defenses South of the Potomac, July 1864–September 1865, vol. 366, p. 390, NARA.

35. Hancock to Halleck, April 15, 1865, RG 393, part 1, entry 2407, NARA.

36. RG 393, part 1, entry 2407, NARA.

37. Hancock to Halleck, April 15, 1865, RG 393, part 1, entry 2407, NARA; *OR*, ser. 1, 46 (3): 774.

38. *OR*, ser. 2, 8:485–86; RG 109, entry 212, box 43, NARA; C. Robertson, *Passport in America*, 65–66.

39. William H. Payne, CSR; Alexander, *Fighting for the Confederacy*, 548; *OR*, ser. 1, 46 (3): 772; Julia Wilbur Diary, April 16, 1865, transcription by Alexandria Archaeology.

40. HQ Provisional Brigade, April 24, 1865, to Maj. Wm. Russell Asst. Adj. Gen. Army of the Shenandoah, RG 393, part 1, entry 2411, Middle Military Division, NARA; George H. Murphy Diary, Manuscripts of the American Civil War, University of Notre Dame Rare Books and Special Collections, http://www.rarebooks.nd.edu/digital/civil_war/diaries _journals/murphy/index.shtml#INDEX (accessed July 17, 2015). The Union detachment included the 1st Rhode Island, 9th New York, 22nd New York, and 12th Pennsylvania Cavalry.

41. HQ Provisional Brigade, April 24, 1865, to Maj. Wm. Russell Asst. Adj. Gen. Army of the Shenandoah, RG 393, part 1, entry 2411, Middle Military Division, NARA.

42. *Journal of Capt. Jed Hotchkiss*, reprinted in *OR*, ser. 1, 46 (1): 521–22.

43. Thomas Munford, "Last Days of Fitz Lee's Cavalry Division," 30, VMHC; *OR*, ser. 1, 46 (3): 813–14. Fitz Lee had secured a brigadier's rank for Munford, but the Confederate Congress had not yet confirmed the appointment (Longacre, *Lee's Cavalrymen*, 322).

44. RG 109, entry 212, box 43, NARA. Included among the 1st Maryland Cavalry (CSA) were companies A, B, D, E, and K.

45. Berkeley and Jefferson Counties both refused to recognize their inclusion into the state of West Virginia. An 1866 mandate by Congress and a Supreme Court case ultimately forced them to become part of the new state (Snell, *West Virginia*, 187).

46. Col. M. A. Reno, HQ Provisional Brigade, April 24, 1865, to Maj. Wm. Russell Asst. Adj. Gen. Army of the Shenandoah, RG 393, part 1, entry 2411, Middle Military Division, NARA. Reno would later achieve fame in the Battle of the Little Bighorn.

47. Berry Benson Papers, journal entries for April 14, 1865, SHC.

48. P. W. Watkins to Sam, April 15, 1865, box 1, folder 6, Elizabeth Seawell Hairston Papers, SHC; Mother [Mary Penn] to My Dear Eliza [Elizabeth Penn Hairston], April 16, 1865, box 1, folder 7, Elizabeth Seawell Hairston Papers, SHC.

49. *Grant's Petersburg Progress*, April 10, 1865.

50. *OR*, ser. 1, 46 (3): 754.

51. RG 393, part 1, entry 2415, Middle Military Division, Telegrams Received August 1864–July 1865, NARA.

52. Bvt. Maj. Gen. Emory, Cumberland, Md., to Morgan, April 13, 1865, RG 393, part 1, entry 2415, NARA.

53. *Grant's Petersburg Progress*, April 10, 1865.

54. *Richmond Whig*, April 17, 1865.

55. *OR*, ser. 1, 46 (3): 774.

56. *OR*, ser. 1, 46 (3): 800. Also in RG 393, part 1, entry 2415, NARA.

57. *OR*, ser. 1, 46 (3): 799; Stanton to Hancock in Winchester, RG 393, part 1, entry 2415, NARA.

58. *OR*, ser. 1, 46 (3): 800. Also in RG 393, part 1, entry 2415, NARA. It is unclear whether this new policy was Grant's or Halleck's idea. But given Grant's questioning of the policy three days later, it seems likely Halleck crafted it on his own.

59. C. Mitchell, *Maryland Voices*, 260–63; Manakee, *Maryland in the Civil War*, 58–59. On

the first vote, citizens voted against the constitution. But when Maryland soldiers in the Union army cast their votes, the new constitution was approved by 375 votes.

60. *OR*, ser. 1, 46 (3): 828. Hancock's letter was from April 18, but he notes in it that he had written Stanton on the sixteenth but had not yet received a reply.

61. Hancock to Halleck, unknown date, Grant Papers, Series 3, Unpublished Materials, box 26, GPL.

62. *PUSG* 14:397. See also *OR*, ser. 1, 46 (3): 818; Sutherland, *Savage Conflict*, 239.

63. While there were individual soldiers from Kentucky and Missouri in the Army of Northern Virginia, by 1865 there were no state units from these states. Maryland was represented in Lee's army during the final spring of the war by the 2nd Maryland Battalion, 1st Maryland Battery, and the 4th Maryland Battery. (Sifakis, *Compendium of the Confederate Armies*.)

64. "John Wilkes Booth's Last Days," *New York Times*, July 30, 1896. This was a postwar account given by Dr. R. B. Garrett, who was twelve years old and a resident of Caroline County, Virginia, in April 1865.

65. *OR*, ser. 1, 46 (3): 804.

66. Kidd, *Personal Recollections*, 444–47.

67. *PUSG* 14:411. See also *OR*, ser. 1, 46 (3): 830–31, 868; RG 109, entry 212, box 43, various folders, NARA; and Kidd, *Personal Recollections*, 447.

68. *PUSG* 14:410.

69. *OR*, ser. 1, 46 (3): 838. For more on the connection between Booth and Mosby, see Wert, *Mosby's Rangers*, 283.

70. King, AAG, to Barnes from War Dept., April 20, 1865, RG 393, part 1, entry 2415, Middle Military Division, NARA; *PUSG* 14:411. See also *OR*, ser. 1, 46 (3): 868; Mosby quoted in Ramage, *Gray Ghost*, 265.

71. Ramage, *Gray Ghost*, 265–66; *OR*, ser. 1, 46 (3): 1396.

72. *OR*, ser. 1, 46 (3): 897; Ramage, *Gray Ghost*, 266.

73. *OR*, ser. 1 46 (3): 880–81.

74. Thomas T. Munford Papers, Special Orders No. 6, April 21, 1865, UVA; Beyond Appomattox database.

75. RG 109, entry 212, box 42, NARA. As of May 1, Hancock reported that 4,100 officers and men of the late rebel army had been paroled by the Middle Military Division alone.

76. Broun, *Dark Days*, 112.

77. *Rockingham Register*, April 21, 1865.

CHAPTER 7

1. Kena King Chapman Diary (1049-z), April 9–18, 1865, SHC. Provost Marshal General Patrick had issued orders that nonresidents would not be permitted to stay in Richmond (Patrick to Maj. Charles Warren, April 16, 1865, RG 393, part 2, entry 1656, vol. 236, NARA).

2. Diary of Edward Valentine Jones, April 16–17, 1865, Going Home Research Files, APCO; RG 393, part 2, vol. 124, Special Orders at Petersburg, April–July 1865, NARA.

3. Kena King Chapman Diary (1049-z), April 19, 1865, SHC; Mushkat, *Citizen-Soldier's Civil War*, 258, diary entry April 26, 1865; Lucy Muse Walton Fletcher Diary, April 12, 1865, DU; Bruce, *Capture and Occupation of Richmond*, 21–23; Diary of Edward Valentine Jones, April 17, 1865, APCO; Phillips, *Diehard Rebels*, 180.

4. Lucy Muse Walton Fletcher Diary, April 22, 1865, DU.

5. Litwack, *Been in the Storm So Long*, 168–72; *Christian Recorder*, April 22, 1865; Blackett, *Thomas Morris Chester*, 303–4.

6. Blackett, *Thomas Morris Chester*, 305.

7. *OR*, ser. 1, 46 (3): 718, 724, 749; *PUSG* 14:388; *New York Herald*, April 13, 1865; Cresap, *Appomattox Commander*, 219–21; Patrick, *Inside Lincoln's Army*, 18. The *New York Herald* reported that the thirteen hospitals in the city as of April 3, 1865, were "capable of accommodating between twelve and fourteen thousand patients." Between the city's two largest hospitals, Jackson and Chimborazo, it reported that there were "about four thousand patients." As of April 8, Maj. Gen. Godfrey Weitzel had ordered all the general hospitals broken up and all Confederate patients removed to Jackson Hospital.

8. See Feiss, "Grant's Relief Man," 173, 186–194; Cresap, *Appomattox Commander*, 119; and Bergen, "How the Race to Appomattox Was Won," 22–25.

9. John Francis Heath to Anna Rives Heath, April 19, 1865, Papers Pertaining to Virginia, 1856–1882, accession #10590, UVA.

10. *PUSG* 14:391; *OR*, ser. 1, 46 (3): 762, 778; *Richmond Whig*, April 17, 1865.

11. *OR*, ser. 1, 46 (3): 763; Cresap, *Appomattox Commander*, 224.

12. *Richmond Whig*, April 17, 1865.

13. RG 109, entry 212, box 43, Richmond folder, NARA; Patrick, *Inside Lincoln's Army*, 495, diary entry April 13, 1865; Patrick to Maj. Charles Warren, April 16, 1865, RG 393, part 2, entry 1656, NARA.

14. RG 109, entry 212, box 43, Richmond folder, NARA.

15. Owen, *In Camp and Battle with the Washington Artillery*, 395; Chesson, *Richmond after the War*, 31; Furgurson, *Ashes of Glory*, 52; Lankford, *Richmond Burning*, 17, 137, 222–23; *New York Times*, April 21, 1865; *Richmond Whig*, April 17, 1865.

16. *Richmond Whig*, April 21, 1865.

17. Blackett, *Thomas Morris Chester*, 306–9, 317. An order would not be issued prohibiting Confederate uniforms in Richmond until June 14. RG 393, part 2, entry 1656 — Misc. Lists of the Provost Marshal, 1864–1865, vol. 236, NARA.

18. *OR*, ser. 1, 46 (3): 835, 882–84; *Richmond Whig*, April 21, 1865; *New York Daily Herald*, April 13, 1865.

19. *OR*, ser. 1, 46 (3): 835, 882–84; *Richmond Whig*, April 21, 1865.

20. Alexander, *Fighting for the Confederacy*, 531, 545–47.

21. Grant to Ord, April 18, 1865, *PUSG* 14:406–7. Grant issued similar orders to Wallace on April 20 (*PUSG* 14:421).

22. Ord to Grant, April 19, 1865, *PUSG* 14:412.

23. Grant to Ord, April 19, 1865, *PUSG* 14:411–12. Halleck served as Chief of Staff in Washington until April 19, 1865. After that date, he commanded the Military Division of the James until June 27, 1865.

24. Bvt. Maj. W. L. James to Maj. Gen. Meigs, April 18, 1865, Grant Papers, Series 3, Unpublished Materials, box 26, GPL; Ord to Grant, April 20, 1865, *PUSG* 14:416.

25. Stanfield, *Confederate Diaries and Letters*, diary entries April 18–19, 1865 (no page numbers).

26. Patrick, *Inside Lincoln's Army*, 497, diary entry April 19, 1865; Grant to Ord, April 20, 1865, *PUSG* 14:415. Patrick resigned his post in June.

27. Potts, *Death of the Confederacy*, 15.

28. *OR*, ser. 1, 46 (3): 961.

CHAPTER 8

1. Townsend, "From Petersburg," 110–11, diary entry April 14, 1865.

2. Townsend, 112, diary entry April 15, 1865.

3. Townsend, 112–14, diary entries April 15–17, 1865.

4. Townsend, 114, diary entries April 18–20, 1865.

5. McIntosh Diary, April 10–14, 1865, David Gregg McIntosh Diary and Papers, VMHC.

6. N. Brown, *One of Cleburne's Command*, 163–65.

7. Dunkerly, *To the Bitter End*, 42–43.

8. Bradley, *This Astounding Close*, 135–40.

9. W. H. Andrews, *Footprints of a Regiment*, 178–79.

10. Bradley, *This Astounding Close*, 142–43 (Davis quoted p. 142); Johnston, *Narrative*, 398–99; *OR*, ser. 1, 47 (3): 206–7. The letter was dictated by Davis but signed by Johnston.

11. *OR*, ser. 1, 47 (3): 177; Simpson and Berlin, *Sherman's Civil War*, 857, 859.

12. McIntosh Diary, April 14, 1865, VMHC.

13. Bradley, *This Astounding Close*, 135; McIntosh Diary, April 16, 1865, VMHC.

14. Robert Herriot, "At Greensboro, N.C., in April 1865," *CV* 30 (March 1922): 101–2; Bradley, *This Astounding Close*, 136.

15. Bradley, *This Astounding Close*, 153; Dunkerly, *To the Bitter End*, 46.

16. Bradley, *This Astounding Close*, 153–54; Dunkerly, *To the Bitter End*, 46–47.

17. McIntosh Diary, April 16, 1865, VMHC.

18. Albright Reminiscences, April 15–19, 1865, SHC; personal diary of John Wilson Warr, April 20, 1865, Going Home Research Files, APCO.

19. Albright Reminiscences, no date to this section, SHC.

20. A. Gordon, *Memories and Memorials*, 1: 292–93 (letter dated April 25, 1865).

21. Shoemaker, *Shoemaker's Battery*, 94–95; Lt. Lewis T. Nunnellee, Postwar Memoir and Diary, April 20, 1865, CMLS.

22. Bradley, *This Astounding Close*, 160; Johnston, *Narrative*, 402; Dunkerly, *To the Bitter End*, 50.

23. Bradley, *This Astounding Close*, 160.

24. Dunkerly, *To the Bitter End*, 50; Simpson and Berlin, *Sherman's Civil War*, 856–57; Long, *Civil War Day by Day*, 678.

25. *PUSG* 14:419; Sherman, *Memoirs*, 2:839.

26. Bradley, *This Astounding Close*, 163; Wills, *Army Life of an Illinois Soldier*, 371, diary entry April 17, 1865.

27. *OR*, ser. 1, 47 (3): 238–39.

28. Sherman to Ellen, April 9, 1865, in Simpson and Berlin, *Sherman's Civil War*, 853.

29. Glatthaar, *Soldiering in the Army of Northern Virginia*, 3–4.

30. Chamberlayne to George William Bagby, December 6, 1850, Bagby Family Papers, VMHC. For the argument that this younger generation was more supportive of secession and the war than their elders were, see Carmichael, *Last Generation*.

31. Curran, *John Dooley's Civil War*, xiii–xxv, 364.

32. Sherman, *Memoirs*, 2:840–41; Bradley, *This Astounding Close*, 170.

33. For the specifics of Reagan's proposal, see Bradley, *This Astounding Close*, 170–71 and appendix A.

34. Johnston, *Narrative*, 404–5; Sherman, *Memoirs*, 841; Bradley, *This Astounding Close*,

170–73; Sherman to Grant and Halleck, April 18, 1865, in Simpson and Berlin, *Sherman's Civil War*, 863–64.

35. *OR*, ser.1, 47 (3): 243–45; Johnston, *Narrative*, 406–7; Bradley, *This Astounding Close*, 170–73.

36. Bradley, *This Astounding Close*, 173; Simpson and Berlin, *Sherman's Civil War*, 857; Royster, *Destructive War*, 347–48; Basler, *Collected Works of Abraham Lincoln*, 8:389, 405–7. On April 12, Lincoln clarified he had not intended to allow the Virginia legislature to reconvene; rather, he had said that the "gentlemen who have *acted* as the Legislature" might meet to discuss removing troops from the state.

37. Sherman to Grant and Halleck, April 18, 1865, in Simpson and Berlin, *Sherman's Civil War*, 863–64, and Sherman to Ellen Sherman, April 22, 1865, 871–72.

38. Col. Archer Anderson to Gen. John C. Breckinridge, April 16, 1865, in Chamberlayne and Chamberlayne, *Ham Chamberlayne*, 323.

39. McIntosh to Davis, April 18, 1865, David McIntosh CSR.

40. McIntosh Diary, April 18–20, 1865, VMHC; McIntosh to Davis, April 19, 1865, Pegram-Johnson-McIntosh Papers, section 10, folder 2, VMHC. This letter is dated April 18 in some sources and April 19 in others.

41. Townsend, "From Petersburg," 118, diary entry April 23, 1865.

42. Curran, *John Dooley's Civil War*, 372–75, diary entries April 14–15, 1865.

43. McIntosh to Davis, April 19, 1865, Pegram-Johnson-McIntosh Papers, section 10, folder 2, VMHC.

44. Echols had been appointed commander of the Western Department of Virginia a few days before the fall of Richmond.

45. McIntosh Diary, April 19–22, 1865, VMHC; Special Orders No. 2 and Ham Chamberlayne to Sister, April 21, 1865, in Chamberlayne and Chamberlayne, *Ham Chamberlayne*, 324–25.

CHAPTER 9

1. Murray enlisted in the 17th Virginia Infantry in June 1861 and served with the unit until early 1864, when he was granted a commission as a 2nd lieutenant and assigned to the 1st Battalion of Virginia Infantry. Murray, "Going Home from Surrender"; 1860 U.S. Census, slave schedule for Thomas J. Murray, Fairfax, Virginia; RG 393, part 4, entry 1695, vol. 266, and entry 1465, NARA. Winship was named acting provost for the Defenses South of the Potomac on April 20 (*OR*, ser. 1, 46 [3]: 871). The building that housed Price, Birch & Co. had previously been the Washington office of slave traders Isaac Franklin and John Armfield.

2. Murray, "Going Home from Surrender."

3. For example, Maj. Thomas Goree of Texas initially planned to travel to New York to catch a steamer bound for New Orleans, noting that Lt. Gen. James Longstreet had proposed such a course for himself (Cutrer, *Longstreet's Aide*, 143).

4. Alexander, *Fighting for the Confederacy*, 547–48.

5. RG 393, part 4, entry 1465—Register of Prisoners, November 1862–September 1865, vols. 370–371 (Defenses South of the Potomac—HQ in Alexandria), NARA; *Alexandria Gazette*, April 20, 1865.

6. Williams, *Stonewall's Prussian Mapmaker*, 269–71.

7. Channing M. Smith Diary, April 12, 19–21, 1861, CMLS; Channing Smith CSR; parole pass of Channing M. Smith, Parole Passes and POW Collection Series, CMLS; W. W. Winship, Capt. and AAG at HQ PM Marshal General, Dept. South of the Potomac, to Col. T. Ingraham, April 26, 1865, RG 393, part 4, entry 1457, NARA; Records of the Washington Street Prison, RG 393, part 4, entry 2141, NARA. Smith would be sent from Washington Street Prison to the Prince Street Prison on May 7 by order of a Captain Smith.

8. RG 393, part 4, entry 1457, p. 196, NARA; J. Owen Berry CSR. Berry had been captured in the fall of 1861 but escaped from the Old Capitol Prison before returning to his unit. After his capture in 1865, the secretary of war rejected his application for parole on account of the previous escape. He would be released on June 15 on oath from Sandusky, Ohio.

9. *OR*, ser. 1, 46 (3): 832.

10. *OR*, ser. 1, 46 (3): 842–43 (letter dated April 19, 1865).

11. *PUSG* 14:421–2; Mortenson, *Politician in Uniform*, 6, 115–17, 170, quote on p. 117.

12. *Civilian and Telegraph*, October 13, 1864; Mortenson, *Politician in Uniform*, 124–25.

13. The case was likely *Miles v. Bradford*, decided by the Maryland Court of Appeals on October 29, 1864, on appeal from the Superior Court of Baltimore City, where Judge Robert N. Martin sat. The Superior Court had dismissed a petition by Samuel Miles to issue a writ of mandamus against Governor Augustus Bradford. The governor allegedly rejected votes in an election on the new state constitution because voters refused to take an oath of allegiance (*Miles v. Bradford*, 22 Md. 170, Lexis Nexis and HeinOnline). Special thanks to Daniele Celano for helping me track down this case.

14. Wallace to Grant, April 22, 1865, *PUSG* 14:421–22. John C. King served on the Court of Common Pleas, Hugh L. Bond the Criminal Court, and Robert N. Martin the Superior Court.

15. Letter from Lew Wallace to U. S. Grant, April 22, 1865, RG 107, Letters Received from the President, Executive Departments, and War Department Bureaus, 1862–1870, file G in C 27 EB 11, NARA; Wallace to Grant, April 22, 1865, *PUSG* 14:421–22. A special thanks to Trevor Plante at NARA for help in locating the enclosures.

16. *OR*, ser. 2, 8:518.

17. Confederate secretary of war John C. Breckinridge had worried as early as March 1865 about what the end of the Confederacy would mean for those from Missouri and Kentucky. "But what will become of the Kentuckians and Missourians who have followed us into the war, and who are disbanded far from home, without means, and with no certainty of a friendly reception, even if they should return to their own states?" he asked. (W. Davis, "Confederate Peacemakers," 152.)

18. Grant to Hancock, April 19, 1865, *PUSG* 14:410.

19. *Baltimore Sun*, April 20, 1865.

20. Wallace to Ord, April 19, 1865, Lew Wallace Papers, Indiana Historical Society, Indianapolis, original in RG 107, Telegrams Collected by the Office of the Secretary of War, Unbound, 1860–70, NARA.

21. RG 393, part 1, entry 2407, NARA.

22. *Alexandria Gazette*, April 24, 1865.

23. *Evening Star*, April 22, 1865.

24. *PUSG* 14:423; Bradley, *This Astounding Close*, 207; Welles, *Civil War Diary*, 633–34, entry April 21, 1865.

25. Welles, *Civil War Diary*, 633–34, entry April 21, 1865; *New York Times*, April 23, 1865; Bradley, *This Astounding Close*, 208.

26. The best book on the legal question of secession is Cynthia Nicoletti's *Secession on Trial*. For other legal histories of the war, see Blair, *With Malice toward Some*; Neff, *Justice in Blue and Gray*; and Witt, *Lincoln's Code*. As Nicoletti argues, in April 1865 (and continuing well into the postwar years) it remained unclear as to whether Lee's surrender had in fact settled the question of secession. If secession was legal, Confederates had not committed treason. If secession was unconstitutional, then many of the war powers asserted by the United States—including the seizure of property under the Confiscation Acts—could be questioned.

27. Blair, "Friend or Foe," 27.

28. *PUSG* 14:423–25; Basler, *Collected Works of Abraham Lincoln*, 8:330–31.

29. Wheaton, *Elements of International Law*.

30. *New York Times*, April 23, 1865; Marvel, *Lincoln's Autocrat*, 373.

31. *OR*, ser. 1, 46 (3): 918–20.

32. Sheffer, *Presidential Power*, ix, 43–44; Garrison, "Opinions by the Attorney General," 228. Attorneys general offered opinions when the United States, not government employees or private individuals, had an interest. On April 11, 1865, Speed issued an official opinion on the duty of the attorney general in which he observed that the "Attorney General will not give a speculative opinion on an abstract question of law which does not arise in any case presented for the action of an Executive Department" ("Duty of the Attorney General," 189).

33. *OR*, ser. 1, 46 (3): 918–20; Speed, "Surrender of the Rebel Army."

34. For the dual status conveyed by the *Prize Cases*, see Nicoletti, *Secession on Trial*, 211–13. For more on the cases, see Neff, *Justice in Blue and Gray*, chapter 1; and Blair, *With Malice toward Some*, 73, 77–79, 87–88, 99.

35. *OR*, ser. 1, 46 (3): 918–20.

36. Stanton to Maj. Gen. Dix, April 23, 1865, Grant Papers, Series 3, Unpublished Material, box 27, GPL (originally from RG 107); *OR*, ser. 1, 46 (3): 918–20.

37. *Evening Star*, April 25, 1862.

38. G. Gordon, *War Diary*, 415.

39. *OR*, ser. 2, 8:505.

40. M. Andrews, *Tercentary History of Maryland*, 1:894.

41. *Evening Star*, April 27, 1865.

42. *Daily National Republican*, April 24, 1865; *Civilian and Telegraph*, May 4, 1865.

43. *Wheeling Daily Intelligencer*, May 3, 1865.

44. M. Andrews, *Tercentary History of Maryland*, 1:894; Myers, *Self-Reconstruction of Maryland*, 25.

45. *PAJ* 7:626–27.

46. *Daily National Republican*, April 24, 1865; vol. 8, Maryland, 18, Federal Writers' Project, *Born in Slavery*, Library of Congress. Frederick's resolutions did note that they precluded "all interference with those who under the amnesty proclamation of the late President have grounded the arms of the rebellion, come within the Federal lines, subscribed to the oath of allegiance, and intend to conduct themselves in the future as good and law abiding citizens" (*Frederick [Md.] Examiner*, April 26, 1865).

47. *Civilian and Telegraph*, April 27, 1865; *Valley Register* (Middletown, Md.), May 5, 1865; Myers, *Self-Reconstruction of Maryland*, 26.

48. A. Smith, *Stormy Present*, 46–48, 183, 276n65.

49. *Richmond Enquirer*, November 29, 1859; Link, *Roots of Secession*, 182, 314n15; Kytle and Roberts, *Denmark Vesey's Garden*, 28.

50. A. Smith, *Stormy Present*, 46–48, 183, 276n65; Link, *Roots of Secession*, 207, 216.

51. For more on the public taking matters into its own hands rather than seeking legal redress, see Blair, *With Malice toward Some*, 60–61.

52. *Valley Register*, May 5, 1865.

53. Committee of citizens [Edward Goldsborough and eleven others] of Frederick, Md., to Stanton, submitted to Gen. Hancock on May 6, April 29, 1865, in RG 393, part 1, entry 2411, NARA. Stevenson was the commander of the Department of West Virginia.

54. Noble Thomas CSR; *New York Times*, May 3, 1865; *Evening Star*, April 29, 1865; *Baltimore Sun*, May 1, 1865. He was released from jail on $5,000 bail around June 10. *Alexandria Gazette*, June 10, 1865. He would be transferred on June 21 by verbal orders from Gen. Edward D. Townsend to Washington.

55. *Baltimore Sun*, April 26 and 27, 1865; Lewis Webb CSR.

56. *OR*, ser. 1, 46 (3): 665; Blair, *With Malice toward Some*, 236.

57. Wallace to William A. Nichols, April 26, 1865, Lew Wallace Collection, Indiana Historical Society, original in RG 84, NARA.

CHAPTER 10

1. *PUSG* 14:433.

2. Bradley, *This Astounding Close*, 209–14.

3. Bradley, 215–17; Silkenat, *Raising the White Flag*, 235.

4. Bradley, *This Astounding Close*, 217.

5. *PUSG* 14:434.

6. Albright Reminiscences, no date to this section, SHC; James Albright CSR. In April, the only men from Lee's army paroled by Sherman's men were those who had been detached to Wade Hampton prior to Appomattox. Such was the case for St. George Tucker Mason and Robert L. Judkins of the 13th Virginia Cavalry, who appeared on a list of staff officers and men serving with the headquarters of the Army of Tennessee's Cavalry Corps (Balfour, *13th Virginia Cavalry*, 45; R. L. Judkin CSR; St. George T. Mason CSR).

7. Albright Reminiscences, entry April 20, 1865, SHC.

8. Silkenat, *Raising the White Flag*, 235–36.

9. *Bedford Inquirer*, May 12, 1865.

10. Patrick, *Inside Lincoln's Army*, 497–99, diary entries April 19–21, 1865.

11. RG 393, part 4, entry 1458 — Letters Received and Endorsements Sent, Defenses South of the Potomac, July 1864–September 1865, vol. 366, NARA.

12. A. Gilchrist Capt. and PM to Capt. J. E. Jones, April 23, RG 393, part 4, entry 1647, vol. 210, NARA; Edward Roach CSR.

13. Letters from Andrew Hero Jr. to mother, April 6–26, 1865, Andrew Jr. and George Hero Papers, Hill Memorial Library, Louisiana State University, Baton Rouge; Andrew Hero CSR. Hero was likely required to take the oath because (for unknown reasons) he desired to travel to Baltimore before heading to New Orleans. He reported to the provost marshal's office in Baltimore on May 3. His destination was listed as New Orleans.

14. Telegraph from Capt. A. Gilchrist at Fort Monroe to Gen. Patrick, May 2, 1865, RG 393, part 1, entry 5169, NARA.

15. *OR*, ser. 1, 46 (3): 939–40.

16. *OR*, ser. 1, 46 (3): 940.

17. Alexander W. Vick to Robert E. Lee, April 23, 1865, *PUSG* 14:495–96.

18. Lee first wrote Grant on April 25, 1865, asking that men and officers captured between April 2 and 6 be granted the same terms as those surrendered on April 9. *PUSG* 14:429.

19. Lee to Grant, April 27, 1865, *PUSG* 14:495.

20. *New York Herald*, April 29, 1865.

21. *New York Times*, April 27 and 30, 1865.

22. Blair, *With Malice toward Some*, 187.

23. Jensen, *32nd Virginia Infantry*, 141. In the CSR, Reed's name is spelled alternatively "Read," "Reed," and "Reid." I have selected the spelling that appeared most frequently (William H. Reed CSR).

24. Jensen, 177, 199; *Testimony of Court-Martial in Trial of Hon. Benjamin G. Harris*, 6, 52; William H. Reed CSR.

25. *Testimony of Court-Martial in Trial of Hon. Benjamin G. Harris*, 6, 52–53.

26. *Testimony of Court-Martial in Trial of Hon. Benjamin G. Harris*, 3–5, 12–13.

27. *Testimony of Court-Martial in Trial of Hon. Benjamin G. Harris*, 2–8.

28. *Testimony of Court-Martial in Trial of Hon. Benjamin G. Harris*, 2–17.

29. Diary of Caldwell Calhoun Buckner, entries April 9–May 16, 1865, Papers Chiefly Pertaining to Virginia, 1803–1904, accession #8995, UVA; Armstrong, *7th Virginia Cavalry*, 120. Buckner's diary indicates he had decided to take the oath on May 16, and his papers show that he did so on May 31.

30. RG 393, part 4, entry 1695, vol. 263, Misc. Lists, Provost Marshal, Norfolk, Va., NARA.

31. Dawson, *Civil War Diary*, 610, diary entry May 2, 1865; *Times-Picayune* (New Orleans), April 30, 1865.

32. *OR*, ser. 2, 8:520, 529.

33. Appomattox parole of T. H. Jones, lot 207 of artifact auction site, November 22, 2008, Greg Coco Research Files, APCO.

34. Rosser describes the place as "Swope's Depot," while others refer to it as "Swoope's" (Rosser, *Riding with Rosser*, 74).

35. George W. Munford to Mrs. Elizabeth T. Munford, April 28, 1865, Munford-Ellis Family Papers, DU; General Orders No. 4 issued by Thomas L. Rosser, April 28, 1865, Confederate Military Leaders Collection, CMLS.

36. *Journal of Capt. Jed Hotchkiss*, reprinted in *OR*, ser. 1, 46 (1): 522–23.

37. *OR*, ser. 1, 46 (1): 1322.

38. Munford to Dorsey, April 28, 1865, reprinted in Thomas Munford, "Last Days of Fitzhugh Lee's Cavalry Division," 37–38, VMHC; Scharf, *Chronicles of Baltimore*, 649–50.

CHAPTER 11

1. I. G. Bradwell, "Making Our Way Home from Appomattox," *CV* 29 (1921): 102–3; Lewis H. Andrews, "After the War Was Over," *Atlanta Journal*, May 21, 1904.

2. John W. Bone, "Record of a Soldier in the Late War," 50, Lowery Shuford Collection, NCDAH.

3. *Savannah Daily Herald*, April 20, 1865.

4. A. Gilchrist Capt. & PM Order, April 24, RG 393, part 4, entry 1647, vol. 210, Press Copies of the Letters Sent PMG, Fort Monroe, NARA; *Savannah Daily Herald*, April 27, 1865; Richard Cribb CSR.

5. Andrews, "After the War Was Over," diary entries April 22–27, 1865.

6. Bone, "Record of a Soldier in the Late War," 51, Lowery Shuford Collection, NCDAH.

7. War Diary of R. M. Crumpler, box 4, Papers of Miss Georgia Hicks, Historian, Daughters of the Confederacy, NCDAH.

8. Augustus Dean Memories.

9. Andrews, "After the War Was Over," diary entries April 18–19, 1865.

10. W. T. Hill's account in Polley, *Hood's Texas Brigade*, 279–81.

11. Henry T. Bahnson, "Last Days of the War as Seen by a Private," Henry T. Bahnson Papers, folder 1 and folder 3, SHC.

12. John Wilson Warr diary, April 21, 1865, Going Home Research Files, APCO.

13. E. Andrews, *Wartime Journal*, May 3, 1865, 199.

14. *Edgefield (S.C.) Advertiser*, May 17, 1865; *Daily Constitutionalist* (Augusta, Ga.), April 26, 28, 1865.

15. Spencer, *Last Ninety Days*, 188.

16. Crabtree and Patton, *"Journal of a Secesh Lady,"* 702.

17. E. Andrews, *Wartime Journal*, May 3, 1865, 199.

18. *Daily Constitutionalist*, May 2, 1865.

19. Dowdey and Manarin, *Wartime Papers*, 934–35. For more on food riots and the idea of the social contract, see McCurry, *Confederate Reckoning*, 171, 179, 181.

20. On Confederate support, see Gallagher, *Confederate War*. For historians who have stressed white southern discontent with the Confederacy and challenges to the southern nation posed by slaves and southern Unionists, see, for example, Faust, *Mothers of Invention*, 238–47; Freehling, *The South vs. the South*; and McCurry, *Confederate Reckoning*.

21. Curran, *John Dooley's Civil War*, 374–75, diary entry April 15, 1865.

22. Lightsey, *Veteran's Story*, 45.

23. Townsend, "From Petersburg," 118, diary entry April 24, 1865.

24. William Henry Harder Memoir, April 23–25, 1865, TSLA.

25. William Henry Harder Memoir, April 25, 1865, TSLA.

26. David Champion, Lieutenant in Company G, 14th Georgia Regiment, in Georgia Division of the United Daughters of the Confederacy, *Confederate Reminiscences*, 1:5–21.

27. Hamilton, *History of Company M*, 71–73.

28. Henry T. Bahnson, "Days of the War," 12–13, manuscript in Henry T. Bahnson Papers, SHC.

29. Mixson, *Reminiscences of a Private*, 127.

30. Curran, *John Dooley's Civil War*, 383–84, diary entry April 19, 1865.

31. Asst. Surgeon Robert Pooler Myers, Diary/Letter Copy Book, entries April 22 and 27, 1865, CMLS; Parole Passes and POW Collection Series, CMLS.

32. Rawick et al., *American Slave*, vol. 8, Arkansas, pt. 1, 107.

33. War Diary of R. M. Crumpler, box 4, Papers of Miss Georgia Hicks, NCDAH.

34. Welch, *Confederate Surgeon's Letters*, 119–20.

35. Mixson, *Reminiscences of a Private*, 129.

36. South Carolina narratives, vol. 14, part 4, 14, Federal Writers' Project, *Born in Slavery*, Library of Congress; Rawick et al., *American Slave*, vol. 6, Alabama, 270, and vol. 14, North

Carolina, part 1, 128; Emilio, *History of the Fifty-Fourth Regiment*, 313; Sternhell, *Routes of War*, 166–69.

37. *Savannah Daily Herald*, April 26, 1865.

38. D. L. Geer, "Memories of the War," *Florida Index*, March 23, 1906.

39. Hill account in Polley, *Hood's Texas Brigade*, 280–81.

40. Berlin, Reidy, and Rowland, *Black Military Experience*, 735.

41. A. Gordon, *Memories and Memorials*, 1:292–93 (letter dated April 25, 1865).

42. Pendleton, *Confederate Memoirs*, 79–80.

43. Townsend, "From Petersburg," 122–23, diary entries April 29–30, 1865.

CHAPTER 12

1. Snell, *West Virginia*, 20, 25, 41, 48; Haymond, *History of Harrison County*, 300–321, 324–25, 333. Thomas J. Jackson, then residing in Lexington, was a native of Clarksburg and the most famous local to join the Confederacy.

2. Shaffer, *Clash of Loyalties*, 103–4.

3. *PAJ* 8:10–11. Quoted from Clarksburg Citizens to Johnson, April 26, 1865, Office of Atty. Gen., Lets. Recd., President, RG 60, NARA. Voters from Eagle Township in Harrison County met on April 27 to form a vigilance committee (*Wheeling Daily Intelligencer*, May 2, 1865).

4. *Wheeling Daily Intelligencer*, April 17 and 29, 1865, May 3 and 4, 1865; *West Virginia Journal*, May 17, 1865; Shaffer, *Clash of Loyalties*, 4.

5. These included the cities of Parkersburg, Wheeling (in Ohio County), Fairmont (in Marion County), Charleston, and Morgantown along with the counties of Berkeley, Brooke, Harrison, Kanawha, Monongalia, Pleasants, Preston, Taylor, and Tyler.

6. *Wheeling Daily Intelligencer*, May 6, 1865.

7. *Wheeling Daily Intelligencer*, April 27, 1865.

8. Dayton, *Samuel Woods and His Family*, 5–17; Shaffer, *Clash of Loyalties*, 154.

9. *Wheeling Daily Intelligencer*, May 9, 1865; John Rundle CSR.

10. *Wheeling Daily Intelligencer*, May 5, 1865.

11. *OR*, ser. 2, 8:533. The Congressional Claims Payment Act of July 4, 1864, called for the quartermaster general to settle claims (such as repayment for livestock) submitted by loyal citizens in states not in rebellion. Lincoln stipulated that Maryland, Missouri, Kentucky, Tennessee, and West Virginia were included among those "not in rebellion" on the day the act passed (Davis and Tremmel, *Parole, Pardon, Pass*, 116).

12. Snell, *West Virginia*, 54–55; Sutherland, *Savage Conflict*, 84–96, 160–62, 235–36, 242–45.

13. Curry, *House Divided*, 131–34; Shaffer, *Clash of Loyalties*. 153. There were reintegration resolutions passed by the general assembly in Richmond and eventually a U.S. Supreme Court case where Virginia tried to reclaim Jefferson and Berkeley Counties. In January 1866, a group of ex-Confederates in Hampshire County demanded re-annexation to Virginia, and the general assembly in Richmond subsequently passed reintegration resolutions.

14. *OR*, ser. 1, 46 (3):1104. See also General Orders No. 57, Headquarters Dept. of West Virginia, May 6, 1865 printed in *Wheeling Daily Intelligencer*, May 10, 1865.

15. Samuel McKee to Johnson, May 3, 1865, *PAJ* 8:23–24.

16. *Cleveland Daily Leader,* May 10, 1865.

17. Morgan (HQ MM Division) to Maj. Gen. C. C. Augur, Comdg. Dept. of Washington, May 6, 1865, RG 393, part 1, entry 2407, Telegrams sent March–July 1865, Middle Military Division, NARA.

18. Myers, *Self-Reconstruction of Maryland,* 24.

19. *OR,* ser. 1, 46 (3): 1072.

20. *Baltimore Sun,* May 8, 1865.

21. Joseph D. Sullivan CSR; *PUSG* 15:5.

22. Woolley to Wallace, May 1, 1865, in Joseph D. Sullivan CSR. Woolley's name is sometimes spelled "Wooley."

23. *PUSG* 15:5.

24. *PUSG* 15:5.

25. *PUSG* 14:495–96.

26. Beyond Appomattox database. For Bowling Green references, see Krick, *9th Virginia Cavalry,* 55.

27. RG 109, entry 212, boxes 41–44, NARA.

28. *Journal of Capt. Jed Hotchkiss,* reprinted in *OR,* ser. 1, 46 (1): 522. For more on enslaved men and women seeking out Federal protection at refugee camps during the war, see A. Taylor, *Embattled Freedom.*

29. *OR,* ser. 1, 46 (1): 1322–23; RG 393, part 1, entry 2407, NARA.

30. RG 393, part 1, entry 2076, Military Division of the James, Letters received, April–June 1865, NARA; *OR,* ser. 1 46 (3): 1088–89.

31. W. W. Winship, Capt. and AAG at HQ PM Marshal General, Dept. South of the Potomac, to Col. T. Ingraham, April 26–June 1, RG 393, part 4, entry 1457, NARA; Hyman, *Era of the Oath.*

32. *Army and Navy Journal,* April 29, 1865, reprinted in the *Western Democrat* (Charlotte, N.C.), May 29, 1865; Capt. Albert Leavenworth, 9th Vt. Vol. of the Office of the Provost Marshal General, Dept. of Va., Richmond, to Capt. James C. Slaght [?], April 25, 1865, RG 393, part 1, entry 5162, 5164 — Dept. of Va., PM, NARA.

33. For more on the *Prize Cases* and dual status, see Nicoletti, *Secession on Trial,* 212, 242–47, 252, 263.

34. *OR,* ser. 1, 46 (3): 1001–10.

35. *OR,* ser. 1, 46 (3): 990–91, 1001–10. The constitutionality of these orders was challenged in the Supreme Court; see, for example, *Ex parte Garland* and *Cummings v. Missouri.*

36. Blair, *With Malice toward Some,* 6.

37. Neff, *Justice in Blue and Gray,* 90.

38. Davis and Tremmel, *Parole, Pardon, Pass,* 19, 55–56. Davis and Tremmel point out that neither pardon nor amnesty was defined by the Constitution (p. 22).

39. *OR,* ser. 2, 8:534 (Halleck to Grant, May 5, 1865).

40. *PUSG* 15:6–7, 11. In his reply, Grant replaced "pardon" with "amnesty," perhaps not clear on the precise meanings of each.

41. *OR,* ser. 1, 46 (3): 1105.

42. *OR,* ser. 1, 46 (3): 1109–10.

43. Elizabeth Munford [Richmond] to her husband, George W. Munford, May 2, 1865, Munford-Ellis Family Papers, DU.

44. Blackett, *Thomas Morris Chester,* 301–2.

45. Mrs. A. P. Webb, Baltimore, to Grant, April 29, 1865, in *PUSG* 15:76–77.

46. Grant to Wooley, May 19, 1865, *PUSG* 15:76. On Grant's orders to remove Wooley from his post, see 15:77.

47. *OR*, ser. 1, 46 (3): 1112. Grant likely issued Special Orders No. 215 in response to several queries he received from officers throughout the South, including one from Maj. Gen. George Thomas in Nashville on May 6 (*PUSG* 15:17).

48. *OR*, ser. 2, 8:538; A. E. King, Asst. AAG, HQ Dept of Washington, May 8, 1865, RG 393, part 4, entry 1458, NARA.

49. Channing Smith CSR.

50. *Wheeling Daily Intelligencer*, May 11 and 24, 1865.

51. *Wheeling Daily Intelligencer*, May 17, 1865.

52. Maj. Gen. Wallace, HQ Middle Department, 8th Army Corps, Baltimore, to Lieut. Col. John Woolley, PM, Washington, D.C., May 8, 1865, RG 393, part 1, entry 2411, NARA.

53. *OR*, ser. 1, 46 (3): 1063.

54. Capt. A. Gilchrist PM at Fort Monroe to Gen. Patrick, May 8, 1865, RG 393, part 1, entry 5169, Dept. of Virginia, PM Telegrams sent and received, NARA.

CHAPTER 13

1. *Testimony of Court-Martial in Trial of Hon. Benjamin G. Harris*, 3, 34. As William Blair observes, a court-martial of a congressman was unusual. (Blair, *With Malice toward Some*, 187.) Whereas courts-martial tried Union soldiers accused of breaking army rules and regulations, commissions allowed the military (rather than civil courts) to try civilians under the laws of war. By war's end, the army had conducted between 3,300 and 4,000 hearings. While a handful of the individuals proved to be U.S. soldiers, the overwhelming majority of those tried were civilians, usually described as guerrillas or bushwhackers (Hart, "Military Commissions and the Lieber Code," 15–17; Sheehan-Dean, *Calculus of Violence*, 244, 416n33; Witt, *Lincoln's Code*, 267).

2. *Testimony of Court-Martial in Trial of Hon. Benjamin G. Harris*; Jensen, *32nd Virginia Infantry*, 177.

3. *Testimony of Court-Martial in Trial of Hon. Benjamin G. Harris*, 28. Harris likewise raised an objection that the court was without jurisdiction.

4. *Testimony of Court-Martial in Trial of Hon. Benjamin G. Harris*, 25–26.

5. *Testimony of Court-Martial in Trial of Hon. Benjamin G. Harris*, 25–26.

6. *Testimony of Court-Martial in Trial of Hon. Benjamin G. Harris*, 36–38. The Lieber Code applied only to the U.S. army. But according to paragraph 130, although paroled soldiers were exempt from active duty in the field, the government could call upon them to perform internal services such as recruiting or drilling.

7. *Testimony of Court-Martial in Trial of Hon. Benjamin G. Harris*, 38–39. Emphasis in the original.

8. *Testimony of Court-Martial in Trial of Hon. Benjamin G. Harris*, 27, 48.

9. Jensen, *32nd Virginia Infantry*, 177, 199.

10. Douglas, *I Rode with Stonewall*, 336–37; MM-2040, Henry Kyd Douglas, RG 153, Court-Martial Case Files, NARA.

11. Douglas, *I Rode with Stonewall*, 337; Henry Kyd Douglas CSR.

12. MM-2040, Henry Kyd Douglas, RG 153, Court-Martial Case Files, NARA; Blair, *With Malice toward Some*, 238; Douglas, *I Rode with Stonewall*, 338–39.

13. RG 393, part 4, entry 1695, vols. 263, Misc. Lists, Provost Marshal, Norfolk, Va., NARA.

14. MM-2040, Henry Kyd Douglas, RG 153, Court-Martial Case Files, NARA; Blair, *With Malice toward Some*, 238; Douglas, *I Rode with Stonewall*, 338–39; Henry Kyd Douglas CSR; J. White, "Military Commission Trial." There is some discrepancy in the records as to whether the military commission convened on May 8 or May 10.

15. Kirkland, *Letter to Peter Cooper*, 29.

16. Blackett, *Thomas Morris Chester*, 348.

17. Douglas, *I Rode with Stonewall*, 339–49. Gen. Edward Johnson, Capt. Oscar Hinrichs, and several others were also called as witnesses in Mary Surratt's trial.

18. Blair, *With Malice toward Some*, 236.

19. Julia Wilbur Diary, April 29, 1865, transcription by Alexandria Archaeology.

20. Nicoletti argues that Jefferson Davis's trial provoked this same debate (*Secession on Trial*, 253–61).

21. *The Liberator*, April 28, 1865.

22. Butler to Johnson, April 25, 1865, in *PAJ* 7:634–35; Randall, *Constitutional Problems*, 101.

23. *New York Times* quoted in *Vermont Watchman and State Journal*, April 28, 1865; *PAJ* 7:634–35. For an excellent discussion of the debates between Johnson and Congress over the legal ending of the war, see G. Downs, *After Appomattox*.

24. As early as April 11, Lieber had written Sen. Charles Sumner of his concerns, observing that under the laws of war, a paroled prisoner of war was no longer liable to be charged with treason, having been treated as an enemy belligerent (Lieber to Sumner, April 11, 1865, in Lieber, *Life and Letters*, 357).

25. *New York Times*, May 3, 1865.

26. *Baltimore Sun*, May 22, 1865.

27. *Nashville Daily Union*, May 30, 1865.

28. *The Independent* (New York), May 10, 1865. For more on Lieber's interpretation, see Nicoletti, *Secession on Trial*, 254.

29. *The Independent*, May 10, 1865. Other papers would continue to cite Lieber's analysis throughout the summer, including E. L. Godkin's (see "The Rebel Parole," *The Nation*, August 3, 1865, 133–34).

30. Greg Downs observes that the legal state of war continued for three years after surrender in some rebel states and for more than five years in others (*After Appomattox*, 3).

31. Kirkland, *Letter to Peter Cooper*, 28.

32. Gen. Emory commanding Dept. of West Virginia, Cumberland, Md., to Bvt. Brig. Gen. Morgan, May 6, 1865, and HQ First Infantry, Division Dept. of West Virginia, Grafton, W.Va. to Brig. Gen. Thomas A. [??], May 17, 1865, RG 393, part 1, entry 2411, NARA. The logic of Confederate government sanction for acts of privateers was at issue with the CSS *Savannah*, captured in 1861 (Nicoletti, *Secession on Trial*, 210–11).

33. Gen. Torbert commanding, Army of the Shenandoah, Winchester, May 15, 1865, to Bvt. Brig. Gen. Morgan, RG 393, part 1, entry 2411, NARA.

34. Morgan to Torbert at Winchester, May 17, 1865, RG 393, part 1, entry 2407, Telegrams sent March–July 1865, Middle Military Division, NARA; *OR*, ser. 1, 46 (3): 1091.

35. *OR*, ser. 1, 46 (3): 1091, 1108, 1166; Sutherland, *Savage Conflict*, 274. Grant ultimately extended the grace period for rebels to turn themselves in without being taken prisoner to June 1.

36. Morgan to Torbert, May 3, 1865, RG 393, part 1, entry 2407, Telegrams sent March–July 1865, Middle Military Division, NARA; *OR*, ser. 1, 46 (3): 1082.

37. *OR*, ser. 1, 46 (3): 1104.

38. *OR*, ser. 1, 46 (3): 1117.

39. *PUSG* 15:31. See also ALS (telegraph sent), DNA, RG 107, Telegrams collected, NARA; *OR* ser. 1, 46 (3): 1123; and *Wilmington Herald*, May 13, 1865. In his memoir, written eighteen years after Appomattox, Rosser claimed that Federal troops had surrounded his home in Hanover County and carried him to Richmond as a prisoner (*Riding with Rosser*, 74).

40. *OR*, ser. 1, 46 (1): 1324.

41. Neff, *Justice in Blue and Gray*, 206–8, 216. For other proclamations and executive orders that helped to end the state of war, see Neff, *Justice in Blue and Gray*, 204–11.

42. *OR*, ser. 1, 46 (3): 1134. For a more detailed account of Taylor's surrender, including the role played by Forrest, see Silkenat, *Raising the White Flag*, 240–50.

43. *OR*, ser. 1, 46 (3): 1136.

44. Keen and Mewborn, *43rd Battalion Virginia Cavalry*, 355; William H. Mosby CSR.

45. Patrick, *Inside Lincoln's Army*, 507, diary entry May 16, 1865; Ramage, *Gray Ghost*, 267–281; Mosby to Pauline, May 27, 1865, Papers of John S. Mosby, MSS 7872, UVA: R. E. Lee to George Palmer, June 6, 1865, Lee Family Collection, CMLS. On May 16, Bvt. Brig. Gen. Sharpe, who had just returned to Richmond from testifying in the Harris trial, asked Grant's chief of staff whether Mosby would be eligible for parole along with other officers of Rosser's command, to which he belonged (*OR*, ser.1, 46 [3]: 1158).

46. *PUSG* 15:47–48. It appears that Grant used the term "bound by their solemn oath" in his letter to mean "parole."

47. Lewis Andrews diary published in the *Atlanta Journal*, May 21, 1904.

48. *Burlington Free Press*, May 12, 1865.

49. Polley, *Hood's Texas Brigade*, 280.

50. Parole Passes and POW Collection Series, CMLS; Theodore Hoyt Woodard Letters, May 14, 1865, CMLS.

51. Hamilton, *History of Company M*, 75.

52. Diary of Clayton Wilson, April 23–May 22, 1865, Going Home Research Files, APCO.

53. Chamberlayne and Chamberlayne, *Ham Chamberlayne*, 324, 327–29.

54. George W. Munford to Mrs. Elizabeth T. Munford, May 9, 1865, Munford-Ellis Family Papers, DU; RG 109, entry 212, box 43, Lynchburg folder, NARA; Wiley, *Recollections of a Confederate Staff Officer*, 276.

55. Lewis T. Nunnelee, Postwar Memoir and Diary, entry April 20, 1865, CMLS; John J. Shoemaker CSR.

56. A. Gordon, *Memories and Memorials*, 294 (letter dated May 21, 1865); William Gordon McCabe CSR.

57. Beyond Appomattox database.

58. *Wheeling (W.Va.) Daily Register*, May 30, 1865; Shaffer, *Clash of Loyalties*, 154; *Wheeling Daily Intelligencer*, May 29, 1865.

59. Asst. Surgeon Robert Pooler Myers, Diary/Letter Copy Book, April 9–May 6, CMLS.

60. Kean, *Inside the Confederate Government*, 208–9, entry for June 1, 1865.

61. Freedmen's Bureau agent quoted in G. Downs, *After Appomattox*, 39–40; *Christian Recorder*, July 1, 1865.

62. Redkey, *Grand Army of Black Men*, 172–73.

63. *New York Herald*, May 23, 1865; *Gallipolis (Ohio) Journal*, May 25, 1862. On report that this rumor was manufactured, see *Highland (Ohio) Weekly News*, June 15, 1865.

CHAPTER 14

1. Speed, "Pardoning Power," 227–35.

2. Dorris, *Pardon and Amnesty*, 109–13. A pardon confers individual forgiveness and exoneration for punishment, whereas amnesty is a pardon offered to an entire class of offenders. Johnson issued a second proclamation that same day regarding the provisional government of North Carolina.

3. McKitrick, *Andrew Johnson*, 48–49; *New York Times*, May 30, 1865; Davis and Tremmel, *Parole, Pardon, Pass*, 19–22. Upon assuming the presidency, Johnson had asked Speed whether a new amnesty oath was necessary in the wake of the surrenders. On May 1, Speed issued an opinion that led Johnson to decide on a new proclamation.

4. Dorris, *Pardon and Amnesty*, 153.

5. For one example, see William Pendleton to General Gibbon, June 13, 1865, in S. Lee, *Memoirs of William Nelson Pendleton*, 420.

6. McKitrick, *Andrew Johnson*, 144–48.

7. McKitrick, 145–46; *OR* series 1, 46 (3): 1224.

8. McKitrick, *Andrew Johnson*, 145–46.

9. Kirkland, *Letter to Peter Cooper*, 22.

10. William Pendleton to My Dear Daughter [Susan P. Lee], June 12, 1865, in S. Lee, *Memoirs of William Nelson Pendleton*, 413–14.

11. *OR*, ser. 2, 8:538.

12. *OR*, ser. 2, 8:556; Petition from Prisoners to Grant, May 23, 1865, Grant Papers, Series 3, Unpublished Materials, box 27, GPL.

13. U.S. War Department, *Index of General Orders*, General Orders No. 109, June 6, 1865; *OR*, ser. 2, 8:1002–3; Sanders, *While in the Hands of the Enemy*, 289. The orders also included the release of those in the rebel navy not exceeding the rank of lieutenant.

14. Cimbala, *Veterans North and South*, 11.

15. RG 393, part 1, entry 5162, NARA; Hubbs, *Voices from Co. D.*, 386–92.

16. *Detroit Free Press* (reprinted from the *Petersburg News*), June 19, 1865; *PUSG* 15: 151; Nicoletti, *Secession on Trial*, 184–85, Underwood quote on p. 185; Freehling, *Road to Disunion*, 236–40; Reeves, *Lost Indictment*, 51–52.

17. *New York Daily Tribune*, June 5, 1865; *Memphis Bulletin*, June 16, 1865.

18. *New York Daily Tribune*, June 5, 1865.

19. Spear, *Punishment of Treason*, 20.

20. Dexter, *What Ought to Be Done*, 25–33.

21. Quoted in Chesebrough, *No Sorrow Like Our Sorrow*, 58.

22. G. Smith, *No Treason in Civil War*, 7, 9; Varon, *Appomattox*, 206; Nicoletti, *Secession on Trial*, 258–59.

23. *New York Times*, June 4, 1865.

24. Finding information on the composition of the grand jury has proven difficult. But in *Life and Letters of Gen. Robert Edward Lee*, J. William Jones described it as a "mixed jury of negroes and whites" (383).

25. Federal records, U.S. Circuit Court, Virginia District, *U.S. v. Jefferson Davis* file,

CMLS; Reeves, *Lost Indictment*, 62–63. Not on the list, however, was Jefferson Davis. Both Davis and Breckinridge had been indicted for treason in Washington on May 26 and therefore did not appear on the Virginia indictments. The list compiled by Reeves differs slightly from those included in the files of the CMLS. For more on why the indictments were dropped, see Nicolette, *Secession on Trial*, 140. Early had been dismissed by Lee in March and had thus far refused to seek a parole, perhaps because he feared reprisal for his part in the 1864 burning of Chambersburg. Ewell had been captured at Sailor's Creek prior to Appomattox and imprisoned at Fort Warren.

26. Pryor would be paroled in Richmond on June 21 (Roger A. Pryor CSR; Warner, *Generals in Gray*, 248).

27. Copies of indictments from *U.S. v. Jefferson Davis* file, CMLS; Reeves, *Lost Indictment*, 66–67.

28. *Norfolk Post*, June 22, 1865; *The Standard* (London), June 27, 1865. For other United Kingdom newspapers that published accounts of the indictments, see *Sheffield and Rotherham Independent*, June 27, 1865; *Bradford Observer* (West Yorkshire, Eng.) June 29, 1865; and *Belfast News-Letter*, June 28, 1865.

29. Pendleton to My Dear Daughter [Susan P. Lee], June 12, 1865, and Pendleton to General Gibbon, June 13, 1866, in S. Lee, *Memoirs of William Nelson Pendleton*, 413–20.

30. Meade, *Life and Letters*, 2:278–79; B. Simpson, *Let Us Have Peace*, 104.

31. Ingalls quoted in Cresap, *Appomattox Commander*, 228; Badeau, *Grant in Peace*, 25; B. Simpson, *Let Us Have Peace*, 107. Varon argues that Lee interpreted "the surrender terms as conditional—namely, as imposing conditions pertaining to the respectful treatment of Southerners that Northerners were bound to obey" (*Appomattox*, 200).

32. Lee to Grant, June 13, 1865, in J. Jones, *Life and Letters of Gen. Robert Edward Lee*, 384; Blair, *With Malice toward Some*, 240. Lee did not include the oath of allegiance with his pardon.

33. Lee to Taylor, June 17, 1865, Lee Letter Collection, CMLS (also in W. Taylor, *Four Years with General Lee*, 155). John C. Breckinridge, indicted in D.C., took his chances first in Cuba and subsequently in Canada and Great Britain. Pickett, although not indicted, feared he would be and hightailed it to Canada, leaving behind his wife and young son. Confederate generals from armies other than Lee's likewise left the United States. Joe Shelby, John B. Magruder, Edmund Kirby Smith, Sterling Price, world famous oceanographer Matthew Fontaine Maury, and several governors headed to Mexico at the prompting of Emperor Maximilian.

34. Grant conceded that the oath of amnesty had not accompanied the petition. According to General Ord, the order requiring the oath had not been received in Richmond when Lee sent his letter. It was not until June 7 that Attorney General Speed had informed those of the exempted class who wished to apply for a pardon that they needed to include proof they had taken the oath of amnesty (*PUSG* 15:150; *New York Herald*, June 13, 1865).

35. *PUSG* 15:149–50; *OR*, ser. 1, 46 (3): 1276. For the argument that Grant rejected the notion of the Appomattox terms as a blanket immunity, see Varon, *Appomattox*, 205.

36. Badeau, *Grant in Peace*, 25–26; testimony of Grant, *Impeachment Investigation*, 826; B. Simpson, *Let Us Have Peace*, 108.

37. Testimony of Grant, *Impeachment Investigation*, 826–27; Badeau, *Grant in Peace*, 26; *PUSG* 15:150, 210–11; Young, *Around the World*, 460–61; B. Simpson, *Let Us Have Peace*, 108.

38. Speed to Chandler, June 20, 1865, RG 60, E A1–10 / General Letter Books, Vol. E,

NARA; Young, *Around the World*, 460–61; Chernow, *Grant*, 553. A special thanks to David Langbart at NARA, College Park, for helping me track down the Speed letter.

39. *Norfolk Post*, August 2, 1865; "The Rebel Parole," *The Nation*, August 3, 1865, 133–34.

40. Reeves, *Lost Indictment*, 82–83, quote on p. 83.

41. On wartime as a legal state, see Dudziak, *War Time*; and G. Downs, *After Appomattox*.

42. *PUSG* 15:164–209; B. Simpson, *Let Us Have Peace*, 108.

43. *PUSG* 15:157, 205; Chernow, *Grant*, 556.

44. Some historians estimate that as many as 10,000 Confederates migrated from the South, primarily to Latin America, between 1865 and 1885. Most southern migrants, however, relocated within the United States, opting to move west or even north for employment (Dawsey and Dawsey, *Confederados*, 13).

45. Dawsey and Dawsey, *Confederados*; Harter, *Lost Colony of the Confederacy*.

46. Albright Reminiscences, April 20, 1865, SHC.

47. Beyond Appomattox database.

48. *Macon Journal* reprinted in the *Columbia Daily Phoenix*, June 24, 1865.

49. Beyond Appomattox database.

50. McIntosh Diary, April 9–23, 1865, David Gregg McIntosh Diary and Papers, VMHC; "Last Colonel of the Artillery, A.N.V.," *CV* 25 (May 1917): 224–26. A review of McIntosh's CSR and Confederate Amnesty files suggests that he never received a parole or pardon (accessed through Fold3).

51. R. E. Lee to George Palmer, June 6, 1865, Lee Family Collection, CMLS.

52. Duncan to Patrick, June 12, 1865, and Ordway to Duncan, June 14 and 15, 1865, RG 393, part 1, entry 5169, NARA; *Lynchburg Republican*, June 14, 1865, reprinted in the *Evening Star*, June 21, 1865. According to the paper, there was some misunderstanding in Lynchburg, and Mosby was ordered to leave town immediately.

53. Col. Franklin Gratton to Lt. Col. Albert Ordway, June 22, 1865, and Duncan to Ordway, June 23, 1865, RG 393, part 1, entry 5169, NARA. Despite the address of this letter, Ordway had been promoted to colonel on May 7, 1865.

54. On the restoration of voting rights in Virginia, see Varon, *Appomattox*, 197.

55. Captain quoted in Blair, *Cities of the Dead*, 52; Joseph Addison Waddell Diary, June 26 and July 2, 1865, UVA.

56. *OR*, ser. 1, 46 (3): 1268; RG 393, part 1, vol. 151, book 251, NARA; *Morgantown (W.Va.) Post*, June 24, 1865.

57. Circular from Headquarters of the District of Henrico, Richmond, Va., June 12, 1865, RG 393, part 1, entry 5163, Press Copies of Letters, February–June 1865, NARA.

58. On emancipation enforced by bayonet, see G. Downs, *After Appomattox*, 39–60.

59. *Herald and Torch Light* (Hagerstown, Md.), June 21, 1865; *Frederick Examiner*, June 14 and 28, 1865.

60. Among the many names I searched, I found two exceptions: Laurence Dickinson and Henry Petit. Dickinson applied to Governor Bradford on August 21, 1865, "on account of having served as a private soldier in the late rebel army." In September, he applied directly to Johnson. There is no indication in the file whether or when he was granted a pardon. Petit applied late June 1865. He was pardoned July 26, 1868 (L. Dickinson and Henry Petit, Maryland files, Confederate Amnesty Records, Fold3). Newspapers did occasionally point out men who had applied for a pardon. See, for example, *Valley Register*, July 21, 1865.

61. John T. Wakenight CSR; *Valley Register*, June 30, 1865; *Herald and Torch Light*, July 5,

1865; *Civilian and Telegraph*, June 15, 1865; *Frederick Examiner*, July 12, 1865; *Shepherdstown (W.Va.) Register*, July 29, 1865.

62. *Wheeling Daily Intelligencer*, July 22, 1865.

63. Dayton, *Samuel Woods and His Family*, 17–18.

64. *Wheeling Daily Intelligencer*, June 9 and 15, 1865; Speed, "Arrest of Paroled Rebels by State Process."

65. *Wheeling Daily Intelligencer*, July 29, 1865. George W. Way, for example, was paroled on April 19 in Winchester (George W. Way CSR).

CHAPTER 15

1. *Rockingham Register*, July 7, 1865.

2. R. Moore, *Tragedy in the Shenandoah Valley*, 40.

3. Quoted in R. Moore, 41–46. On the very day that Lusk received orders to seek out the horse thieves, Col. H. B. Reed had issued orders relieving Lusk of his command over the detachment stationed at Rude's Hill (RG 94, Book Records of Volunteer Union Organizations, 22nd New York Cavalry, vol. 1, NARA).

4. Capt. Allen Baker to Lt. Charles Clark, May 12, 1865, RG 393, part 2, entry 1334—Letters Sent and Received—Provisional Cavalry Brigade, Army of the Shenandoah, NARA.

5. RG 393, part 2, entry 1178—Dept. of West Virginia, Register of Charges and Specifications Received and Cases Tried, April 1864–July 1865, vol. 66, NARA; RG 393, part 4, entry 1457—Letters Sent by the Provost Marshal, November 1862–September 1865, vol. 365, Defenses South of the Potomac—HQ in Alexandria, NARA; *Beverly and Tom Lowry Database of Civil War Courts-Martial*. Wright had been captured and sent to northern prisons at least twice during the war, having been released from Fort Warren in Baltimore on May 11, 1865.

6. R. Moore, *Tragedy in the Shenandoah Valley*, 47–57; letter from George Summers, June 27, 1865, published in *CV*, 14 (September 1906): 403; letter from I. N. Koontz, June 1865, published in *Shenandoah (Va.) Herald*, March 9, 1906.

7. *Rockingham Register*, July 7, 1865; *Staunton (Va.) Spectator*, July 11, 1865; *Times-Picayune*, July 29, 1865; *Daily Empire* (Dayton, Ohio), July 24, 1865; *Daily Progress* (Raleigh, N.C.), July 31, 1865.

8. Bvt. Brig. Gen. H. H. [Wells?] and [?], Dept. South of Potomac to Col. J. H. Taylor, Chief of Staff and A. A. Genl., from Alexandria, Va., June 19, 1865, RG 393, part 1, entry 2411, Middle Military Division, NARA.

9. RG 393, part 2, entry 1322—Letters Sent, March–August 1865—Army of the Shenandoah Valley, NARA; Col. H. B. Reed to Maj. William Russell, May 11, 1865, RG 393, part 2, entry 1334—Letters Sent and Received—Provisional Cavalry Brigade, Army of the Shenandoah, NARA.

10. On the demobilization of Union troops, see Jordan, *Marching Home*, 9–40; and Holberton, *Homeward Bound*, 53–80.

11. Reid, *Ohio in the War*, 2:737.

12. *Daily National Republican*, April 14, 1865.

13. *Rockingham Register*, July 28, 1865. Emphasis added.

14. *New York Times*, June 12, 1865. The pace with which Johnson would grant individual pardons accelerated dramatically by the fall (McKitrick, *Andrew Johnson*, 145–46).

15. Nicoletti, *Secession on Trial*, 93–94.

16. Nicoletti observes that former Confederates also offered justifications on the right of secession often framed in the language of "trial by battle," i.e., that the battlefield had rendered a verdict on the constitutional question of secession (Nicoletti, 93–94).

17. Thomas L. Rosser, Confederate Amnesty Papers, Texas, Fold3.

18. Richard S. Ewell, Confederate Amnesty Papers, Virginia, Fold3; *PUSG* 15:154–55.

19. William H. Payne, Confederate Amnesty Papers, Virginia, Fold3.

20. Lee to Ordway, June 21, 1865, *PUSG* Documents, vol. 14, GPL.

21. *PUSG* 15:222–23.

22. *OR*, ser. 2, 8:683; *PUSG* 15:223.

23. *OR*, ser. 2, 8:683. Stanton initially approved the order but then suspended it.

24. Lt. Harshorn's Ledger of Destitute Rations Issued to Parole Prisoners, Virginia, May 30 to June 10, 1865, VMHC. Special thanks to Emma Gaier for helping me create a database of those receiving rations at Lynchburg.

25. Passes for Thomas G. Wallingford and W. F. Wharton, Parole Passes and POW Collection Series, CMLS; William F. Wharton CSR.

26. *Progress-Index* (Petersburg, Va.), July 10, 1865; *Memphis Bulletin*, June 9 and 16, 1865; Janney, *Burying the Dead*, 43. Winchester was the only locale I have been able to locate that formed a Ladies' Memorial Association in the spring of 1865. Most others seem to have formed in the spring of 1866.

27. Dennett, *South as It Is*, 2–3; Trowbridge, *Desolate South*, 51.

28. Eppa Hunton to his wife, May 26, 1865, Hunton Family Papers, VMHC; *OR*, ser. 2, 8:709–10.

29. *OR*, ser. 2, 8:709–10; Blair, *With Malice toward Some*, 242. Stephens would not be released from Fort Warren in the Boston Harbor until October 1865. Clement Clay remained imprisoned at Fort Monroe until April 1866.

30. Lee to Reverdy Johnson, July 27, 1865, in R. Lee, *Recollections and Letters*, 175.

31. *PUSG* 15:211–12.

32. Lee to Fitzhugh "Rooney" Lee, July 29, 1865, in R. Lee, *Recollections and Letters*, 177–78.

33. On June 27, 1865, the Middle Military Division was discontinued. That same day its former commander, Hancock, assumed command from Wallace of the Middle Department, which now included parts of the Departments of Washington, Pennsylvania, West Virginia, the Potomac, Delaware, and West Virginia.

34. *OR*, ser. 2, 8:715; *Baltimore Sun*, August 2, 1865.

35. *Cincinnati Enquirer*, August 2, 1865.

36. Lieber to Charles Sumner, August 4, 1865, in Lieber, *Life and Letters*, 358.

37. *Norfolk Post*, August 2, 1865; Wise, *Life of Henry A. Wise*, 371. For more on refugee camps in the spring and summer of 1865, see A. Taylor, *Embattled Freedom*, 209–38.

38. *National Republican* (Washington, D.C.), August 11, 1865; *Daily Progress*, August 22, 1865; *Reynold's Newspaper* (London), August 27, 1865.

39. *National Republican*, August 11, 1865.

40. *Norfolk Post*, August 2, 1865.

41. Freedmen's Bureau agent quoted in G. Downs, *After Appomattox*, 39–40; *Christian Recorder*, July 1, 1865. For more on the atrocities and murders committed against African Americans in the wake of Appomattox, see Blair, *Murders and Outrages*.

42. Chamberlayne and Chamberlayne, *Ham Chamberlayne*, 333.

43. *Vermont Standard* (Woodstock), September 8, 1865; *Bradford Reporter* (Towanda, Pa.), September 14, 1865; Bradley T. Johnson pardon application, July 8, 1865, box 2, Bradley T. Johnson Papers, UVA; letters in support of Bradley Johnson, Confederate Amnesty papers of Bradley T. Johnson, accessed through Fold3. The other men included George Freanor, John G. Honard, Thomas Fitzhugh, and S. G. Gillmore, "the guerrilla" (*Times-Picayune*, September 10, 1865). Johnson was married to the daughter of a prominent North Carolina congressman.

44. *PUSG* 15:143–44; Bradley Johnson to President Johnson, February 12, 1866, and J. A. Noonan to dear Judge, March [?], 1866, box 2, Bradley T. Johnson Papers, UVA; Confederate Amnesty papers of Bradley T. Johnson, accessed through Fold3; Fessenden, Grimes, et al., *Report of the Joint Committee on Reconstruction*.

45. *Baltimore Sun*, March 28, 1866. Johnson had served under Jubal Early in the Shenandoah Valley campaign. When Lee dismissed Early in March 1865, Johnson was sent to Salisbury, North Carolina.

46. *Baltimore Sun*, April 6, 1866; *PUSG* 16:143–44; Grant to Speed quoted in B. Simpson, *Let Us Have Peace*, 132; Nicoletti, *Secession on Trial*, 196; Confederate Amnesty Papers of Bradley T. Johnson, accessed through Fold3. In March 1866, Grant again interceded on behalf of a Confederate general, this time George E. Pickett, who was to be charged with war crimes. For more on this see *PUSG* 16:148–50.

47. *Weekly Standard* (Raleigh, N.C.), March 7, 1866; *New Orleans Crescent*, March 2, 1866; *PUSG* 16:85–86. Initially, it appears that Grant considered applying the surrender terms to Gee's case. But for unknown reasons, in his response to Johnston, he refused to do so. Gee was acquitted of all charges in 1866.

48. Johnson quoted in Wert, *Longstreet*, 409; *PUSG* 15:401–2; Reeves, *Lost Indictment*, 90–91.

49. Nicoletti, *Secession on Trial*, 196n31. Davis would be indicted in 1865 but never brought to trial. For an excellent discussion of why, see Nicoletti, *Secession on Trial*.

50. Blair, *With Malice toward Some*, 235; Randall, *Constitutional Problems*, 97.

51. William H. Payne CSR.

52. *PUSG* 15:212–13, emphasis added; *Raleigh Sentinel*, August 14, 1866. The parole was issued by Maj. George K. Leet. He likewise issued a new parole for Custis and likely for Rooney. The *Raleigh Sentinel* notes that "Custis and Fitzhugh Lee" attended, but this is most likely Lee's son William Henry Fitzhugh "Rooney" Lee rather than his nephew, as the paper refers to the men as brothers.

53. *Nashville Telegraph and Union*, January 13, 1867; Confederate Amnesty Papers for James Longstreet, Fold3. Longstreet was pardoned on June 17, 1867, "by order of the President."

54. Second Amnesty Proclamation, September 7, 1867, *PAJ* 13:40–43; M. Summers, *Dangerous Stir*, 177–78. The second proclamation reduced the number of exemptions from fourteen to three: "chief executive officers, including the President and Vice President" of the Confederacy; those who had mistreated prisoners of war; and all persons "legally held to bail either before or after conviction," including those engaged in Lincoln's assassination.

55. Bergeron, *Andrew Johnson's Civil War*, 210–11; Nicoletti, *Secession on Trial*, 299–300.

56. Nicoletti, *Secession on Trial*, 294–300; Reeves, *Lost Indictment*, 168.

57. Nicoletti, *Secession on Trial*, 294–300; *Aegis and Intelligencer* (Bel Air, Md.), February 19, 1869; *Brooklyn Union*, February 12, 1869.

58. For example, see Fessenden, Grimes, et al., *Report of the Joint Committee on Reconstruction*, 2:33, 3:15.

59. M. Summers, *Ordeal of the Reunion*, 67–73.

60. "The Rebel Parole," *The Nation*, August 3, 1865, 133. In September 1865, Forrest was indicted for treason by Chief Justice Chase, but he was never arrested or tried. U.S. forces arrested Raphael Semmes, commander of the CSS *Alabama*, in December 1865. Some considered him a guerrilla of the high seas for sinking more than sixty U.S. ships. Semmes claimed that he was included in the Johnston-Sherman surrender. He was eventually released in April 1866 (Blair, *With Malice toward Some*, 242).

61. Blair, *With Malice toward Some*, 243.

62. Beyond Appomattox database. As of December 2020, I have found 16,997 paroles at sites other than Appomattox between April 10 and July 15, 1865.

EPILOGUE

1. Bradley T. Johnson, "The Maryland Confederate Monument at Gettysburg," *SHSP* 14:429–31.

2. There is a vast literature on the Lost Cause. For several overviews, see Janney, *Remembering the Civil War* and *Burying the Dead*; Blight, *Race and Reunion*; Foster, *Ghosts*; Wilson, *Baptized in Blood*; Gallagher and Nolan, *Myth of the Lost Cause*, 1–34; Gallagher, *Lee and His Generals*; Blair, *Cities of the Dead*; Brundage, *Southern Past*; and Cox, *Dixie's Daughters*. For the argument that the Lost Cause began before Appomattox, see Gallagher, "Shaping Public Memory of the Civil War," in Gallagher, *Lee and His Army in Confederate History*, 255–82.

3. B. Jones, *Under the Stars and Bars*, 263–64.

4. Quoted in Bushong and Bushong, *Fightin' Tom Rosser*, 184.

5. Phillips, *Diehard Rebels*, 178.

Bibliography

PRIMARY SOURCES

Manuscript Collections

Appomattox Court House National Historic Park, Appomattox Court House, Va.
    Going Home Research Files
    Greg Coco Research Files
    Library Files
Atlanta History Center, Ga.
    Abbie M. Brooks Diary
Hill Memorial Library, Louisiana State University, Baton Rouge
    Andrew Jr. and George Hero Papers
Historical Society of Pennsylvania, Philadelphia
    John Gibbon Papers
Huntington Library, San Marino, Calif.
    Diary of Annie G. Dudley Davis
    Manley Ebenezer Rice Papers
Indiana Historical Society, Indianapolis
    Lew Wallace Papers
Library of Congress, A People at War Collection (microfilm)
    John Rumsey Brincklé Papers
Louisiana Historical Association Collection, Howard-Tilton Memorial
    Special Collections, Tulane University, New Orleans
    Frank Lobrano Diary
Massachusetts Historical Society, Boston
    Henry J. Millard Letters
    Jane Norton Wigglesworth Grew Correspondence
Mississippi Department of Archives and History, Jackson
    William M. Abernathy, "Our Mess: Southern Army Gallantry
        and Privations, 1861–1865" (typed manuscript)

National Archives and Records Administration, Washington, D.C., and College Park, Md.
  RG 60 — General Records of the Department of Justice
  RG 94 — Records of the Adjutant General's Office
  RG 92 — Records of the Office of the Quartermaster General
  RG 107 — Records of the Office of the Secretary of War
  RG 109 — War Department Collection of Confederate Records
  RG 110 — Records of the Provost Marshal General's Bureau
  RG 153 — Records of the Office of the Judge Advocate General
  RG 393 — Records of the War Department
North Carolina Division of Archives and History, Raleigh
  Personal Diary of John Willis Council
  Papers of Miss Georgia Hicks
  Benjamin Sims Journal
  John W. Bone, "Record of a Soldier in the Late War," Lowery Shuford Collection
Perkins Library, Special Collections Library, Duke University, Durham, N.C.
  Lucy Muse Walton Fletcher Diary
  Munford-Ellis Family Papers
  Diary of John R. Porter
Small Special Collections, University of Virginia, Charlottesville
  John Moncure Daniel Papers
  Papers of John W. Daniel and the Daniel Family
  Bradley T. Johnson Papers
  Lewis and Latane Family Papers
  Hodijah Baylies Meade, "Memoirs of a Confederate
      Surgeon in the Army of Northern Virginia"
  Papers of John S. Mosby
  Thomas T. Munford Papers
  John L. Nau III Collection
  Thomas L. Rosser Papers
  Joseph Addison Waddell Diary, 1855–1865
  Papers Chiefly Pertaining to Virginia, 1803–1904
  Papers Pertaining to Virginia, 1856–1882
Southern Historical Collection, Wilson Library, University of North Carolina, Chapel Hill
  James W. Albright Diary and Reminiscences
  Edward Porter Alexander Papers
  William D. Alexander Diary
  Henry T. Bahnson Papers
  Berry Benson Papers
  Kena King Chapman Diary
  Thomas Pollock Devereux Papers
  Elizabeth Seawell Hairston Papers
  Fries Shaffner Papers
  J. E. Whitehorne Diary
State Archives of North Carolina, Raleigh
  Reminiscences of Mrs. James W. (Martha Sarah Purvis)
      Albright (North Carolina Digital Collections)

Tennessee State Library and Archives, Nashville
  William Henry Harder Memoir
Ulysses S. Grant Presidential Library, Starkville, Miss.
  Appomattox Subject File
  Grant Papers, Series 3, Unpublished Materials
  Ord Subject File
  PUSG Documents (organized by volume)
Virginia Museum of History and Culture (previously the Virginia Historical Society), Richmond
  Bagby Family Papers
  Early Family Papers
  Confederate Memorial Literary Society Collection
    Confederate Military Leaders Collection
    Hiram W. Harding Diary
    Lee Family Collection
    Lee Letter Collection
    Capt. Henry Carter Lee Pocket Diary
    Asst. Surgeon Robert Pooler Myers, Diary/Letter Copy Book
    Lewis T. Nunnelee, Postwar Memoir and Diary
    Parole Passes and POW Collection Series
    Roster of Officers and Members of the R. E. Lee Camp
      No. 1 Confederate Veterans (January 1, 1913)
    Maj. Thomas J. Rowland Letters
    Channing M. Smith Diary
    U. S. v. Jefferson Davis file
    Theodore Hoyt Woodard Letters
  Charles Bickem Fields Diary
  Lt. Harshorn's Ledger of Destitute Rations Issued to Parole Prisoners
  Hunton Family Papers
  R. E. Lee Headquarter Papers
  Osmun Latrobe Diary
  William Andrew Mauney, "A Diary of the War Between the States" (typescript)
  David Gregg McIntosh Diary and Papers
  Thomas Munford, "Five Forks . . . The Last Days of
      Fitz Lee's Cavalry Division" (typescript)
  Daniel T. Nelson Papers
  Pegram-Johnson-McIntosh Papers
  POW Collection Series

                              Online Databases

Alexandria Archaeology. Transcription of Julia Wilbur Diary accessed online at https://
  www.alexandriava.gov/uploadedFiles/historic/info/civilwar/JuliaWilburDiary1860
  to1866.pdf.
Augustus Dean Memories. http://batsonsm.tripod.com/deanaa.html.
Fold3.com. Used to access CSRs and Confederate Amnesty Papers. https://www.fold3.com.
Library of Congress. *Born in Slavery: Slave Narratives from the Federal Writers' Project,*

1936–1938. Federal Writers' Project, Slave Narrative Project, 17 vols. https://www.loc
.gov/collections/slave-narratives-from-the-federal-writers-project-1936-to-1938/about
-this-collection/.

Printed Primary Sources

Acken, J. Gregory, ed. *Blue Blooded Cavalryman: Captain William Brooke Rawle in the Army
of the Potomac, May 1863–August 1865*. Kent: Kent State University Press, 2019.

Albright, James W. *Greensboro, 1808–1904: Facts, Figures, Traditions, and Reminiscences*.
Greensboro, N.C.: Jos. J. Stone, 1904.

Alexander, Edward Porter. *Fighting for the Confederacy: The Personal Recollections of General
Edward Porter Alexander*. Edited by Gary W. Gallagher. Chapel Hill: University of
North Carolina Press, 1989.

Andrews, Eliza Frances. *The Wartime Journal of a Georgia Girl*. New York: D. Appleton,
1908.

Andrews, Matthew Page. *Tercentary History of Maryland, 4 vols*. Chicago: S. J. Clarke, 1925.

Andrews, W. H. *Footprints of a Regiment: A Recollection of the 1st Georgia Regulars, 1861–
1865*. Atlanta, Ga.: Longstreet Press, 1992.

Arnold, William B. *The Fourth Massachusetts Cavalry in the Closing Scenes of the War for the
Maintenance of the Union*. Boston, 1910.

Badeau, Adam. *Grant in Peace: From Appomattox to Mount McGregor; A Personal Memoir
by Adam Badeau*. Hartford, Conn.: S. S. Scranton, 1887.

Basler, Roy P. *Collected Works of Abraham Lincoln*. 8 vols. New Brunswick, N.J.: Rutgers
University Press, 1953.

Benson, Susan Williams, ed. *Berry Benson's Civil War Book: Memoirs of a Confederate Scout
and Sharpshooter*. Athens: University of Georgia Press, 2007.

Berlin, Ira, Joseph P. Reidy, and Leslie S. Rowland, eds. *The Black Military Experience*.
Ser. 2 of *Freedom: A Documentary History of Emancipation, 1861–1867*. New York:
Cambridge University Press, 1982.

Bernard, George S. *War Talks of Confederate Veterans*. Petersburg, Va.: Fenn & Owen, 1892.

Blackett, R. J. M., ed. *Thomas Morris Chester, Black Civil War Correspondent: His Dispatches
from the Virginia Front*. Baton Rouge: Louisiana State University Press, 1989.

Brinton, John H. *Personal Memoirs of John H. Brinton, Major and Surgeon U.S.V., 1861–1865*.
New York: Neale Pub., 1914.

Broun, Catherine Hopkins. *Dark Days in Our Beloved Country: The Civil War Diary of
Catherine Hopkins Broun*. Edited by Lee Lawrence. Warrenton, Va.: Piedmont Press and
Graphics, 2014.

Brown, Norman D., ed. *One of Cleburne's Command: The Civil War Reminiscences and Diary
of Capt. Samuel T. Foster, Granbury's Texas Brigade, CSA*. Austin: University of Texas
Press, 1980.

Bruce, George A. *The Capture and Occupation of Richmond*. United States: N.p., 1918.

Buck, Stuart H., ed. "With Lee after Appomattox: Personal Experiences from Diary of
Samuel C. Lovell." *Civil War Times Illustrated* 17, no. 7 (November 1978): 42–43.

Burrage, Henry S. *History of the Thirty-Sixth Regiment Massachusetts Volunteers, 1862–1865*.
Boston: Rockwell and Churchill, 1884.

Calkins, Chris, ed. "Final March to Appomattox: The 12th Virginia Infantry, April 2–12,
1865, an Eyewitness Account." *Civil War Regiments* 2, no. 3 (1992): 236–51.

Chamberlain, Joshua. "Appomattox: Paper Read before the New York Commandery, Loyal Legion of the United States, October Seventh, 1903." In *Personal Recollections of the War of the Rebellion: Addresses Delivered by Military Order of the Loyal Legion*, by A. Noel Blakeman, 274–75. 3rd ser. New York, 1907.

———. *Bayonet! Forward: My Civil War Reminiscences*. Gettysburg, Pa.: Stan Clark Military Books, 1994.

Chamberlayne, John H., and C. G. Chamberlayne. *Ham Chamberlayne, Virginian: Letters and Papers of an Artillery Officer in the War for Southern Independence, 1861–1865*. Richmond: Dietz Print. Co., 1932.

Claiborne, John Herbert. *Seventy-Five Years in Old Virginia: With Some Account of the Life of the Author and Some History of the People amongst Whom His Lot Was Cast,— Their Character, Their Condition, and Their Conduct before the War, during the War, and after the War*. New York: Neal Publishing Company, 1904.

Clark, Walter, ed. *Histories of the Several Regiments and Battalions from North Carolina in the Great War, 1861–65, Written by Members of the Respective Commands*. 5 vols. Goldsboro, N.C.: Nash Brothers, 1901.

Coker, James Lide. *History of Company G, Ninth S.C. Regiment, Infantry, S.C. Army and of Company E, Sixth S.C. Regiment, Infantry, S.C. Army*. 1899. Reprint, Bethesda, Md.: University Publications of America, 1990.

Confederate States of America. *Journal of the Congress of the Confederate States of America, 1861–1865*. 7 vols. Washington, D.C., 1904–1905.

Crabtree, Beth G., and James W. Patton, eds. *"Journal of a Secesh Lady": The Diary of Catherine Ann Devereux Edmondston, 1860–1866*. 1979. Reprint, Raleigh, N.C.: Division of Archives and History, 1995.

Craig, Tom Moore, ed. *Upcountry South Carolina Goes to War: Letters of the Anderson, Brockman, and Moore Families, 1853–1865*. Columbia: University of South Carolina Press, 2009.

Curran, Robert Emmett, ed. *John Dooley's Civil War: An Irish American's Journey in the First Virginia Infantry Regiment*. Knoxville: University of Tennessee Press, 2012.

Cutrer, Thomas W., ed. *Longstreet's Aide: The Civil War Letters of Major Thomas J. Goree*. Charlottesville: University Press of Virginia, 1995.

Davis, Jefferson. *The Papers of Jefferson Davis*. 14 vols. Baton Rouge: Louisiana State University Press, 1971.

Dawson, Sarah Morgan. *The Civil War Diary of Sarah Morgan*. Edited by Charles East. Athens: University of Georgia Press, 1991.

Dennett, John Richard. *The South as It Is*. Edited by Caroline E. Janney. 1866. Reprint, Tuscaloosa: University of Alabama Press, 2010.

Dexter, Henry Martyn. *What Ought to Be Done with the Freedmen and with the Rebels? A Sermon Preached in the Berkeley Street Church, Boston, on Sunday April 23, 1865*. Boston: Nichols and Noyes, 1865.

Douglas, Henry Kyd. *I Rode with Stonewall: Being Chiefly the War Experiences of the Youngest Member of Jackson's Staff from the John Brown Raid to the Hanging of Mrs. Surratt*. Chapel Hill: University of North Carolina Press, 1940.

Dowdey, Clifford, and Louis H. Manarin, eds. *The Wartime Papers of R. E. Lee*. Boston: Little, Brown, 1961.

Emilio, Luis F. *History of the Fifty-Fourth Regiment of Massachusetts Volunteer Infantry, 1863–1865*. Boston: Boston Book Co., 1891.

Fessenden, W. P., James W. Grimes, et al., eds. *Report of the Joint Committee on Reconstruction*. U.S. 39th Congress, 1st Session, 4 parts. Freeport, N.Y.: Books for Libraries Press, 1971.

Fulton, William Frierson. *The War Reminiscences of William Frierson Fulton II, 5th Alabama Battalion, Archer's Brigade, A. P. Hill's Light Division, A. N. V.* Gaithersburg, Md.: Butternut Press, 1986.

Georgia Division of the United Daughters of the Confederacy. *Confederate Reminiscences and Letters, 1861–1865*. 15 vols. to date. Atlanta: United Daughters of the Confederacy, Georgia Division, 1995–2001.

Gibbon, John. *At Gettysburg and Elsewhere (Expanded and Annotated): The Civil War Memoir of John Gibbon*. N.p.: Big Byte Books, 2016.

———. "Personal Recollections of Appomattox." *Century Magazine* April 1902, 936–43.

———. *Personal Recollections of the Civil War*. New York: G. P. Putnam's Sons, 1928.

Gordon, Armistead C. *Memories and Memorials of William Gordon McCabe*, vol. 1. Richmond: Old Dominion Press, 1925.

Gordon, George. *A War Diary of Events in the War of the Great Rebellion: 1863–1865*. Boston: J. R. Osgood and Co., 1882.

Graf, LeRoy P., and Ralph W. Haskins, eds. *The Papers of Andrew Johnson*. 16 vols. Knoxville: University of Tennessee Press, 1967–2000.

Grant, Ulysses S. *The Papers of Ulysses S. Grant*. Edited by John Y. Simon et al. 32 vols. Carbondale: Southern Illinois University Press, 1967–2012.

———. *The Personal Memoirs of Ulysses S. Grant*. 2 vols. 1885. Reprint, Old Saybrook, Conn.: Konecky and Konecky, 1992.

Graves, Rev. Joseph A. *The History of the Bedford Light Artillery*. Bedford City, Va.: Press of the Bedford Democrat, 1903.

Haley, John W. *The Rebel Yell and the Yankee Hurrah: The Civil War Journal of a Maine Volunteer*. Edited by Ruth L. Silliker. Lanham, Md.: Down East Books, 2014.

Harwell, Richard Barksdale, ed. *A Confederate Diary of the Retreat from Petersburg, April 3–20, 1865*. Atlanta: The Library, Emory University, 1953.

Haymond, Henry. *History of Harrison County, West Virginia: From the Early Days of Northwestern Virginia to the Present*. Morgantown, W.Va.: Acme Publishing, 1910.

Hewett, Janet B., and others, eds. *Supplement to the Official Records of the Union and Confederate Armies*. 100 vols. Wilmington, N.C.: Broadfoot, 1994–2000.

Hinson, William G. "Diary of William G. Hinson during the War of Secession." Edited by Joseph Ioor Waring. *South Carolina Historical Magazine* 75 (April 1974): 111–20.

History of the Thirty-Fifth Regiment Massachusetts Volunteers, 1862–1865: With a Roster. Boston: Mills, Knight and Co., 1884.

Hopkins, William P., and George B. Peck. *The Seventh Regiment Rhode Island Volunteers in the Civil War, 1862–1865*. Providence: Snow and Farnham, Printers, 1903.

Hotchkiss, Jedediah. *Make Me a Map of the Valley: The Civil War Journal of Stonewall Jackson's Topographer*. Edited by Archie P. McDonald. Dallas: Southern Methodist University Press, 1973.

Hubard, Robert T. *The Civil War Memoirs of a Virginia Cavalryman: Lt. Robert T. Hubard, Jr.* Edited by Thomas P. Nanzig. Tuscaloosa: University of Alabama Press, 2007.

Hubbs, G. Ward. *Voices from Co. D: Diaries by the Greensboro Guards, Fifth Alabama Infantry Regiment, Army of Northern Virginia*. Athens: University of Georgia Press, 2003.

Hunton, Eppa. *Autobiography of Eppa Hunton*. Richmond: William Byrd Press, 1933.

Impeachment Investigation: Testimony Taken before the Judiciary Committee of the House of Representatives in the Investigation of the Charges against Andrew Johnson. Washington, D.C.: Government Printing Office, 1867.

Johnston, Joseph E. *Narrative of Military Operations Directed during the Late War between the States*. New York: D. Appleton and Company, 1874.

Jones, Benjamin Washington. *Under the Stars and Bars: A History of the Surry Light Artillery, Recollections of a Private Soldier in the War between the States*. Richmond: E. Waddey, 1909.

Jones, J. William. *Life and Letters of Gen. Robert Edward Lee, Soldier and Man*. 1906. Reprint, Harrisonburg, Va.: Sprinkle Publications, 1986.

Kean, Robert Garlick Hill. *Inside the Confederate Government: The Diary of Robert Garlick Hill Kean*. Edited by Edward Younger. 1957. Reprint, Baton Rouge: Louisiana State University Press, 1993.

Kidd, James Harvey. *Personal Recollections of a Cavalryman: With Custer's Michigan Cavalry Brigade in the Civil War*. 1908. Reprint, Alexandria, Va.: Time-Life Books, 1983.

Kirkland, Charles P. *A Letter to Peter Cooper, on "The Treatment to Be Extended to the Rebels Individually," and "The Mode of Restoring the Rebel States to the Union." With an Appendix Containing a Reprint of a Review of Judge Curtis' Paper on the Emancipation Proclamation, with a Letter from President Lincoln*. New York: A. D. F. Randolph, 1865.

Lane, David. *A Soldier's Diary: The Story of a Volunteer, 1862–1865*. N.p., 1905.

Lee, Robert E. *Recollections and Letters of General Robert E. Lee by His Son, Captain Robert E. Lee*. New York: Doubleday, Page, and Company, 1905.

Lee, Susan P. *Memoirs of William Nelson Pendleton, D.D.: Rector of Latimer Parish, Lexington, Virginia; Brigadier-General C.S.A.; Chief of Artillery, Army of Northern Virginia*. 1893. Reprint, Harrisonburg, Va.: Sprinkle Publications, 1991.

Lieber, Francis. *The Life and Letters of Francis Lieber*. Edited by Thomas Sergeant Perry. Boston: J. R. Osgood and Company, 1882.

Lightsey, Ada C. *The Veteran's Story*. Meridian, Miss.: Meridian News, 1899.

Longstreet, James. *From Manassas to Appomattox: General James Longstreet*. 1896. Reprint, Boston, Mass.: Da Capo Press, 1992.

Lynch, Charles H. *The Civil War Diary 1862–1865 of Charles H. Lynch, 19th Conn. Vol's*. Privately printed, 1915.

Marshall, Charles. *An Aide-de-Camp of Lee: Being the Papers of Colonel Charles Marshall, Sometimes Aide-de-Camp, Military Secretary, and Assistant Adjutant General on the Staff of Robert E. Lee, 1862–1865*. Edited by Sir Frederick Maurice. 1927. Reprint, Lincoln: University of Nebraska Press, 2000.

———. "Appomattox Court House—Incidents of the Surrender, as Given by Charles Marshall in His Address on the Anniversary of the Birthday of General R. E. Lee at Baltimore, Md., Jan. 19, 1894." *Southern Historical Society Papers* 21 (1893): 353–60.

McCarthy, Carlton. *Detailed Minutiae of Soldier Life in the Army of Northern Virginia, 1861–1865*. Richmond: C. McCarthy and Company, 1882.

Meade, George Gordon. *The Life and Letters of George Gordon Meade: Major General United States Army*. 2 vols. New York: Charles Scribner's Sons, 1913.

Mitchell, Charles, ed. *Maryland Voices of the Civil War*. Baltimore: Johns Hopkins University Press, 2007.

Mixson, Frank M. *Reminiscences of a Private*. Columbia, S.C.: State Company, 1910.

Montgomery, Walter Alexander. *Appomattox and the Return Home*. United States: N.p., 1938.

Moore, Edward Alexander. *The Story of a Cannoneer under Stonewall Jackson in Which Is Told the Part Taken by the Rockbridge Artillery in the Army of Northern Virginia*. Lynchburg, Va.: J. P. Bell Company, 1910.

Mosby, John S. *The Memoirs of Colonel John S. Mosby*. Edited by Charles Wells Russell. Boston: Little, Brown, and Company, 1917.

Murray, Thomas Jefferson. "Going Home from Surrender." *Fare Facts Gazette* 12, no. 2 (Spring 2015).

Mushkat, Jerome, ed. *A Citizen-Soldier's Civil War: The Letters of Brevet Major General Alvin C. Voris*. DeKalb: Northern Illinois University Press, 2002.

Myers, William Starr. *The Self-Reconstruction of Maryland, 1864–1867*. Baltimore: Johns Hopkins Press, 1909.

Nevins, Allen, ed. *A Diary of Battle: The Personal Journals of Colonel Charles S. Wainwright, 1861–1865*. San Francisco: Pickle Partners, 2014.

Owen, William Miller. *In Camp and Battle with the Washington Artillery of New Orleans*. Boston: Ticknor and Company, 1885.

Palmer, Beverly Wilson, ed. *The Selected Letters of Charles Sumner*. Vol. 2. Boston: Northeastern University Press, 1990.

"Paroles of the Army of Northern Virginia: Statement of Brigadier General W. P. Roberts as to His Staff and Command." In *Southern Historical Society Papers*, vol. 18, 386–88. Edited by J. William Jones et al. Richmond: Southern Historical Society, 1890.

Patrick, Marsena Rudolph. *Inside Lincoln's Army: The Diary of Marsena Rudolph Patrick, Provost Marshal General, Army of the Potomac*. Edited by David S. Sparks. New York: T. Yoseloff, 1964.

Pearce, T. H., ed. *Diary of Captain Henry A. Chambers*. Wendell, N.C.: Broadfoot, 1983.

Pendleton, William Frederic. *Confederate Memoirs: Early Life and Family History [of] William Frederick Pendleton [and] Mary Lawson Young Pendleton*. Edited by Constance Pendleton. Bryn Athyn, Pa., 1958.

Polley, Joseph B. *Hood's Texas Brigade: Its Marches, Its Battles, Its Achievements*. New York: Neale, 1910.

Potts, Frank. *Death of the Confederacy: The Last Week of the Army of Northern Virginia as Set Forth in a Letter of April, 1865*. Richmond: privately printed for A. Potts, 1928.

Quarles, Garland R. *Diaries, Letters, and Recollections of the War between the States*. Winchester, Va.: Winchester-Frederick County Historical Society, 1955.

Rawick, George P., et al., eds. *The American Slave: A Composite Biography*. 41 vols. Westport, Conn.: Greenwood Press, 1972–79 (Series 1, 7 vols.; Series 2, 12 vols.; Supplemental Series 1, 12 vols.; Supplemental Series 2, 10 vols.).

Reid, Whitelaw. *Ohio in the War: Her Statesmen, Generals, and Soldiers*. 2 vols. Cincinnati: R. Clarke Co., 1895.

Resolutions Adopted by Bratton's Brigade, South Carolina Volunteers, January 30, 1865. Richmond: Confederate States of America, 1865.

Richardson, Albert Deane. *A Personal History of Ulysses S. Grant: And Sketch of Schuyler Colfax*. Hartford, Conn.: American Publishing Co., 1868.

Rosser, Thomas L. *Riding with Rosser*. Edited by S. Roger Keller. Shippensburg, Pa.: Burd Street Press, 1997.

Scharf, J. Thomas. *The Chronicles of Baltimore*. Baltimore: Turnbull Brothers, 1874.

Sheridan, Philip Henry. *Personal Memoirs of P. H. Sheridan, General, United States Army.*
2 vols. New York: C. L. Webster, 1888.

Sherman, William T. *Memoirs of General W. T. Sherman.* 2 vols. 1885. Reprint, New York:
Library of America, 2007.

Shingleton, Royce Gordon, ed. "South from Appomattox: The Diary of Abner Cox's."
South Carolina Historical Magazine 75 (October 1974): 238–44.

Shoemaker, John J. *Shoemaker's Battery: Stuart Horse Artillery, Pelham's Battalion,
Afterwards Commanded by Col. R. P. Chew, Army of Northern Virginia.* 1908. Reprint,
Gaithersburg, Md.: Butternut Press, 1983.

Smith, Gerrit. *No Treason in Civil War: Speech of Gerrit Smith at Cooper Institute, New York,
June 8, 1865.* New York: American News Company, 1865.

Smith, J. L. *Antietam to Appomattox with 118th Penna. Vols. Corn Exchange Regiment: With
Descriptions of Marches, Battles, and Skirmishes, Together with a Complete Roster and
Sketches of Officers and Men.* Philadelphia: J. L. Smith Map Publisher, 1892.

South Carolina Division of the United Daughters of the Confederacy. *Recollections and
Reminiscences, 1861–1865 through World War 1.* 12 vols. South Carolina: South Carolina
Division, United Daughters of the Confederacy, 1990–2002.

Spear, Samuel. *The Punishment of Treason.* Brooklyn: Union Steam Presses, 1865.

Speed, James. "Arrest of Paroled Rebels by State Process." In *Official Opinions of the
Attorneys General of the United States.* Vol. 11, *Containing the Opinions of Hon. Edward
Bates, of Missouri, [and] Hon. James Speed, of Kentucky,* edited by J. Hubley Ashton, 240.
Washington, D.C.: W. H. and O. H. Morrison, 1869.

———. "Duty of the Attorney General." In *Official Opinions of the Attorneys General of
the United States.* Vol. 11, *Containing the Opinions of Hon. Edward Bates, of Missouri, [and]
Hon. James Speed, of Kentucky,* edited by J. Hubley Ashton, 189–92. Washington, D.C.:
W. H. and O. H. Morrison, 1869.

———. "The Pardoning Power." In *Official Opinions of the Attorneys General of the United
States.* Vol. 11, *Containing the Opinions of Hon. Edward Bates, of Missouri, [and] Hon.
James Speed, of Kentucky,* edited by J. Hubley Ashton, 227–37. Washington, D.C.: W. H.
and O. H. Morrison, 1869.

———. "Surrender of the Rebel Army of Northern Virginia." In *Official Opinions of the
Attorneys General of the United States.* Vol. 11, *Containing the Opinions of Hon. Edward
Bates, of Missouri, [and] Hon. James Speed, of Kentucky,* edited by J. Hubley Ashton,
204–9. Washington, D.C.: W. H. and O. H. Morrison, 1869.

Spencer, Cornelia. *The Last Ninety Days of the War in North Carolina.* New York:
Watchman Publishing Company, 1866.

Stanfield, Pamela. *Confederate Diaries and Letters.* N.p.: CreateSpace Independent
Publishing Platform, 2015.

Stewart, Robert L. *History of the One Hundred and Fortieth Regiment Pennsylvania
Volunteers.* Philadelphia: Published by authority of the Regimental Association, 1912.

Stone, DeWitt Boyd, Jr., ed. *Wandering to Glory: Confederate Veterans Remember Evans'
Brigade.* Columbia: University of South Carolina Press, 2002.

Stonebraker, Joseph R. *A Rebel of '61.* Albany: Wyncoop, Hallenbeck, Crawford Co., 1899.

Summers, Festus P., ed. *Borderland Confederate.* Pittsburgh: University of Pittsburgh
Press, 1962.

Taylor, Walter H. *Four Years with General Lee.* Edited by James I. Robertson. 1962. Reprint,
Bloomington: Indiana University Press, 1996.

—————. *General Lee: His Campaigns in Virginia, 1861–1865.* 1906. Reprint, Lincoln: University of Nebraska Press, 1994.

Testimony of Court-Martial in Trial of Hon. Benjamin G. Harris. 39th Congress, 1st Session, House of Representatives, Ex. Doc. No. 14.

Thomas, Benjamin P., ed. *Three Years with Grant: As Recalled by War Correspondent Sylvanus Cadwallader.* New York: Knopf, 1955.

Townsend, H. C. "From Petersburg to Appomattox, Thence to Join Johnston in North Carolina, Diary of H. C. Townsend, January, May, 1865." In *Southern Historical Society Papers,* vol. 34, edited by R. A. Brock, 99–127. Richmond: Southern Historical Society, 1906.

Trowbridge, J. T. *The Desolate South, 1865–1866: A Picture of the Battlefields and of the Devastated Confederacy.* Edited by Gordon Carroll. New York: Duell, Sloan and Pearce, 1956.

U.S. Bureau of the Census. *Eighth Census of the United States, 1860.* Washington, D.C.: GPO, 1864.

U.S. Congress, Joint Committee on Reconstruction. *Report of the Joint Committee on Reconstruction.* 39th Cong., 1st sess. Washington, D.C.: GPO, 1866.

U.S. War Department. *Index of General Orders, Adjutant General's Office, 1865.* Washington, D.C.: GPO, 1866.

—————. *War of the Rebellion: A Compilation of the Official Records of the Union and Confederate Armies.* 128 vols. Washington, D.C.: GPO, 1880–1901.

Vattel, Emmerih de. *The Law of Nations: Or, Principles, of the Law of Nature, Applied to the Conduct and Affairs of Nations and Sovereigns.* Philadelphia: T. & J. W. Johnson, 1849.

Waddell, Joseph A. *Annals of Augusta County, Virginia, from 1726 to 1871.* 1902. Reprint, Harrisonburg, Va.: C. J. Carrier, 1979.

Walters, John. *Norfolk Blues: The Civil War Diary of the Norfolk Light Artillery Blues.* Shippensburg, Pa.: Burd Street Press, 1997.

Welch, Spencer Glasgow. *A Confederate Surgeon's Letters to His Wife.* New York: Neale Publishing, 1911.

Welles, Gideon. *The Civil War Diary of Gideon Welles: Lincoln's Secretary of the Navy.* Edited by William E. Gienapp and Erica L. Gienapp. Urbana: Knox College Lincoln Studies Center and the University of Illinois Press, 2014. First published in 1911 by Houghton Mifflin.

Wheaton, Henry. *Elements of International Law.* 2nd annotated ed. London: S. Low, 1863.

Wiatt, Alex L., ed. *Confederate Chaplain William Edward Wiatt: An Annotated Diary.* Lynchburg, Va.: H. E. Howard, 1994.

Wiley, Bell Irwin, ed. *Recollections of a Confederate Staff Officer.* Jackson, Tenn.: McCowat-Mercer Press, 1958.

Williams, Richard Brady, ed. *Stonewall's Prussian Mapmaker: The Journals of Captain Oscar Hinrichs.* Chapel Hill: University of North Carolina Press, 2014.

Wills, Charles Wright. *Army Life of an Illinois Soldier: Including a Day by Day Record of Sherman's March to the Sea; Letters and Diary of the Late Charles W. Wills, Private and Sergeant 8th Illinois Infantry; Lieutenant and Battalion Adjutant 7th Illinois Cavalry; Captain, Major, and Lieutenant Colonel 103rd Illinois Infantry.* Washington, D.C.: Globe Printing Company, 1906.

Wise, Barton Haxall. *The Life of Henry A. Wise of Virginia, 1806–1876: By His Grandson, the Late Barton H. Wise.* New York: Macmillan, 1899.

Young, John Russell. *Around the World With General Grant: A Narrative of the Visit of General U.S. Grant, Ex-President of the United States to Various Countries in Europe, Asia, and Africa in 1877, 1878, 1879.* Vol. 2. New York: American News Company, 1879.

Periodicals

Aegis and Intelligencer (Bel Air, Md.)
Alexandria Gazette
Atlanta Journal
The Atlantic
Baltimore Sun
Bedford (Pa.) Inquirer
Belfast News-Letter
Bradford Observer (West Yorkshire, Eng.)
Bradford Reporter (Towanda, Pa.)
Brooklyn Union
Burlington Free Press
Christian Recorder
Cincinnati Enquirer
Civilian and Telegraph (Cumberland, Md.)
Cleveland Daily Leader
Columbia Daily Phoenix
Confederate Veteran
Daily Constitutionalist (Augusta, Ga.)
Daily Empire (Dayton, Ohio)
Daily National Republican
    (Washington, D.C.)
Daily Progress (Raleigh, N.C.)
Detroit Free Press
Edgefield (S.C.) Advertiser
Evening Star (Washington, D.C.)
Florida Index (Lake City)
Frederick (Md.) Examiner
Gallipolis (Ohio) Journal
Grant's Petersburg Progress
Greensboro (N.C.) Times
Herald and Torch Light (Hagerstown, Md.)
Highland (Ohio) Weekly News
The Independent (New York)
*Journal of the Congress of the
    Confederate States of America*
The Liberator
Lynchburg Republican
Memphis Bulletin
Morgantown (W.Va.) Post
Morning Post (Raleigh, N.C.)

Nashville Daily Union
Nashville Telegraph and Union
The Nation
National Republican (Washington, D.C.)
New Orleans Crescent
New York Daily Herald
New York Daily Tribune
New York Evangelist
New York Herald
New York Times
Norfolk Post
Petersburg News
Philadelphia Inquirer
Progress-Index (Petersburg, Va.)
Raleigh Sentinel
Reynold's Newspaper (London)
Richmond Enquirer
Richmond News Leader
Richmond Times Dispatch
Richmond Whig
Rockingham Register (Harrisonburg, Va.)
Savannah Daily Herald
Sheffield and Rotherham Independent
Shenandoah (Va.) Herald
Shepherdstown (W.Va.) Register
South Carolina Historical Magazine
Southern Historical Society Papers
Southern Magazine
The Standard (London)
Staunton (Va.) Spectator
Times-Picayune (New Orleans)
Valley Register (Middletown, Md.)
Vermont Standard (Woodstock)
Vermont Watchman and State Journal
Weekly Standard (Raleigh, N.C.)
West Virginia Journal (Charleston)
Western Democrat (Charlotte, N.C.)
Wheeling (W.Va.) Daily Intelligencer
Wheeling Daily Register
Wilmington Herald

Akers, Anne Trice Thompson. "Colonel Thomas T. Munford and the Last Cavalry Operations of the Civil War in Virginia." Master's thesis, Virginia Tech, 1981.

Armstrong, Richard L. 7th Virginia Cavalry. 2nd ed. Lynchburg, Va.: H. E. Howard, 1992.

Ayers, Edward L. The Thin Light of Freedom: The Civil War and Emancipation in the Heart of America. New York: W. W. Norton, 2017.

Balfour, Daniel T. 13th Virginia Cavalry. Lynchburg, Va.: H. E. Howard, 1986.

Bergen, William. "How the Race to Appomattox Was Won." In Petersburg to Appomattox: The End of the War in Virginia, edited by Caroline E. Janney, 13–40. Chapel Hill: University of North Carolina Press, 2018.

Bergeron, Paul H. Andrew Johnson's Civil War and Reconstruction. Knoxville: University of Tennessee Press, 2011.

Blair, William A. Cities of the Dead: Contesting the Memory of the Civil War in the South, 1865–1914. Chapel Hill: University of North Carolina Press, 2004.

———. "Finding the Ending of America's Civil War." American Historical Review 120 (December 2015): 1753–66.

———. "Friend or Foe: Treason and the Second Confiscation Act." In Wars within a War: Controversy and Conflict over the American Civil War, edited by Joan Waugh and Gary W. Gallagher, 27–51. Chapel Hill: University of North Carolina Press, 2009.

———. Murders and Outrages: Contesting the Denial of Racial Violence in the South, 1865–1868. Chapel Hill: University of North Carolina Press, 2021.

———. Virginia's Private War: Feeding Body and Soul in the Confederacy, 1861–1865. New York: Oxford University Press, 1998.

———. With Malice toward Some: Treason and Loyalty in the Civil War Era. Chapel Hill: University of North Carolina Press, 2014.

Blight, David. "The Civil War Isn't Over." The Atlantic, April 8, 2015.

———. Race and Reunion: The Civil War in American Memory. Cambridge, Mass.: Harvard University Press, 2000.

Bradley, Mark L. This Astounding Close: The Road to the Bennett Place. Chapel Hill: University of North Carolina Press, 2000.

Brown, Maj. Gary D. "Prisoner of War Parole: Ancient Concept, Modern Utility." Military Law Review, vol. 156 (1998): 200–23.

Brundage, W. Fitzhugh. The Southern Past: A Clash of Race and Memory. Cambridge, Mass.: Harvard University Press, 2005.

Buck, Paul. The Road to Reunion. Boston: Little, Brown, 1937.

Burrell, Charles Edward. A History of Prince Edward County Virginia, from Its Formation in 1753, to the Present. Richmond: Williams Printing Co., 1922.

Bushong, Millard K., and Dean M. Bushong. Fightin' Tom Rosser, C.S.A. Shippensburg, Pa.: Beidel Printing House, 1983.

Caldwell, J. F. J. The History of a Brigade of South Carolinians, Known as "Gregg's" and Subsequently as "McGowan's Brigade." Marietta, Ga.: Continental Book Co., 1951.

Calkins, Chris M. The Appomattox Campaign: March 29–April 9, 1865. Conshohocken, Pa.: Combined Books, 1997.

———. The Battles of Appomattox Station and Appomattox Court House, April 8–9, 1865. Lynchburg, Va.: H. E. Howard, 1987.

————. *The Final Bivouac: The Surrender Parade at Appomattox and the Disbanding of the Armies, April 10–May 20, 1865*. Lynchburg, Va.: H. E. Howard, 1988.

Camp, Stephanie M. H. *Closer to Freedom: Enslaved Women and Everyday Resistance in the Plantation South*. Chapel Hill: University of North Carolina Press, 2004.

Carmichael, Peter S. *The Last Generation: Young Virginians in Peace, War, and Reunion.* Chapel Hill: University of North Carolina Press, 2005.

————. *The War for the Common Soldier: How Men Thought, Fought, and Survived in Civil War Armies*. Chapel Hill: University of North Carolina Press, 2018.

Catton, Bruce. *Never Call Retreat*. New York: Doubleday, 1965.

————. *A Stillness at Appomattox*. Garden City, N.Y.: Doubleday, 1954.

Cauble, Frank. *The Proceedings Connected with the Surrender of the Army of Northern Virginia.* Appomattox, Va.: Appomattox Court House National Historical Park, 1962; revised 1976.

————. *The Surrender Proceedings, April 9, 1865, Appomattox Court House*. Lynchburg, Va.: H. E. Howard, 1987.

Chernow, Ron. *Grant*. New York: Penguin Press, 2017.

Chesebrough, David B. *No Sorrow Like Our Sorrow: Northern Protestant Ministers and the Assassination of Lincoln*. Kent: Kent State University Press, 1994.

Chesson, Michael. B *Richmond after the War, 1865–1890*. Richmond: Virginia State Library, 1981.

Cimbala, Paul. *Soldiers North and South: The Everyday Experiences of the Men Who Fought America's Civil War*. New York: Fordham University Press, 2010.

————. *Veterans North and South: The Transition from Soldier to Civilian after the American Civil War*. Santa Barbara: Praeger, 2015.

Clampitt, Bradley R. *Occupied Vicksburg*. Baton Rouge: Louisiana State University Press, 2016.

Coffman, Richard M., and Kurt D. Graham. *To Honor These Men: A History of the Phillips Georgia Legion Infantry Battalion*. Macon, Ga.: Mercer University Press, 2007.

Coski, John M. "We Are All to Be Paroled." *Museum of the Confederacy*, Fall 2010, 5–9.

Cox, Karen L. *Dixie's Daughters: The United Daughters of the Confederacy and the Preservation of Confederate Culture*. Gainesville: University Press of Florida, 2003.

Cresap, Bernard. *Appomattox Commander: The Story of General E. O. C. Ord*. San Diego: A. S. Barnes, 1981.

Curry, Richard Orr. *A House Divided: A Study of Statehood Politics and the Copperhead Movement in West Virginia*. Pittsburgh: University of Pittsburgh Press, 1964.

Davis, Burke. *To Appomattox: Nine April Days, 1865*. New York: Rinehart, 1959.

Davis, William C. "Lee, Breckinridge, and Campbell: The Confederate Peacemakers of 1865." In *Petersburg to Appomattox: The End of the War in Virginia*, edited by Caroline E. Janney, 138–69. Chapel Hill: University of North Carolina Press, 2018.

Davis, John Martin, Jr., and George B. Tremmel. *Parole, Pardon, Pass and Amnesty Documents of the Civil War: An Illustrated History*. Jefferson, N.C.: McFarland, 2014.

Dawsey, Cyrus B., and James M. Dawsey, eds. *The Confederados: Old South Immigrants in Brazil*. Tuscaloosa: University of Alabama Press, 1998.

Dayton, Ruth Woods. *Samuel Woods and His Family*. Charleston, W.Va.: Hood-Heserman-Brodhag Company, 1939.

Dilbeck, D. H. *A More Civil War: How the Union Waged a Just War*. Chapel Hill: University of North Carolina Press, 2017.

Dorris, Jonathan Truman. *Pardon and Amnesty under Lincoln and Johnson: The Restoration of the Confederates to Their Rights and Privileges, 1861–1898.* 1953. Reprint, Westport, Conn.: Greenwood Press, 1977.

Downs, Gregory P. *After Appomattox: Military Occupation and the Ends of War.* Cambridge, Mass.: Harvard University Press, 2015.

Downs, Jim. *Sick from Freedom: African-American Illness and Suffering during the Civil War and Reconstruction.* New York: Oxford University Press, 2012.

Driver, Robert J., Jr. *First and Second Maryland Cavalry, CSA.* Charlottesville, Va.: Rockbridge, 1999.

Dudziak, Mary L. *War Time: An Idea, Its History, Its Consequences.* New York: Oxford University Press, 2012.

Duncan, Richard R. *Beleaguered Winchester: A Virginia Community at War, 1861–1865.* Baton Rouge: Louisiana State University Press, 2007.

Dunkerly, Robert M. *To the Bitter End: Appomattox, Bennett Place, and the Surrenders of the Confederacy.* El Dorado Hills, Calif.: Savas Beatie, 2015.

Earle, Jonathan Halperin, and Diane Mutti Burke, eds. *Bleeding Kansas, Bleeding Missouri: The Long Civil War on the Border.* Lawrence: University Press of Kansas, 2013.

Emberton, Carole. *Beyond Redemption: Race, Violence, and the American South after the Civil War.* Chicago: University of Chicago Press, 2013.

Faust, Drew Gilpin. *Mothers of Invention: Women of the Slaveholding South in the American Civil War.* New York: Vintage Books, 1996.

Feiss, William B. "Grant's Relief Man: Edward O. C. Ord." In *Grant's Lieutenants: From Chattanooga to Appomattox,* edited by Steven E. Woodworth, 173–94. Lawrence: University Press of Kansas, 2008.

Foote, Lorien L. *Yankee Plague.* Chapel Hill: University of North Carolina Press, 2016.

Foster, Gaines M. *Ghosts of the Confederacy: Defeat, the Lost Cause, and the Emergence of the New South.* New York: Oxford University Press, 1987.

Freehling, William W. *Road to Disunion: Secessionists Triumphant, 1854–1861.* Vol. 2. New York: Oxford University Press, 2007.

———. *The South vs. The South: How Anti-Confederate Southerners Shaped the Course of the Civil War.* New York: Oxford University Press, 2001.

Freeman, Douglass Southall. *R. E. Lee: A Biography.* 4 vols. New York: Charles Scribner's Sons, 1934–35.

Furgurson, Ernest B. *Ashes of Glory: Richmond at War.* New York: Alfred A. Knopf, 1996.

Gallagher, Gary W. "An End and a New Beginning." In *Appomattox Court House,* by U.S. National Park Service, 27–81. Washington, D.C.: Division of Publications, Harpers Ferry Center, National Park Service, and U.S. Department of the Interior, 2002.

———. *The Confederate War: How Popular Will, Nationalism, and Military Strategy Could Not Stave Off Defeat.* Cambridge, Mass.: Harvard University Press, 1997.

———. *Lee and His Army in Confederate History.* Chapel Hill: University of North Carolina Press, 2001.

———. *Lee and His Generals in War and Memory.* Baton Rouge: Louisiana State University Press, 1998.

———. *The Union War.* Cambridge, Mass.: Harvard University Press, 2011.

Gallagher, Gary W., and Alan T. Nolan, eds. *The Myth of the Lost Cause and Civil War History.* Bloomington: Indiana University Press, 2000.

Garrison, Arthur H. "The Opinions by the Attorney General and the Office of Legal Counsel: How and Why They Are Significant." *Albany Law Review* 76 (2013): 217–51.

Glatthaar, Joseph T. *Forged in Battle: The Civil War Alliance of Black Soldiers and White Officers.* Baton Rouge: Louisiana State University Press, 1990.

———. *General Lee's Army: From Victory to Collapse.* New York: Free Press, 2008.

———. *Soldiering in the Army of Northern Virginia: A Statistical Portrait of the Troops Who Served under Robert E. Lee.* Chapel Hill: University of North Carolina Press, 2011.

———. "A Tale of Two Armies: The Confederate Army of Northern Virginia and Union Army of the Potomac and Their Cultures." *Journal of the Civil War Era* 6 (September 2016): 315–46.

Greenberg, Amy. *A Wicked War: Polk, Clay, Lincoln, and the 1846 U.S. Invasion of Mexico.* New York: Alfred A. Knopf, 2012.

Grimsley, Mark. "Wars for the American South: The First and Second Reconstructions Considered as Insurgencies." *Civil War History* 58 (March 2012): 6–36.

Hamilton, D. H. *History of Company M, First Texas Volunteer Infantry, Hood's Brigade, Longstreet's Corps, Army of the Confederate States of America.* Waco, Tex.: W. M. Morrison, 1962.

Hart, Gideon M. "Military Commissions and the Lieber Code: Toward a New Understanding of the Jurisdictional Foundations of Military Commissions." *Military Law Review* 203 (April 2010).

Harter, Eugene C. *The Lost Colony of the Confederacy.* Jackson: University Press of Mississippi, 1985.

Henderson, Timothy J. *A Glorious Defeat: Mexico and Its War with the United States.* New York: Hill and Wang, 2007.

Holberton, William B. *Homeward Bound: The Demobilization of Union and Confederate Armies, 1865–1866.* Mechanicsburg, Pa.: Stackpole Books, 2001.

Hsieh, Wayne Wei-Siang. "Lucky Inspiration: Philip Sheridan's Uncertain Road to Triumph with the Cavalry of the Army of the Potomac." In *Petersburg to Appomattox: The End of the War in Virginia,* edited by Caroline E. Janney, 110–37. Chapel Hill: University of North Carolina Press, 2018.

Hurt, R. Douglas. *Agriculture in the Confederacy: Policy, Productivity, and Power in the Civil War South.* Chapel Hill: University of North Carolina Press, 2015.

Hyman, Harold Melvin. *Era of the Oath: Northern Loyalty Tests during the Civil War and Reconstruction.* Philadelphia: University of Pennsylvania Press, 1954.

Janney, Caroline E. *Burying the Dead but Not the Past: Ladies Memorial Associations and the Lost Cause.* Chapel Hill: University of North Carolina Press, 2008.

———. *Remembering the Civil War: Reunion and the Limits of Reconciliation.* Chapel Hill: University of North Carolina Press, 2013.

Jensen, Les. *32nd Virginia Infantry.* Lynchburg, Va.: H. E. Howard, 1990.

Jones, T. Cole. *Captives of Liberty: Prisoners of War and the Politics of Vengeance in the American Revolution.* Philadelphia: University of Pennsylvania Press, 2020.

Jordan, Brian Matthew. *Marching Home: Union Veterans and Their Unending Civil War.* New York: Liveright Publishing, 2014.

Keen, Hugh C., and Horace Mewborn. *43rd Battalion Virginia Cavalry, Mosby's Command.* Lynchburg, Va.: H. E. Howard, 1993.

Krick, Robert K. *Lee's Colonels: A Biographical Register of the Field Officers of the Army of Northern Virginia.* Dayton, Ohio: Morningside Bookshop, 1979.

————. *9th Virginia Cavalry*. Lynchburg, Va.: H. E. Howard, 1982.

Kytle, Ethan J., and Blain Roberts. *Denmark Vesey's Garden: Slavery and Memory in the Cradle of the Confederacy*. New York: New Press, 2018.

Lang, Andrew F. *In the Wake of War: Military Occupation, Emancipation, and Civil War America*. Baton Rouge: Louisiana State University Press, 2017.

Lankford, Nelson D. *Richmond Burning: The Last Days of the Confederate Capital*. New York: Viking, 2002.

Levine, Bruce. *Confederate Emancipation: Southern Plans to Free and Arm Slaves during the Civil War*. New York: Oxford University Press, 2007.

————. *The Fall of the House of Dixie: The Civil War and the Social Revolution That Transformed the South*. New York: Random House, 2013.

Link, William A. *Roots of Secession: Slavery and Politics in Antebellum Virginia*. Chapel Hill: University of North Carolina Press, 2003.

Litwack, Leon F. *Been in the Storm So Long: The Aftermath of Slavery*. New York: Vintage Books, 1979.

Long, E. B., with Barbara Long. *Civil War Day by Day: An Almanac, 1861–1865*. Garden City, N.Y.: Doubleday, 1971.

Longacre, Edward G. *Fitz Lee: A Military Biography of Major General Fitzhugh Lee, C.S.A.* Boston, Mass: Da Capo Press, 2006.

————. *Lee's Cavalrymen: A History of the Mounted Forces of the Army of Northern Virginia, 1861–1865*. Mechanicsburg, Pa.: Stackpole Books, 2002.

Manakee, Harold R. *Maryland in the Civil War*. Baltimore: Maryland Historical Society, 1961.

Marrs, Cody. *Nineteenth-Century American Literature and the Long Civil War*. New York: Cambridge University Press, 2015.

Martinez, Jaime Amanda. *Confederate Slave Impressment in the Upper South*. Chapel Hill: University of North Carolina Press, 2013.

Marvel, William. *Lee's Last Retreat*. Chapel Hill: University of North Carolina Press, 2002.

————. *Lincoln's Autocrat: The Life of Edwin Stanton*. Chapel Hill: University of North Carolina Press, 2015.

————. *A Place Called Appomattox*. Carbondale: Southern Illinois University Press, 2008.

Mayers, Adam. *Dixie and the Dominion: Canada, the Confederacy, and the War for the Union*. Toronto: Dundurn, 2003.

McCurry, Stephanie. *Confederate Reckoning: Power and Politics in the Civil War South*. Cambridge, Mass.: Harvard University Press, 2010.

McFall, F. Lawrence. *Danville in the Civil War*. Lynchburg, Va.: H. E. Howard, 2001.

McKitrick, Eric L. *Andrew Johnson and Reconstruction*. New York: Oxford University Press, 1960.

McPherson, James M. *Battle Cry of Freedom: The Civil War Era*. New York: Oxford University Press, 1988.

Mitchell, Reid. *Civil War Soldiers*. 1988. Reprint, New York: Penguin Books, 1997.

Moore, Robert H. *Tragedy in the Shenandoah Valley: The Story of the Summers-Koontz Execution*. Charleston, S.C.: History Press, 2006.

Morris, George S., and Susan L. Foutz. *Lynchburg in the Civil War: The City — the People — the Battle*. Lynchburg, Va.: H. E. Howard, 1984.

Morrison, James L., Jr. *"The Best School in the World": West Point, the Pre–Civil War Years*. Kent: Kent State University Press, 1986.

Mortenson, Christopher R. *Politician in Uniform: General Lew Wallace and the Civil War.* Norman: University of Oklahoma Press, 2019.

Neely, Mark E., Jr. *Southern Rights: Political Prisoners and the Myth of Confederate Constitutionalism.* Charlottesville: University Press of Virginia, 1999.

Neff, Stephen C. *Justice in Blue and Gray: A Legal History of the Civil War.* Cambridge, Mass.: Harvard University Press, 2010.

Newhall, Caroline Wood. "'Under the Rebel Leash': Black Prisoners of War in the Confederate South." PhD diss., University of North Carolina at Chapel Hill, 2020.

Nicoletti, Cynthia. *Secession on Trial: The Treason Prosecution of Jefferson Davis.* New York: Cambridge University Press, 2017.

Nine, William G., and Ronald G. Wilson. *The Appomattox Paroles, April 9–15, 1865.* Lynchburg, Va.: H. E. Howard, 1989.

Noe, Kenneth W. "'Disturbers of the Peace': The Kidnapping of John D. Hale and the Long Civil War in Kentucky." *Register of the Kentucky Historical Society* 117, no. 2 (Spring 2019): 267–81.

Oakes, James. *Freedom National: The Destruction of Slavery in the United States, 1861–1865.* New York: W. W. Norton, 2013.

Phillips, Jason. *Diehard Rebels: The Confederate Culture of Invincibility.* Athens: University of Georgia Press, 2007.

Powers, J. Tracy. *Lee's Miserables: Life in the Army of Northern Virginia from the Wilderness to Appomattox.* Chapel Hill: University of North Carolina Press, 1998.

Ramage, James A. *Gray Ghost: The Life of Col. John Singleton Mosby.* Lexington: University Press of Kentucky, 1999.

Randall, J. G. *Constitutional Problems under Lincoln.* Rev. ed. Gloucester, Mass.: Peter Smith, 1963.

Reardon, Carol. *With a Sword in One Hand and Jomini in the Other: The Problem of Military Thought in the Civil War North.* Chapel Hill: University of North Carolina Press, 2012.

Redkey, Edwin S., ed. *A Grand Army of Black Men: Letters from African American Soldiers in the Union Army, 1861–1865.* New York: Cambridge University Press, 1992.

Reeves, John. *The Lost Indictment of Robert E. Lee: The Forgotten Case against an American Icon.* New York: Rowman and Littlefield, 2018.

Robertson, Craig. *The Passport in America: The History of a Document.* New York: Oxford University Press, 2010.

Robertson, James I., Jr. "Danville under Military Occupation." *Virginia Magazine of History and Biography* 75 (July 1967): 331–48.

Royster, Charles. *Destructive War: William Tecumseh Sherman, Stonewall Jackson, and the Americans.* New York: Knopf, 1991.

Sanders, Charles W. *While in the Hands of the Enemy: Military Prisons of the Civil War.* Baton Rouge: Louisiana State University Press, 2005.

Savage, Kirk. *Standing Soldiers, Kneeling Slaves: Race, War, and Monument in Nineteenth-Century America.* Princeton: Princeton University Press, 1997.

Shaffer, John W. *Clash of Loyalties: A Border County in the Civil War.* Morgantown: West Virginia University Press, 2003.

Sheehan-Dean, Aaron. *The Calculus of Violence: How Americans Fought the Civil War.* Cambridge, Mass.: Harvard University Press, 2018.

Sheffer, Martin S. *Presidential Power: Case Studies in the Use of Opinions of the Attorney General.* Lanham, Md.: University Press of America, 1991.

Sifakis, Stewart. *Compendium of the Confederate Armies: Kentucky, Maryland, Missouri, the Confederate Units and the Indian Units.* New York: Facts on File, 1995.

Silkenat, David. *Raising the White Flag: How Surrender Defined the American Civil War.* Chapel Hill: University of North Carolina Press, 2019.

Simpson, Brooks D. *Let Us Have Peace: Ulysses S. Grant and the Politics of War and Reconstruction, 1861–1868.* Chapel Hill: University of North Carolina Press, 1991.

Simpson, Brooks D., and Jean D. Berlin, eds. *Sherman's Civil War: Selected Correspondence of William T. Sherman, 1860–1865.* Chapel Hill: University of North Carolina Press, 1999.

Simpson, Harold B. *Hood's Texas Brigade: Lee's Grenadier Guard.* Fort Worth: Landmark Publishing, 1970.

Skelton, William B. *An American Profession of Arms: The Army Officer Corps, 1784–1861.* Lawrence: University Press of Kansas, 1992.

Smith, Adam I. P. *The Stormy Present: Conservatism and the Problem of Slavery in Northern Politics, 1846–1865.* Chapel Hill: University of North Carolina Press, 2017.

Snell, Mark A. *West Virginia and the Civil War.* Charleston, S.C.: History Press, 2011.

Sternhell, Yael A. *Routes of War: The World of Movement in the Confederate South.* Cambridge, Mass.: Harvard University Press, 2012.

Styple, William B. *Generals in Bronze: Interviewing the Commanders of the Civil War.* Kearny, N.J.: Belle Grove, 2005.

Summers, Mark W. *A Dangerous Stir: Fear, Paranoia, and the Making of Reconstruction.* Chapel Hill: University of North Carolina Press, 2009.

————. *The Ordeal of the Reunion: A New History of Reconstruction.* Chapel Hill: University of North Carolina Press, 2014.

Sutherland, Daniel E. *A Savage Conflict: The Decisive Role of Guerrillas in the American Civil War.* Chapel Hill: University of North Carolina Press, 2009.

Tarbell, Ida M. "Disbanding the Confederate Army." *McClure's Magazine,* April 1901, 526–38.

Taylor, Amy Murrell. *Embattled Freedom: Journeys through the Civil War's Slave Refugee Camps.* Chapel Hill: University of North Carolina Press, 2018.

Tripp, Steven Elliott. *Yankee Town, Southern City: Race and Class Relations in Civil War Lynchburg.* New York: New York University Press, 1997.

Trudeau, Noah Andre. *Like Men of War: Black Troops in the Civil War, 1862–1865.* Edison, N.J.: Castle Books, 2002.

————. *Out of the Storm: The End of the Civil War, April–June 1865.* Boston: Little, Brown, 1994.

Ural, Susannah J. *Hood's Texas Brigade: The Soldiers and Families of the Confederacy's Most Celebrated Unit.* Baton Rouge: Louisiana State University Press, 2017.

U.S. National Park Service. *Appomattox Court House.* Washington, D.C.: Division of Publications, Harpers Ferry Center, National Park Service, and U.S. Department of the Interior, 2002.

Varon, Elizabeth R. *Appomattox: Victory, Defeat, and Freedom at the End of the Civil War.* New York: Oxford University Press, 2013.

————. "The Last Hour of the Slaveholders' Rebellion." In *Petersburg to Appomattox: The End of the War in Virginia,* edited by Caroline E. Janney, 138–69. Chapel Hill: University of North Carolina Press, 2018.

Warner, Ezra J. *Generals in Gray: Lives of the Confederate Commanders.* Baton Rouge: Louisiana State University Press, 1959.

Waters, Zack C., and James C. Edmonds. *A Small but Spartan Band: The Florida Brigade in Lee's Army of Northern Virginia*. Tuscaloosa: University of Alabama Press, 2010.

Waugh, Joan. "'I Only Knew What Was in My Mind': Ulysses S. Grant and the Meaning of Appomattox." *Journal of the Civil War Era* 2 (September 2012): 307–36.

———. *U. S. Grant: American Hero, American Myth*. Chapel Hill: University of North Carolina Press, 2009.

Wert, Jeffry D. *General James Longstreet: The Confederacy's Most Controversial Soldier*. New York: Simon and Schuster, 1993.

———. *Mosby's Rangers*. New York: Simon and Schuster, 1990.

White, Jonathan W. "The Military Commission Trial of Maj. Henry Kyd Douglas, C.S.A.: A Picture of Treason." *Military Images* 32 (Spring 2014): 30–33.

White, Ronald C. *American Ulysses: A Life of Ulysses S. Grant*. New York: Random House, 2016.

Wilson, Charles Reagan. *Baptized in Blood: The Religion of the Lost Cause*. Athens: University of Georgia Press, 1980.

Winik, Jay. *April 1865: The Month That Saved America*. New York: HarperCollins, 2001.

Witt, John Fabian. *Lincoln's Code: The Laws of War in American History*. New York: Free Press, 2012.

Woodward, Colin Edward. *Marching Masters: Slavery, Race, and the Confederate Army during the Civil War*. Charlottesville: University of Virginia Press, 2014.

Index

Page numbers in italics refer to illustrations.

transportation for former Confederates, 119–20; releases POWs, 217, 240–41; role in Johnston's surrender, 145–49, 157–58; supports amnesty for Lee, 191; at surrender conference, 27–32; surrender terms offered by, 12–13, 21–27

Great Britain, 15, 297n33

Greensboro, N.C., 10–11, 40, 70, 85, 124–29, 135, 159, 168, 170, 172, 175, 178, 227

Griffin, Charles, 29, 92

Grimsley, Daniel A., 19, 38

guerilla warfare, 15, 44, 47, 50, 79, 104, 132, 134, 135, 205, 207, 235, 237–38; in border states, 46, 101, 181, 185, 190; Union fears of continuing after Appomattox, 4, 88, 100–101, 105–6, 128, 131, 151, 189, 207, 224, 237–38, 254. *See also* John S. Mosby

Halleck, Henry W., 43, 45, 97, 102–4, 119–21, 134, 143, 158, 160, 190–92, 205, 206, 230

Hancock, Winfield Scott, 42–47, 189, 205, 238; commander of Middle Military Division, 142; on return of former Confederates to border states, 139, 143–45, 244; role in Mosby's surrender, 45–47, 96–97, 102–6, 205–7

Harris, Benjamin G., 162, 164–65, 196–99, 217

Holcombe, James P., 91

Hunton, Eppa, 33, 221, 240, 243

Illinois military units: 103rd Infantry, 130

international laws of war: belligerent rights for Confederates under, 146, 190, 204–7, 220; civilian trials under, 293n1; Grant's knowledge of, 23–27; paroled soldiers under, 49, 66, 14; violations of, 45, 196, 247

James River, 18–19, 36, 38, 40, 51, 60, 101, 109–11, 137, 240, 255

Johnson's Island, Ohio, 92, 98, 132, 142, 175, 200, 221, 240, 251

Johnson, Andrew, 4, 93, 95, 134, 145–47, 151–52, 173, 180, 181, 185, 191–92, 202, 203, 207, 213–14, 216, 217, 218, 219, 222, 223, 224–25, 227, 239, 240, 243, 244, 248–53;

256; amnesty proclamations of, 229, 231–32, 247, 251, 252

Johnson, Bradley T., 248–52, 255

Johnson, Reverdy, 223, 243

Johnston, Joseph E., 7, 105, 123–24, 126, 128, 150, 157, 166, 207, 208, 229, 250, 255; Army of Northern Virginia soldiers attempt to join, 12, 15, 35, 37–38, 41–42, 48, 52, 123, 159, 209; conference with Beauregard, Breckinridge, and Davis, 125; surrender conferences with Sherman, 129–30, 132–34, 145, 158, 224, 249. *See also* Army of Tennessee

Jones, A. C., 69

Jones, Benjamin Washington, 51–52, 255

Jones, Edward Valentine, 54, 56, 68, 74, 77–78, 109–10

Jones, T. H., 166

Klipstein, E. Augustus, 8, 17

Kentucky, 6, 92, 104, 118, 119, 139, 142, 144, 158, 174, 186, 193, 195, 205, 231, 232, 233, 241. *See also* border states

Kentucky military units (CSA): 2nd Cavalry, 280n15; 14th Cavalry, 280n15

Koontz, Isaac Newton, 234–37

Koontz, Jacob, 235

Ladies' Memorial Associations, 242

Ladies' Soldiers Aid Society of Richmond, 242

laws of war, 23, 25, 26, 27, 45, 49, 66, 146, 149, 190, 196, 204, 205, 207, 220, 247, 293n1, 294n24

Lee, Fitzhugh, 14, 18–19, 55, 59, 116, 221, 240

Lee, G. W. Custis, 12, 163, 221, 240, 252, 301n52

Lee, Robert E., 2, 7, 8, 12–13, 28, 31, 37, 40, 42, 43, 46, 50, 54, 57, 61, 65, 87, 91, 99, 101, 106, 108, 114, 118, 128, 132, 155, 163, 191, 225–26, 240, 245, 251–52, 255–56; decision to surrender, 14–23, 26; farewell order (General Orders No. 9), 53, 56–57, 162, 172, 216, 255–56, 272n5; indictment of, 221–23, 243–44, 253; intercedes on Mosby's behalf, 207–8, 229; perceived by Unionists as a traitor, 202, 216, 219–20;

questions travel restrictions, 159–62, 188; surrender conference, 27–32; takes oath of allegiance, 251–52

Lee, W. H. F. "Rooney," 221, 240, 244, 252

Leonardtown, Md., 101, 164–65, 196

Letcher, John, 221, 234, 243

Lewis, John W., 73

Lexington, Va., 206, 216, 244, 251

Lieber, Francis, 66, 203–5, 220, 245, 269n25, 294n24

Lieber Code. *See* General Orders (USA): No. 100

Lincoln, Abraham, 17, 27, 133, 143, 146, 149, 152, 180, 184, 219; assassination of, 2, 10–11, 78, 93–98, 102, 104–6, 107, 114, 116, 118, 129–31, 137, 138–39, 140, 142, 151, 162, 165, 170, 175–76, 181, 185, 186, 201, 207, 217, 218, 219, 237, 251; plan for Confederate surrender and Reconstruction, 25–26, 191, 224; Proclamation of Amnesty and Reconstruction (1863), 25, 132, 156, 188, 191, 213–14

Lincolnton, N.C., 18, 40, 41, 122–23, 173, 179, 267n33

Lomax, Lunsford, 35, 206

Longstreet, James, 13–14, 29, 32–34, 55, 63, 76, 91, 173, 215, 221, 250–53, 269n21

Lost Cause ideology, 56, 64, 111, 242, 255–57, 272n2

Louisiana, 57, 70, 79, 116, 176, 208, 237

Louisiana military units: 30th Infantry Regiment, 79; Donaldsonville Artillery, 63; Washington Artillery Battalion, 36, 83, 89, 90, 92, 116, 160

Libby Prison, 12, 112, 231

Lightfoot, C. E., 18

Luray Valley, Va., 235

Lynchburg, Va., 1, 3, 12, 14, 18–20, 35–40, 41, 49, 64, 71, 89–93, 97, 99, 107, 122, 129, 132, 160, 198, 207, 209, 229–30, 234, 241, 244–45

Mackenzie, Ranald S., 19, 58, 90, 99, 106Mahone, William, 221, 240

Maine military units: 1st Light Artillery Battery, 42

Manassas, second battle of, 132

Marshall, Charles, 17, 21, 28, 56, 160

Maryland, 6, 42, 43, 44, 46, 48, 88, 97, 101, 102–4, 140, 150–56, 162–64, 182, 193, 196, 197, 204, 247; Confederate soldiers from, 89, 95–96, 99–100, 103–4, 119, 139, 143–45, 150, 152, 154–56, 158, 167, 174, 186–88, 199, 201, 231–32, 241–42, 244, 248–49, 251, 255. *See also* border states

Maryland military units (CSA): 1st Cavalry Battalion, 20, 37, 99–100, 167, 241–42; 1st Artillery Battery, 155; 2nd Infantry Battalion, 282n63; 2nd Artillery Battery (Baltimore Light Artillery), 90; 4th Artillery Battery, 282n63

Massachusetts military units: 4th Cavalry, 65; 36th Infantry, 279n6; 54th Infantry (USCT), 177

McCabe, William Gordon, 13–14, 18, 41–42, 52, 129, 131, 168, 178–79, 209

McIntosh, David G., 1–2, 48, 123, 124, 126, 128, 131, 134–36, 168, 178, 229

Meade, George Gordon, 29, 55, 61, 222

Merritt, Wesley, 14, 29

Mexico, 13, 27; as destination for Confederates, 178, 223, 254, 297n33; threat of war with French, 178, 226; war with United States, 23–25

Michigan military units: 5th Cavalry, 45; 17th Infantry, 95

Middle Department (USA), 95–96, 142–45, 150, 155, 161, 244

Middle Military Division (USA), 42, 96, 142–44, 205

Military Division of the James (USA), 119, 160, 205

Mississippi, 48, 70, 116, 209, 248; soldiers from, 173, 208; violence against African Americans in, 247–48

Mississippi military units: 17th Infantry, 64; 48th Infantry, 91

Mississippi River, 24, 28, 37, 125, 175, 179, 207–8, 229

Missouri, 6, 44, 92, 103–4, 144, 193, 208, 231, 232, 244. *See also* border states

Missouri military units: Merrick's Missouri Regiment, 280n15

Moorman, Marcellus N., 20, 35

Morton, Oliver, 143
Mosby, John S., 43–47, 46, 49, 52, 98, 102, 104–7, 205–8, 221, 229–30, 237, 246–47
Mosby's Rangers (43rd Virginia Battalion Cavalry), 34, 43–50, 52, 88, 98, 102–7, 139, 144, 207
Mount Jackson, Va., 98, 99–100, 236
Munford, Elizabeth, 192
Munford, Thomas T., 19, 33, 36–37, 99, 123, 167, 192; failure to surrender at Appomattox, 18–20; surrender of, 209; troops of, 18, 20, 229; urges troops to fight on, 106–7

New Jersey, 199
New Jersey military units: 14th Infantry Regiment, 71
New Market, Va., 99–100, 234
New Market Heights, battle of, 79
New Orleans, 69, 92, 93, 114, 119, 120, 158, 160, 165, 166, 170, 178, 195, 202, 208, 225, 241, 285n3
New York, soldiers from, 71
New York City, 114, 118, 140, 141, 160, 161, 162, 165, 199, 204, 218, 223, 243
New York military units: 9th Cavalry, 281n40; 13th Cavalry, 142; 16th Cavalry, 47; 22nd Cavalry, 167, 189, 234–35, 237–38, 281n40
Norfolk, Va., 73, 96, 107, 150, 161, 165, 201, 206, 218, 219, 222, 227, 246, 247
North Carolina, 2, 5, 7, 10, 11, 18, 28, 34, 35, 37, 40, 41, 47, 48, 50, 52, 57, 69, 74, 76, 79, 82, 84, 85, 100, 119, 122–23, 127, 135, 147, 157–59, 167, 169, 170, 171, 173, 177, 178, 179, 188, 209, 211–12, 218, 221, 227, 234, 241, 248–49, 250, 252; soldiers from, 58, 60, 64, 82, 93, 116, 168, 175
North Carolina military units: 1st Sharpshooters Battalion, 88; 4th Infantry, 57, 80; 13th Battalion Artillery, 11; 16th Infantry, 75, 76; 27th Infantry, 89; 30th Infantry, 93, 169, 176; 47th Infantry, 79

oaths: of allegiance to U.S., 25, 102–4, 142–43, 154–56, 160–63, 184–90, 217–18; of

amnesty, 191–95, 213–15, 241, 297n34; of parole, 25, 49
Ohio military units: 12th Cavalry, 176; 192nd Infantry, 235–38
Old Capitol Prison (Washington, D.C.), 95, 98, 196, 201, 286n8
Oldham, Williamson S., 74
Ord, O. E. C., 61, 112–14, 113, 116–21, 160, 191, 198, 201, 205, 223, 231, 269n21
Ordway, Albert, 240

pardon: executive power to, 219–20, 296n2; under Lincoln's 1863 proclamation, 25, 132, 191; under Johnson's 1865 proclamation, 213–15, 223–25, 231–32; under Johnson's 1867 proclamation, 252; under Johnson's 1868 proclamation, 253
Parker, Ely, 22, 268n4
parole lists, 53, 55, 58, 63, 66, 97
parole passes, 57, 58, 66, 72–75, 86, 100, 109, 137–38, 159, 164, 166, 188, 218, 241, 255
paroles: as blanket amnesty or pardon, 66, 155, 202, 224, 297n35; differ from pardons, 215; Grant's decision to employ, 25–26, 34; history of, 25; as military status, 190–91, 198; penalty for breaking, 26, 49, 96, 110, 166, 204, 244; protection afforded by, 66, 202–4, 215, 220, 223–24, 227, 240, 244–45, 253–54; terms of at Appomattox, 22–23, 27–28, 95–96, 97, 222, 225; violations of, 159, 200–201, 216, 235. *See also* General Orders (USA): No. 73; prisoners of war; and provost marshals
partisans. *See* guerrilla warfare; John S. Mosby
Patrick, Marsena R., 112, 114–16, 119–20, 159–60, 195, 207–8, 240, 282n1
Payne, William H. F., 19, 97–98, 221, 240, 251, 267n37
Pegram, William J., 80
Pemberton, John C., 24–26
Pendleton, William Frederic, 178, 179
Pendleton, William N., 29, 122, 216, 221–22
Peninsula campaign, 40
Pennsylvania, 23, 100, 188
Pennsylvania military units: 3rd Heavy

MIX
Paper from
responsible sources
FSC® C008955

2-2-22